Conversations at Little Gidding

The Janssen portrait of Nicholas Ferrar

CONVERSATIONS AT LITTLE GIDDING

'*On the Retirement of Charles V*'
'*On the Austere Life*'

DIALOGUES BY
MEMBERS OF THE
FERRAR FAMILY

EDITED WITH INTRODUCTION
AND NOTES BY

A. M. WILLIAMS

CAMBRIDGE
AT THE UNIVERSITY PRESS
1970

Published by the Syndics of the Cambridge University Press
Bentley House, 200 Euston Road, London N.W.1
American Branch: 32 East 57th Street, New York, N.Y.10022

Library of Congress Catalogue Card Number: 78–85741

Standard Book Number: 521 07680 3

Printed in Great Britain
at the University Printing House, Cambridge
(Brooke Crutchley, University Printer)

To Linda, my late wife, and Hannah, our daughter,
without whose patient indulgence for my long
preoccupation with the Little Academy this
work could not have been accomplished

Contents

Plates

Preface

During the 1630s, under the direction of Nicholas Ferrar, members of his family held 'conversations' in which nearly every phase of contemporary society was a cause for discussion—and dismay. The first of the two conversations reproduced here reflects the fascination with the retirement of Charles V which permeated a good deal of the thought and literature of the early seventeenth century. The second conversation shows the increasing concern of thoughtful contemporaries with the luxury and self-indulgence which helped prepare the way for Cromwell. The Ferrars were intelligent and outspoken critics of life under the Stuarts, sure in their condemnation of the declining morality of the upper classes, of the licentiousness common to both literature and dress, of the sybaritic luxury of the wealthy, and of the pernicious influence of imports from the New World, especially tobacco. In their defence of the old-fashioned virtues of honesty, modesty, hard work, and simple living they have much to say to our tempestuous times.

What follows is the best attempt that I can make to reproduce the two hitherto unpublished manuscripts at Clare College and in the British Museum. The task of transcribing the originals was considerable. I have been as accurate as I possibly can be, but the number of different scribes—each with his personal idiosyncrasies of spelling and punctuation—and the fact that the same scribe was by no means consistent in his own practices may open me to the charge of carelessness. In the printing of the manuscript, superior letters have been brought down to the line and the orthography has been expanded and amended where necessary. With these exceptions the text is as exact a transcript as modern methods of printing can reasonably produce.

As for the Introduction and notes, their purpose is to give the reader background and help in understanding only the two manuscripts here reprinted, not to tell the whole Little Gidding story. There are gaps; there is speculation; there is work still to be done. There may be errors and, although I am indebted to several for help, the mistakes are of my own making.

For scholarly and editorial advice I want especially to express my very deep gratitude to the late Alan Maycock, whose books *Nicholas Ferrar of Little Gidding* and *Chronicles of Little Gidding* are the sources of nearly all factual information about the Ferrars and whose personal interest in my undertaking greatly deepened my long-held admiration and affection for him. Leicester Bradner, professor emeritus of Brown University in Providence, Rhode Island, has made suggestions for the Introduction.

For the tangible and intangible kinds of help without which I should have had neither the opportunity nor the time to complete this volume, I thank the Trustees of St Mark's School, Southborough, Massachusetts, and the former Headmaster, William W. Barber, Jr. It was through them that I was able to spend six months in England under a grant most generously provided for Masters of St Mark's by the Honourable Hugo Loudon, for whose generosity I am most grateful.

A. M. WILLIAMS

St Mark's School
Southborough, Massachusetts

NOTE: Page references in the Introduction refer to page numbers of the present volume, not to those of the manuscripts. Within the text which follows, folio numbers of the manuscripts are inserted in caret brackets at the end of each folio. All the material of the 'Dialogue on the Retirement of Charles V' except Part II (see head-note) is found in the Clare College manuscript (see Bibliography). All the material in the 'Dialogue on the Austere Life' is found in B.M. Add. MS. 34659.

Introduction

If you came at night like a broken king,
If you came by day not knowing what you came for,
It would be the same, when you leave the rough road
And turn behind the pig-sty to the dull façade
And the tombstone. And what you thought you came for
Is only a shell, a husk of meaning
From which the purpose breaks only when it is fulfilled
If at all. Either you had no purpose
Or the purpose is beyond the end you figured
And is altered in fulfilment.

.   .   .   .   .   .

                    A people without history
Is not redeemed from time, for history is a pattern
Of timeless moments. So, while the light fails
On a winter's afternoon, in a secluded chapel
History is now and England.

T. S. Eliot, 'Little Gidding', *The Four Quartets*

My fascination with the Ferrars is an interest which has endured since I first read the last of T. S. Eliot's *Four Quartets*—to which he gave the title 'Little Gidding'. Being something of an Eliot-man, I set out to learn what this place was which he had described and why it had such significance for him. It was not long before I was deep in Alan Maycock's biography of Nicholas Ferrar, son of the strong-willed old lady who in 1625 established a retreat for herself and her family at the manor of Little Gidding in a remote section of Huntingdonshire. It was from this biography that I learned of the existence of four manuscript volumes in which were recorded the conversations of 'The Little Academy', a discussion group formed by members of the Ferrar family to instruct both themselves and their audience in matters moral and intellectual.

I discovered that at least one of the 'Story Books' had been published in 1899 by Miss E. Cruwys Sharland, who described it as Volume I, and that she had also included half of what she called Volume II. As I leafed through the discussions, I became impressed by the wide reading of the participants, their ability to design artistic dialogues, their command of a vivid but still direct prose style, and by the inevitable intrusion of personal and contemporary comment in the midst of solemn attempts at moral improvement.

Next, Blackstone's *The Ferrar Papers*, published a bit later than Maycock's book, came to hand; it completed the second half of the folio published in part by Miss Sharland and known as Volume II. This is the section that includes the grimly amusing, Donnesque dialogue on the winding sheet and the idyllic re-creation of life free from lawyers on the Isle of Man. It was in these discussions that the Ferrars first became thoroughly live to me as human beings, bearing the scars of their deep involvement with the life of the first quarter of the seventeenth century and, by way of reaction, dedicated to a life of retreat and retirement, of self-discipline and unselfish service.

Miss Sharland's volume had indicated the existence of an earlier long dialogue (now published for the first time) devoted entirely to discussions centred around the retirement of the Holy Roman Emperor Charles V, and considering his resignation as a commentary on the corruptions of the world, on the necessity for private and personal renunciation, and on the superficiality of the unexamined life. Many years ago I traced this manuscript volume to the library of Lady Eleanor Langman, a descendant of the Ferrars, but it was not until she gave it to Clare College, Cambridge, that it became readily available for study.

A fourth manuscript is part of the British Museum collection and is now also published for the first time. Although ostensibly concerned with questions of abstinence and diet, and inspired by the Ferrars' imminent preparations for the celebration of Christmas, the discussions frequently become a free-swinging commentary on the licence and luxury of their day. Personalities clash, the nobility are castigated, contemporary life and literature condemned, translations of the Bible compared, and great quibbles take place over the nature of gluttony—and of raisins. The Little Academy showed itself to be a vigorous, imaginative, well-informed, and amazingly outspoken group of disputants.

Fascination with the Ferrars has led me a long way from Eliot's *Four Quartets*—and the present volume is the unexpected result. When as an Eliot-man I first began my researches, I thought I knew what I had come for, but 'the purpose is beyond the end figured and is altered in fulfilment'.

THE FAMILY BACKGROUND

In May 1625 at the age of seventy-four, Mary Woodnoth Ferrar, widow of Nicholas Ferrar senior, an important member of the Virginia Company, purchased the manor of Little Gidding for £6,000. There she and her bachelor son, Nicholas, gathered around them many members of their family, including Mrs Ferrar's eldest child, Susanna Collett, her husband John, and nine children, Mary, Anna, Susanna, Hester, Margaret, Elizabeth, Ferrar, Joyce and Judith. Nicholas's elder brother John Ferrar also retired to Little Gidding with his second wife, Bathsheba (his first wife having died childless in 1613), and their son Nicholas, the third of that name. Two other children—Virginia and John— were later born into this family.

At the time of their arrival at Little Gidding, the grand-children of Mrs Ferrar can be grouped roughly by age: Hester Collett was approaching twenty and her sisters Mary, Susanna, and Anna were increasingly older; Margaret and Elizabeth were between ten and fifteen and Ferrar, Judith and Joyce as well as Nicholas Ferrar, John's son, were ten or under.

Old Mrs Ferrar may have been the dominant personal force behind this gathering together of her family, but her son, Nicholas, who had long dreamed of retreat from the distracting world of

London business and society, was its spiritual guide. He had had a
brilliant scholarly career at Clare College, Cambridge, from
which he had received his B.A. in 1610 at the age of eighteen.
He became a fellow of the college with the intention (perhaps
partly motivated by his own uncertain health) of studying
medicine. Even as an undergraduate he had frequently resorted to

Members of Little Gidding Community

MOTHER, FOUNDER, GRANDMOTHER	Mary Woodnoth Ferrar (1550–1634)
MODERATOR	Susanna Ferrar Collett (1581–1657), daughter of Mrs Ferrar
RESOLVED	John Collett (1578–1650), husband of Susanna
CHIEF, later MOTHER	Mary Collett (1601–80)
PATIENT	Anna Collett (1603–38)
GOODWIFE	Susanna Collett Mapletoft (m. 1628 before establishment of Little Academy; d. 1657)
CHEERFULL	Hester Collett Kestian (m. 1635)
AFFECTIONATE	Margaret Collett Ramsay (m. 1636)
	Elizabeth Collett Woodnoth
SUBMISSE	Joyce Collett Wallis
OBEDIENT	Judith Collett Mapletoft
GUARDIAN	John Ferrar (1590–1657), elder son of Mrs Ferrar
	Bathsheba Owen Ferrar, wife of John Ferrar (d. 1659)
	Nicholas Ferrar (1620–40)
	Virginia Ferrar (1626–87)
	John Ferrar (1632–1719)
VISITOR	Nicholas Ferrar (1592–1637), younger son of Mrs Ferrar

the home of his married sister Susanna in nearby Bourn to recover his strength and energies and to escape the damp discomforts of Clare Hall. There

he began a work of piety that was to bear abundant fruit in the future. It was one of his chief delights to talk to the Collett children about the wonders of the Christian faith, training them up in the daily reading of the Scriptures and in memorising the Psalms of David. In all good things he made himself their guide and director. In years to come this association, begun when Nicholas was a boy in his 'teens, was to be deepened and enriched beyond measure; to these children he 'continued to his dying day their true spiritual friend and father'.[1]

With the spring of 1613 came a dramatic shift away from what was a very promising academic career. Nicholas was advised that in order to preserve his health, perhaps even his life, he must seek a complete change of climate abroad. An opportunity came for him to join the entourage of the Princess Elizabeth Stuart and the Elector Frederick V on their wedding trip and triumphal return to Heidelberg. Although he had intended to stay with the royal party until it reached its destination and despite the possibility of becoming a secretary to the princess, Nicholas soon set out on his own. He did not return to England until five years had passed and until he had seen nearly all the principal cities of Holland, Germany, Austria, Italy and Spain.

When he did return in the late summer of 1618 he brought with him a large collection of books, a proficient knowledge of several languages, and the results of two years' study of medicine at Padua. He must also have brought back with him a habit of self-discipline and a love for solitude, requisites for those who, although in poor health, desire to accomplish something in the world. Most important of all, he brought with him considerable first-hand experience with the Counter-Reformation.

The recovery of the interior life of prayer; the purifying of religious practice and observance; a new austerity and dignity in public worship;

[1] Maycock, p. 29.

a wonderful flowering of charitable works in the care of the sick, the education of children and reform of prisons; the restoration of the proper ideals of the priesthood—these are, in the Christian sense, the true fruits of the sixteenth century in Catholic Europe.[1]

Despite his preference for quiet and solitude, Nicholas immersed himself in family business affairs and especially in the complicated struggles of the Virginia Company until that valiant venture lost all its privileges in 1624. It was doubtless the deep concern felt by all members of the family over their financial troubles that explains their familiarity with the language of law and business and their genuine scepticism about the possible benefits to be derived from contact with the New-found World.[2]

By study, by nature and by experience, Nicholas became convinced that he could find fulfilment only in a life devoted to the service of his fellow man and to the worship of God. With the demise of the Virginia Company, he must have felt that he had fulfilled all the worldly demands required of him. He had refused one after another several enticing opportunities—a readership at Gresham College, an offer of marriage which included a £10,000 dowry, an important diplomatic post and, after taking orders as deacon, advancement within the Church. His mind must have been determined long ago; now his own and his family's affairs were in order—and he was released.

And so it came about that after a year or so devoted to the search for a remote and suitable retreat, Little Gidding was purchased in May 1625. The plague which ravaged London during the spring and summer of that year hastened members of the Ferrar family in their decision to escape the city; some first took refuge with Mrs Collett at Bourn and others later at Little Gidding. Characteristically, Nicholas stayed on in London to help the plague-stricken until early autumn, when he joined his

[1] Maycock, p. 48.
[2] For a full discussion of the Ferrars' involvement with the Virginia Company and with the plantations of the New World see Maycock, Chapter IV, and *Clare College, 1326–1926*, Chapter IX.

mother and family in the great work of restoring the chapel, main house and outbuildings of the dilapidated Little Gidding manor. His final renunciation of all worldly concerns was consummated on Trinity Sunday 1626 when he was ordained deacon at Westminster Abbey by Bishop Laud. On that day

towards evening he returned home to his mother and entreated her to hear him read somewhat he had written . . . It was the solemn vow he had made to Almighty God, that 'since he had been afforded so many gracious deliverances from so many perilous attempts of the devil and man upon his soul and body, and since now his family was rescued from a ruin so deplorable and unavoidable, if God had not been infinitely good to them;—he would now separate himself to serve God in this holy calling, to be the Levite himself in his own house, and to make his own relations, which were many, his cure of souls'.[1]

THE LITTLE ACADEMY

The restoration of the buildings, the organization of the school (which was later to include other children in addition to those of the resident families), the establishment of a dispensary for medicine and food to the neighbouring poor, and the inauguration of the hourly weekday Offices in the Great Chamber of the manor house and of the Night Watches in the chapel or oratories demanded the full attention of the Ferrars in their early years at Little Gidding. At first there could have been no time for the preparation of the elaborate conversations which were later carried on by the group to be known as 'The Little Academy'. A daily custom was established, however, which obviously provided the foundation and inspiration for the formalized dialogues later initiated in 1631. In his life of his brother Nicholas, John Ferrar describes the family meal-time practice.

Grace said, all standing, after some time they all sat down, and one whose turn it was read at dinner and suppertime some part of history, such as was appointed, either some chronicles of nations, journeys by

[1] Mayor, pp. 226–7.

land, sea-voyages, and the like. The reasons and the methods of them I shall for the better satisfaction of the historian set down.

Finding silence at meals' time unpleasant and common discourse for the most part unprofitable, it is agreed that there shall be always something read during meal-times. And because the mind, then being in most men altogether intent upon the refreshment of their bodies, doth not willingly admit any serious speculation, it is thought fit that the reading shall be always of some easy and delightful matter, such as are history and relations of particular actions and persons, such as may not only furnish the mind with variety of knowledge in all kinds, but also stir up the affections to the embracements of virtue. The performance of this shall be by two young daughters and four boys, every one in their course, whereby a particular benefit is hoped will arise to the whole, and they shall by these means be brought to read any book well and gracefully ... For the better retaining in memory of that which shall be read, it is agreed that a summary collection shall be kept in writing of those things, which are judged worthy of observation out of that book. The drawing of this abstract shall be the work of one of the parents or masters, but the transcribing of it fair may be by any of the children; and every noon, presently after collation, shall be made a repetition of that which was formerly read. The manner of this repetition, whether it shall be by examination of the younger, or by the elders relating it and application of things, is left to the judgement of the directors of those exercises to proceed according as the nature of the subject, time, persons and other occasions shall require. The ordinary and constant charge of this matter is committed to John and Mary Ferrar, and for assistance and supply, when they cannot, Susanna Collett; the mother and the elder daughters are desired always, as occasion serves, to give their help. Some other orders and directions were given, but this as a taste may suffice. And by this means it came to pass, that though they seemed to live privately and had not much commerce with people, yet they were well acquainted with the former and latter passages of the world, and what was done in it at home and abroad, and had gained knowledge of many actions of note and passages of consequence and the manners of other countries and nations and affairs of their own country.[1]

From the education of the young to the edification of their elders was not a great step. It must have been out of the interest

[1] Mayor, pp. 40–2 and below, pp. 241 and 248.

created by the meal-time readings and a desire for more serious discussion and more mature application than such occasions permitted that the Little Academy came into being on the Feast of the Purification, 2 February 1630/1. By this time most of the manual work of restoration would have been completed and the spiritual and charitable routines established. Jebb describes the purpose and nature of the Little Academy both in his own words and in those of Francis Peck.

They were equally diverted and instructed by divine interludes, dialogues and discourses in the Platonic way, that admirable way of drawing the truth out of another's ignorance. These innocent and profitable entertainments and recreations he [Nicholas Ferrar] introduced to wean the family off from the Christmas games and wilder sports which could hardly exist without riot and extravagant license ... On All-Saints'-Day they began, and at Christmas on every holiday they proceeded in gracefully repeating and acting their Christian histories, taken out of both ancient and modern historians ... These he formed into colloquies, with forcible applications of all to their own circumstances ... Mr. Ferrar himself compiled and wrote them with his own hand, to be transcribed by the actors that had parts in them.[1]

Ascetic conversations interspersed with sundry admirable examples and tales in honour of virtue and piety; as discoursed and related (in the time of k. Ch.I.) in the sisters's chamber by the seven virgin ladies and others ... of the religious academy at Little Gidding in Huntingdonshire: first drawn up for their use by their Visitor, the pious Mr. Nicholas Ferrar, Gent ...[2]

That the Ferrars in their isolation and retirement chose to tell themselves stories and to form out of their family members an organized 'Little Academy' can surprise no one familiar with the classical, medieval, and Renaissance prototypes with which the Little Gidding community was familiar. Some of the sources later to be discussed—the Oratories of St Philip Neri and the

---

[1] *Ibid.*, pp. 273–5. See also Sharland, p. 75, for evidence that written stories were read out at the meetings of the Little Academy.

[2] Mayor, p. 294. For the confusing bibliographical background, see Maycock, Appendix II.

conversations of Valdesso with his friends—could have directly inspired the Ferrars in their determination to encourage by group discussion the 'more ready and fervent prosecution of virtues and the better performance of all such duties as . . . should be required of them' (p. 5). On occasions when 'storying' became partly intended for amusement as well as for edification, a comparison (and, one might add, a contrast) with the pleasures of other isolated groups—Boccaccio's plague-driven refugees and Chaucer's road-weary pilgrims—is tempting but to be avoided. Socratic dialogue, which came to be a favourite device to encourage lively participation by members of the Ferrar family, was as old as Plato and served as a common means of instruction in many 'academies' that flourished after him, as well as a popular framework for the examination of literary, political, and philosophical problems. To suggest that the Little Academy was also in the tradition of the Courts of Love and that Mary Collett is an Eleanor of Aquitaine turned anchorite would be open to question. Blackstone, however, traces the dialogues to a wholly Elizabethan

court tradition, as it were baptised and purged of vanity, yet recognisably part of the pastoral convention. Nicholas surrounded by the Sisters . . . is but a variation on the shepherd with his swains and nymphs; the names of Phyllis, Corydon and Chloe are exchanged for those of Learner, Patient and Humble; the quaint conceits, the elaborate compliments and courtly euphuisms are the same, though they adorn a theme higher and more solemn than was ever discovered in Arcadian valleys.[1]

STORYING

The original Little Academy, made up as it was of participants ranging in age from less than fifteen to nearly eighty, was an ambitious undertaking and one (even when undertaken by such determined people as the Ferrars) doomed to fall far short of its ideal. At first, daily meetings were contemplated, and may

---

[1] Blackstone, pp. xiv–xv.

indeed have been held, but if they were, the discussions were considered unworthy of preservation.

They agreed every day at a set hour to confer together of some subject as should tend either to the information of the understanding or to the exciting of the affections, to the more ready and fervent prosecution of virtues and better performance of all such duties as in their present or other course of life hereafter should be required of them. (p. 5)

Later their intentions were augmented to include an attempt to entertain as well as to instruct. 'It is a hard task . . . that we must likewise endeavour to profit them in the way of virtue as well as to please them.'[1] Finally an additional demand was made upon the storytellers—compensation for a cheerless Christmas. The stories told at Christmastide 1632 were required not only to instruct and please but also to quiet the belly in 'its grudgings for those delicacies which you have robbed it of'.[2]

Subjects for discussion were at first planned ahead, and assignments were made of material to be worked up by the participants, although there were occasional deviations and surprises (p. xli). It was doubtless Nicholas Ferrar and Mary Collett who decided upon the topic and organized the illustrative material. Care had to be taken, for the sessions of the Little Academy were attended not only by the participants, but also by other members of the household and frequently by guests. The writer of the narrative links (Nicholas Ferrar) remarked on one occasion that there was 'a necessity of handling some choice subject because of the presence of certain friends whom dearest affection forced to admit and worth required to entertain with more than ordinary preparations' (pp. 15–16).

The Ferrars were fascinated by history and deeply read in the events of the recent past, in which they searched for the working

[1] Sharland, p. 19.
[2] *Ibid.*, p. 246. The first stories told in this Christmas season were lurid accounts of the torturing of ancient and modern martyrs. They seem to have been chosen for their narrative appeal as well as to honour those saints whose martyrdom is recalled at this time.

out of God's plan and purposes as well as for convincing examples that goodness, piety, and noble actions were still possible. As a result, a large number of their stories concern nearly contemporary men and events and at times draw on their own experience.

But because old stories move not so much, either because they have been often heard formerly, or perhaps not so fully credited, I shall desire that our instances may be of later times, and that you, dear Patient, make entrance by the recompting of that incomparable history touching the death of the last king of Spain, Philip the third, than which I have never heard a more convincing proof of this world's vanity and of the worth of God's service. (p. 17)

In keeping with their preference for modern rather than ancient stories was their sceptical attitude toward many practices and beliefs, both public and private, which had the sanction of tradition but, to their minds, lacked the blessing of God.

Finding in themselves and observing in others that do sincerely pursue virtue that the greatest bar of perfection was ignorance of the truth, whereby through misapprehension many prejudicial things were embraced and many most behoveful to their ends and most delightful in performance were not only neglected but abhorred, which having in many particulars experimented in themselves, doubting that they were abused in most of those things which we have received from our fathers, they determined ... to make a particular survey of those opinions and practices which the world recommends or disallows, weighing them not in the scales of common judgement but of true and right reason according to the weights and by the standard of the Scriptures. (pp. 4–5)

Once when the Cheerfull seemed to be particularly obtuse in grasping the correction of a common error, the Chief reprimanded her, saying

God hath given you an understanding capable of deeper points than these and he hath seconded it with a heart that dares not, I know, be against the truth. But you have been so long rooted and fortified in the common error of the world that I see you have taken it up for a main principal of truth so as you are loath to admit any question about it. (p. 56)

The words of the Chief invite comparison with those of Francis Bacon in *Novum Organum*.

The Idols and false notions which are now in possession of the human understanding, and have taken deepest root therein . . . so beset men's minds that truth can hardly find entrance . . . The formation of ideas and axioms by true induction is no doubt the proper remedy for the keeping off and clearing away of Idols.[1]

Bacon's desire to clear away the Idols is very closely paralleled by the Affectionate's remarks in the abstinence dialogue: 'The authorities indeed that you alleged are great and evident. But experiment [experience], a more infallible argument, proves the contrary' (p. 192). Bacon, however, wrote for the instruction of man; Mary Collett advocated the glorification of God.

In order to keep the attention of a group which varied greatly in age, intelligence and interests, the Chief recommended stories not only of 'later times', but also of men of ordinary stature.

Dim eyes see better in a shady light than in the brightness of the sun, and middling examples and arguments more prevail with weak and feeble minds than those that are more excellent in all other kinds, so especially in matters of virtue. That which must strongly move to imitation must not be too far removed from hope of matching in some good proportion. Wonder not, therefore, if now and then you hear that which may seem but ordinary. It's purposely contrived, as coarser dishes are served in greatest feasts, that there may be that which may be pleasing and proper for every man's liking and constitution.[2]

This sentiment is also reflected in later words by the Moderator.

The examples of saints (said the Moderator) works little but upon those that endeavour to become saints, or find themselves plain sinners. The first are taken with conformity of that profession which themselves long after, and the last are troubled with deformity of their own vices in the light of others' virtues. But worldly men that think themselves Christians good enough for heaven, whilst none can touch them with open enormities, make but a jest of the authority or examples of holy men, when they are alleged either to prove or persuade that which they

---

[1] Bacon, *Novum Organum*, 1620, Sections 38 and 40.   [2] Sharland, p. 21.

please not to believe or follow. I would rather, therefore wish to hear, if it might be, the confirmation of this new doctrine (for so it will be counted) by the testimony of some such persons as there lies no exception of partiality against by reason of any great eminency of holiness.[1]

It is not surprising that the Little Academy needed guidance in their undertaking and that, when such guidance was lacking, things fell apart and the centre could not hold. The first crack appeared when the group allowed their fascination with Charles V—and perhaps the Chief's insistence that they hear all about him—to alter their plan to have a number of participants tell a variety of stories.

The Charles V discourse was a departure from their original intent as it is for the most part a long monologue by the Chief. The discussion became general only when toward the end the Moderator insisted upon its becoming personal and introduced a long digression: her lively attack on the keeping of unnecessary servants, although related to Charles's preference for the simple life, was really centred about the problem of the Submisse, who aspired to become a lady-in-waiting.

The firm direction of Nicholas seems missing, and we learn from Maycock that the Visitor was absent from Little Gidding a good part of the time during that summer.[2] It is also possible. of course, that foreseeing his absence Nicholas planned the introduction of the subject and turned the meetings of the Little Academy over to the Chief with the assurance that she could keep the recently organized group intact and interested. Planned or not, the Charles V discussion shows that when the control exerted by Nicholas was absent and that of the Chief proved ineffective, the Ferrars had the unfortunate failing of most human beings—to give way to personalities and gossip when they became bored with more elevated topics.

[1] Sharland, p. 53.
[2] 'In June 1631 he [Nicholas Ferrar] was appointed to serve on a Royal Commission to consider the condition of Virginia. Its activities were not extensive; but its sessions necessitated his presence in London for some six weeks in that summer, and probably on later occasions.' (Maycock, p. 157.)

Order was restored at Christmastide 1631 and the storying at that time went on according to the original plan and doubtless under Nicholas's direction. These conversations of the Little Academy, published by Miss Sharland, are among the most artful, finished, and impersonal of the dialogues. There is no evidence, however, that the group met again until St Luke's Day (18 October) in 1632, when the Chief lamented their infrequent meetings and when, as the result of her criticism, she was elected Mother.[1] Speeches and the giving of gifts in her honour occupied all of that meeting and part of next session on All Saints' Day (1 November). By St Andrew's Day (30 November) planned storying was resumed only to be interrupted by the Cheerfull, who wanted to convince the family that Christmas be celebrated —if celebrated is the word—in an austere fashion.

At Christmastide 1632 the Little Academy made another attempt to return to the good ways of the past, but it was short-lived and no session is recorded after Holy Innocents' Day (28 December) until some time after Mrs Ferrar senior's death in May 1634. They met then to honour her many requests that the discussions be renewed; and the rather few participants, having assumed new names,[2] managed to produce the previously mentioned dialogues on the winding sheet and life on the Isle of Man. These conversations seem completely spontaneous and free from the restraint of any director, but Ferrar art and artifice have not disappeared. The Learner (probably Mary Collett) had just finished a story about which the Register (perhaps Mrs Collett) remarked, 'With death you went off and with death you come on, and by a Conrad bring us back again to the same place from whence by a Conrad you lead at first away. Whether it be by art or by chance . . . I will not enquire.'[3]

---

[1] Sharland, p. 164.   [2] Blackstone, p. 111.
[3] *Ibid.*, p. 200. In the dialogue called 'The Winding Sheet', after the opening discussion of the gift of the winding sheet and the digression on life on the Isle of Man, the emphasis fell on men and women who had made a 'good' death. The name of Conrad III (1093–1152), King of Germany, was introduced

Nor can we enquire whether it is by art or by chance that the last recorded words of the Ferrars' storying, uttered by the same speaker a few lines later, are so reminiscent of their opening words four years earlier. 'You have my opinion and purpose, and I think it to be suitable to that which we intend. That is, the bettering of ourselves by the knowledge of truth and the practice of virtue. The least progress in which is more to be esteemed than the perfection of all the arts and learning.'[1]

CHRONOLOGY OF THE STORY BOOKS

One must not be misled by the traditional and more or less arbitrary numbering of the 'Story Book' volumes as I, II, III and IV. Such numbers have very little to do with the order in which the discussions took place. In other words, Miss Sharland's description of what she printed as Book I and half of Book II is misleading, especially when considered in conjunction with her subtitle, *Being the Religious Dialogues Recited in the Great Room, 1631-2*. An examination of the texts of all four manuscript volumes will show the logical development of the Little Academy's thought and reveal interrelationships among the subjects discussed which on first glance seem not to exist.

The reasons for the foundation of the Little Academy (as Nicholas Ferrar expressed them) and its early conversations are recounted in Miss Sharland's book, pages 2-10. These passages were copied on manuscript pages 1-16 to serve as an introduction to the 'Dialogue on the Retirement of Charles V'. In chronological order of recitation, however, this conversation, for the

(Blackstone, pp. 165-7) and, more to the point, the example of Conrad I, who just before his death in 918 made public repentance for the wars and bloodshed in which he had taken part, was treated at length (Blackstone, pp. 167-73). At the end of the discussion (Blackstone, p. 200) Conrad II is mentioned in preparation for the account of another death-bed pronouncement; but the discussion (which may never have taken place) was omitted in favour of a graceful ending for the manuscript volume.

[1] Blackstone, p. 201.

most part really a monologue, was also preceded by Sharland, pages
11–18 and 61–9.[1] This material is here restored to its proper place,
for without it the 'Dialogue on the Retirement of Charles V'
would appear to be unmotivated and references in it to these earlier
stories would not be understood. That the Charles V conversations followed those on Ash Wednesday 1630–1 and preceded
those on St Stephen's Day 1631 is apparent from the manuscript:
'The story of Charles the Fifth's relinquishment of the world
having grown already to a volume, and yet not perfected,
although as much as is done was recited in the summer, is here
omitted, and we pass on to the setting down of the Christmas
Stories . . .' (p. 28 n. 1) Since the Ferrars were self-consciously
aware of their own life *in contemptu mundi*, the story of the retirement of Charles V proved of such interest to them that the
Chief's monologue was seldom interrupted. The balance of what
Miss Sharland printed as the first volume of the manuscript follows
along quite nicely after the note of explanation which precedes
the St Stephen's Day conversation.

As has been seen, the Little Academy did not convene again
until St Luke's Day (18 October) 1632;[2] the conversation on that
occasion was the first entry in a new manuscript volume, which
Miss Sharland called Book II. The discussion had nothing to do
with St Luke, but rather with the concern of the Chief, Mary
Collett, over their long neglect of 'those many excellent works
we had in hand'. It may be presumed that Mrs Ferrar senior was
now too aged to participate in the affairs of the Little Academy,
and it is true that Nicholas had been away a good deal. The
upshot of their self-examination was to elect Mary Collett to the
office of Mother to succeed her grandmother, Mrs Ferrar. The
rest of the conversation for that day as well as the first part of the
subsequent conversation on All Saints' Day (1 November) was
devoted to matters of reorganization and to the formal installation
of Mary in her new office. St Andrew's Day (30 November) was

---

[1] Sharland, pp. 13–14, and see below, p. 17.   [2] Sharland, p. 154.

celebrated with a number of stories; no more were recorded until those told at Christmastide.

A comparison of the opening paragraph of the Christmas stories of 1631 with the similar passage of 1632 sustains an important deduction. Mary Collett, the Chief, is the speaker in both instances.

ST STEPHEN'S DAY 1631. It is a hard task that is imposed on us, most honoured Grandmother and Founder of our Little Academy, that we should make supply of delights to your family for those vain pastimes of cards and the like, which you have so Christianly deprived them of. But when it is added that we must likewise endeavour to profit them in the way of virtue, as well as to please them, in requiring of two things that scarce stand together, there is a great surcharge of difficulty to the work and pains to us.[1]

CHRISTMASTIDE 1632. It is a hard task, beloved Cheerefull, that is upon us, and *double to that which was last year enjoined.* To outvie idle pastimes by worthy stories was not much; the pleasure lies the same way in both these matters. It's the delight of mind that's sought by gaming, and, therefore, when a better satisfaction was offered in the same kind, it was no great difficulty to content them from whom we took the less. But the belly, you know, hath no cares; and therefore I know not how you can apply your stories to quiet its grudgings for those delicacies which you have robbed it of. They must be very material stories that can recompense for the loss of so much good cheer as your austere temperance hath retrenched.[2]

Something had clearly changed—and the Cheerfull was held partly responsible. It is a very likely conjecture that the discussion of temperance initiated by the Cheerfull had already taken place —and that this cheerless Christmas was the result. A complete manuscript volume is given over to the problems of diet appropriate to the health of body and soul and to the evil results of self-indulgence in both drink and food. This volume begins in haste:

CHEERFULL: Pardon me if I seem importunate in occasioning this meeting so much before your expectation. Not only the earnestness of

---

[1] Sharland, p. 19.   [2] *Ibid.*, p. 246. Italics mine.

mine own desires, but the necessity of the thing itself admits no longer delay.

MOTHER: You say very true. For except you now give us the better satisfaction we may no longer forbear the making of our Christmas provisions.

CHEERFULL: Call them as they be, I pray, carnal excesses and spiritual prejudices that corrupt the body, defile the soul, and waste the estate. (pp. 159–60)

When the textual evidence is assembled and evaluated, the suggestion that the discourses on temperance took place in Advent 1632 is difficult to refute.

Miss Sharland ended her book with the Christmastide 1632 colloquies, which make up only the first half of the manuscript volume in which they appear. The latter half, printed by Blackstone in *The Ferrar Papers*, is the transcript of a discussion which occurred two years later, i.e. some time after the death of Mrs Ferrar senior and after a second reorganization of the Little Academy and the adoption of new names by its members.

THE NATURE OF NAMES

Which of the former actors these were is not to be enquired. The desire of concealing this point was one of the reasons of the alteration of names, though not the principle. The truth is, however, their intents were not, at least as they themselves thought when they took these specious titles of virtues and abilities with which they were first styled, to procure honour in others' esteem, but rather to animate themselves in the pursuit and practice of those things which were most necessary and proper for them; yet finding a secret kind of complacency arising in their hearts upon the sounding of such magnifique attributes in their ears and feeling a manifest failing, that I may not say, flat contradiction in their dispositions and actions to them, they began to be afraid in good earnest least they should by the use of them, though it were not in dead earnest, incur not only the unpardonable guilt of usurpation of that which they had no right unto, but the irreparable damage of impairment and happily of the utter overthrow of that humility which they ought above all others to pursue.[1]

---

[1] Blackstone, pp. 111–12.

These are the words of Nicholas Ferrar, the anonymous narrator, as he introduced the last of the series of conversations which the Little Academy held. Except for the elevation of the Chief (Mary Collett) to the title of Mother,[1] the original names had been retained and used with scrupulous care from the beginning.

There is a valid distinction to be made between the significance of the names assumed by or given to the adults of the group and those which the adults assigned to the younger members. The titles of Mrs Ferrar senior, who is styled variously as Founder, Grandmother, or Mother, were objectively descriptive of her position and relationship. Her eldest child, Susanna Ferrar Collett, was known as the Moderator. Although not always equable and sweet-tempered, Susanna, as mother of a family of more than twelve, doubtless merited the appellation. Her husband, John Collett, was called the Resolved. Perhaps 'Resigned' would have been a more accurate description since Maycock describes him as 'completely dominated by his wife'.[2] He speaks little and seems perhaps to be resolved only in his determination to keep peace in the family.

John Ferrar, Nicholas's older brother, as titular head of the household was addressed simply as the Guardian. The title, one can be sure, is not specious (p. 146) despite his unguarded financial ventures which nearly lost the family fortune. Nicholas, the Visitor, although he attended as well as supervised a majority of the meetings, had least to say of any member of the older group. When he does speak, the manuscript identifies him merely as 'one of the company'.

Fitting, formal, and respectful as the names of the older generation seem to be, those of the younger members of the Little Academy were clearly bestowed, with one great exception, with a touch of pious hope and a bit of wishful thinking. The exception, of course, was Mary Collett, known at first as the

---

[1] Sharland, p. 164; Maycock, p. 179.   [2] Maycock, p. 172.

Chief, an office which as mistress of ceremonies she clearly fulfilled. It was she who voiced concern over the failure of the Little Academy to convene and she who claimed that she must accept certain burdens out of 'conformity of name' (p. 23). It is interesting to note that, when she assumed the role of Mother, she received as a gift seven children that she might 'truly be invested in the reality of motherhood in particular, as well as in name and generality thereof'.[1]

That Mary's title of Chief or Mother was an honourable exception among the names given the young is corroborated not only by the quotation with which this section of the Introduction opened but also by the words of the Moderator in a passage found in the discussion of Charles V. 'There's none here perhaps answers to their names, as an expression of their natures, but as a testimony of their desires and endeavours, that they would fain be such as they are called.' (p. 136)

Of the younger group, first in order of age after Mary was Anna Collett, known as the Patient. That her title may very well be a sincere one is ably argued by Maycock,[2] but there is considerable evidence within the Story Books themselves to suggest that she was also capable of impatience. After a long digression in the 'Dialogue on the Retirement of Charles V', the narrator (Mary Collett, still known as the Chief) asked where she left off.

Why, upon departure (said the Patient) from his little nephew. And because you told us at the first, he made such haste, we suppose he is by this time come to the end of his journey, and now settled in his long desired rest, wherewith I pray proceed.

Ah, dearest Patient (said the Chief and laying her hand on hers) how doth the unwonted impotency of desires transport you to the prejudice of themselves and all here, whilest too impatiently you require accompt of his retirement and quiet. (pp. 117–18)

At a later meeting, the Guardian, in commenting on the weaknesses of his nieces, said: 'I would assign . . . want of wisdom, or

---

[1] Sharland, p. 179.   [2] Maycock, p. 182.

rather of consideration, to the Patient.' And she replied, 'Let it be plain indiscretion.'[1]

If knowledge and influence are a reflection of age, the Cheerfull must be the next younger sister after Anna and may with more or less certainty be identified as Hester Collett. Her age may also be deduced from the fact that in the first session of the Little Academy she was called upon to recite after the Patient and before the Affectionate. She freely confessed the fault of self-will imputed to her by the Guardian,[2] and such was her determination that she was instrumental in imposing on the community what amounted to a Christmas fast in 1632. In the 'Dialogue on the Austere Life', which preceded that ascetic Yuletide, the Cheerfull showed remarkable knowledge of the literature of abstinence and of the subtleties of debate.

By the same reasoning the Affectionate may be identified as Margaret Collett. She was too young to take much part in the early meetings of the Little Academy, and even two years later in the abstinence dialogue she confessed that her years were not many nor her experience great (p. 307). Although the worst fault that the Guardian could find in her was idleness,[3] the unexpected vehemency with which she commented on her stories of the two popes (pp. 22–3) showed a vigour of spirit and a control of irony surprising in one of her years. Margaret is indeed a puzzling young woman: Maycock cites evidence to substantiate his suggestion that she was not happy in the atmosphere of the Little Gidding household[4] and that she was of almost defiant independence of mind.[5] In a dialogue at Christmas time, 1631, her words lack warmth and humanity, and she speaks with puritanic positivism when she offers to tell a story 'in confirmation of this latter point, that strict judgement and severe punishment shall follow wicked deeds after this life'.[6] Outspoken, precocious,

---

[1] Sharland, p. 160.
[2] *Ibid.*
[3] *Ibid.*
[4] Maycock, pp. 176–7.
[5] *Ibid.*, p. 286.
[6] Sharland, p. 78.

intelligent and, as later evidence will show, not entirely kindly-affected towards her sister, the Submisse (p. 144), the Affectionate was perhaps least inclined to be such as she was called.

Conclusive evidence that the assigned names were indicative of the hope that they might become descriptively accurate rather than of the fact that they already were is found in the case of the most refractory of the Collett girls, 'the Submisse'. We learn that she refused to wear a habit (p. 136) or a veil (p. 138), and that her present behaviour and ambitions for the future, which are fully discussed in the first half of Part x of the Charles V dialogue, caused great concern to the whole community. The Submisse was apparently, at least at the time, the most unsubmissive daughter of the Colletts—she was probably Joyce—of whom her father remarked, 'I perceive this lovely name is not imposed on our Submisse for desert; but instruction to teach her what she ought to be rather than to tell others what she is.' (p. 136) The nature of names could not be more clearly revealed.

DE CONTEMPTU MUNDI

The leading actors of the 'Dialogue on the Retirement of Charles V'

The members of the Little Academy—actors as they called themselves—who took part in the 'Dialogue on the Retirement of Charles V' were seven in number: the Chief, Patient, Cheerfull, Guardian, Affectionate, Resolved, and Moderator. Three other persons were obviously present at some of the meetings—the Grandmother or Mother, the Visitor, and the Submisse—as well as unknown members of the audience. An arbitrary division of the manuscript reveals the following participants or auditors (titles of the latter are in parentheses):

Part I   Chief, Patient, Cheerfull, Guardian, Affectionate
            (Grandmother, Visitor)

Part II   Chief, Patient, Cheerfull, Guardian, Affectionate
            (Visitor)

Nicholas Ferrar, the Visitor, was the stage-manager of most of the early sessions of the Little Academy; and although he was not a named participant in the 'Dialogue on the Retirement of Charles V', his presence at the beginning is obvious. It was his deep sympathy with Charles's renunciation of worldly position, a parallel to his own retirement, that brought about the discussion. Doubtless he guided the Chief in composing her opening remarks on happiness for the second session (p. 16), and it must be he (referred to as 'one of them smiling') who at the conclusion of that session insisted that no dismissal of the possibility of happiness in this world could be complete or convincing without an examination of the opinions of the all-powerful Charles (p. 23).

After the Chief had sketched in the many reasons which Charles V had for being the happiest of men, 'one of the company rising with a sober countenance' promised that if she proved Charles was unhappy, he might be counted 'a fool of four and twenty carats that thinks out of the gleanings of some few clusters in a petty fortune to extract that wine of gladness and content which Charles the Fifth could not do out of the whole vintage of human felicity' (p. 60). To which the Chief replied that he had already followed the example of Charles in his contempt for worldly delights and that now he must lead others as they strove to follow him.

The Charles V manuscript reflects both Nicholas's fascination with the subject of retirement as well as his sense of artistic unity. His care for the form of the finished manuscript led him to change the order of stories (p. 17), and to write a brief history of the Little Academy by way of introduction. Nicholas seems to have enjoyed thoroughly the role of author–editor, and he betrays a certain delight in his consciously mannered literary style (p. 15).

Like many bachelor sons of studious habits, Nicholas was deeply devoted to his mother and moved easily in a society largely composed of women and girls. His high opinion of them was attested by the Chief when, commenting upon the retirement of Charles V's sisters along with him, she saw this act as 'A happy instance of the honourable proposition, which our Visitor hath so often engaged himself to maintain: that there was never excellent person nor action wherein woman's virtue had not a share.' (p. 80)

Nicholas's esteem for womankind was completely justified in the person of the Chief, Mary Collett, his devout but warmly human niece who dominated the discussion of the retirement of Charles V. From the very first meeting of the Little Academy, Mary, wearing a veil and dressed in her friar's gown, acted as mistress of ceremonies. She proposed the topic, 'a serious confirmation of our well chosen resolutions' (p. 6), and introduced each of the participants with words of encouragement as they proceeded to tell their assigned stories to illustrate the evils of procrastination. That she was a sensitive, appreciative, yet firm chairman is well illustrated by the passage with which she managed the transition from a story by the Cheerfull to one by the Patient (p. 10).

Nicholas's descriptions of Mary's behaviour reveal her almost morbidly modest, self-conscious, and shy personality. We read that she 'for a good space set her eyes upon the ground' (p. 9) and that she 'made a second stop and with a bashful view running over the countenances of her auditors as if she would fain know and yet durst not stay to examine in their faces the judgement of their minds, drawing part of her veil before her to hide the flashing blush which the encounter of so many eyes with hers had bred' (p. 33). The Guardian remarks that the Chief was endued with 'indefatigable abilities of both memory and voice' (p. 104), an observation made after her monologue which constitutes Parts v, vi and vii of the present work when the Chief feared that she had bored the company and lost their attention.

That this suggestion was met with vigorous denial may be in part traced to her mastery of the art of dialogue. She suggested the first Socratic dialogue (p. 51) and on many other occasions by well-timed pauses, enigmatic remarks, or autocratic statements elicited the participation of her audience. She was capable of vivid and impassioned speech (see especially Part vii on the vices and follies of the gentry), of puns and word play and, when occasion demanded, of irony and invective; one example must suffice.

To spend the whole day in managing of a horse, in training of a hound, or in manning of a hawk is a noble employment both of time and mind. But to spend the least minute in the direction of a godly life, to take the least care touching their consciences, or to bestow the least pains in the spiritual culture of their family, why it savours of the pedant. It is not only discharge of his own duty, but matter of merit in a parent and master to send his household to the church and his children to the school there to learn what belongs to the soul and mind. The information and accompt touching matters of religion and education are put over to the parson and schoolmaster as too mean and base for excellent spirits and understandings to descend unto. (pp. 102–3)

Her deep disapproval of the artificiality and emptiness of society, her contempt for worldly success, and her hatred for ostentation and luxury are everywhere evidenced. By contrast we find her sincere belief in the inability of this world to furnish happiness (p. 16) and her conviction that God manifests His will through human agents as directly nowadays as He did in the times of Christ and His later saints. Charles V was sent as a new Solomon (p. 66), the exploration and exploitation of the New World was reserved especially for his times (p. 69), and even Charles's shortcomings and failures were witnesses of God's desire to use this monarch both as a warning and as an exemplar to mankind (pp. 37 and 42). Not only could every event be interpreted as a sign of God's providence—an idea which Protestant groups later developed into a sort of inhuman humanitarianism— but even more significant was the Chief's conviction that God directly rewards the good and, by implication, punishes the bad. Her belief that prosperity was the result of Godliness—or that Godliness was rewarded by prosperity[1]—is close to the Puritan emphasis on the doing of good works as witness of God's love or as a means of obtaining God's grace. In speaking of the direct benefits of Charles's piety, the Chief said, 'So that perhaps we shall do no wrong to conclude that in God's merciful acceptance and reward of his true goodness, they [Charles's descendants] have since upheld that great prosperity, which else, it may be, by worse deserts and courses they had forfeited.' (pp. 44–5) The Guardian much later returned to this subject and developed it at length.

Let me by solemn acknowledgement of my excess of happiness in a weak and private fortune add a ball to the confirmation of that undeniable inference which our Chief made upon the transcendent prosperity of our Charles and his royal family. That there is no surer way to multiply a man's own than by the promotion of many others' good. (p. 108)

Mary Collett was blessed with great strength of mind and character, surprising intelligence and wide learning. Of all her many graces and virtues, her humility and sincerity are those that

---

[1] Sharland, p. 55 and below, pp. 44–5.

impress us most and are perhaps best revealed in the words with which she closed her discussion of Charles's short-comings.

But let me walk always the royal path of uprightness, not only conforming my words and actions to my intents, but explaining them to others' apprehension making them answer not my own cunning interpretations but what they did confidently expect. And let it be my portion, Oh Lord, rather to have mine own plainness abused by others subtlety than by fineness of will to work out mine own ends upon others' simplicity. (p. 41)

The supporting cast

It would be unreasonable to maintain that the assigned stories told in the formal sessions of the Little Academy under the direction of Nicholas Ferrar reflect in any significant way the personalities of the narrators. In the Charles V manuscript, however, except for the first two parts, the Chief is the only story teller; the other actors speak spontaneously to demand clarification, to offer amplification, or to apply the problems raised by the Chief's monologue to their own circumstances. It is therefore reasonable to assume that the personalities of the three youthful speakers and of their parents and uncles are directly revealed by their comments and contributions in Parts IV, VIII, IX and X.

In the first two parts of the present work the Patient tells her assigned stories of ambitious Trajan, of Philip III of Spain on his death-bed, and of Charles V's reception of the news of victory over Francis I. Later, when she can speak spontaneously, her love and sympathy for her sister Mary are touchingly recorded by her words and deeds after the Chief's long diatribe against the keeping of unnecessary servants (p. 131) and by her Thoreau-like renunciation of worldly luxury.

Henceforth by God's assistance my cares, my desires, my endeavours shall be more seriously bent to the despising than formerly they were to the longing pursuit of these seeming excellencies. Whatever offer itself to pretence of adding greatness to my condition, either in apparel, diet, dwelling or attendance shall find churlish refusal at my hands, as a deceitful enemy of my peace, however it may put on the glozing visor of friendship. As for others misprision, it's but a childish bugbear and shall not make me start, I hope, however frightful it come dressed. What neighbours talk or the world censureth, if I strive not to make the best show, shall no more trouble me than the Bo-ohs where-with nurses terrify their little ones. (pp. 133–4)

Although the Patient seemed not to care what others thought, she was concerned to win them to her way of action. She is so passionate in her analysis of the dangers and futility of trying to correct backsliders that one suspects that someone, perhaps the Submisse, had told her to mind her own business. Certainly frustration and hurt feelings motivated such a passage as the following.

To suffer for well doing is so infallible a condition as he must needs have small experience in the world that hopes to bring any good business to effect without his own prejudice. He must quit all desires, not only attempts of virtuous performance, that resolves not to part with his quiet and patiently undergo the ill will at least of those whose good he chiefly endeavours. (p. 145)

Over-eagerness remained her besetting weakness to the end. After the Chief had long remained silent and Charles V was almost forgotten, the Patient tried to put herself forward as the leader of a new discussion, a prolonged investigation of the evils of servant-keeping, but when she rashly attempted to interrupt the dialogue between her mother, the Moderator, and her uncle, the Guardian, her importunity was sharply rebuked. 'Your turn comes shortly (said the Moderator) and all that we are now about is but to clear the place from the encumbrances that you may more freely exercise your skill in [knowledge of] this miscreated profession.' (p. 155) Her turn never did come, and she must have had a new occasion for frustration and hurt feelings.

The Cheerfull played no significant part in the Charles V discussion: in addition to a story of the wealthy mother of a bishop (pp. 11-12), an episode from the life of Henry IV (pp. 20-1), and perhaps a story illustrating Charles V's devotion to his sister (pp. 27–8), she contributed only a few innocuous remarks which reveal nothing of her personality. John Ferrar, to whom she was deeply devoted, took a fatherly interest in her and in his eagerness for her advancement suggested that she as Scholar take part in a Socratic dialogue with the Chief (pp. 51–2), in which she was forced to attempt to uphold the position that happiness is to be found in worldly success and that Charles must have been the happiest of men.

Although the Affectionate was 'prized as a good historian' (p. 23), only three stories were assigned her: the story of the fines (pp. 12–13); the short account of the two popes (pp. 22–3); and the story of Charles V's 'surpassing patience' (pp. 26–7). On a later occasion she showed a strange control over the language of gambling and an unsisterly eagerness to continue the excoriation of the Submisse.

Nay, if we mean not to lose all as the match is made (said the Affectionate). For the saving of our own stake seems much more doubtful to me than our Guardian conceives. Many a man for want of good play looseth the game that fair casting had certainly made him master of. Haste makes waste is an old saw . . . I shall therefore devise to make all sure to stay the administration of this physic to the Submisse, whereunto her own indisposition of mind and many opportunities so well served at this present, as I doubt we shall afterwards repent if we do not at this time make use of them. (p. 144)

From evidence in the present dialogue, one must assume that it was the Submisse who was the least tractable of the maiden sisters. She is the chief subject of discussion in Part x, in which her intention of becoming a gentlewoman-in-waiting is severely condemned. We have already noted her stubbornness in refusing to conform in dress to the custom of her sisters, and she seems in addition to have been sulky and petulant. Although she remained silent, her face betrayed annoyance over the criticism directed at her: 'I read in her countenance the challenge of both unkindness and revenge for so public an imputation in a matter in which she thinketh herself perhaps most free.' (p. 136) One must remember that Joyce was so young, about thirteen or fourteen when the Little Academy first met, that no story was assigned her until some six months later on St Stephen's Day, 1631. On that occasion she told a story of the divorce of Henry VIII and Catherine of Aragon—a recital which so shocked her uncle and half-hearted defender, the Guardian, that he was led to remark, 'This story is indeed an honour to your sex, but a shame to your age.'[1] Despite these adolescent outbreaks, the Submisse came around to the family's way of thinking—and married a clergyman, as all the Collett girls were expected to do.

The Guardian, Moderator, and Resolved, the three senior members, were assigned no stories in the first meetings of the Little Academy; their roles in the 'Dialogue on the Retirement of Charles V' are limited to comment and commendation. Usually gentle and a bit slow-witted, the Guardian, John Ferrar, made soothing and complimentary remarks when the Chief was tired or discouraged (pp. 9 and 104), and his kindness came to the fore when the Submisse's parents seemed too harsh in their judgement of her (pp. 136–7). Later his good-natured desire to avoid angry words and family arguments led him to give in, albeit somewhat grumpily, to the desire of the others to continue the discussion of servitude which, because of its difficulty, he deemed a waste of time (p. 144).

As for making all men parties that shall any way appear against you in the cause which the Patient aims at, though perhaps it may have much truth on its side, yet it will find so little belief amongst indifferent men as adds no encouragement at all for me to enter that league, which I see you have all agreed upon to the overthrow of this matter, which in mine eye seems one of the most impregnable that amidst all the several conditions of men's lives you could have undertook. (pp. 145–6)

Good and simple man that he was, on occasion the Guardian was capable of annoyance with others and of a feeling of being

[1] Sharland, p. 37.

unappreciated himself. At least once he was driven to twit his sister when she complained of her large family and her lack of means.

Alas (said the Guardian) how strangely misshapen must the inward features of our minds needs be when the richer and better proportioned the garment of God's cutting out, the worse it fits and becomes us in our fancies. Why verily it was the emulation of your happiness in this kind that most of all other thoughts and affections was all this while so seriously on work in me. And were it not that in yours I have as great an interest, I will not say as you, but as in yourself, my dearest sister, I doubt not whether it might not pass on to envy. (p. 113)

Not only did he look upon the Moderator's children as his own, but he also took a fatherly interest in the Cheerfull, his adopted daughter (p. 52) and in the Chief's adopted son (p. 116), all of whom, he, following the example of Charles V, agreed to educate along with his own children.

The world of Little Gidding must have offered a happy refuge for John Ferrar for, according to Maycock's evidence, he had been something less than successful as a business man and owed his extrication from complete bankruptcy entirely to the efforts of his brother Nicholas.[1] John's vehement denial of regret over the waste of his fortune reflects his sincerity and humility of spirit, as does his claim to have found true happiness in service honourably given to God and man (pp. 108–9). Even more indicative of the Guardian's simple philosophy was his fear that his own former love of comfort and even luxury might by example corrupt others. He shamefully admitted his

great folly in the lavish disbursements of those incomes which should be applied to more necessary use; of ambitious vanity in seeking to match the pomp and state of great personages; and of many wanton appetites and desires touching ease and pleasure, however valid under the pretence of conveniency and comeliness . . . That waste should be repaid with necessity, that pride should have a fall, and vain delights closed up with bitter sufferings were but the just recompense and fruits

---

[1] Maycock, p. 108.

of this misdoing . . . And this I could wish graven on the frontispiece of the house for a caveat, that none of weak and troubled states should by our errors be encouraged to the like prodigal excess. (p. 110)

The Resolved, John Collett, was remarkably similar in temperament to his brother-in-law, John Ferrar. Like him he was kindhearted, unassertive, at times bumblingly obtuse, and almost always completely overshadowed by the quick-witted, strongwilled women of the Little Academy. His most striking characteristic was a self-conscious metaphor-madness. His first words in the 'Dialogue on the Retirement of Charles V' praised the Chief for the richness of the catch which the net of her discourse might bring in and urged her to 'launch out again cheerfully . . . and prepare the nets and trim the sails which you began to strike' (p. 105). A couple of pages later, he offered his services as a midwife who will

endeavour, if you yourself please, to deliver you of this burthen by helping forth these conceptions of yours which have attained their just perfection and by a quiet return of those other that are not yet perhaps fully shapen to the womb of your further meditation, that in due time they may receive a happy birth. (p. 106)

He will be an archer and 'adventure a second arrow' (p. 109) and later a party to an attack on a garrison (p. 146). Involved as his own images sometimes became, his slowness in deciphering the Guardian's figures of 'the house' and 'the plantation' aroused the Moderator's annoyance: 'A blind man (said the Moderator upon the Resolved's longsome pause) may feel day at the light of this cranny, and therefore our Resolved thinks it not worth his discovery.' To which the henpecked Resolved graciously replied: 'Since you are so confident, gentle Moderator, I shall gladly leave it to your hands.' (p. 112)

The discussion of gentleman and lady attendants shows the Resolved at his well-meaning best—or worst. Perhaps more sensitively aware than the others that Nicholas himself had spent several months as a gentleman usher in the entourage of the

Princess Elizabeth, he objected to the harsh condemnation of such service.

However strange you make it, I am sure (said the Resolved) your own judgement testifieth it will be necessary to call back those passionate disgraces wherewith through the sides of feeble wasting women you have contemptuously affronted the whole order of free and gentlemen attendants, which compriseth a far greater number, as I suppose, of well born and well educated persons of both sexes than any other profession whatsoever. (p. 140)

He confessed his honest and perhaps rather stupid confusion over the trend of the argument, charging that 'The contradiction of your discourses . . . intangle my thoughts as in a labyrinth.' To this his wife rather testily replied, 'The mountain has at last brought forth a mouse . . . It's not for yourself, I am sure, you thus dally in picking up straws; you see others' weakness and therefore will have the way clear without any colour of rub.' (p. 141) When the specific problem of the Submisse's plans for entering service was discussed, the Resolved revealed himself as a sufficiently strong and devoted father to stand up for his daughter, the Submisse, against the harshness of his wife, the Moderator.

His last contribution to the colloquium voiced his doubt of the value of Socratic dialogue—a form for which he had no skill and little sympathy.

The pains and care which the learner makes spare of in this way which you have chosen (said the Resolved) returns with double travail on the instructor's head. Whilest therein he takes on him not only his own, but the burden of him whom he teacheth, by skilful art endeavouring as well to induce the ready apprehension, as the right proposal of the matter, with much more difficulty of a study perhaps fitting the truth to the learner's capacity and affections than he took on himself to find or declare it. (p. 148)

The wife of the Resolved and the mother of a large family of girls, Susanna Ferrar Collett, the Moderator, must be forgiven if the strain occasionally showed. John's slowness of mind and easy-going ways understandably called forth her impatience; on one occasion she quite frankly accused him of allowing his mind to dry up like an unused pump (p. 107). Even her gentle and generous brother fell victim to her sharp tongue: in her carping concern for the future of her large family, which included seven unmarried daughters, she charged the Guardian with lack of sympathy and solicitude (p. 113). Although her objections to the Submisse's intention of becoming a lady-in-waiting arose from motherly concern for the temptations which this difficult child would face —and to which she might gladly succumb—a large part of her disapproval was based on a philosophic conviction that any kind of service was ugly and degrading. The closing words of her diatribe against servitude reflect her truly democratic spirit.

Love to our neighbours and humility in ourselves by being profitably employed to common benefit and by painful diligence kept low in our own appraisements, whilst we see ourselves but fellow labourers with the meanest of God's household, are these two main ends whereunto in every calling God chiefly directs us. But the love of preeminence is the Devil's condemnation and whatever condition of life sets up to utter this sort of ware must do it by patent from him, for no vocation of God's ordinance hath any privilege of traffic therein. Equality is man's virtue. To be above belongs to God, and no man may take this honour to himself but he that is called God. (pp. 142–3)

Nicholas Ferrar could not better have expressed his own social philosophy nor more succinctly stated the basic tenets which guided the Ferrar family in their life at Little Gidding.

The judicious Thuanus

For her stories about Charles V the Chief relied heavily on the work of the French historian Jacques-Auguste de Thou (1553–1617), referred to by the Ferrars as Thuanus. His *Historia sui Temporis* appeared in sections in Latin during his lifetime and, along with his *Mémoires*, in a complete edition, also in Latin, in 1620. Both the parts and the whole encountered violent opposition from the Roman Catholic Church, which placed the second volume when it appeared on the Index.

It is difficult to avoid a digression on the life and works of de Thou, but restraint must be practised. As a confidential minister to Henry III and later to Henry IV of France, he was in a most advantageous position to gather material for the writing of contemporary history, an undertaking to which he devoted the last quarter of his life. Not only was he concerned with events of which he had first-hand knowledge, but he also consulted the best available primary sources in order to give objective accuracy to his year-by-year account. His work covered the period from 1546 to 1584 in such a lively and detailed manner that it immediately became a classic and was eventually translated into German, English and French. Perhaps the flavour of the *Historia* is best reflected in de Thou's introductory remarks.

I hope to transmit to posterity the most memorable events in all parts of the world, commencing my account a little before the death of Francis I and continuing up to the time of writing. I declare that my intention is to stick closely to the truth and to avoid partialities begotten by favour and dislike. But before engaging myself in such a great enterprise, it seems to me to the point to go back to the source of events by explaining briefly what was the state of affairs and the character of leaders; what were the plans of princes, their resources, passions, and interest. And since France and Spain had become so dominant that the destiny of other states depended absolutely on these two great powers, it is with them that I am going to begin.[1]

On occasion, the Chief seems to translate directly from de Thou, but for the most part she relies on paraphrase or synopsis. Much of her praise of Charles's personal characteristics and many virtues is very close to the eulogy which de Thou wrote when he recorded the emperor's death. Her accounts of the ceremonies connected with Charles's abdication, of his return to Spain, of the

---

[1] This passage as well as all other quotations from de Thou is my translation from the French translation published in London in 1734. The quotation is found in Book I, p. 5.

heralds who announced the news to the Spanish people, and of his simple journey to Juste are so close to de Thou's descriptions in Books XVI and XVII of his history that one could believe that the Chief had the volume before her as she talked.

The Ferrars seem to refer to two other historians—'the Prince of Historians' (p. 26) and 'the grave Florentine' (p. 127). The account of Charles's sober and dignified reception of the news of the defeat of Francis I, attributed to the 'Prince of Historians', cannot be traced to de Thou; a footnote to Robertson's description of the incident gives as sources for the passage Prudencia de Sandoval's *Historia de la Vida y haches del Emperador Carlos V* and Alfonso de Ulloa's *La Vita dell'invittissimo Carlo Quinto*.[1] Both these accounts as well as the one in Juan de Mariana's *Historia de rebus Hispaniae* probably find their ultimate source in the *Historia del Emperador Carlos V*, by Pedro Mexia, Charles's personal historiographer and most likely an eyewitness to the event. All the descriptions are similar and any one might serve as the basis of the Patient's paraphrase; in none, however, can I find the original of what seems a direct quotation. As for the 'grave Florentine', said to have been so greatly moved by the modest retinue of Charles V, I can find no positive identification. The passage is not to be found in de Thou, nor does the epithet fit him or any of the other historians mentioned above.

Of retreat and reformation

De Thou's comments on Charles's retirement are worth quoting not only because he offers a counterbalance to the Ferrars' somewhat dewy-eyed, apologetic rationalizations (pp. 65-9; 74-6), but because he includes a long list of precedents for Charles's action.

It was then that the emperor—either moved by the death of his mother or disgusted with the world because of his lack of success, and realizing moreover that his physical infirmities increased daily—seriously considered retiring to Spain . . .

[1] Robertson, II, 92-3.

The emperor was especially distressed over the decline of his under-takings. Since he could see only with sorrow that they were failing along with himself, he resolved to retire to Spain in order to escape further embarrassment, to recover his health (which far from returning, caused him perpetual suffering) and to set up his son's somewhat renewed good fortune against a king already powerful and up to this moment always successful. In contemplating his abdication, he could bring to mind many examples of great men who, having arisen to an equal degree of importance, had spent their final days in retirement . . .

There follows a catalogue of the retirements of various emperors, most of whom reigned during the period of the domination of the Byzantine Empire by the Comnenus dynasty. De Thou concludes these examples by commenting:

Because it is true that most of these princes resigned from the empire quite unwillingly and even with the understanding that after their abdication no one would disturb their peace in any manner, the retire-ment of Lothair, son of Louis the Debonnaire, is more remarkable. After he had brought his son Louis into Imperial partnership with him, he retired of his own free will in 855 at the end of fifteen years to the monastery at Pruim, which he had had built and to which he had given great revenues.

Confirmed in his intention by all these examples which I have just reported, and by many others, and resolved to divest himself of all his estates, on the fifteenth of October the emperor had letters drawn up which he signed with his own hand and sealed with his own seal by which he ceded to his son Philip, whom he had already declared King of Naples and Sicily, his rights in all other kingdoms and in all that he possessed.[1]

It is possible but not really very likely that such historical precedents were influential in leading Charles to a decision; certainly they could have meant nothing to Nicholas Ferrar. It is, however, quite probable that Charles's abdication reflected philosophical sympathy with the actions of two of his con-temporaries and that Nicholas's retirement can be attributed

[1] De Thou, Book XVI, pp. 661–3.

in part to his admiration for these same men as well as for Charles.

Charles was intimately aware of the career of St Ignatius of Loyola (1491–1556), founder of the Society of Jesus, in whose early persecutions he as emperor took some part. Ignatius, a courtier and gallant, joined the army in 1517 and, while recuperating from a nearly mortal wound in 1521, underwent a mystical conversion as the result of reading a collection of the lives of the saints, there being no romances immediately available to him at that time. After an unsuccessful attempt to live in Jerusalem, and after years of preparatory study undertaken at the request of his superiors, Ignatius, along with six of his followers, was ordained in Venice in 1537. Most of the remainder of his life, however, was spent in Rome, where the Society of Jesus was recognized by Paul III in 1541 and where Ignatius published the *Spiritual Exercises* in 1548.

The men associated with Ignatius took vows of poverty and chastity; they dedicated themselves to education, ministering to the sick, and imitation of the life of Christ. Although later to assume the title of general of a group directly submissive to the pope, Ignatius was twice arrested by the Inquisition in the early days of his preaching and proselytizing. It was on one of these occasions in 1528 that Francis of Borgia (1510–71) saw and pitied him.

The influence of Francis over the emperor was much more direct than that of Ignatius. He was a cousin of the emperor, a trusted and capable courtier who, despite the deep impression made on him by the sight of the persecuted Ignatius, continued as friend and confidant of Charles and Isabella. The death of the empress, to whom Francis had been especially devoted, hastened his decision to retire from the court and reinforced his contempt for worldly position and success. He returned to his inherited duchy of Gandia, where he made many reforms—social, ecclesiastical and legal—and where he gave refuge to the Jesuits. After the death of his wife in 1550, he accomplished a long-held ambition: with the emperor's consent, he gave over his duchy together with all his titles and estates to his eldest son and, after having joined Ignatius in Rome, was ordained in 1551. A dynamic preacher, he won many disciples from the highest ranks of society and upon his return to Spain in 1554 was put in charge of all Jesuit missions. When Charles returned to Spain in 1556, he again sought out his old friend, whose precedent so exactly paralleled his own actions. For the last two years of Charles's life the courtier-turned-Jesuit became the close companion and adviser of the emperor-turned-recluse.

It was only sixty years later that Nicholas Ferrar returned to England after five years spent travelling on the Continent, where he had been widely exposed to the thought and accomplishments of the Counter-Reformation. Consciously as well as unconsciously he brought back with him something of the feeling and philosophy of this movement which had scarcely touched the Church in England, a country in which reformation was a term more accurately indicative of an outward and juridical change than of an inward and spiritual purification. If the Reformation in England had been more spiritual and less political in tone, Protestantism might have been saved from the many dissensions by which it is still unhappily beset.

There is no reliable evidence that Nicholas had direct and personal contact with any of the religious thinkers or monastic establishments in Italy or Spain. As a student not only of medicine but also of men, he read widely and observed carefully; his notebooks and letters must have been as crammed as his luggage with evidence of the impact of new ideas and new philosophies. What books he brought back with him it seems we shall never know. Jebb's footnote provides only a tantalizing clue: 'Many scarce books in various languages, chiefly treating of a spiritual life and of religious retirement, together with prints by the best masters relating to scripture subjects, all of which he had collected in his

1

travels, reached England before him. Of these only a few prints escaped in the devastation of Giddings' in 1646 by Puritan soldiers.[1]

It is quite beyond the scope of this Introduction to speculate at length on the many books and persons that might have influenced Nicholas Ferrar's life and thinking. Two or three have already been mentioned; a few others demand attention; a scholar-reader, however, can doubtless supply more and perhaps more direct influences.

In Italy, Nicholas lived in an atmosphere that since the days of St Catherine of Siena had encouraged a spirit of Christian humanism and had already produced groups not unlike the family retreat that was to be established at Little Gidding. The Oratories established by St Philip Neri in the years after 1550 seem almost to be prototypes for the meetings of the Little Academy. Baronius, a disciple of Neri, in *De Origine Oratorii* outlined the general pattern of meetings.

After some time spent in mutual prayer, one of the brothers read a spiritual book, and in the middle of the reading, the Father who super-intended the whole, discoursed upon what was said, explaining it with greater accuracy, enlarging upon it, and inculcating it into the hearts of the hearers. Sometimes he desired one of the brothers to give his opinion on the subject and then the discourse proceeded in the form of a dialogue; and this Exercise lasted an hour to the great consolation of the audience. After this, one of his own people at his command mounted to a seat raised a few steps above the rest and, without any adornment of language, discoursed upon some approved *Lives* of the saints, illus-trating what was said by passages of Scripture or sentences from the Fathers.[2]

It is also interesting to note another similarity: the Oratories were started for the benefit of laymen to help them use leisure

---

[1] Mayor, p. 201 n. 1. The problem of reconstructing possible contents of the Little Gidding library is further complicated by the bonfire of his books of 'comedies, tragedies, love hymns, heroical poems, and such like' that Nicholas ordered to be kindled on his future grave before his death (Mayor, p. 54).
[2] Addington, pp. 7–8.

time constructively and to test whether a life of perfection were possible for those living outside a cloister. The establishment of the Oratories, Addington asserts, marked the revival of 'Christian society of the early ages with its simplicity, its faith, and its charity'. When Nicholas Ferrar was in Italy, five Congregations had already been founded. The Rule was printed in 1612, a year before Ferrar's arrival.

Also close to the ways of Little Gidding were the practices of the Brethren of the Common Life. Founded by Geert de Groote (1340–84), out of disgust for his former self-indulgent and luxurious living, the Brethren provided a quasi-monastic retreat for men, and later, in separate houses, for women of similar experience and like mind. The organization grew under Florentius Radewins (1350–1400), under whom a rule was adopted, and chapters soon spread throughout the Low Countries and the Rhine valley. No vows were required; the emphasis was on teaching and the production of books for the use of schools, on the care of the poor, and on the leading of simple religious lives free from the extremes of ritual, fasting, penance, and un-worldly mysticism. Although the order was rapidly falling into decay when Nicholas visited the Low Countries in 1613, he might have visited one of the houses; certainly an interest in à Kempis, who received his education from the Brethren, would have led him to a study of their practices.

In Spain Nicholas breathed the air which had nourished the spirits of many given to mystic visions, baroque asceticism, and monastic retirement. Following closely upon the examples of St Ignatius Loyola and of St Francis of Borgia were the lives and works of St Teresa of Avila (1515–82) and of her follower, St John of the Cross (1542–91). First published in 1587, the writings of St Teresa—a visionary and ascetic who attributed the spread of the Reformation to the relaxed discipline of the monastic order— included the *Way of Perfection* and the *Castle of the Soul*. The *Spiritual Works* of St John, although completed in the 1570s, were not published until 1619, the year Nicholas Ferrar returned from Spain to England.

A catalogue of all the manuals of devotion and rules for monastic orders which might have come into Nicholas's hands would be a tedious and vain undertaking. There is, however, incontrovertible evidence that the Ferrars were acquainted with the writings of Juan de Valdes (1490?–1541) and of Francis of Sales (1567–1622). *The One Hundred and Ten Considerations* of Valdes, although originally written in Spanish, was first published in Italian at Basle in 1550. Exactly how and when Nicholas obtained a copy is a question, but that he valued the book highly is beyond doubt. In 1632 he finished a translation of it for which his friend George Herbert wrote a preface.[1] The poet-priest found some things in the *Considerations* to which exception might be taken, but he went on to remark:

Nevertheless I wish you by all means to publish it, for these three eminent things observable therein: First, that God in the midest of Popery should open the eyes of one to understand and express so clearly and excellently the intent of the Gospell in the acceptation of Christ's righteousness . . . a thing strangely buried and darkened by the Adversaries and their great stumbling block. Secondly, the great honour and reverence which he everywhere bears towards our dear Master and Lord . . . and setting his merit forth so piously for which I do so love him that were there nothing else, I would print it that with it the honour of my Lord might be published. Thirdly, the many pious rules of ordering our life about mortification and observation of God's kingdom within us, and the working thereof, of which he was a very diligent observer. These three things are very eminent in the author, and overweigh the defects (as I conceive) towards the publishing thereof.[2]

Juan de Valdes, brother of Alfonso (who was attached to the court of Charles V and became a severe critic of the corruption of the papacy and of the policies of Clement VII), fled Spain in

---

[1] The book did not appear until 1638 after the deaths of both Ferrar and Herbert. See Maycock, pp. 271–2. [2] Valdes, p. lix.

horror of the Inquisition in 1530 and eventually settled in Naples, where he surrounded himself with a spiritual court not unlike the Oratories of St Philip Neri, which were to be established a couple of decades later.[1] 'At his country house Valdes received on the Sunday a select number of his most intimate friends, and they passed the day' in the morning by first hearing Valdes comment on Scripture or 'some "divine consideration" which had occupied his thought during the week' and then by discussing his remarks. In the afternoon similar attention was given to themes proposed by members of the group.[2]

The Sunday conversations of Valdes and his friends were similar in content as well as in form to the sessions of the Little Academy. Underlying the discussions of the workings of Divine Grace and of the nature of Original Sin were the assumptions that concern for the things of this world inhibited purity of mind and body, and that, according to advice given a woman by Valdes, one must believe as if by faith alone one could be saved, and one must work as if salvation depended on works.[3] 'Valdes's faith was, in fact, sincere but unspecific, flexible and protean, harmless in any other age, centred upon a personal search for God and that "imitation of Christ" which humanism had reduced to identity with the Stoic virtues.'[4]

In particular, the Ferrars must have found two passages of the *Considerations* especially stimulating and comforting.

CONSIDERATION XVII ... A man should courageously, and generously resolve himself touching the world, turning his back to all the honour thereof, and to all the estimation thereof...[5]

CONSIDERATION LVII ... The proper exercise of a Christian is to attend unto *Mortification*. Attending unto it he feels, that the profit of it consists in this, that a man mortifying his affections and appetites goes by little and little comprehending that divine Christian perfection...[6]

---

[1] In his life of George Herbert, Walton confuses Juan de Valdes with his brother Alfonso.   [2] Valdes, p. xiii.   [3] *Ibid.*, p. xv.
[4] Elton, p. 111.   [5] Valdes, p. 55.   [6] *Ibid.*, p. 206.

A minor curiosity in relation to the *Considerations* is the strangely direct appeal that the publisher, Curio, all unwittingly, made to a man like Nicholas Ferrar. Nicholas would scarcely have to have read further to know that here was his book.

And you that waste all your time idly in reading of Boccace his hundred Novelties, and the like, lay them a while aside, and read these considerations of Valdesso, which are indeed true Novelties. For in them is treated of the great Divine and joyful new and gladsome tidings of the Gospell of Jesus Christ, of the great Pardon for Sins, of the reconciliation made with God by the death of the Sonne of God. Here you shall find the true & holy Enamourments of God and of Christ with mankind. Here you shall understand the true Embraces and the true Kisses given by meanes of the Holy Spirit. And last of all you shall find where the true delights and pleasures of those soules are, which are enamoured of God and of Christ and disenamoured of the world.[1]

Valdes's thought as it was spread by his disciples later became influential among the circles of public Protestantism, but his message, like that of Francis of Sales, was largely personal and offered a guide to the methods and practices of the private religious.

Francis of Sales's *Introduction to the Devout Life* was published in 1608 and, according to Maycock, 'we can be quite sure that Nicholas knew it and came to love it, for it was one of the many books bound by the sisters at Little Gidding'.[2] The life of St Francis offers an almost perfect paradigm for those who have been moved by a contempt for the things of this world. Born to wealthy and noble parents, he received an education from the Jesuits and later studied at Padua, where he pursued law to please his father and theology to please himself. He entered the priesthood against family opposition, became Bishop of Geneva, one of the founders of the Order of the Visitation, and an important figure of the Counter-Reformation. For him Nicholas must have felt some innocent envy and great admiration.

[1] *Ibid.*, p. xiv.   [2] Maycock, p. 49.

Unfortunately a spirit similar to that of the Counter-Reformation was raised in England too feebly and too late to be effective. The Ferrars were conscious of the wide gulf between their ways and the ways of the world and had only the weakest hope that they could win others to adopt the pattern of their life and thought. Like the latter-day Quakers, with whom they have much in common, the Ferrars chose the way of personal example rather than the way of politics or polemics.[1] Something might have been done to prevent the chaos of modern Protestantism had a churchman with the convictions of Ferrar and the passion of Milton arisen a hundred years earlier. But now it was too late. The Church of England was being attacked by such powerful forces from without that the struggle was for its life rather than for its soul. Not that Nicholas was alone; there were those who shared his condemnation of the practices of many of the people and some of the clergy, many who found consolation only in retirement, and some who, like Hamlet, could consider death—however abstractly—as 'a consummation devoutly to be wished'. Again it will be possible to select only a few instances, but they provide ample proof that disaffection with the world about them was not unusual among courtiers and commoners in the days of Elizabeth I and her immediate successors and that the example of Charles V was frequently cited.

'The slings and arrows of outrageous fortune'

The Ferrars themselves quote from an unimpeachable authority to prove that in this world 'all is vanity and vexation of spirit'.

In the year 1586 Queene Elizabeth told the whole state in the representative body of the Parliament, that Happines was so farre estranged from this world that the first step towards it was to bee quickly gone out of the world. Heare her own words. I am not ignorant of all kinds

---

[1] See below, pp. 171–3. Walton remarks in his life of Herbert, 'And 'tis fit to tell the reader that many of the clergy that were more inclined to practical piety and devotion than to doubtful and needless disputations did often come to Gidden Hall and make themselves part of that society . . .' (pp. 311–12).

of Lives: for I have obeyed, and I have governed: I have had good Neighbours and also evill: I have found trechery where I trusted: I have evill bestowed benefitts, and I have been evill reported of when I have done well. When I call these things past to mind, see and behold the things present, and expect future things, I think them most happy who dy soone. I think them most happy who dy soone: this is her censure, which addeth to that you have heard. Meethinks wee may boldly conclude that what is thus jointly ratified by the Defender of the Faith, the Christian and Catholick kings, must needs be an orthodox Christian, Catholick verity, that this world is a vale of misery, and that there is no true and solid Comfort to bee found, whilst wee are here on earth, but in the Faithfull service of God.[1]

If there is a certain Boethian flavour about the thoughts of Elizabeth and the appended comments of the Guardian, it is not at all surprising. Elizabeth herself translated the *De Consolatione Philosophiae*, and the Ferrars must also have been students of this widely popular work of Boethius. Elizabeth's speech invites comparison with Boethius's lament in prison over the evil effects of doing good, and the words of the Guardian echo the conclusion of Boethius as to the locus of happiness in this world: 'Our happiness itself is God.'[2] In fact, much of the Ferrars' investigation into the nature of happiness (especially the Socratic dialogue in Part IV of the Charles V volume) is closely parallel to the dialogues of Books III and IV of the *De Consolatione*. The Ferrars could also call upon Boethius to reinforce their condemnation of luxury in food and dress and the ostentatious keeping of many servants. It is Philosophia, not the Chief, who concludes that the comforts and pleasures of the body 'which can neither perform that they promise, nor are perfect by having all that is good, do neither, as so many paths, lead men to happiness, nor make men happy of themselves'.[3]

Nor was Elizabeth alone among English monarchs who expressed attitudes and ideas compatible with those of the Ferrars. King James himself wrote a condemnation of the use

---

[1] Sharland, p. 70.   [2] Boethius, III, 10.   [3] *Ibid.*, III, 8.

of tobacco (*Counterblast to Tobacco*, 1604) and Charles, his successor, was a personal and sympathetic friend of members of the Ferrar family, one who on several occasions visited Little Gidding.[1]

Public disgrace and sudden fall from power were misfortunes which sometimes resulted from close association with the English crown. The experience of Robert Devereux, Earl of Essex, caused many to doubt that worldly success and royal honours led to lasting happiness unless, like Elizabeth, one was convinced that such happiness could be achieved only in the world to come. Francis Bacon, whose rise to power had begun with his part in the prosecution of Essex, his former patron and friend, in 1618 became the Lord Chancellor and was created Viscount St Albans in 1621—the same year in which he later was convicted of bribery and forced into retirement. It was he who remarked in his essay 'Of Great Place', 'Certainly great persons had need to borrow other men's opinions to think themselves happy; for if they judge by their own feelings they cannot find it.' The Little Academy arrived at an almost identical conclusion in its dialogue on the nature of happiness and would surely concur with Bacon's pronouncement in 'Of Empire': 'We see also that kings that have been fortunate conquerors in their first years . . . turn in later years to be superstitious and melancholy; as did Alexander the Great, Dioclesian, and in our memory, Charles the Fifth . . .'

Sir Henry Wotton (1568–1639), another associate of Essex, considering his patron's sudden commitment to the Tower,

thought prevention by absence out of England a better security than to stay in it, and there plead his innocency in a prison. Therefore did he, so soon as the Earl was apprehended, very quickly, and as privately glide through Kent to Dover . . . and was by the help of favourable winds and liberal payment of the mariners, within sixteen hours after his departure from London, set upon the French shore.[2]

---

[1] See the fourth of T. S. Eliot's *Four Quartets*. For a full account of Charles I's association with the Ferrars see Maycock, especially pp. 276–82.

[2] Walton, pp. 108–9.

After the death of Elizabeth, Wotton enjoyed a brilliant career as foreign ambassador under James I and was rewarded in 1624 by being appointed provost of Eton College, a post he held until he died.

Wotton was a minor poet of some ability. In 1613 he had written the delicate lyric 'Ye meaner beauties of the night' in praise of the Princess Elizabeth upon the occasion of her marriage to the Elector Frederick V, and he later wrote 'The Character of a Happy Life', in which he found the happy man was he

> Who hath his life from rumours freed;
> Whose conscience is his strong retreat;
> Whose state can neither flatterers feed,
> Nor ruin make oppressors great;
>
> Who God doth late and early pray
> More of His grace than gifts to lend;
> And entertains the harmless day
> With a religious book or friend;
>
> —This man is freed from servile bands
> Of hope to rise or fear to fall:
> Lord of himself, though not of lands,
> And having nothing, yet hath all.

Happy indeed was Wotton's retirement to Eton which, says Walton, was 'to his mind as a quiet harbour to a sea-faring man after a tempestuous voyage . . . where he might sit in a calm, and looking down, behold the busy multitude turmoiled and tossed in a tempestuous sea of troubles and dangers'.[1] Persuaded that his new office required it, he was 'made Deacon with all convenient speed'. When congratulated on this act by a friend, Sir Henry replied:

I thank God and the King by whose goodness I now am in this condition; a condition which that Emperor Charles the Fifth seemed to approve: who after so many remarkable victories, when his glory was great in the eyes of all men, freely gave up his crown and the many

[1] *Ibid.*, p. 129.

cares that attended it ... making a holy retreat to a cloisteral life, where he might by devout meditations consult with God ... And after a kind of tempestuous life, I now have the like advantage ... even from my God, whom I daily magnify for this particular mercy, of an exemption from business, a quiet mind ... even in this part of my life, when my age and infirmities seem to sound me a retreat from the pleasures of this world, and invite me to contemplation, in which I have ever taken the greatest felicity.[1]

In 1626, two years after Wotton's retirement to Eton, both Nicholas Ferrar (1592–1637) and his close contemporary George Herbert (1593–1633) became deacons. The circumstances leading to Ferrar's decision are familiar; Herbert entered the Church only after being frustrated in his attempts at the kind of career that Sir Henry so successfully followed. In his Preface to Herbert's *The Temple*, Nicholas wrote, 'Quitting both his deserts and all the opportunitie that he had for worldly preferment he betook himself to the Sanctuarie and Temple of God, choosing rather to serve at God's Altar, then to seek the honour of State-Employments.' Walton, whose biography of Herbert includes several pages on the Ferrars of Little Gidding, gives a somewhat less flattering explanation, claiming that Herbert hoped that 'he might in time attain the place of a Secretary of State, he being at that time very high in the King's favour ... This, and the love of Court-conversation mixed with a laudable desire to be something more than he then was drew him often from Cambridge, where he held the post of Orator for the University.' But 'God ... did in a short time put an end to the lives of two of his most obliging and powerful friends ... and not long after King James died also, and with them, all Mr. Herbert's Court-hopes.'[2] Most modern biographers, including Hutchinson in his introduction to the *Works of George Herbert*, take the more lenient view of Nicholas Ferrar and point, as does Douglas Bush, to the close parallel between Herbert's career and that of his friend Ferrar, 'who in

---

[1] Walton, pp. 129–30.　　　　[2] *Ibid.*, p. 276.

1625 had turned his back upon auspicious worldly prospects to fulfill his deepest desires by establishing a religious community at Little Gidding'.[1] When Herbert was later inducted to the priesthood, he is reported by Walton to have remarked: 'I can now behold the Court with an impartial eye, and see plainly that it is made up of fraud and titles and flattery and many other such empty, imaginary, painted pleasures: pleasures that are so empty as not to satisfy when they are enjoyed: but in God and His service is a fulness of all joy and pleasure, and no satiety.'[2]

Born two years after Herbert, Robert Herrick (1591–1674) also came late to his vocation and only after some years of attendance not only on the king but on Ben Jonson as well. He enjoyed the patronage of Endymion Porter, whose influence at court was perhaps second only to that of the Duke of Buckingham, to whose household Porter was attached. After a belated education (1613–17) at St John's College, Cambridge, it was still not until 1623 that Herrick was ordained. In 1627 he went as chaplain with Buckingham on an expedition to the Ile de Ré. After Buckingham was assassinated in 1628, Porter lost his influence at court, and Herrick, now without a patron, accepted the vicarage of Dean Prior from Charles I. He took up his duties there in 1630 and stayed on in 'the dull confines of the drooping west' until 1648, when he was ejected by the Puritans, not to return again until 1660. His expressed dislike for his rustication may not have been any more sincere than his literary passion for Julia, Anthea, or Prue. It is significant that the poems voicing his discontent precede immediately his ouster by the Puritans,[3] and it is certainly obvious that he found a sort of anacreontic fulfilment in distant Devonshire where, in the words of Douglas Bush, 'in a troubled age he [Herrick] is largely content to mirror a timeless Epicurean Arcadia'.[4]

[1] Bush, p. 137. For further discussion of the relationship between Ferrar and Herbert see Maycock, especially pp. 233–5.   [2] Walton, p. 289.
[3] Moorman, p. 79 and Herrick, *Poetical Works*, ed. Martin, Chronological Tables.   [4] Bush, p. 112.

If for Wotton and Herbert and Herrick the life of a clergyman seemed attractive in part because it offered a refuge from the more turbulent world in which they had formerly moved and in which they could no longer find happiness, for Richard Hooker (1544?–1600) in an earlier age, a promising career even within the Church itself brought with it such personal misery that retreat to the country was preferable to success in the City. Hooker, a meek, quiet-loving Oxford scholar, became a priest in 1581 and, as the result of well-meant interference by his friend and former pupil, Edwin Sandys, was called from his country parish to be Master of the Temple,

a place which he accepted rather than desired; and yet here he promised himself a virtuous quietness . . . that so he might bring forth in peace the fruits of peace and glorify God by uninterrupted prayers and praises . . . but Almighty God did not grant it, for his admission into this place was the very beginning of those oppositions and anxieties, which till then this good man was a stranger to . . .[1]

Walton goes on to summarize the 'oppositions and anxieties' of a churchman in Elizabeth's times and to sketch the background for Hooker's involvement in the defence of the Church of England against the attacks of Walter Travers, a protégé of the Earl of Leicester and a powerful defender of the Calvinist faction. The clash between Hooker and Travers became a public scandal; charges and counter-charges were made; and Hooker emerged a famous man who 'grew daily in respect with the most learned and wise of the Nation'[2]—and a man who now had many enemies among the chief Benchers. To put an end to heated controversy and to solidify the position of the Church of England, Hooker conceived his great work, *The Laws of Ecclesiastical Polity*, and begged for a country parish so that he could complete his studies. To the archbishop he wrote:

When I lost the freedom of my cell, which was my college, yet I found some degree of it in my quiet country parsonage: but I am weary of

---

[1] Walton, pp. 181–2.   [2] *Ibid.*, p. 207.

the noise and oppositions of this place; and indeed, God and Nature did not intend me for contentions, but for study and quietness [so that I may] pray for God's blessing upon my endeavours and keep myself in peace and privacy, and behold God's blessing spring out of my Mother Earth and eat my own bread without oppositions.[1]

In 1591 Hooker left London for a parish in Boscombe near Salisbury; in 1595 he moved to Bishopsbourne near Canterbury, where, says Walton, 'he continued his customary rules of mortification and self-denial, was much in fasting, frequent in meditation and prayers, enjoying those blessed returns which only men of strict lives feel and know, and of which men of loose and godless lives cannot be made sensible; for spiritual things are spiritually discerned'.[2]

In *Puritan and Anglican*, Edward Dowden wrote, 'Men who were concerned for the life of the soul, if they did not carry that concern into public strife and become zealots of a party, were tempted to retreat from the world of action like the devout company of Little Gidding.'[3] To be involved in Anglican apologetics was as uncongenial a task for Hooker as dedication to Puritan controversy must have been later for Milton. Whether 'L'Allegro' and 'Il Penseroso' reflect personal convictions or not is here beside the point: they exist as expressions of the allurements of the rural and private life free from involvement with the affairs of men and party, the kind of life which Milton himself lived at Horton and on the Continent for ten years or so following his graduation from Cambridge and before setting aside his literary ambitions to become embroiled in religious and political pamphleteering.

Young men like Milton born in the early years of the seven-

---

[1] *Ibid.*, p. 209.

[2] *Ibid.*, p. 214. Close as Hooker's regimen was to that practised by the Ferrars at Little Gidding, and familiar as they doubtless were with Hooker's thought (see below, p. 4 n. 1), there is no trace of direct references to or borrowings from Hooker.

[3] Dowden, p. 5.

teenth century were blown by the rising winds of religious contention and political storm into ports of refuge more strange and more remote than those open to their predecessors. Ferrar and Herbert, separated only by some fifteen or twenty years from the stresses which faced Milton and Crashaw, were able to find their peace within the Anglican Church. For the two younger men the *via media* was closed: one became the great defender of Cromwell's cause; the other died a Catholic priest in Loreto.

Richard Crashaw (1612?–49) was—perhaps not strangely—attracted to Roman Catholicism in part because of his friendship with the High Anglican Ferrar family. After his graduation from Pembroke College he was made a fellow of Peterhouse, where he became tutor to Ferrar Collett, nephew of Nicholas Ferrar. Crashaw frequently visited Little Gidding, participated in the vigils and watches, and came to study and love the works of the Spanish mystics, especially the writings of St Teresa, about whom while still a Protestant he wrote one of his best poems. He also greatly admired Herbert's *The Temple* (of which Nicholas Ferrar was the editor) and later called a collection of his own poems *Steps to the Temple* as a tribute. Perhaps it was at Little Gidding that Crashaw became familiar with the writings of Lessius and wrote a short poem 'In Praise of Lessius', which was printed among the commendatory poems prefacing Nicholas's translation of the *Hygiasticon*, which appeared in 1634.[1] The poem was later somewhat revised, given the title 'Temperance' and printed in Crashaw's *Carmen Deo Nostro*. Although Crashaw was translating in part from *Argenis*, a Latin political novel by John Barclay, his poem 'Description of a Religious Life and Condition of Life' described a religious foundation not unlike that of Little Gidding. In Crashaw's life and poetry the circle closes, for again the same influences were at work which had earlier moved Nicholas in the course of his Continental studies and travels. Crashaw's rejections, however, were more dramatic and com-

---

[1] See below, pp. lxxviii, lxxxi–lxxxiv.

plete: he abandoned his Church and his country as well as his
secular career.

In an age in which melancholia was anatomized by Burton
from his quiet study in Oxford and dramatized by Shakespeare
on the London stage, it is not surprising that preachers and poets
and public figures all voiced doubts about the ability of this world
to produce true happiness. The misery of man's life is reflected by
Donne in his *Devotions* and by Taylor in his *Holy Dying*:

As our life is very short, so it is very miserable; and therefore it is well
it is short. God, in pity to mankind, lest his burden should be in-
supportable, and his nature an intolerable load, hath reduced our state
of misery to an abbreviature; and the greater our misery is, the less
while it is like to last. (Chapter I, Section IV)

Many of the best lived away from the noise of success and preferment; many, like Donne, chose the Church as a career when the
way of the world seemed to offer no future; and more, unlike
the Dean of St Paul's, sought the obscurity of small and quiet
parsonages. To several, including Donne, the fall of Essex in 1601
was a body-blow and the marriage of James I's daughter, the
Princess Elizabeth, in 1613, the last bright moment.[1]

In 1612 Donne, who was travelling with Sir Henry Wotton,
wrote home shortly before attending ceremonies in connection
with the election of Frederick V:

I go thither [the Palatinate] with a great deale of devotion for me
thinkes it is a new kinde of piety, that as Pilgrims went heretofore to
places which had been holy and happy, so I go to a place now, which
shall be so, and more by the presence of the worthiest Princess of the
world, if that marriage proceed. I have no greater errand to the place
then that at my return in to England I may be fitter to stand in her
presence and that after I have seen a rich and abundant country in his
best seasons, I may see that Sun which shall always keep it in that
height.[2]

[1] As a young diplomat, Donne was closely associated with Essex from 1596 until
the latter's execution in 1601. Donne was secretary to Lord Egerton, Lord
Keeper of the Great Seal, into whose charge Essex was remanded in 1601.
[2] Donne, Letter XXVI.

In honour of the wedding, which occurred on St Valentine's Day, 1613, Donne wrote a graceful epithalamium addressed to St Valentine and comparing the bride and groom to two phoenixes.

> Till now, Thou warm'dst with multiplying loves
> > Two larks, two sparrows, or two doves,
> > > All that is nothing unto this,
> For thou this day couplest two Phoenixes;
> > Thou mak'st a taper see
> What the sun never saw, and what the Ark
> (Which was of fowls and beasts the cage and park,)
> Did not contain, one bed contains, through Thee,
> > Two Phoenixes, whose joinèd breasts
> Are unto one another mutual nests,
> Where motion kindles such fires, as shall give
> Young Phoenixes, and yet the old shall live.
> Whose love and courage never shall decline,
> But make the whole year through, thy day, O Valentine.

But it was that other Donne, the one who two years earlier saw in the death of Elizabeth Drury a sign of the world's sickness and decay, who spoke more truly for 'men who were concerned for the life of the soul' in the early seventeenth century.

> And learn'st this much by our Anatomy,
> That this world's general sickness doth not lie
> In any humour, or one certain part;
> But as thou sawest it often at the heart,
> Thou seest a hectic fever that hath got hold
> Of the whole substance, not to be controlled,
> And that thou hast but one way not t'admit
> The world's infection, to be none of it.

> *The players cannot keep counsel;*
> *They'll tell all.*

In the foregoing discussion of the early seventeenth-century malaise and world-weariness, the emphasis has been not so much on the words as on the lives of men. But if what we are told by

Aristotle in the *Poetics* is valid—that 'Poetry is more philosophical and more serious than history, for poetry deals with things in a universal way, but history with each thing for itself'—then we must look to poetry for the final truth about the period in which the Ferrars formed their opinions and took up their way of life. If we may also assume that the greatest poet of the age will tell us the most truth, we may limit our investigation to Shakespeare—and only to as many of his plays as is necessary to make the point.

Shakespeare, too, had been caught up in the fall of Essex, partly because of the close relationship between his patron, the Earl of Southampton, and Robert Devereux, Earl of Essex. Southampton accompanied Essex on several military and naval expeditions, including the successful attempt to capture Cadiz in 1596. In 1599 he was with Essex in Ireland and was present during the subversive talk between the English leader and the Earl of Tyrone. Finally, Southampton was so deeply involved in Essex's rebellion in 1601 that he was sentenced to death, a penalty changed to life imprisonment, from which in turn he was released by James I in 1603. Shakespeare could not have watched the sure but slow decline of his patron towards disgrace and death without great personal sorrow. Moreover, he had written in the prologue to Act v of *Henry V* a description—prophetic in intention, but ironic in result—of the triumphant return of Essex from Ireland, likening that event to Henry's return from victory at Agincourt.

> As, by a lower but loving likelihood,
> Were now the General of our gracious Empress—
> As in good time he may—from Ireland coming,
> Bringing rebellion broached on his sword,
> How many would the peaceful City quit
> To welcome him!

Even more disturbing to Shakespeare was the use of his play *Richard II*, first produced in 1595, to stir up enthusiasm for Essex's rebellion, for this was presumably the history play put on

by Shakespeare's own company on the afternoon of 7 February
1601, the day before the uprising which sent Essex to the block
and Southampton to the Tower. Shakespeare and his actors
were cleared from any complicity, but Queen Elizabeth was
not unaware of the implications in the play: she wrote to
William Lambarde in August 1601, 'I am Richard II, know ye
not that?'

With disillusionment, disappointment, uncertainty, and danger
so deeply embedded in the lives of many public and private
figures of Shakespeare's time, it is not surprising that several of
Shakespeare's protagonists take action not unlike that of the
Emperor Charles V when he renounced his throne. Lear is
perhaps the best example of royal resignation. It was his 'fast
intent to shake all cares and business' from his old age and, like
Charles, to divest himself of 'interest of territory, cares of state',
and 'all the large effects that troop with majesty'. Richard II
seemed equally eager to shuffle off the responsibilities and burdens
of office and, moreover, to take up a monastic life: 'I'll give my
jewels for a set of beads, my gorgeous palace for a hermitage.'
Richard resigned almost willingly and with words and actions
that recall those of Charles V.

> Now mark me how I will undo myself.
> I give this heavy weight from off my head
> And this unwieldy sceptre from my hand,
> The pride of kingly sway from out my heart.
> With mine own tears I wash away my balm,
> With mine own hands I give away my crown,
> With mine own tongue deny my sacred state,
> With mine own breath release all duteous oaths.
> All pomp and majesty I do forswear;
> My manors, rents, revenues, I forgo.

Even the great Mark Antony, in whose 'name lay a moiety of the
world', could abandon the public duties of a triumvir in Rome
for the private joys of a lover in Egypt in the conviction that any
other life was emptiness:

> Let Rome in Tiber melt and the wide arch
> Of the rang'd empire fall. Here is my space.
> Kingdoms are clay; our dungy earth alike
> Feeds beast as man.

To Hamlet life was a burden to be endured, a burden possible to bear as a student in Wittenberg but heavy beyond belief for the Prince of Denmark, to whom death with all its horrible uncertainties was almost preferable to life in the corrupt and corrupting Danish court. For the most part, only the evil, the greedy, or the mad—a Macbeth, a Cassius, a Richard of Gloucester—would covet power or state; the good and sensitive would gladly live with Prospero on his idyllic island or with Duke Senior in the forest of Arden.

> Hath not old custom made this life more sweet
> Than that of painted pomp? Are not these woods
> More free from peril than the envious court?

Some had even retired without resigning. In *The Tempest*, Prospero, Duke of Milan, had really retired while he still held office and long before he had created the paradise of the magic island; he admits 'Those [the liberal arts] being all my study, the government I cast upon my brother and to my state grew stranger.' Prospero's return to Miranda's 'brave new world', peopled not only by a Ferdinand and an Alonso but also by an Antonio and a Sebastian, is the result of his love for his daughter, not of his reconciliation to the world of men.

> I'll bring you to your ship, and so to Naples,
> Where I hope to see the nuptial
> Of these our dear-belov'd solemnized;
> And thence retire me to my Milan, where
> Every third thought shall be my grave.

The Tempest was among the six plays by Shakespeare chosen to be given in honour of the marriage of the Princess Elizabeth to the Elector Frederick V in February 1613. Although possibly written as early as 1611, it was not printed until the 1623 Folio. The negotiations for the marriage had been so prolonged and their success so eagerly anticipated that we may believe equally easily either of two attractive theories. It may be that Shakespeare anticipated a joyful outcome to the embassy of Wotton and Donne and so wrote the wedding masque as part of the original play; or it may be that the masque was inserted (or even merely elaborated) to honour the Princess and her fiancé. Regardless of the circumstances of composition, the words of Juno were a warm wish for happiness for the royal couple in their brightest moment.

> Honour, riches, marriage blessing,
> Long continuance, and increasing,
> Hourly joys be still upon you!
> Juno sings her blessings on you.

DE CONTEMPTU CORPORIS

The new Little Academy

In contrast to the 'Dialogue on the Retirement of Charles V', the discussions on abstinence and the austere life include fewer participants; however, the group as a whole is more active in its contributions, Socratic investigations are more frequent, and no one speaker dominates the conversation—not even the Cheerfull, who initiated it.

In the ten arbitrary divisions of the manuscript the following members of the Ferrar family took part:

Part I	Cheerfull, Mother, Affectionate; brief remarks by Patient, Guardian and Moderator
Part II	Cheerfull, Mother, Affectionate, Patient; minor comments by Guardian and Moderator
Part III	Affectionate and Cheerfull in Socratic dialogue following earlier speeches by Mother, Patient, and Guardian

DE CONTEMPTU CORPORIS

Nicholas seems not to have been present nor is any reference made to him; the Resolved (John Collett) is mentioned only once; the Submisse is not mentioned at all. The Moderator makes only occasional contributions which, in contrast to her somewhat sharp-tempered intrusions in the Charles V sessions, seem relaxed and tolerant. Early in the proceedings she shows herself sceptical of the strictness of some of the Cheerfull's censures of Christmas celebration (p. 162) and later suggests that mankind wishes 'for as much content on earth as can well stand without loss of Heaven, and as many of God's temporal blessings as may possibly be enjoyed with His good will' (p. 176). Although clearly opposed to gluttony, resulting as it does in lascivious discourse (p. 278) and lust (p. 281), the Moderator seems to remain convinced that one must accept the common opinion that 'nothing keeps love and friendship more alive and flourishing in the world than this practice [of moderate good cheer] doth' (p. 262).

The Patient, too, seems to have overcome a certain impatience with others. Nowhere is she upbraided for unwarranted interruptions, but rather she reflects increasing maturity in her comments on the observations of her elders. Her youngness does show in minor ways: she fears that so long as there are other tongues to speak and other ears to listen she will fall into the vice of gossip (p. 293), and she continues to insist that those who attempt to do good to others will suffer for their virtuous intentions (p. 166). She seems convinced in her dedication to temperance (p. 190) and quotes Solomon (p. 226), Socrates (p. 217), and St Basil (p. 182) as witnesses for her own condemnation of gluttony.

In the two years which separate the discussion of Charles V from the 'Dialogue on the Austere Life', the Affectionate (Margaret Collett) graduated to active membership in the Little Academy. Her most significant contribution is that of an almost suspiciously able devil's advocate in Socratic dialogue with the Cheerfull in Parts III and IV. Her defence of good cheer rests largely on the 'opinion and custom of the best and wisest men of the world' (p. 186) and on 'the great force and virtue which good cheer hath for the maintenance and increase of mutual love and friendship' (p. 259). That her defence is partly specious, a tribute to her intelligence rather than evidence of her convictions, is made clear by recollection of her first words in this dialogue in which she cautioned: 'We are doubly bound to beware that neither the errors of any example, however authorized, mislead us from our stableness; nor the violence of any opposition, however intended, cause us to run into the same excess of riot.' (p. 160)

But unresolved ambiguities are present. The Affectionate seems to have had great skill in cooking—and dainty and rich food, at that (p. 248)—and despite her youth, some experience with intemperance. When the Cheerfull asked, 'How find you yourself affected and disposed after good cheer?' she boldly answered, 'Why, good for nothing.' (p. 195)

One wonders also at times whether Margaret was not discouraged by what she considered the wordiness and perhaps not complete sincerity of certain members of the Little Academy and if her preference for the more relaxed life at Margaretting[1] was not a frustrated reaction. Her long diatribe on gossip with which this volume concludes may well stem from disgust with the pettiness which must at least occasionally have broken the peace of such a closely knit community. Certainly when she urges fearless action, disregard for the opinion of the world, and willingness to serve as a light to others, hers is the voice of an independent, determined, almost coldly logical young woman:

We are afraid to go alone. Let us not think so. There are others of our minds if they had an example to allege for their opinion. We shall have them that will follow in the way as soon as they know there's any gone before. But we are loath to be the foremost. Why, that's advantage if we well mark it. We shall thereby have a double benefit; not only our own but others well doing in imitation of us shall run to our accompt. We want an example? Let's make one. We shall have run some hazard at first. We shall certainly reap more honour, more reward from God and good men at the last. And yet perhaps the danger that affrights us is nothing so bad as it makes show of. The wounds that we expect are but words; the sufferings that we shall feel but in conceit. (p. 172)

Although the Cheerfull (Hester Collett) plays a central part in the 'Dialogue on the Austere Life', she reveals little of herself—and that little is quite unattractive. The suddenness with which she called the Little Academy together ('Pardon me if I seem importunate in occasioning this meeting so much before your expectation'), her insistence on abstinence and austerity in place of the moderation which had been the Ferrars' congenial practice, betray a mind excessively self-righteous and narrow. The Cheerfull seems to carry all questions of restraint in eating and drinking to extremes: Christmas provisions are carnal excesses (p. 160); all eating is a necessary evil (p. 219); wine is neither a meat nor drink, but a medicine. She is intolerant of delay and discussion

---

[1] Maycock, p. 177.

('Shall we be recommending good examples every day, I may say almost all the day long and never go about to follow them?' (p. 171)), but does not succeed in controlling the dialogue until Part III when she pleads, 'Give me leave to continue therein without any more digressions' (p. 191). She welcomes the suggestion of Socratic dialogue with the Affectionate, for she had already learned something of that art in the Charles V meetings (pp. 51–9) and had come by her own knowledge of temperance in that manner (p. 192). The dialogue continues with occasional interruptions from Parts IV to VII as the Guardian and the Mother succeed the Affectionate as partners and eventually take over the discussion themselves. Throughout, the Cheerfull reveals a rather narrow mind of no great learning or originality, but of a dogged stubbornness which drives her assumed opponents to ridiculous quibbling and logically illogical admissions. In Part VII, when the interest shifts away from abstinence to a consideration of the effects of over-indulgence and the evils of ostentation, the Cheerfull no longer participates in the discussion.

The humane and tolerant Guardian, John Ferrar, plays a more active and constructive part in this dialogue than he did in the earlier one devoted to the retirement of Charles V. Unlike the others, he probably had had considerable experience with high living and was not without pleasant memories of merry company and good cheer. When the Cheerfull suggests that wine is properly to be considered only a medicine, the Guardian replies, 'It is a pleasant medicine, if it be a medicine' (p. 225), and proceeds to defend its use for the relief of sorrow by quoting appropriate passages from the Bible (pp. 225–6). Compared with the Cheerfull, he is a relativist and a humanitarian: he does not want the words of the Scripture stretched beyond the intention of the writer (p. 235) and feels that within limits 'No man ought to be restrained from his liberty either of judgement or practice in this case'—that is, the matter of drinking wine. He shows considerable skill and pleasure when driven into a casuistic debate on the meaning of 'much and little wine' (pp. 236–8) and must have been quite pleased when he was able to remark,

For much cheerfulness will cause much mirth and jollity and much appetite and digestion will draw down the more meat. But since meat and mirth are really good, why the more of them should not be accompted the better, as long I mean as they grow not to excess, I see no reason and I am sure I have the greatest part of the world on my side. (p. 238)

As the gratuitous phrase with which he concludes these remarks might indicate, the Guardian rather enjoyed gently baiting his auditors; certainly he took a quiet satisfaction in luring the Cheerfull into quibbles and corners by a logical extension of the condemnation of wine to an attack on grapes and raisins (pp. 244–50).

During the course of the dialogue he cites a wide variety of sources—Sir Philip Sidney, Aristophanes, Busbequius, St Francis of Sales, Pico della Mirandola, St Jerome—as pertinent authorities. At the close, however, with great sincerity and humility he speaks from personal experience on the sins of backbiting and slandering (pp. 295–306). He refuses to consider wine as the ultimate cause of evil-speaking and when the Patient asks, 'But shall we say that this is a natural effect of good cheer?' he wisely replies, 'No, verily, but a necessary consequence of the evil disposition of the mind wherewith men ordinarily come into it.' (p. 265) Here as everywhere the Guardian is the welcome voice of wisdom, tolerance, and human understanding. Aware of his own shortcomings and appreciative of the weaknesses of all mankind, he relies simply and unquestioningly on God's all-embracing Grace.

I therefore give my ball to the advancement of this self same end which you have all agreed upon, setting up by resolution for myself and humble prayers for all the rest of the family the growth in Grace and in the knowledge of our Lord and Saviour Jesus Christ, to whom be glory both now and forever, for the main end, sole rule, sure guide, and overruling mistress of all our opinions, desires, and actions in this world . . . (pp. 178–9)

Mary Collett, known as the Chief in the 'Dialogue on the Retirement of Charles V', was elected Mother after the death of old Mrs Ferrar (p. xxxi). The change was only nominal: she remained the humble, sympathetic, no-foolishness kind of intellectual and spiritual leader that she had always been. In the course of the abstinence discussion she reveals new but not unexpected intellectual skills and reflects an attitude toward wine and good cheer not as intolerant as that of the Cheerfull nor as liberal as that of the Guardian.

There is no doubt that she strenuously objected to the pagan qualities of the pastimes and celebrations by which her contemporaries observed the Christmas season (p. 170) and that she herself to her great comfort had already made some progress in self-denial and temperance.

I am therefore come to a resolution, God willing, to undergo whatever in this kind shall be needful, and so much the rather as I find by that little essay which through God's mercy I have made of this virtue there is no likelihood of disadvantage or loss any way... There is scarce one meal in the week that bread itself relisheth not more pleasant in my taste than formerly the greatest delicacies that art or nature could afford. And I find it most true that I heard of old and could not believe: that the pleasantness of the meat lies not in the costly steam of a dainty dish but in the pure keenness of a well-ordered appetite. (p. 189)

Temperance, however, is not prohibition. Wine is permissible, she says, because 'it naturally cheers up the heart and ought not to be generally restrained in this vale of misery' (p. 258). When the austere Christmas that the Cheerfull imposed on the family came to be observed a few weeks later, the Mother was a bit resentful and urged the Cheerfull to bring forth a 'banquet of stories ... and that answerable to the festival, rich and plentiful with dainties, that our guests may report they have Christmas fare for the mind at least, albeit but ordinary entertainment for their bellies'.[1]

[1] Sharland, p. 248.

It is in the course of her insistence on discovering the true intention of Scripture and on avoiding wilful misinterpretation that the Mother shows her remarkable knowledge of ancient and modern translations of the New Testament (pp. 231–5). She cites not only many of the earlier English translations but also Greek, Latin, Italian, Dutch, Flemish, and German Bibles in her attempt to clarify the meaning of the phrase 'given to much wine' as it appears in Titus ii, 3.

As her final contribution to this session of the Little Academy, she delivers the first of the meditations on gossip and slander (pp. 284–93) and in true humility condemns herself as having been of the devil's party.

Thus I condemn myself and less I cannot suspect of others touching this matter, an ordinary, indeed, but an abominable practice which I now as much hate as I have heretofore little understood, finding the venom to lie chiefly in that which is commonly reputed the virtue thereof. Because it is intended to the increase of love and ministers much satisfaction to distempered minds, I thought it a trim piece of art and, pleasing myself in the opinion of much charity as well as policy made the revealing and discanting upon others faults the ordinary manner of patching up mine own reconciliation with offended friends. (p. 285)

Mary Collett, however, was in no way narrowly concerned with her own salvation. She, perhaps more than any other member of the Ferrar community, had great but failing hope that the ways of the world might change and the example of Little Gidding might be a force in the true reformation of England.

Our example may perhaps hearten on some others. Let us not blame either our sex or our condition, as disabled for the advancement of God's kingdom. We have a talent and great one committed to us, if we be careful to employ it. Not in the tongue, no—that belongs to the ministry; but in the hands and in the feet—that's common to all Christians. We may tread out the way to heaven and we may lead on by good works though we cannot teach by words. And perhaps that real kind of instruction [that] hath in all ages been the most forcible is in this the most necessary where there are many masters but few guides, a dearth of patterns in an exuberance of rules. (pp. 171–2)

An exuberance of rules

Master George Herbert of blessed memorie, having at the request of a Noble Personage translated it [*Discorsi della vita sobria*] by Luigi Cornaro into English, sent a copie thereof, not many months before his death, unto some Friends of his [the Ferrars], who a good while before had given an attempt of regulating themselves in matter of Diet: Which, although it was after a very imperfect manner, in regard of that exact course therein prescribed; yet it was of great advantage to them, inasmuch as they were enabled, through the good preparation that they had thus made, to go immediately to the practise of that pattern, which Cornarus had set them, and so have reaped the benefit thereof, in a larger and eminenter manner than could otherwise possibly have been imagined in so short a space.

Not long after, Lessius his book, by happie chance, or, to speak better, by gracious providence of the Author of Health and all other good things, came to their hands: Whereby receiving much instruction and confirmation, they requested from mee the Translation of it into English. Whereby hath ensued what you shall now receive.[1]

The book for which T. Smith wrote these introductory remarks comprised a translation of Leonard Lessius's *Hygiasticon* (Louvain, 1613), Herbert's translation of Cornaro's *Discorsi* (Venice, 1558), and an anonymous (and insignificant) *Discourse translated out of the Italian, That a Spare Diet, is better than a Splendid and Sumptuous*, which Smith describes as 'a banquet of Junkets after a solid Feast. The Author thereof was an Italian of great reputation, living in the same age which Cornarus did.'

Luigi (or Ludovici) Cornaro (1467–1566) was a pleasure-loving, high-living Venetian nobleman who, in middle life becoming discouraged with the efforts of medical men to restore his health, resolved to experiment with the effects of a regulated diet. He not only cured himself but lived to be nearly a hundred,

---

[1] Lessius, 'To the Reader, The Preface of the Publisher' by T. S[mith].

thereby giving the lie to a forty-year-old prophecy that he had only a few months left. When he wrote his book, Cornaro was a lively and delightful octogenarian, enthusiastic in his praise of moderation and more especially in his delight with his healthy, prosperous, and active old age. He speaks of the pleasure he has in his houses, his gardens, his friends, and his grandchildren—and in his reading, his writing, and his interest in the theatre. Like Bacon's, this approach to abstinence is humanistic and even materialistic: life is desirable for the sake of living it fully; and if moderation will enable one to achieve that end, then moderation is desirable. 'If', he wrote, 'this world consist of order, if our corporall life depend on the harmonie of humours and elements, it is no wonder that order should preserve, and disorder destroy.'[1] After many years of experiment and with increasing age, he came to achieve this order by allowing himself only twelve ounces of food and fourteen ounces of liquid daily. He realized, however, that such stringency in diet was not a universal rule—that each man should devise his own regimen.

Wherefore since an orderly life is so profitable, so vertuous, so decent, and so holy, it is worthy by all means to be embraced; especially since it is easie and most agreeable to the nature of Man. No man that follows it, is bound to eat and drink so little as I: No man is forbidden to eat fruit or fish, which I eat not: For I eat little, because a little sufficeth for my weak stomack: and I abstain from fruit, and fish, and the like, because they hurt mee. But they who find benefit in these meats, may, yea ought to use them: yet all must take heed, lest they take greater quantitie of any meat or drink (though most agreeable to them) then their stomack can easily digest: So that he which is offended with no kinde of meat and drink, hath the *quantitie* and the *qualitie* for his rule.[2]

Francis Bacon had already mentioned Cornaro in his *Historie of Life and Death* (1623) in a passage reprinted by T. Smith in his Preface in order to still narrowly Protestant objections to the

---

[1] Cornaro, p. 22.   [2] *Ibid.*, pp. 32–3.

publication of works by Roman Catholics—and one a Jesuit, at that.

It seems to be approved by experience, that a slender Diet, and well-nigh Pythagorian, or such as is answerable to the severest Rules of Monasticall life, or to the institutions of Hermites, who had Necessitie and Scarceness for a Rule, doth produce long life. And to this course appertains drinking of water, cold aire, slender food (to whit, of roots and fruits, and poudered and pickled flesh and fish, rather than that which is fresh and hot) the wearing of hair-cloth, often fastings, frequent watchings, and seldome enjoyment of sensuall pleasures, and the like. For all these do diminish the spirits, and reduce them to that quantitie, which sufficeth merely to the service of life, whereby the consumption of the Radicall humour and Vitall heat is abated. But if the Diet be somewhat more choice then these rigours and mortifications allow, yet if it bee always equall, and after one constant proportion, it will afford the same benefitt: Which was evidently demonstrated by the Regiment and Diet which the Venetian Cornarus used, who ate and drank so many yeares by one just weight; by which means he came to live above an hundred yeares, continuing an able man both in strength and senses.[1]

How the Ferrars came to know of Cornaro is a matter for speculation, but Smith's implication that the book was unknown to them until Herbert made his translation seems as questionable as the suggestion that it had much help to offer them. Both in theory and practice the Ferrars had already advanced beyond the self-denials recommended by the genial Venetian gentleman. That the Ferrars were already familiar with the work of the rigorous and Jesuitical Lessius before they learned of Cornaro, and that it was Lessius who helped determine their 'rule' seem likely not only from their practice but also from examination of the following chronology:

1. Nicholas Ferrar was travelling in the Low Countries in 1613.
2. Lessius's *Hygiasticon* was published in 1613 in Louvain.

[1] See above, p. lxxviii n.

3 The regimen of Cornaro was known in England before 1622, when Bacon referred to it.

4 The Cheerfull initiated the abstinence discussions in Advent 1632, by which time the Mother had already made considerable progress in the practice of self-denial (p. 189).

5 Scattered throughout the Charles V dialogue, which took place in the summer of 1631, and especially in the prefatory remarks which date back to February of that year, there is considerable evidence that ascetic practices were already common to some members of the Little Academy.

6 Robert Mapletoft wrote to Nicholas Ferrar, on 30 January 1633, that 'Lessius will be finished some time tomorrow'.[1]

7 George Herbert died on 1 March 1633 and had sent a copy of his translation of Cornaro 'not many months before his death'.[2]

8 As a tribute to his close spiritual friend, Nicholas included Herbert's translation with his own translation of *Hygiasticon* when it was published in 1634.

Leonard Lessius was born at Brecht in 1554 and died at Louvain in 1623. A brilliant student and teacher, a spiritual force highly esteemed by many, including St Francis of Sales, he was a professor of theology at Louvain from 1585 to 1623. In the *Hygiasticon*, written ten years before his death, Lessius freely admits his debt to Cornaro[3] although his approach to the purpose of abstinence was essentially disciplinary, ascetic, and spiritual: 'For that which I principally intend, is to furnish religious persons, and those who give themselves to pietie, with such a way and manner of living, as they may with more ease, cheerfulness, and fervencie apply themselves to the faithfull service of the Great God,

---

[1] Maycock, p. 272 n.   [2] See above, p. lxxviii.   [3] Lessius, p. 9.

and our Saviour, the Lord Jesus Christ.'[1] The practice of self-denial is the only means by which one may attain this end: 'Abstinence is an outward, secondarie, and ministeriall foundation, inasmuch as it removes those things which breed impediment to the exercises of Faith, and to the functions of the Intellectual facultie, or makes them full of difficultie, unpleasant and tedious.'[2]

A few pages later he follows these generalizations with this paragraph which must have found fervent acceptance by the Little Gidding community.

For besides that this [a disciplined and clear intellect] is very pleasant in its own nature, it brings along with it, if so be we desire it, a very great spiritual commoditie: For then, by long experience of forepast age, the vanitie of the world is better discerned, and becomes more contemptible; heavenly matters begin to relish us better, and earthly to be despised: Those everlasting future things which hang over our heads, are always before our eyes, and call upon us to make fitting preparation for them: All knowledge and experience which we have gotten from our youth up untill that time, turns greatly to our advantage, and we reap the sweet thereof. And then the affections and perturbations of our mindes being calmed, we can with great ease and pleasure, give ourselves to Prayer, Meditation of divine matters, Reading of scripture and the works of the holy Fathers. Then we may with delight always busy our mindes with pious cogitation, and, as the holy Fathers were wont, be alwayes ruminating upon some one or other divine sentence out of Gods Word, and with great reverence and devotion be constantly partakers of the Prayers, and other publick duties which the Church enjoynes us unto.[3]

Unlike Cornaro, Lessius was writing not the autobiography of an abstinent, but advice for all those who would encourage the spiritual life of man. As a result partly of this quite different intention and partly of a quite different personality, Lessius tends to enumerate, subdivide, and categorize in a schoolteacher-like fashion. He finds that a sober life brings five 'commodities' to the body and five more to the soul. The physical

[1] Lessius, p. 11.   [2] *Ibid.*, pp. 174–5.   [3] *Ibid.*, pp. 181–3.

advantages discussed in Chapter VII include freedom from most diseases, resistance to disease, mitigation of the effects of disease, prolongation of life and promotion of agility. As for the soul (Chapter VIII), abstinence strengthens and invigorates the senses, diminishes the force of the passions and affections, preserves the memory, helps the wit and understanding, and extinguishes the fury of lust. Much of this, to be sure, is merely Cornaro codified. When Lessius came to devising rules for obtaining these ends, however, his prescriptions were not as absolute as the measures of food recommended by Cornaro; rather they were based on a relative scale in which the constitution of the individual would determine in part the maximum amount of food permissible or desirable. In limiting his diet, each individual was to follow these guides:

1 Not to eat so much as to impair the operation of the superior faculties of the mind.
2 Not to eat so much as to feel dull at any time.
3 To decrease the amount eaten as experience with self-denial increased.
4 To take no care for the quality of food.
5 To avoid variety in food and 'such as are curiously and daintily dressed'.
6 To avoid the sight of feasts and dainites. Think of the bad smells generated by rich eating.
7 To eat once a day preferably, but never more than twice.
8 For the elderly and those of weak constitutions, twelve to fourteen ounces of food and liquid each day are sufficient.

Lessius discusses the relationship between food, lust, and choler in terms which the Ferrars were later to echo: 'The appetite doth not onely desire that which is necessarie to the conservation of the Bodie but also that which may serve for Procreation . . . [but] it oftentimes longs after more then is any way proportionable . . .

for the nourishment of the Bodie, or for the matter of Propagation.'[1]

Such self-defeating over-indulgence results 'by reason of the condiments and Lickorish cooking of the meats themselves, which by their varietie and new relishes do go on continually provoking the Appetite, and stirring up Gluttony'[2] and choler. In fact, one can almost hear the voice of the Cheerfull in one of the last passages of the *Hygiasticon*: 'What can be more vile and undecent for a man then to be a slave to his belly? And what greater madness, then to renounce and quit our interest in all those excellent benefits which Sobrietie brings forth both to Soul and Bodie for a little tickling delight in the throat?'[3]

Clearly, the Ferrars knew the *Discorsi* and *Hygiasticon*, but the tantalizing and oblique references that the participants in the dialogue make to other sources tease the reader out of thought. Some of their ideas may derive from Richard Burton's *Anatomy of Melancholy* (1621)—and, indeed, Burton may be the 'most worthy author of our times' cited below, page 212, but I cannot find the reference. In the *Anatomy* (Part I, Sect. II, Mem. II, Subs. I) 'Bad Diet' is discussed among the other causes of melancholy, and in Subsection II of the same division Burton has something to say about surfeiting and drunkenness, which could well have served the Ferrars as a point from which to expand their discussion. In Subsection III, 'Custom of Diet'—in which, by the way, Busbequius is mentioned (p. 217)—Burton explains how men may become used to strange food and still maintain control of their minds and bodies. A similar point is made by the Cheerfull in the 'Dialogue on the Austere Life' (p. 195). Finally, Burton suggests cures for melancholy through Diet Rectified in Substance and in Quantity and both Lessius and Cornaro are mentioned as sources (Part II, Sect. II, Mem. II, Subs. I and II).

Many of the pertinent passages in Burton refer to Galen, who in turn owed much to Pliny. The Ferrars could have read both

---

[1] Lessius, p. 191.   [2] *Ibid.*, p. 194.   [3] *Ibid.*, p. 207.

of these ultimate sources in the original languages; much of Pliny, however, was available in English through the efforts of that indefatigable Elizabethan translator, Philemon Holland, whose *Natural History* appeared in 1601; and Latin translations of Galen, the work of Thomas Linacre some hundred years earlier, were to be had. So many classical and medieval sources exist and are cited so informally by the Ferrars that it has proved impossible to discover direct borrowings.

One is next tempted to trace the Ferrars' thought to English predecessors, the early English mystics and hermits such as Walter Hilton, Julian of Norwich, and the unknown authors of *The Ancrene Riwle* and *The Cloud of Unknowing*. But the search is fruitless: the discussions reflect the common concerns of those living in monastic or semi-monastic retreat, and the emphasis falls on simplicity and austerity in thought, word, and deed, in dress, food, and conversation. The Ferrars seem to have had no realization that they had distinguished pattern-makers in their own country, even such a recent one as William Bullein, author of *A Dialogue Against the Fever Pestilence* (1564) and *The Government of Health* (1595). Fascinating and lively dialogues that they are, they reveal only an occasional similarity of thought and a common reliance on the traditional sources, especially Galen and Pliny. The latter work is interesting principally for the songs sung by Humfrey, the teacher, to help John, his young interlocutor, remember various rules of health: his 'small song of the foure complections' ingeniously traces the properties of food to the humours and ages of man, and to the seasons of the year. The tone throughout is light and informal; the result, a breath of fresh air reminiscent of the atmosphere created by Cornaro.

That the Ferrars were directly familiar with a wide variety of the ascetic literature of the past and that Nicholas Ferrar, a former medical student, would accumulate a library of treatises on medicine and health must be granted. That they had any specific sources is yet to be discovered. That they covered their tracks well—and perhaps intentionally—is clear from such interspersed phrases as 'your master, whoever he may be' (p. 293) and 'he from whom I have received it' (p. 181), a remark which also indicates a possible oral source—perhaps direct instruction by Nicholas—for the Cheerfull's defence of temperance which follows. Both the Cheerfull and the Mother seem to have taken part in earlier Socratic dialogues which they drew on for the instruction of the Little Academy. The Cheerfull introduces the discussion between herself and the Affectionate as following 'the same way wherein I was taught myself' (p. 192), and the Mother offers with the help of the Guardian to instruct the Little Academy 'after the same manner that I learned it' (p. 228). During the last sessions of the meetings devoted to the discussion of temperance, the Mother in the course of her attacks on slander and back-biting, close as they are in spirit and frequently in word to Sections 27 to 29 of *The Devout Life* of St Francis of Sales, clearly indicates reliance on a master (again possibly Nicholas) who, she remarks, is confident 'not in his own strength . . . but in the mercy of God' in his determination to avoid malicious gossip (p. 294). Whatever their sources, whoever their authorities and masters, the Ferrars seem to have assimilated them so thoroughly that they could speak with all the force of original discovery and deep personal conviction.

As for the Practitioners, they forbid any more to be spoken of them then this, That they find all the benefits, which are promised by Cornarus and Lessius most true and reall; so by God's mercie they find no difficultie at all in the observation of this course. They are sufficient witnesses in their own affaires, and I hold them to be faith-full: And therefore making no doubt of the truth of the latter part of their report, as I can abundantly give testimony of the veritie of the former, I commend both to thy belief and consideration; and so commit thee to God's grace.[1]

In these words in his address 'To the Reader' T. Smith bids the Ferrars farewell and gives both them and us God's blessing.

[1] See above, p. lxxviii n.

ON THE RETIREMENT
OF CHARLES V

Part I

The narrator, Nicholas Ferrar, relates the considerations which led to the founding of the Little Academy at the behest of the Maiden Sisters on the Feast of the Purification, 2 February 1630/1, and comments on its early struggles. The first dialogue recorded took place on Ash Wednesday of that year, but the extended discussion on Charles V did not begin until the end of May. The Chief proposes the topic—that 'our well chosen resolutions' should be confirmed by immediate action —and tells a story of Pyrrhus who, deaf to advice to seek peace and happiness, died by accident after years of warfare and suffering. She applies the moral to Christians who postpone the fulfilment of promises made to God and to themselves—those who, while intending to lead austere and godly lives, devote themselves to 'foolish employments of minds and times in gauds and trifles'. The Patient tells a story of Trajan, and the Cheerfull one of a bishop's wealthy mother. The Affectionate concludes this section by a short story illustrating how the foolish defence of errors can multiply guilt.

NOTE: These stories as well as the introductory remarks are also included in B.M. Add. MS. 34657 and were printed by Miss Sharland in *The Story Books of Little Gidding*, pp. 2–10.

It was the same day wherein the Church celebrates that great Festival of the Purification [2 February], that the Mayden Sisters longing to bee Imitatours of those Glorious Saints, by whose Names they were called (for All bare Saints Names, & she that was elected Cheif that of the Blessed Virgin Mary) hauing entered into a ioynt Couenant between themselues & some others of Neerest Bloud (which according to their seueral Relations they stiled Founder, Guardian, & Visitour) for the performance of diuers Religious Exercizes, Least as sweet Liquours are oftentimes corrupted by the sowreness of the vessels wherein they are infused, there should arise in their hearts a Distaste or Abuse of those Excellent things, which they proposed: They therefore resolued together with the Practize of Deuotion to intermingle the study of Wisedome, Searching & Enquiring diligently into the knowledge of those things, which appertaine to their Condition & Sex; Finding in themselues and obseruing in others, that doe sincerely pursue vertue, that the Greatest barre of Perfection was Ignorance of the Truth, whereby through misapprehension many preiudicial things were embraced, & many most behovefull to their Ends & most delightfull in performance ⟨1⟩ were not only neglected but abhorred. Which hauing by many particulars experimented [experienced] in themselues, doubting that they were alike abused in most of these things, which wee haue receiued by Tradition from our Fathers, they determined with firm promises each to other to make a particular survey of those Opinions & Practizes, which the World recommends or disallows, weighing them not in the Scales of Common iudgement, but of true & right Reason[1] according to the weights & by the

[1] Right reason—the exact definition of this phrase, even when used by more careful philosophic writers than the Ferrars, is very difficult. Douglas Bush in *English Literature of the Earlier Seventeenth Century*, p. 35, defines it as 'the eternal and harmonious law of God and nature written in every human mind and heart'. The same writer remarks in *Paradise Lost in our Time*, p. 37, 'Right reason is not merely reason in our sense of the word; it is not a dry light, a nonmoral instrument of inquiry. Neither is it simply the religious conscience. It is a kind of rational and philosophic conscience which distinguishes man from the beasts and which links man with man and with God. This faculty was implanted by God in all men, Christian and heathen alike, as a guide to truth and conduct.' Although the Cambridge Platonists flourished in a period too late to have a direct influence over the Ferrars, their appeal to 'right reason' and the 'light of nature' had been anticipated by Richard Hooker, as Basil Willey points out in his *Seventeenth-Century Background*, p. 121. Hooker died in 1600 and his thought and works must have been familiar to the Ferrars. Professor Willey also remarks, *op. cit.* p. 72, 'Reason... was for the Platonists the ultimate source of authority in matters of faith; and the function of Scripture was to illuminate and confirm its dictates, never to contradict them. Revelation is not confined to the pages of holy writ nor to the age of the prophets and apostles, for Reason, a "seed of deiform nature", is "Natural revelation"' (pp. 72–3). This comment should be considered in relation to the many instances in which the Ferrars traced the working of God's hand in the lives and actions of nearly contemporary persons.

For a full discussion of right reason the reader is referred to *Right Reason in the English Renaissance* by Richard Hoopes. Hoopes quotes a passage from

Standard of the Scripture, wherein they being excellently versed so as they were able to repeat by heart both the Booke of Psalmes & most part of the New Testament: they found that there was neither Action nor Opinion that could be propounded but might receiue a Cleare Solution & direction from that Booke. Wherefore not vpon Presumption of their own Abilities but on Confidence of Gods Gracious Assistance to their humble & diligent Endeauours they agreed euery day at a sett houre to conferre together of some such subiect, as should tend either to the Information of the Vnderstanding[1] or to the Exciting of the Affections[2] to the more ready and fervent prosecution of vertues, & better performance of all such duties ⟨2⟩ as in their present or other Course of Life hereafter should bee required of them.

The First Proceedings, as it alwaies happens in great Attempts, that haue no Presidents [precedents] to direct, were both in forme & substance farre short of that whereunto they were in the end reduced.

Wherefore as Artists vpon the full accomplishment of their works Cast aside the first Draughts so silencing what was lesse exactly done I shall goe on with the Recording of things, from that time, which themselues accompt the beginning being about the end of May. Only by way of Introduction, as Porches were anciently sett in the Fronts of greater Buildings, I will sett down the Passages of Two or Three seuerall daies, which may well serue for a preface to the Reader of this Following Booke, as in truth they were maine arguments to the Confirmation of their minds, who were the Actours of this & other Noble Vndertakings.

Reasons Academy (1605), which he attributes to Robert Mason rather than to Sir John Davies: "'Since then the knowledge and vse of Reason is the onely salue to cure these reasonless infirmities, it is not amisse in this little Dispensatorie, to show the true manner of this composition, that every man knowing the ingredients and their naturall operations, each man may be his owne physition, and cure those maladies which make the world run mad with toyes and fantasmes.'" This passage is very close in thought to the spirit of the Little Gidding discussions.

[1] Vnderstanding—the mind or intellect.
[2] Affections—natural inclinations.

On Ash Wednesday therefore Although for the better suiting of their Bodies to their Hearts, & their Hearts to the Meditations of the day they forbore the refreshment of Corporal Food, yet so much the more desirous to Feast their minds in the ⟨3⟩ Fast of their Bodies meeting at their appointed time & place together with that other Company, which were alwaies Auditours & sometimes, at least some of them, partner Actors in their Exercizes, The CHEIF began thus.

My Dearest Sisters & sweet Companions the Solemnitie of this Day inviting vs to sober Thoughts, I shall desire our Stories may be such As both befitts the Season & tend to a serious Confirmation of our well-Chosen Resolutions. And that so much the rather, because if you shall agree thereunto, wee will Make this Day the Beginning of our Exercize accompting this week already past, but as the Tuning of Instruments before Musick, harsh Iarring to sweet Harmonie. The whole Companie seeming by Cherefull gesture to approue the matter, The GVARDIAN in all their behalfs made answere.

Faire Cheif: The motion is like your self most Acceptable & worthy to be so. Wherefore in Gods Name, doe you make Entrance, & wee will to the best of our Abilities, second you both in Cloth & Colour [offer similar examples] as the Proverb is. Wherevpon She thus proceeded:—⟨4⟩

That Braue King & Captaine Pirrhus,[1] whom Hannibal iudged the worthiest Cheiftaine next Alexander, that euer the World had, Boyling with Ambitious desires of Enlarging his Dominions & Encreasing his Honours, brought one Day into Consultation amongst his Captaines & other Freinds, the Resolutions of Warring vpon some of his Neighbours, against whom he had rather made then found iust Quarrel. The whole Counsel gaue their votes according to the Kings mind, Onely one excepted

---

[1] Pirrhus—Pyrrhus, 318–272 B.C., King of Epirus. His story is told by Plutarch, but comparison of their version with that in North's translation shows that the Ferrars relied here on one of the many Latin editions which had earlier appeared.

Named Cineas a man of Long Robes, who excusing his Ignorance in Martial matters, besought his Maiestie, that wauing all Arguments touching that subiect he might freely demand some few questions of him. To which the King gratiously condescending Cineas sayd: Sir, when you haue ouercome these against whom you are now bent, what will your Grace farther doe? Marry quoth the king, if wee herein proue successfull, the whole state of Greece must submitt to our Empire. Bee it so, sayth Cineas, will you rest there? Nay verily, quoth Pirrhus, but then immediately will wee goe against the Romans, & if wee ouerthrow them, then Italy shalbe the Fruit of our Labour & Hazard. A Noble & Happy Conquest ⟨5⟩ sayd Cineas. But when this shalbe effected, what shall wee then doe? Why then quoth the King wee shall not doubt to sett on the Carthaginians. And suppose you haue ouercome them, sayd Cineas, what then? Why then quoth he, All Africa shalbe ours. In a Blessed houre replied Cineas. And what shall wee then doe? Pirrhus now grown aweary, half in Anger, half in Mirth, Oh Cineas, sayd he then will wee giue our selues to Rest & Quiet, to Banquets & Games, & enioy all the Happiness, which wee shall haue purchased. If that (sayd hee), Dread Soueraigne, be the vpshott of your Intents & Aimes, who forbids you now to accomplish the same, with the sauing of all that Labour and Hazard, which wee shall vndergoe & perhaps be ouerwhelmed with? How can it be Conformable to your Excellent Wisedome to fetch a large & wearisome Course about for the Attainment of those pleasures, into the Fruition whereof you may immediately enter, if you please. If a happy & delightfull Life bee that you Aime at in the end, why doe wee not without delay take our part thereof? This sayd Cineas. And though Pirrhus could not gainsay, yet could he not follow the Prudent Advice of this wise Counseller, but led on stiffly by his ⟨6⟩ Confused & blind desire after some yeares spent in Extremities, Toyle, & Anguish of mind & Body was miserably slaine by a peice of Timber cast from the top of a House by a womans hand. But this Tragical End is not that, which I have recompted this story for. But the proposal of Cineas his Argument to convince [show] the madness of vs Christians. That professing the seruice of God out of a pure heart & a good Conscience to be the maine & vpshott of all our desire & Aimes doe not withstanding all by a ioynt Conspiracy, as it were, in folly sett that part to be performed in the Catastrophe of our Life, giuing our youth & present times to the pursuite of Vanities, spending the strength & vigour both of mind & body in a violent Race cleane contrarie to that path, at the head whereof the Prize is sett, which wee pretend to seek. But let vs no more, my Dearest Sisters, be as Children tossed to and fro with euery windy & frothy Argument of the Louers of this World, but come to a cleare & stable Resolution touching the Leading of our Liues henceforth. If this seruice of the World & the Flesh be good & beneficial, & worthy our souls, that fetch their original from heauen, why then let vs sett seriously thereabout, loosing no time gett what we may ⟨7⟩ of the Pleasures & Profitts they afford & perhaps offer a liberal tast unto vs: & herein Let vs sett vp our rest. If we say Nay, but though for a while wee shalbe glad to be partakers of this Worlds delight, yet on no hand will wee take them for our portion but purpose in the End, bidding adue to them all. (As with greatest Honour to her & Ioy to ourselues, wee see our Dearest Grandmother to haue done.) Why then what silly fondness will it be not to begin euen from this very instant to follow the Course, which in the End wee resolue to take & to endeauour the Attainment of those things, which wee know only to be worthy keeping, Wisedome, Temperance, Patience, Meeknes, Humilitie & the rest of those heauenly ornaments. As for the vaine Fancies in Apparrel, the Licorish Appetites[1] in diet, Foolish imployment of our minds & times in Gauds & Trifles, peeuish venting of Humours & all the like infirmities, which vex our weaker sex. Why should wee not from this very houre bid an vtter defiance vnto them, since at the last wee meane with

---

[1] Licorish Appetites—appetites for dainty and fancy food.

shame to Casheere them, as our Reproach & danger. If it wilbe Honourable & good in our gray haires, how much more now in youth, to be wise & vertuous? ⟨8⟩

Here the CHEIFE stayd, & hauing for a good space sett her Eies on the ground. At last with a Cheerfull Eie veiwing the Company round about, Your thoughtfull Countenances (sayd she) giue a Testimonie, that I haue sayd too much & perhaps in other manner then I ought, & therefore I will no further encrease your wearines or my own fault.

Not so (Replied the GUARDIAN) most worthy Cheif: But rather the Excellency of the matter & your answerable handling of it, hath bred this solleme Alteration on our parts, so as though wee could gladly heare your discourse, till the starres should appeare, yet that wee may not at present ouercharge your nor our own memories, desirous to beare away that, which you haue already sayd wee are Content to yeeld to your desires.

Wherevpon the CHEIF arose & took the Patient by the Hand & sett her down in the Chaire, saying, To you it belongs, Deare Sister, by some better recompted story to make satisfaction for that which I haue been wanting in. To whom the PATIENT Replied. Whatsoeuer shall this day, Worthy Cheif, be sayd on this subject, must be but descant on the song, which you haue now sett. And in proof thereof I ⟨9⟩ shall tell you an Example tending to that purpose. That Euery man in his place should be carefull to performe his own offices without delay:

Traian[1] that Incomparable Emperour, being on a day in speedy March against some Barbarians, that had broken into the Roman Pale, A Poore Widdow pressing through the midst of his Guard, Casting herself on her knees took hold of his stirop, & with a shower of Teares, that poured from her Eies, besought him to doe her iustice of one, that had cruelly murdered her only Son. The

[1] Trajan—Roman Emperor from A.D. 98 to 117. This story is told by Dante in the *Purgatorio*, Canto x, and in the *Fiore di Filosofi* attributed to Brunetto Latini.

Emperour bad her rise saying, that at his return he would doe her
iustice to the full. But now, Mother, sayd hee, my hast is too
great. Wherevpon the old Woman replied. Suppose you Come
not back againe, Who then shall doe mee right? That shall my
Successour, sayd Traian. Alas Sir, sayd she, if hee should fail me
too, shall not you then remaine indebted to iustice & to mee? But
put case, that thy successour doe mee right, shall his iustice free
thee? Nay shall it not rather augment thy fault? Happy will it be
for him if all, that he can doe suffice to discharge himself. Which
is more, as ⟨10⟩ thou perceiuest then thou now canst doe. The
Emperour hearing this dismounted presently, & sent for the
Accused, did the Widdow iustice according to her desire & his
own duty. And afterwards discomfited his Enemies & returned with
great Honour. This was one of those Noble Acts, which made this
Emperour so famous & beloued, as After-Ages out of Compassion
that such incomparable vertues should be damned fained Traians
soul to be returned out of Hell by St Gregorie the Greats
Prayers. But surely where euer his soul be, the Wisdome & Worth
of his Action ought to be imitated by vs neuer putting off the
doing of right & iustice which wee are bound to performe.

The Patients story was of all much Commended. & the CHEIF
taking the Cheerfull by the hand, Although (sayd she) the mends
of my defects be already made by this Renowned story, yet that
it may be with greater Advantage, I shall desire you, Sweet
Sister, to fitt vs with some of those Excellent ones, which you are
Mistresse of.

Wherevpon the CHEERFULL made Answere. I am at the most
but a steward, that keeps others Wealth, but because I know with
their good liking I may make vse of ⟨11⟩ that, which is in my
store, I shall tell you an Example to perswade vs not to deferre the
bestowing of our Almes & the Exercize of our Charitie (as the
manner of too many is) to the period of our Liues, but whilst
opportinitie serueth to be ready to distribute & willing to Communicate [share with others] according to the Apostles Counsell

& Encouragement. Laying vp in store a good Foundation against the time to come.[1] To this purpose shall my story bee. Whereof howeuer the Fact may be doubtfull, the moral I am sure is most profitable.

A Great Lady high both in Bloud & Riches but much more high & happy in the vertues of Her Son by Dignitie a Bishop & in holy Conuersation a Saint, being oftentimes pressed by him to the Exercize of Charitie in an ouerflowing measure, still put him off with the large bequest that she intended in her will to Good Vses, which she conceiued would be as acceptable to God & profitable to herself as any present distribution. Her good son perceiuing that by solid Arguments he was not able to perswade her, bethought himself by a more plaine & material kind of proof to convince her. One night therefore hauing invited her to supper at his ⟨12⟩ Palace, which he studiously protracted. At her getting into the Coach to returne home it being very late & dark she called for torches to attend & guide the way. The Bishop who had purposely commanded there should be none ready desired her to lett the Coach driue on easily. To which when she made answere that all the way being bad needed light, but especially the passage of the Bridge, which was very perilous. The Bishop Counselled her to proceed saying that hee would send the lights after, which should ouertake her by that time shee came to the Bridge. Whereunto with much passion she replied. That will I not hazzard sayd shee, by any meanes. For suppose wee should bee on it, before we are aware. There would then perhaps need more then Lights to help vs out againe, & to remedy the hurt, that might befall us. I will not therefore stirre, sayd shee, till I haue the Torches before mee. The Bishop seeing that it wrought as he wished, with great Humilitie besought her to Consider, whether it were not fitt to obserue the same Course in that, which was of farre more importance, sending her good works & Almes deeds

[1] I Timothy vi, 18 and 19.

before her by the performance of them in her life time rather then to leaue them till the last houre, which might happily, as it did many others, ⟨13⟩ by sudden approach prevent her Expectation. Which if it should Madame, sayd hee, I cannot say how certainly you might promise your self to accomplish what you intend. Many more & greater hazards of disappointment must needs be vndergone then that, which you now feare from mee. But howsoeuer this I am certaine, that at the best the light can but follow, which will be nothing like either for Comfort or safetie in so dreadfull a passage as to haue it brightly shining before you. The good Lady being a woman of deep vnderstanding after she had well pondered the matter told her son. That the cases were indeed so like, that she meant to hold the same Course in both. And therefore sayd shee, let mee now haue the torches alongst with mee to prevent bodily danger, & come you to morrow & take order for the prouiding of asmuch light as may be for the conducting of my soul in that dark & fearfull passage of death.

You haue, Deare Cheerfull, (sayd the GUARDIAN) passed our Expectations in this storie.

Let vs heare (sayd the CHEIFE) what the Affectionate intends & then I doubt not, Honoured Guardian, But you shall have further matter of Commendation. ⟨14⟩

My storie (sayd the AFFECTIONATE) being short & to perswade the sparing of Faults, I should make a double one to trouble you with a Preface.

A Certaine Courtier hauing obtained of the Prince towards the repaire of his decayed Fortunes a Charter to Exact a Penny for euery defect in man or Beast, that passed the Gates of the Citty, His officers seeing one come Limping by, called to him for their due. He pretending it was but a Casual streine refused to pay. Wherevpon drawing neerer to him the officers perceiued a blemish in his Eies. & so required Two pence. He offered the first penny. For the last he began stoutly to maintaine, that seeing his sight was perfect, the Blemish was not in Compas of their Charter. They as resolutely claiming as he denying, by misfortune his hatt fell off, & much scurf and some soreness appearing on his head they then told him they would haue three pence. Whereat growing enraged, he striuing to be gone & they haling him back againe in their strugling they perceiued he wore a trusse for Burstnes [hernia]. Where upon they told him he must now pay foure pence, which in the end the poore man was forced to doe, that might at first haue ⟨15⟩ gone cleare for a penny. How often hath it happened so with mee in the foolish defence of Errours multiplying the Guilt & putting vpon myself the Necessitie of discompting [discounting] by Foure-fold sorrow & shame that, which at first a light acknowledgement would haue redeemed. Its best therefore at first to make the amends of that, which is done amisse. So I counsell you & God willing shall myself practize. Paying my Penny at the first demand to saue further Arrerages. ⟨16[1]⟩

[1] The rest of this folio is blank in the MS.

Part II

It is surprising that the stories told at Eastertide 1631 and found in the manuscript volume printed by Miss Sharland were not also included in the present manuscript by way of introduction to the 'Dialogue on the Retirement of Charles V', for it was at that time that Charles was first mentioned as the most convincing witness 'that all this world yields is nothing but vanity and vexation of spirit'. These stories are printed here because they lead into the discussion of Charles V, which preceded by some eight months the bulk of the stories in the Sharland volume. Without them, the opening words of the Chief in Part III would seem abrupt and unmotivated.

In his curiously ambiguous editor's link (in which he seems both to deplore and welcome the coming of spring), Nicholas Ferrar voices the theme of nearly all future meetings of the Little Academy—'the insufficiency of all earthly things to give content'. The Chief's story of the insatiable ambition of Alexander the Great illustrates Nicholas's point; but because 'old stories move not so much as new', the Chief urges the Patient to tell the story of the death of Philip III as a modern and more cogent example. The hand of Nicholas as editor is again apparent when he acknowledges shifting the next three stories to a later occasion; they are here restored to their chronological position. The Patient's story of Philip's death-bed denunciation of 'all things that are in this world to be but vain things' is followed by an episode from the life of Henry IV of France to illustrate 'the insufficiency of all worldly things to breed comfort'. The Affectionate adds the example of two popes, Marcellus and Adrian, to reinforce the disillusionment reflected by the two kings. Nicholas now suggests that fully convincing proof of the hollowness of worldly power and great possessions must take into account the 'transcendent power and dignity' of the Holy Roman Emperors. The Chief takes her cue and promises to examine the case of Charles V, the mightiest emperor of them all. On the next day, however, finding herself unprepared, she tells only of his pious motto. The Patient recounts Charles's great restraint upon hearing of the defeat of Francis I, and the Cheerfull cites an example of Charles's devotion to his sister, Mary of Hungary.

NOTE: The manuscript page numbers refer to B.M. Add. MS. 34657. The stories may also be found in Sharland, pp. 11–13, 61–6, 14–18.

In the like kind were there appointed houres dayly spent, till after Easter. When the whole frame of this Lower World, where in ⟨33⟩ wee are bounded, seeming to sett it self forth with all manner of brauery to entertaine the approaching Sun her Paramour, least the outward glory & pleasure, that every way offered it selfe, should by Rauishment of the sences steale away their hearts from the pursuit of those farre more rich, though lesse euident beauties & delights, which they were enamoured of, this Sober Companie resolued, both for a Counterpoyze to the Common Iollity of that season, & for a wholesome restraint of their weaker Affections (that they might not melt away through too much sweetnes in an vnparalelled Prosperity, which God had euery way crowned them with) by the Choyse of more sad & solemne meditations & discourses to allay that lightnes & excesse of Cheerefulnes, which too much happines doth vnhappily breed in most mens minds, Perswading themselues, that in a moderate & temperate enioyment of their outward Comforts they should both better confirme the fruition of them, & more certainly attaine those Benefitts to which Prosperity, when it is conferred by Gods Loue & fauour, is intended. Which in their Iudgement they determined to bee not the debauchment of the soule through a dissolute surfetting in those vanities & pleasures, which the World sucks out of Gods blessings, but rather the composing of mens minds by the experiment [experience] of the ⟨34⟩ Insufficiency of all earthly things to giue Content to a right esteeme & vse of them, Not as things, wherein our desires should rest and settle themselues, but whereby they should bee carried vp to the Contemplation & pursuit of those true eternall & absolute good things, whereof all, that seemes good here below, is but as a beame or rather a glimpse of light to the body of the sunne it selfe.

These great thoughts working in the minds of this little society, & a necessity of handling some Choise subiect being occasioned by the presence of Certaine Freinds, whom Dearest affection enforced to admitt, & worth required to entertaine with more then ordinary preparations, the CHEIFE thus gaue vent to their ouer-flowing thoughts.

The desire of happines is one & the same in all men, but the apprehensions & pursuits thereof are almost as many as the men themselues. Some few select soules agree, that it is not else where to bee found but in God. But the most part deceiued by false appearances or rather shaddows hope to attaine it in the Heaping vp of Riches, Honours & pleasures. Hence ariseth that continuall restlesse toyle of mind & body, with which wee find all men ouerwhelmed, whilest they seeke to multiply the store & possession of these things to themselues, wherein they conceiue ⟨35⟩ happines to be included. And although they find their expectation still frustrated of that Content, which they imagined, yet bewitched with the glorious prospectiue of things, which are before them, they are led on both with vnsatiable desires & vnwearied attempts in the following of these vanities, euer imputing the want of their Content to the want of some one thing or other. Whereas in truth if all whatsoeuer the World hath from its beginning afforded in matter of Riches, Honour & Pleasure were molded into one Lumpe, & giuen to any one Man to enioy, it were not able to satisfy his soule, but he would still find an emptines or rather an increase of anguish. It's a well knowne story of Alexander the great,[1] that hauing conquered the greatest part of this world, and vndoubtedly possessed himself of all the good in it, hearing talk of more Worlds hee fell aweeping. So little was all that, which hee had, able to satisfy his desires, that it could not keepe him from lamenting his miserable Estate. Questionlesse if wee did seriously weigh, as wee must Necessarily beleiue the truth of this, wee should not bee so violently & vainely led on to the spending of ourselues in the seeking of the things of this world. I suppose therefore, that there can bee

---

[1] Alexander the Great—Plutarch tells this story in *Sayings of the Romans* (207 D) in the *Moralia*, of which Phileman Holland published his translation in 1603.

nothing more profitable either to the disturning of our minds from the ouer-greedy pursuit of things here below, or to inflame them to the endeauour after those things, which are aboue, then to add to the con⟨36⟩tinuall experiment of the insufficiency of these things, which euery one findeth in their owne soules by Dayly tryall, the often refreshment of those illustrious examples, which God hath continually sett forth before our eies for the full reformation of our vnderstanding touching the Vanity of all earthly things, still making this application to our owne hearts, That if the mighty men of the World could not attaine Ioy nor Content in the right & fulnes of all things, that this world affords, It will bee mere madnesse for vs to hope to find it in the offalls & scraps of meaner fortunes. & if they were forced at last to goe to God, & to seeke their happines in his service, how much Wisedome & Happines wilbe in vs to beginne timely, whither they all in the end striue. But because old stories moue not so much, either because they haue beene often heard formerly, or perhaps are not so fully Credited, I shall desire, that our instances may bee of later times & that you Deare Patient would make the enterance by the recompting of that Incomparable History touching the Death of the Last King of Spain Philip the third, then which I haue neuer heard a more convincing proofe both of this Worlds Vanity & of the worth of Gods seruice.

The stories of King Phillip, Henery the fourth of France, ⟨37⟩ & the two Popes Marcellus & Adrian, being this day told by the PATIENT, CHEERFULL & AFFECTIONATE, are here omitted, being brought in afterwards to serue for INNOCENTS DAY.

But the conclusion of this day prouing the beginning of a large & painefull work to the Cheife,[1] I haue thought fitt to insert here that passage, which it brought on, the rather to enforce the performance & perfection of the same.[2] ⟨38⟩ [MS. p. 38 cont. p. 23.]

[1] The examination of the life of Charles V, which begins in Part III.
[2] The three stories to which reference is made and which were told on Holy Innocents' Day (28 December) 1631 are here restored to their original position.

PATIENT. When King Phillip[1] lay desperately sick, hee caused Florentius his Confessour & Preacher of his Court to bee thrice sent for at midnight. Who presently came vnto him with the Provinciall of Castile, & bringing with him Father Ignatius his Chirograph,[2] who discoursed with the King of his approaching death, exhorted him to submitt himselfe to the Diuine Pleasure of God. The King gaue Florentius his Confessour great thankes for such Comforts, & turning towards him, Truely (sayd hee) my Florents, I am much obliged vnto thee for those wholesome admonitions, which thou hast continually raysed vp & refreshed my soul in thy sermons. Florents made Answere, that hee had nothing more in his wishes, if God prolonged his life, then that hee should now vow, that hee would build a Chappell in the Honour of the Holy & Immaculate Conception of the Virgin Mary, & perswade the Pope, that he should at last decide the Contraversy, which had beene so long debated thereabout.

To whom the King. Doe not you remember (sayd hee) in your ⟨127⟩ sermon on Ashwednesday, that one of your Auditours should finish his last Day this present Lent. That touched mee, & now that fatall houre is vpon mee. But shall I bee partaker of euerlasting Felicity? & then great heauines & Anxiety surprized his mind. & then hee presently sayd to his Confessour, Thou hast not hitherto vsed the right course of healing mee. Which when the Confessour vnderstood of the medicining for the body, the King added, I am not solicitous of my body & temporal disease, but of my soul. To whom the Confessour I haue done what I could. That, which remaines, is to be left to Gods Providence. And vpon this Occasion Florentius did largely discourse of the mercies of God, & brought vnto his remembrance those things, which hee had Laudably performed for Christian Religion. But the King answered, Ah how happy had I beene, if I had liued in a Desert

---

[1] King Phillip—Philip III of Spain (1578–1621). The Ferrars must have used a very recent source for their account, possibly the memoirs of the French ambassador Bassompierre.

[2] Chirograph—one who drew up formal documents.

these three & twenty yeares, wherein I haue held this kingdome. To whom Florentius sayd, that his Maiestie might performe euen now also an acceptable duty to God, if hee would cast downe all earthly things, his Kingdome, dignity, Life & salvation at the feet of his Crucified Sauiour Jesus Christ, & committ all to his will. Then, the King sayd, very willingly will I ⟨128⟩ doe this. & euen in this very moment, Whateuer God hath giuen mee, my Principalities, my Power, & my Life it selfe, I lay downe at the feet of Jesus Christ the Sauiour crucified for mee. Whose image he did kisse with singular affection, & further sayd to Florentius, Now truly then thou hast ministered egregious Comforts to my soul, & shall hence forth endeauour, that it may bee openly signified to the people, that I at the point of death haue acknowledged all things, that are in this world, to bee but vaine things, & this very Kingly Dignity, which during Life may bee splendent & pleasant, but in the point of death it is very bitter & troublesome. & so hee did ioyfully render vp his spirit to God the heauenly Father as became a Christian King. Before his death hee did likewise exhort his Sonnes to all Piety & in especiall his Eldest Borne. Hee admonished, that hee should well weigh, that hee also was mortall, & therefore should so institute both his Life & the administration of his kingdome, that it might not repent him at his end of his Kingly power & Dignity, as it now befell him, breathing out his soul. That hee should bee a Father of the poore and of the Common-wealth. That hee should bee enflamed with the zeal ⟨129⟩ of Gods Glory. & that hee should account the dishonour done to the Diuine Maiesty to be put vpon himselfe. Then hee gaue him a sealed Codicill, & charged him exactly to obserue all that, which was therein contained. & presenting him likewise the image of Christ crucified, hee sayd this Image thy great Grandfather Charls the fift gaue my Father, which now I doe, as it were by will, bequeath vnto thee. Thou shalt reuerence it as a Christian & Catholick King, & by the beholding thereof remember thine owne Mortality.

As concerning his will hee bequeathed nothing else therein, then Admonitions belonging to Piety, & diligently recommended to his Sonne the Monastery at Madrill built by his Mother, & the Colledge of the Jesuites, which is at Salamantica, & gaue Commandement that his Body should bee buried with slender Pompe or with out many or Magnificent Ceremonies, & that it should not bee prepared with spices. For being so great a sinner I accompte my selfe vnworthy a Buriall at all, sayd hee. This was the End of that great Monarch, whose Deuotion, that it was not righter sett in many Particulars deserues mee thinks rather Teares then Censures; but euen where hee went most wrong himselfe, there perhaps hee may most ⟨130⟩ confirme vs in the truth. But leauing him to Gods mercy, touching his soules estate I wish, that the Remembrance of his Acknowledgement touching this worlds vanities may euer remaine fresh in mine owne & all your minds.

The Patient hauing ended after a good Pause allowed for Consideration of this wonderfull History, the CHEEREFULL began.

A Concurrent to King Phillip of Spaine was Henry the fourth in France,[1] the Father of our Royall Queene Mary. How his tragicall end made proofe of the misery of humane Condition is too well vnderstood to bee repeated in this Company. But that, which went before his death is not perhaps so generally knowne, though farre more observable in my Iudgement & most sutable to the Theme propounded by the Patient.

Whateuer on Earth Could bee deuised for the affording of Content & Ioy might iustly seeme to bee vnited in the Person & prosperity of this Prince. A large faire flourishing kingdome, more honour from abroad, more Loue at home of his subiects then euer any of his predecessours had. A strong Body, a faire

---

[1] Henry IV (1533–1610) was assassinated by a religious fanatic.

⟨131⟩ Issue, aboundance of treasure, a setled peace, & what could bee imagined to giue Content that hee wanted? Besides a Festivall time, the Queenes Coronation being then solemnized, debarred out all Cares & businesses, & in a thousand kind of vanities brought in mirth & Iollity into the Court.

How full of ioy & comfort may wee deeme this Prince. & yet alas it is all otherwise. His heart is swallowed vp with griefe & Melancholy, though hee knows not why. Hee riseth early from his wearied bed, & goes to masse. That hee heares deuoutly; at his returne they bring him his Children, & amongst others the Duke of ——[1] whom hee loued dearely, & in whom he tooke great delight; but then very pensiuely hee bid carry the child to breakfast, & turning himselfe away sadly casteth himselfe vpon his Bed to sleepe, if hee might. But rest forsakes through anguish of mind, which makes him rise & fall on his knees in prayer to God from him to find Comfort, which no where else he could. Then againe hee lies downe, & againe riseth to praier. This he did three times. In the end to shift by change of Place the wearisomenes of his owne thoughts, hee goes to walke in the Gallery till dinner. Costly victualls restore his body, but they refresh not his mind. Thats still encombred with perplexity. Which the Nobelmen perceiuing ⟨132⟩ & pittying striue by diuers merry passages to allay, themselues mutually laughing to draw him on to mirth. With much adoe they force a fained smile or two from him, though naturally of a most pleasant disposition. In the end hee breakes of [off] all with a French Proverb, Wee haue laughed enough for Friday, wee may well weepe on Sunday. And so they did indeed. But of his death I meane not to speake at this time. Its the insufficiency of all worldly things to breed comfort, that I haue told this story. In proofe of which I suppose wee may read, as it were in text Letters, & withall where indeed true happines is to bee found. Which hee seeking it in Gods service & particularly in praise, directeth vs vnto.

[1] Blank in manuscript.

The Cheife seeing the Story ended, & by the fixed eies of all the Auditours perceiuing, that they esteemed silence the fittest Descant on so sad a Tragedy, conforming her Demeanour to their solemne Countenances & stillnes, did by a gentle Invitation of her hand direct the AFFECTIONATE to the Chaire. Who with great reuerence to her & all the rest thus began & proceeded.

My Sisters haue seuerally told you of two Kings. I shall ⟨133⟩ bring two Popes to serue on this Iury, Adrian the sixt,[1] & Marcellus the second.[2] It is not much aboue a hundred yeares agoe, that the first, & little aboue halfe the time, that the other liued. Both of them for Wisedome, Learning, & Integrity passing any of that Rank that went before them many hundreds of yeares, & both of them advanced from low degree. Which should haue made their happines seeme the greater to themselues, which to all others seemed the very Crowne of humane Felicity. But heare the Euidence, that themselues giue. Adrian wills it to been grauen on his Tombe, That hee esteemed nothing to haue befallen him more vnhappily, then that hee had raigned.

And Marcellus euen in the heat of the Congratulation, which all the world offered him, grows into so deepe displeasure with that, which others terme soueraigne happines, That repeating Pope Adrian his Epitaph, hee brake of [off] his dinner, & smiting his hand on the Table hee cries out, I see not how they, that hold such high dignities can be saued.

Goe now & seeke for Content & happines in the propriety of a few acres of land, or in the Command of a Few silly people, or in the wantonnes of a few vaine pleasures, which neither Kings nor Popes could find in all what their royall Estate afford. ⟨134⟩ Is hee not a mad Man, that hopes to fill himselfe in the shallow

---

[1] Adrian VI (1459–1523), the former tutor of Charles V, served as regent of Spain in 1520. He was crowned pope in August 1522, and died in September 1523.

[2] Marcellus II (1501–55) served as pope for only three weeks before his death.

pitts of Ciuill or Ecclesiasticall Dignity, when hee sees that the ouerflowing Riuers of Crownes & triple Miters leaue their possessours soules as dry & thirsty of Content, as the sands of Arabia are of Moysture? If neither Kings nor Popes can find Ioy or Happines, who can hope to doe it in this world? ⟨135⟩

Both the vehemency of spirits and the abruptnes of the Period, with which the Affectionate closed, made the Company for a while to expect her further proceeding, which by her rising from the Chaire perceiuing to bee otherwise, ONE OF THEM[1] smiling, as though hee would make beleiue, that the Affectionate, whom they prized for a good Historian, was but a bad Herald, stayed her saying, Your Conclusion is not necessary; because your Induction is not full, hauing left out that, which is the Chiefe, the Imperiall Diademe, which perhaps by its transcendent power & Dignity circles in that perfect happines & content, which those lesser Orbs of Kings & Popes Crownes cannot.

The Affectionate turning her eies to the Cheife as admonishing her of her Cue, That part, (sayd the CHEIFE) is imposed on mee for the conformity of Name not for the proportinablenes of abilities:[2] for it might haue beene performed better by some others. And although in re⟨38⟩gard of the worth & weight of the subiect it requires a more curious hand then mine, yet that I may shew that iust obedience to your authority, which I shall require in the like kind from you, I shall recount a true & fresh History, which shall serue as a seale to your Confirmation of all, which my Sisters by their former stories haue endeauoured to perswade themselues & vs.

Is it possible, sayd the GUARDIAN, that wee should heare any more convincing proofes & examples then those which haue already beene told.

---

[1] ONE OF THEM—doubtless the speaker was Nicholas Ferrar, the Visitor, who is here guiding the discussion so that the Chief, Mary Collett, can show her command of a subject that was dear to the hearts of both uncle and niece.

[2] That part—the consideration of the 'Imperial diadem', that is, the chief part.

Yes verily (sayd the CHIEFE) by how much the excess of Dignity, the Excellency of personal worth, & the more liuely manner of bearing euidence (hee hauing put in execution those Conceptions, which these former recompted Princes vttered onely in word). By so much doe I esteeme Charles the V a more pregnant testimony, that all, which this world yeelds, is nothing but Vanity & Vexation of spirit.

The name of Charles stilled not onely the tongues, but the thoughts of the whole Company, who settling themselues with great attention, seemed with much earnestnes to require the Cheifes performance of her promise & satisfaction of their desires. But shee drawing back from the Chaire to which shee had all this while sett next, ⟨39⟩ The time, sayd shee, is too farre spent at present, nor am I provided as I wish. Besides the Story itselfe is worthy of an Intire Day. The Company yeelding to the iustnes of her Excuses with out further reply dissolued at that time.

The next Day meeting at their ordinary Place & Houre the CHEIFE finding herselfe vnfurnished for the discharge of her promise, casting about with witt to salue what indeed proceeded of want, as if it had beene of deliberate Choise, what was indeed Constreyned by Necessity beganne thus.

Least as it happens in Royall Bankets, when they come too thick the greatest dainties are not sett by, so it should proue in our Royall Stories. I suppose it not amisse for the better preparing of our minds to receiue them with that due attention & affection, which they deserue to giue a little respitt to the digesting of those, which haue beene yesterday told, least perhaps else, as hony to a full stomacke, they should proue lesse regardfull in our minds. Wherefore by your good leaue wauing for the present the performance of my purpose & your expectation touching Charles the V his Relinquishment of this Worlds vanity, I shall tell you a particular Act of his, which as it was perhaps a preparation to these excellent Resolutions, which he at last vndertooke, so it shall serue mee for a preface to the recompting them. ⟨40⟩ Hauing ouercome John Fredericke of Saxony[1] & Maurice of Silesia[2] in a most vnexpected manner, when all the World sang the applause of his invincible prowesse, wisedome, & good Fortune, comparing him to Iulius Caesar in the greatnes of his attempts, & particularly in the happy achieuement of this victory, attributing to him, as of right, that famous Motto, which Iulius Caesar used, I came, I saw, & ouercame. Hee, striking out the last word as too full of arrogancy, added a Couple of farre more truth & sobriety, making it thus to runne, I saw, & I came, & God ouercame. By his Humility & wisedome farre more deseruing admiration then by his victory. The Cheife hauing ended her story, the PATIENT thus seconded her.

There is no Meddow more abundant of sweet & Beautifull Flowres then this Noble Princes Life of faire Actions & vertues. Wherefore I desire since wee are in so rich a Garden for beauty & delight, that wee should not seeke any further to finish this daies work. Our Cheife hath told you a passage of his humility to God-ward; I shall tell you one of the monstrations of his mind towards his aequalls & enemies. As hee was going to Euensong, News was brought him that his great & present enemy Francis the first[3] was ouerthrowne & taken prisoner by his Captaines. When his Counsellours and Courtiers ⟨41⟩ attending on him broke out into great reioycings & Boastings, hee with a seuere Countenance stilling all their vnseasonable mirth, kept on his course to Church, where commanding Publick thanks to be giuen in a solemne manner for the victory, which hee had obtained, hee did streightly forbid all those expressions of publique mirth, which

---

[1] John Frederick, Elector of Saxony and ardent Lutheran, was captured by Charles at Muhlberg, 24 April 1547.

[2] Maurice of Silesia had been won over to his side by Charles and joined the latter in his attack on John Frederick, whom he succeeded as Elector of Saxony in 1548.

[3] Francis the First (1494–1547), King of France, was defeated at Pavia on 25 February 1525 by the armies of Charles V, who was in Spain at the time. He married Eleanor of Austria, Charles's sister, in 1530.

by fires, Bells, & other waies were intended in the Citty, Deeming the effusion of so much Christian bloud & the Calamity of so great a Prince to deserue rather teares & Compassion, then mirth or insultation. The next morning he receiued the sacrament with euident tokens of great devotion & went accompanied with the whole Court in procession. Neither in words or deeds, sayth the Prince of Historians,[1] did he discouer any spice of vnfitting mirth or swelling thoughts. To the Congratulations of Embassadours & other great Persons about him his answere was, that hee could not but much reioice by the manifest assistance of the Diuine Power to haue receiued a certaine earnest of Gods fauour towards him, & to be made confident, though most vnworthy, that hee was in his grace from whom hee had obtained so singular mercy. For the rest hee no further reioyced then that there was thereby opportunity offered him to settle peace in Christendome, to turne their ioynt Armies against the Common Enemies of our Faith, & together with ⟨42⟩ these greater designes to bee able to benefitt his Freinds, & to pardon his enemyes, & in Confirmation of these intents hee did then receiue the Iustification of certaine states, which had highly offended him, although as hee professed their excuses were altogether insufficient & by this occasion hee had gained much advantage to right himselfe. But he rather chose to follow St Pauls example, vsing the Authority, which God had giuen him, to aedification & not to Destruction.[2]

   Yet all this, mee thinkes, seemes little, sayd the AFFECTIONATE, in point of Moderation in regard of that surpassing Patience which this Heroycall Emperour showed, when at the seige of Metz[3] a souldier of Base Ranke, but baser condition, after the bitter imputation of their Common Miseries to his folly called him to

---

[1] Prince of Historians—I have not been able to find this passage in de Thou. Robertson repeats it almost verbatim and gives both Sandoval and Ulloa as sources. See Introduction, p. xlvii.

[2] II Corinthians x, 8.

[3] Siege of Metz—in 1553 Henry II of France checked Charles's advance with the assistance of the ever-vacillating Maurice of Saxony.

his face the sonne of a madwoman.[1] How great a magnanimity was there in his brest, that could with out disquiet passe ouer such an affront, which, to that Anguish of mind hee then endured in the greatest of all Calamities, that euer befell him, must needs bee like the powring of scalding oyle vpon smarting wounds. The reproaches against Prosperity & Innocency are but the beating of the garments. That cuts to the soule, that are true & giuen vpon advantage. I commend him of generousnes, that contemneth that Iniury, which hurts him not. ⟨43⟩ But I admire him, that holds his hand, when as his heart is peirced to the quick, & restraines the power of Reuenge, when hee is offended, out of presumption of weakenesse.

The Cheerefulls story at that time being more proper to another head, & hereafter to bee remembered, In supply take that, which was told the next day as more sutable to the former peices, being of the selfe-same Charles, & Mary the widdow-Queene of Hungary,[2] his Sister in Bloud & vertue during life, & his Companion in death & in the selfe-same resolutions of abandoning the world, whilest they liued in it.

After her husbands the King of Hungarys Death shee returned home to her Brother the Emperour, & continued with him in presence counselling & assisting, & in his Absence gouerning some of the most noble parts of his large spreading Empire. It so happened a Gentleman of Noble birth & great estate corrupted one of her Maides of Honour, which shee tooke so heynously, as the Gentleman was faine to fly to the Emperour, beseeching him to mediate the pardon of his offence, which the Emperour louing the Gentleman very dearely, did in most effectuall manner. But the royall Lady standing constant in her Iudgement would by no

---

[1] Sonne of a madwoman—Charles's mother, Queen Joanna (La Loca), third child of Ferdinand and Isabella of Spain, died 11 April 1555, after forty-nine years of confinement.

[2] Mary the widdow-Queene—Charles appointed his sister Mary, widow of Louis II of Hungary, regent of the Netherlands after the death of his aunt, Margaret of Austria. The story is found in de Thou, Book XXI, p. 297.

meanes be entreated. The Emperour, hoping that time & Importunity might perswade her ceased not with all ⟨44⟩ earnestnes to solicite her Reconciliation. Shee seeming wearied therewith besought her Brother the Emperour no more to trouble her in that matter, which was vnworthy for him to meddle with who being the fountaine of Iustice ought rather to vrge the execution thereof, then the perversion. But, sayd shee; as it becomes a sister for the supply of what is defectiue on your part, I vow to God & you, that if euer hee come neere mee, though it bee in your owne company, I will cause him to be hanged on the next tree, that can be found. Whether this Austere Loue of Chastity & vndaunted Courage in the punishment of vice were greater in this Noble Queene, or the Moderation & vnpartial mind of the Emperour, that could both patiently endure the disappointment of his earnest desires & the generous reproofe of his Sister I leaue to your Iudgement, to mee they seeme both worthy of highest praise & Imitation.[1] ⟨45⟩

[1] Miss Sharland printed the concluding paragraph of folio 45 as the first paragraph of the stories told on St Stephen's Day 1631. The paragraph reads, 'The story of Charles the fifths relinquishment of the world, being grown already to a volume, & yet not perfected, although as much as is done, was recited in the summer, is here omitted, & wee passe on to the setting downe of the Christmas Stories. The occasion whereof is expressed by the Cheif in the introduction, which shee then made, & here next follows.'

Part III

The Chief is now prepared for her examination of the life of Charles V. She finds Charles so blessed in every way—kindred and friends, health and vitality, wisdom and courage, counsellors and followers—that one could not imagine a happier man, as the historian Thuanus himself asserts. He was courteous, well-tempered, devout, and self-disciplined; he never boasted of his marital infidelities, but rather his shame led him to conceal the name of his daughter Margaret's mother and to acknowledge his illegitimate son, Don John, only on his deathbed. His actions both in victory and defeat were marked by magnanimity, courage, and humility. His generosity was shown in the distribution of titles, honours, and wealth during his lifetime; and, although mistakes can be cited, his integrity and justice were admirable. The Chief speaks of the lesson that God's punishment of Charles for insincerity and captious words offers and instances this punishment as an example of God's love for Charles. She then upholds Charles's love for God as his greatest 'capability' for perfect happiness in this world and draws a moral from his actions applicable to daily life: as in Charles's case, devotion to God may well ensure our own worldly prosperity and that of our children; all of us in a small way can experience a similar rise to fortune with God's blessing. The Chief concludes her inventory of Charles's virtues and accomplishments by asking 'Whether by all these titles . . . Charles may as justly lay claim to the possession of happiness as ever any mortal could do?'

If Happiness were to be found in things of this World, or Man's heart capable thereof, whilest he is here below, wee might as iustly expect to haue discouered it in Charles the Fift as in any of the sons of Adam whosoeuer.

Search all the Records of Antiquitie & you shall not bee able to produce an Example to match him in the Abundance of outward goods, & in the right Composure of an Inward Disposition to inioy them:

The Family of Charles V

PHILIP I (1478–1506)—JOANNA OF CASTILE (1479–1555)

ELEANORA (1498–1558)
m. (1) Manuel I of Portugal (1469–1521)[a]
m. (2) Francis I of France (1494–1547) in 1530[b]

ISABELLA (1501–25)
m. Christian II of Denmark (1481–1559)

FERDINAND (1503–64)
m. Anna of Hungary (1503–47)

MARY (1505–58)
m. Louis II of Hungary (1506–26)[c]

CATHERINE (1507–78)
m. John III of Portugal (1502–57), son of Manuel I by his first marriage[d]

CHARLES (1500–58) m. (1526) ISABELLA OF PORTUGAL (1503–39) daughter of Manuel I and sister of John III

MARY (1528–1603)
m. Maximilian II of Austria (1527–76), son of Ferdinand I and Anna, in 1548

JOANNA (1535–73)
m. Prince John of Portugal (d. 1554), son of John III and Catherine

PHILIP (1527–98)[e]
m. (1) Mary of Portugal, daughter of John III

DON CARLOS (1545–68)

MARGARET OF AUSTRIA (1522–86)[f]

DON JOHN OF AUSTRIA (1545–78)[g]

---

a Manuel's first wife was Isabella, daughter of Ferdinand and Isabella of Spain. His second wife, Maria, sister to his first wife, was the mother of John III.

b Francis's first wife, Claude of Brittany, died in 1524.

c Mary's brother Ferdinand married Louis's sister, Anna of Hungary.

d John was the brother of Isabella, Charles V's wife.

e Philip married (2) Mary of England in 1554. She died in 1558 and he married (3) Elizabeth of Valois in 1559.

f Margaret was born before her father's marriage to Isabella of Portugal. According to de Thou her mother was the Princess Marguerite de Medici, but modern historians give the credit to Joanna van der Gheenst.

g John was born after the death of Isabella, Charles's wife. His mother was Barbara Blomberg of Regensburg.

The Nobilitie of his Bloud, the Dignitie of his Crown, the Vastness of his Dominions, the Richnes of his Treasures, the Mightines of his Power, & the Greatness of his Actions, would I am perswaded in Equal Ballance weigh down the most splendid Glory of any of the Ancient Monarchs whatsoeuer. Neither Ninus in the Assirian, nor Nabuchadnezar in the Chaldeen, nor Cyrus in the Persian, nor Alexander in the Grecian, nor Augustus in the Roman Empyre passed our Charles in the Eminencie of any of these things.

But these perhaps may some say tend rather to Greatnes then to Happines, which dwells in the middle Region. These Transcendent Excellencies rather fill the Beholders eies with a dazleing Lustre, then his heart, that enioys them with Content. Crowns & Scepters ⟨17⟩ are others Benefitts rather then the wearers being alwaies thicker sett with Troubles & Dangers then with precious Stones. Its the personal & priuate Comforts, that make men happy. They are our own & full of sweetnes. And who then so Abundant in them, as this mighty Emperour? The Grandchild by both sides of the most Excellent Princes, that many Ages before had seen. The Husband of a most vertuous Wife and by her the Father of a most Royall issue, seeing with his own Eies his son & Two Daughters settled in Royal Thrones with as much obedience submitting to him, as Commanding others.

And that, which was yet farre more admirable, most happy & honorable euen in the Errours of his Bed. His daughter Margaret becomming the Founder of a Princes house in Italy and euery way by her own vertues approuing her self worthy of so great a Father. And that Natural son of his, whom he could scarce for blushing acknowledge on his Deathbed (& then he first acknowledged him) prouing the brauest man of his times, The Great Don John of Austria.

Nor was he lesse happy in Collateral Relations: Hauing three Great Queens for his Sisters & his Brother Ferdinand by his Loue & Bounty Ascending into the Imperial Seat. ⟨18⟩

It would be too tedious to relate the seuerel Princely Dignities of a multitude of Nephews & Neices all conferred or helped forwards by him. That, which hath been already particularized riseth to greater summe, then can be equalled by any other Example, as I suppose. But when to the Number, Worth, & Greatnes of such a kindred the sincere Loue & Honour wherewhith all [of] them prosecuted him [followed him with honour] shalbe added, approouing themselues ready and Loyal Ministers & Assistants in his Affaires & faithfull Freinds & Sharers both in his prosperous & Adverse Fortunes. When all shall be put together, may I not boldly conclude: That wee haue found one Blessed with more comforts in this kind, then but by instancing in him could haue been imagined euer to haue really befallen any man.

Nor was hee lesse happy in the Perfection & Excesse of all other Domestick Loues & Personal Affections. More Noble Captaines in warre, more prudent Counsellours in peace, more able ministers, more faithfull servants, & more sincere Freinds cannot I beleive be produced to haue euer attended or assisted any Prince. As for Vniversal Loue the fairest floure of Humane Felicitie. Let estimate be taken by that Name, which ordinarily both souldiers & the common people in Germanie vsed when speaking of ⟨19⟩ him, they termed him Our Father, which he not only accepted from the meanest sort, but requited with great tendernes & Familiaritie calling them Sons & stiling himself their Father. Here the CHEIF made a long Pause & then as if she had recollected her thoughts followed on her discourse in this wise.

Hauing Eagle-like mounted to the height of what the most Ambitious heart could wish towards the attainment of the worlds Happines, I will not bring down either mine own or your thought to the suruey of Lower matters, Pompes or Pleasures, or other such like Vanities, Which are indeed but Carrion & they, that haue an eie to them, howeuer by their Lofty soaring with swelling words they may seeme Birds of Heauen, yet are they indeed but Crows & Kites of the Dunghills. Let it suffice to haue thus touched them. What euer the world can afford of this Nature must of Necessitie, you know, be included in the Circumference of those other transcendent goods, which wee haue before inventoried. There remaineth now only the scrutinie of the Person himself, whom vndoubtedly wee may pronounce as complete in all other Abilities of mind & body, which are required to make the enioyment of all these things Happy to the Possessours as could bee wished. ⟨20⟩

Hee was of a strong Complexion & an Actiue strength. No man more gracefully sate his Horse, nor more stoutly bare the weight of his Armes. No man lightlier endured the Distempers of heat & Cold, nor more patiently vnderwent Labours & travaile, then Charles did in his youth.

Hee was precizely regular in his Diet & very spare in all bodily pleasures. Of a comely presence though but of midling stature & rather of Royal then of Beautifull Visage, somewhat Hawk nosed. His Eies of a greyish blew full of modestie euen to shamefastnes, but such as was manly. Of a cheerfull countenance & of an Affable speech, oftentimes in the warres descending to familiar Conference with ordinary souldiers. Of so sure memory, that he neuer forgot a person or busines, that he treated of, nor time, nor place, nor almost any other Circumstance, yet was the goodnes more Admirable then the greatnes. Hee, that lost no other thing, neuer kept the Remembrance of Iniuries.

Here the CHEIF made a second stop, & with a bashfull veiw running ouer the Countenances of her Auditours, as if shee would faine know & yet durst not stay to examine in their faces, the iudgement of their minds, drawing part of her vail before her to hide the flashing blush, which the Encompter of so many eies ⟨21⟩ with hers had bred, after a small, but as appeared very serious bethinking of her selfe, letting her vail fall, & looking vp cheerfully, I perceiue (sayd she) by the Affectionatenes of your Countenances, that there is a Fire of Loue kindled in your hearts towards the memory of this Heroical Prince. But you haue yet seen the Case only, the Iewel itself is within. That which hath been hitherto presented is but the Clothes & the Corps. The mind is the man & the Perfections of the soul are those things, which properly & principally belong to Charles & our present Contemplations. With all this & more (for more may be sayd though perhaps more could not be had) might a man be miserable, if he were vitious in his Vnderstanding or Affections. There is nothing so sweet, that Folly turns not into bitterness, nothing so good, that vice corrupts not. Sardanapalus & Nero & Heliogabalus & all the rest of that suit & Colour [kind], were in all mens Esteeme so much the more wretched by their own inward wickedness, as they had the greater outward provisions for Happiness.

Wisedome & Vertue alone make a man Happy so Philosophers conclude, but together with the Abundance of all other things there is none els will deny.[1] And how certainly, how surpassingly Happy must wee expect this man to haue been? Blessed with so great ⟨22⟩ Abilities of Natural Wisedome & Courage as hee seemed worthy & likely (sayth the Noble Historian)[2] though he had not at first had it, to haue in the end obtained by his own vertue what euer he inherited by Birth or Succession.

Could he say more, think you, then this? Yet because it neither satisfied him, nor, I see it, contents not you to Coast so large and faire a shore with so breif a Card [survey], Heare what the same Author adds.

In this Prince Fortune stroue with vertue, that vpon his deserts she might sett the very Crown of Felicitie. Neither doe I think (sayth hee) that either our own or the memorial of forepast Ages can propose for imitation to them, which by the way of vertue aspire to soueraignitie, the Example of any Prince more liuely drawn to the Image of complete Vertue.[3]

---

[1] None els will deny—so the manuscript. The probable meaning is that when wisdom and virtue are combined with all other advantages, no one would deny that a man ought to be happy.

[2] Noble Historian—de Thou; see the discussion immediately following and Introduction, p. xlv.   [3] See de Thou, Book XXI, p. 292.

I read in your Looks the Demande of his Name, that giues so large a Testimonie: It is the most Iudicious Thuanus.

There is no doubt but he wrott what he thought. & I make no question but to perswade you to think what he wrott, if you giue mee Leaue to take some few peices of this rich frame into Consideration. But where shall I begin? With that, which to mee seemes most difficult in vnlimited Power: The moderation of mind, ⟨23⟩ which kept him free not only from Iniurie of deeds, but from all Insolencie of words. He was neuer perceiued either in suddaine Choler or settled Reuenge to haue been transported beyond the bounds of seemly grauitie. I cannot temper [restrain] my self from one Admirable Instance of his Temper herein. Which because you haue not heard before giue mee Leaue here to insert. When John Frederique[1] was brought before him Luis de Auila his much Fauoured Chamberline riding close to the Emperour rounded [whispered to] him thus in his Eare.

Let not mighty Prince the heat of mind or body through this hard & newly gained Battaile nor the freshnes of the Saxons great offences prouoke you to doe that, which you neuer yet did to any other by giuing him harsh words.

To which he readily & cheerfully made answere. God willing they shall not. And indeed he royally performed it not only forbearing all vpbraidings & threatenings, but with singular modestie & Curtesie Commanded the Afflicted Prince to keep his Horse, when he was about in Humilitie to light, commiserating the double Distresse of his Enemies fainting through wounds and thirst, rather then Exacting his own due.

Neither was his moderation in Pleasures lesse then that, which you ⟨24⟩ haue heard touching his Passions. From his very childhood being trayned vp in serious matters, his while Life was a continual Exercize of Heroical Industry in most Noble & weighty Affaires. Pervse the Historie of those times you shall scarce euer find him mentioned but either in Armes or at Counsell. When

---

[1] See above, p. 25 n. 1.

you find him in Bankets or Triumphs you shall find it was the condescending to others desires, not the Choise of his own mind, out of Curtesy to please others rather then himself. Hee staies and Accepts the Magnifique Intertainment of the French King at Paris, Affords his Presence cheerfully, spends his time freely, & seemes liberally to partake in the Brauery & Iollitie of those Royal Games & Sports. But his own servants know, that he recouers in the night what was robbed from him in the day, & spy him in his Closett euery morning a whole houre long at his Prayers to God on his bended knees. That you may well beleiue that he was not ouer much rauished either with the Glorie or Delight of the Pompes or Pleasures of this world, that was so constant in the Exercize of his own Humilitie & Contemplation of spiritual matters. How little may wee think these Earthly things took him, that was so frequent & willingly Conversant in Heauenly? ⟨25⟩

As for those Blemishes of Chastitie, which you heard before touched, others may perhaps say much, but it neither becomes you nor mee to heare any thing in defense or Excuse thereof: How shall Our Virgin Bashfulness admitt the discourse of these matters, which he himself could neuer remember without blushing? Though in an vncontrolled height of Power & in the throng of a Polluted Generation, yet is not our Charles led by the Errour of the wicked to Glory in his shame. But though through Humane Frailtie he loose the First prize of Perfect & Vninterrupted Chastitie, yet he carryeth away the second of vnparalelled Modestie, & becomes a greater Example by his fall then perhaps he could haue been by his Integritie.

The Name of Margarets Mother could neuer be learned. Those few that had been priuy to the Errour hauing their lips sealed vp close by Fidelitie & he himself by shamefastnes. By his own Confession he giues the first notice of Don John of Austria to the World but not till himself was going out of it. On his Death-bed he acknowledged him for his Child & recommends him to his son

Phillip, but by the mediation of Freinds. Hee had not the heart to declare with his own mouth, no not when he was a dying.[1]
⟨26⟩

What a check doth his secret Concealment so long, and his shamefast manner of Revealing it at the last giue to the Brazen Impudency of this Filthy Age when euery parcel [insignificant] Gallant dare in the open Eie of Heauen boast of that, which Charles the Fift durst scarce confesse in his Chamber to his Freinds & Servants.

If you haue sufficiently veiwed his Moderation in Passions & Pleasures, turn your Eies to his Patience & Magnanimitie. Neither Dangers nor Difficulties nor Calamities euer changed his Countenance. But they, that looked on him took themselues heart from the Courage & Cheerfulnes, that shined out in his face.

He is forced to fly from Inspruch by Torchlight in a Cold & dark Night through narrow & deep waies so vnprovided as without Bootes. And yet there's none of all the Company, that sheweth so little feare as hee, that was only sought to be surprized [taken prisoner]. His Courage cheers vp all the rest, that needed not haue been otherwise affrighted but for his Danger. Hee hath the Advantage of an Horse, & yet outgoes not the Company on foot. With a Trunchion in his hand he rides vp & down ordering & Encouraging them to make ⟨27⟩ speed without affrightment. That you may know it is the same vertue, that performes both Great & small matters, you might haue seen Charles as carefully & nobly performing the office of an Vnder Martial as he was wont of a mighty Emperour.

Hee comes thus in hast & alone & yet strikes a Terrour into the Venetian state by his approach, that they immediately arme as though their best defences were all too little against his single Prowesse.

There was no Victorie euer made him iudged more Invincible then his retreat. Nor euer happened a more Illustrious proof of

[1] See de Thou, Book XXI, p. 297.

the Incomparable Loue & Esteeme that hee had in all mens minds. When John Frederique[1] the greatest Example of seueritie, that euer Charles made, chose rather as a Voluntarie Prisoner to accompany him then to gaine his Libertie by others Curtesie or his own Indeauours. What think you? Whether was more Admirable the Fidelitie of the Captiue Prince, or the worth of the Emperour, that drew this braue man to follow him in his Flight, by whom he had been ouercome in battail. & made him not willing to leaue Charles in Distresse, by whom he had been despoiled of Honour, State, & Libertie. What a Treasure of ⟨28⟩ Worth & Vertue did he conceiue to be in Charles his Freindship, that was able to make recompence for so many & inestimable dammages.

Answerable to what you may haue heard was all this Heroical Prince's Demeanour in the Infortunacy at Algeers, in the distresse at Metz, in the Tempest that droue him on the English Coast, in all the other like Accidents, & many they were, that befell him. There was neuer the least disproportion to be found between his mind & his Title. Hee proued himself alwaies euery way, A Caesar.

In a word, that wee may be induced to beleiue, that no man was euer made more for Happiness. He was endued with that Wisedome & Courage, as he was able euen out of Adversitie to extract Honour & Comfort by the greatnes of his Patience & Magnanimitie.

You are rather wearied I see then satisfied with the splendour & richnes of these iewels. I will therefore with the more speed passe ouer the rest. Although in truth mee thinks its too much niggardlines to be scanty in that wherein he was so large: Royal Bounty. That's it, which next appeares of the greatest Number of Carats & the most Orient Colour, that euer you saw Pearl in ⟨29⟩ this kind. What so honourable, what so pleasant to a generous heart, as to be continually making others honourable & full of

---

[1] See above, p. 25 n. 1.

Comfort. And where shall wee find a Match for our Charles in the Number, worth, & happy Bestowing of highest Benefitts & Fauours? What Crown in Heraldry can be brought forth, that his Greatnes & Bounty sett not vpon some or others head? His Brother by his Cession becomes Adorned with the Emperial Diademe. His sone by Resignation the mightiest King on Earth. The House of Medices receiues the title of Great Dukes, & that of Saxonie that Electorate from his hand. Numberlesse is the Number of Inferiour Dignities. That you may know that he was mounted to the highest pitch, That all Humane Greatnes & Honour should be subordinate to his Beneficence. His scholemaster Adrian[1] doth by his meanes, Ascend into the Papal Chaire. But Honours perhaps are the lesser proof of Bounty. The Excellencie & Happines of Liberalitie is best seen in the Distribution of Riches. Money, as the world deemes, includes with all good things. Hee, that is rich, is Blessed in that he receiues. How much more Blessed then must the Giuer bee both in the Abilitie & ready will to make others rich. Will you know in a word ⟨30⟩ the Exuberant Happines of our Charles in this kind. Neuer more nor more mighty Rich men grew vp vnder any Princes Bounty & Prosperitie, then did vnder his. What the vnknown Treasures of Solomon came to, wee know not: but take the greatest summe, that stands registred in Historie to haue been bestowed by any one Prince, & you shall not find them to amount to so much as Charles the Fift gaue & was by his Grant enioyed.

But that which makes both this of Liberalitie & all other vertues transcendent in him was the Eminency of Iustice and Pietie. These Two in the Royal Crown are like the Two great Lights in Heauen, whence all other things receiue their Lustre. Euen Beauty it self is but dimme without it be Enlightened by the Glory of the sun.

Without Iustice Bountie turnes to Crueltie & oppression & Vertue it self proues but the greater Instrument of malice. And

---

[1] See above, p. 22 n. 1.

all the Comforts of Life & World, if they be not by the Constant Exercize of Pietie grafted into the Hopes of Euerlasting Ioy, are but like troubled slumbers in hott diseases, full of disquiet, whilest they are taken, & leauing the heart & head more sick when they are broken off. ⟨31⟩

The Feare of Death to a Guiltie Conscience bitters all the sweetnes of this world euen to Wormewood & Gall. That your suspicions this way may not preiudice the Necessitie of my Conclusions, you shall know, that not only, if you search the high Thrones of Princes, but euen amongst the Lower formes of Priuate Persons you shall scarce find a heart more ennobled with Iustice towards men, or more enriched & confirmed with Deuotion to Godward then our Charles had.

Perhaps there may be cast in the way an Errour one or Two against the Precize Rules of Iustice & Integritie. The Eluding of Anna Mamorantze's[1] too much Credulitie & the ouer-reaching of the Lantzgraue[2] by a Captious Subtiltie. But when wee find it to haue been acted rather by the violence of others Cauilling Heads, then by the Freedome of his owne Counsels, & when in so large a life & so many great advantages as were offered, wee cannot discouer aboue a Couple of Aberrations, I shall deeme him not only ignorant of all History, but of the Common Frailty of man's Nature, that would goe about to barre Charles from the highest prize of Fidelitie & Iustice. Let them be amplified as much as Envy can, yet they will not at most be found of ⟨32⟩ greater blemish to his Immortal Fame, then wee see a mole in the Neck or a wart in the Forehead are to a most accomplished Beauty, though in themselues disgracefull, yet much more setting out the Beauty & fauour of all the other Perfections. But I mention these things now not so much to cleare a mortal mans Reputation, as to Advance the seueritie and Impartialnes of the Diuine

---

[1] Anna Mamorantze—Anne, Duc de Montmorency (1493–1567). See de Thou, Book XXI, p. 293.
[2] Lantzgraue—Philip, Landgrave of Hesse (1504–67), father-in-law of Maurice, Elector of Saxony (1521–53).

Iustice, which turned a witty & Advantageable sophistrie, as Charles thought, when he caused it, to the greatest disturbance of his quiet & ouerthrow of his Counsells & designes, that could bee.

Slights and Cunning where plaine dealing is expected, may perhaps benefitt at the instant: but in the end ruine him, whosoeuer he be, that vseth them.

If Charles the Fift payd so dearely for a little insinceritie, Let him, that will, practize it. There's no Dammage so vntolerable, that Ile redeeme, nor no Benefitt so great, that Ile purchase at that Rate.

Let Merchants haue their Policies, Lawyers their Reseruations & Pretences, Tradesmen their Mysterie, & euery man their meaning. But let mee walk alwaies the Royal path of Vprightnes, not only conforming my words & ⟨33⟩ Actions to my intents, but explaining them to others apprehension, making them Answere not mine own Cunning Interpretations, but what they did Confidently Expect. And let it be my Portion, Oh Lord, rather to haue mine own Plainnesse abused by others subtletie then by Finenes of witt to work out mine own Ends vpon others simplicitie. But I offer too great preiudice to the Excellencie of this subiect & your Patience by this intermingling of my priuate thoughts. Pardon mee. The Remembrance & obseruation of that, which cheifly perhaps brought Charles to God, hath carried vp my meditations with it, as little sparks ascend in greater flames. It is not so much Pleasure by Admiration of God's wonderfull Contriuements, that wee ought to seek in great mens Liues & Actions, as the Bettering of our selues by particular application of that, which concernes vs to imitate in their Heroical Vertues, or to Expect from the impartial hand of God neuer failing with Rewards to cherish & with punishments to reuenge the performance or breach of his Holy Commandement.

Let it suffice Charles did amisse by the Policie of Captious words ouer-reaching those, who vpon too much ⟨34⟩ securitie of his Royal Fidelitie had lesse carefully & Cautelously [cautiously] prouided for themselues & Charles by Gods just awarde becomes deceiued where himself most trusted. Vngratefully requited by whom he had been most beneficial vnto, & Endangered by what he most contemned. Yet think him not the lesse but the more beloued of God. A sharp Chastisement is an Argument of Gods present Fauour, when it improoues vs to Vertue.

But before I bring the proof of Gods Loue to him, let mee giue you the say of his Loue to God. That's only now resting to find him compete in all the Capabilities for Perfect Happines. Deuotion & Pietie make a man Happy in the miseries of this World. How much more shall they adde to him, that enioyed all the Felicitie, that the whole Circumference thereof affords. And verily, whether you consider the Priuate Affections of his soul, or the publick Endeauours of his Royal Condition you shall perceiue him most Admirable in his Loue to God & in his Confidence of God's Loue & favour towards him.

You expect I see for the more perfect Finishment of this discourse, that I should bring an Instance or two. You shall haue them, & such as you haue not yet heard, that your satisfaction ⟨35⟩ may be the more, whilest by Addition of New proofs you haue the former confirmed.

Whilest Braue John Frederique retyred with speed equal to Flight, & Charles in Company of the men at Armes pursued him on a maine trott, he spied (according to the Custome still vsed amongst the Lutheran Protestants) a Crucifix sett vp in the high way which by some bold hand had newly receiued a Muskett shott in the brest thereof. At which spectacle Charles first stopping as amazed, Afterwards lifting up his Eies to Heauen with an afflicted voice & Gesture, Thou knowest, Lord (sayd hee) that this Bullett hath peirced my heart. How rightly informed his knowledge was is not now to dispute. But if you beleiue him on his word, as I doe, you will with mee conclude, that his Deuotion

& Loue must needs be very fervent to the Lord himself, that was so affected with the conceit of Dishonour to the Representation.

But there was a strong mixture of superstition in this Act? Bee it so. But let them, that dare therevpon condemne Charles, well advise, whether his erring zeal shall not rise vp hereafter to convince [convict] the world now a daies of stone coldnes. That cannot only with Patience, but with smiles ⟨36⟩ broake the Profanation of that Holy Name, whereby wee are called, & without any great trouble dayly see the precious bloud, & sacred wounds of our Sauiour by fearfull oaths & Execrations with greater smart & offense refreshed to him now in heauen, then they were with cruel paine at first inflicted on his body here on Earth.

Let vs to the true remembrances & Pledges of our invisible Lord his Holy Name, & sacred Mysteries sett the same seal of Deuout Affections, when euer they come in our waies, as Charles did to his Picture. Or els let vs grant as it is in truth. That our hearts be as farre short of his true & sincere Loue towards our Redeemer, as our Vnderstandings are better informed by right & sound knowledge, then Charles his was.

But Particular Actions are not it may be so infallible proofs of sincere Religion. There are few excellent dispositions, that wee shall not perceiue either by chance or Art oftentimes venting the strongest of their Natural Desires & Passions in the outward Forme & Dresses of Pietie, especially when it may tend to the improuement of their Honours or Furtherance of their Designes. To doe good sometimes to outward veiw inferres no necessitie of inward Godlines. ⟨37⟩ There's a Firmnes of Intention to make it his principal end, there's a constancy of Actions to make it his continual busines, that is required to seal the Assurance of Pietie & Religion to a man's own heart & to giue warrantie thereof to others. If this suffice then it is vndeniable on Charles his part. That I may not make it lighter by giuing it in my own, or lesse pregnant by Addition of more, Ile giue you the Confirmation of this in the very words of a witnesse against whom no exception can ly. The Noble Thuanus, who no doubt would on his oath had it been required, haue deliuered what hee now averres on his Honour.

Wee may without Flatterie affirme (sayth hee) that after Charles his Exaltation to the Empyre the study of Pietie was so cheifly in him, that almost all things, that hee did either in warre or peace ought to be referred to that end. Hee giues as a particular Instance of this General, His restlesse indeauour for the Celebration of a Lawfull Counsell, That the Reformation of corrupted manners & the revnitement of diuided opinions in the Church of Christ might haue been by this meanes effected, as he & most others had hope. Which purpose of his (sayth Thuanus) although it was either ⟨38⟩ by the insinceretie of the Popes, or by the Eruption of French warres continually hindered, yet was it continually by him reassumed againe & constantly prosecuted to the End. So that no man need marveil (sayth hee) that all Charles his Counsells, words & Actions should be made so glorious by the Present Aide & Assistance of the Diuine Power, Considering the Holy purposes & intentions, that he alwaies had in his heart. Pietie & Iustice (adds this Great Statesman) were the Aime of all Charles his Life.[1]

And if his obseruation erre not, the Fairest Flowers both of worth & happines, which haue since adorned his Descent, haue sprung from the vigour of his Example & the vertue of his Fauour with God.

A zealous Promotion of God's seruice & a Faithfull discharge of his place haue in Thuanus his Iudgement (& who will dare oppose so great Authoritie) ministred euer since Nourishment to that Royal Family.

So that perhaps wee shall doe no wrong to Conclude, that in God's mercifull Acceptance & Reward of his True Goodnes, they

[1] See de Thou, Book XXI, p. 293.

haue since vpheld that great Prosperitie, which els, it may be, by worse deserts & Courses they had forfeited. ⟨39⟩

But howeuer in this particular wee must restraine our Censures as too dull ey'd to trace God's Footsteps exactly in paths so farre aboue our veiws, as Kings & Princes Liues are, yet can wee not too boldly apply the obseruation to our selues. That the Abounding in God's seruice & the Enlarging of our Affections toward Common good is the surest way to reare high our own proper Happines & to Establish it firme to our Posteritie.

How many Fathers may wee think haue cutt short their Childrens Prosperitie by drawing it out too long, & haue cheifly ouerthrown it by too much & only intending it.

There's no Flourishing Estate on Earth, that is not founded in Vertue. That which is planted by the Contriuements of a partial Head & heaped vp by the Toyl of a Niggard hand, besides that it grows vp a staruelíng Tree neuer out liues the memorie of the Founder.

Mark it well. You shall scarce see the ruine of any of these kind of Fortunes, but you shall immediately heare the Builders guilt testified by Eie & Eare wittnesse. That you may be assured, it is but a Mushrom of a Nights growth & nourished by Earthly Damps whateuer Honour, wealth & Greatnes shootes vp from these stemmes. ⟨40⟩ It's the Dew from Heauen, the Blessing of God only, that makes great & happy euen in this World. And that Blessing is best procured by the Neglect of our selues for the Advancement of his seruice, & the Equal Esteeme & Indeauour for others for vniversal good as for our own. The Assurances of this being approoued in the Royal height of Charles his tran-scendent Estate shalbe proportionably confirmed in the Pros-peritie of euery mans Lower Fortunes. If Pietie & Iustice bee as seriously intended, Euery mans Condition may bee made as flourishing to himself & his, as Charles his was. Whom hauing now on all sides & in all respects, by which any dimension of Happiness is to be taken, presented to your veiw before I can proceed further, I am to require the free declaration of your Iudgements touching that, which I layd for the foundation of this Long Discourse.

Whether by all these Titles, which you haue now heard alledged Charles may not as iustly lay claime to the Possession of Happines as euer any mortal man could doe?

The question is weighty & the Solution on either side of highest Consequence. Take leasure & bethink you well.

Part IV

After a solemn pause the Guardian, using figures derived from the language of exploration, praises the Chief's description and agrees that Charles may aptly be called the happiest of men. To the Guardian's annoyance, the Chief teasingly refuses to concede that Charles was happy and, forced by the entreaty of others to explain, asserts that he was not happy because 'There's no happiness at all in this world.' When the Guardian refuses to be put off by this obvious answer, the Chief proposes that a dialogue be arranged between one of her companions and herself to examine the true nature of happiness. Eager that she should win the reputation of a scholar, the Guardian proposes the Cheerfull, his 'adopted' daughter, as a partner with the Chief (CH.) in Socratic dialogue. Two admissions are drawn from the Scholar (SC.): that for a man to be truly happy both himself and others must agree that he is happy; and that she believes the common error that, as the Chief phrases it, 'there is a certain measure of happiness in this world' found in those things which 'Charles did so amply enjoy'. The question of a fit judge of Charles's happiness is raised; and after the Scholar has been drawn in to setting up qualifications, she is forced to accept Charles himself as the only candidate. The dramatic tension of the dialogue (which in the latter pages of this section rises to the height of conscious art) mounts until 'one of the company' (Nicholas Ferrar) solemnly promises that if the Chief proves Charles was not happy, he will never again seek after the things of this world. The Chief affirms that he has already made great progress in this spiritual voyage, wishes him further success and, expressing herself in the language of navigation, promises that she—and she hopes others—will soon follow his example.

----◆----

The Cheif hauing thus spoken, as if either her thoughts ⟨41⟩ were full of intricacy; or by her own seriousness she would invite the Company to a solemne Consideration of the matter, Crossing her Armes & fixing her Eies in the ground she continued a good space in an vnmouable Posture although the reasoning of the Company

47

on Euery side some aloude & some in soft whisperings seemed to enforce her Eie & Eares to their Attention.

At last the Guardian rising vp from his Chaire, & laying his hatt, which till then had couered his head on the Table by him. Her mind, which by the former noyse of talking could not be diuerted, seemed by the suddaine silence of the Company & the Guardians motion to be reuoked [called back to attention]. Where vpon lifting vp her eies, when she perceiued by the bowing of himself & the preparation to speak, that both the Reuerence & words were directed vnto her, dying her face with a scarlett blush, as being out of modestie ashamed of so vnexpected Honour she likewise rising vp with great Reuerence sett herself to receiue his Answere. But He beckning with his hand, that shee should againe take her place began thus.

But that your intimation to the contrary (most Worthy Cheif) ⟨42⟩ breeds a demurrer amongst vs, that in nothing neither can nor will be contrary vnto you, wee should by a ioynt Consent giue vp our Verdict.

That this man had embraced in his Armes the whole orbe of Felicity. Neither can wee find any thing wanting to him nor any thing without that, which he had, that is necessarie to this Worlds Happines.

We are too well skilled in those Cardes [surveys], which the wise masters of this World haue drawn touching Humane Felicitie. Our Loue & Folly haue made vs too long students, too great Proficients in this schoole of Vanitie. But what wee haue there gazed on by way of Prospectiue you haue represented vnto vs in substance.

Wee cannot though wee curiously search find either Creek, that you haue not run vp, or Headland, that you haue not Compassed or Channel, that you haue not sounded. You haue made a perfect discouery of the whole bay of this worlds Happines, & your Charles appeares rightly & fully Enfeoffed in [put in possession of] the whole & Euery part thereof.

How many Millions would think themselues most Happy with the Hundred part of that, which he enioyed touching the ⟨43⟩ Blessings of this Life? How Blessed without any of them at all, would the better sort of men (those I meane of pure souls & Elevated Vnderstandings) esteeme themselues in any meane Conformitie to his Excellent Vertues & in any weak Participation of those Certain Pledges, which he had of being partaker of that better life aboue.

To be Happy here in the fruition of all the Good, which Earth affords, & withall to be invested into the succession of Heauen. To haue this world's Felicitie to the vttermost & Gods Blessing both together, Why this cannot but be perfect double Happines. But not to be Happy euery way in himself alone, but in the continuance of Admirable Prosperitie to his Children & Family, & that as their Bloud flowing from his Bloud, deriued from his Worth, Why that is such a rare straine of Felicitie as wee see Thousands of kind & tender-hearted Parents willingly Embracing their own miserie to reach thereunto, Gladly content to accept at Gods hands Sorrow & Affliction for their own Portion, that they may leaue ioy & Comfort to their Posteritie. But Charles hath for himself & leaues to his House the fatt & the sweet of this world & this Life. And yet wee are not at an End. Had his Happines died with ⟨44⟩ himself, or had it liued only in his Children the Brauer spirits of Mankind would haue put in a Caueat against him. That though he might be iudged happy in his own Generation yet not in ours. Perpetuitie is by them required to Happines & rightly, if they rightly vnderstood it. He neuer was Happy, that ceaseth to bee Happy euen in himself. Its an Euerlasting memory, that must sett the seal to all. And herein, whom can they produce more Happy then Charles liuing still fresh & euery day, whilst day shall last likely to grow increasing in Glorious Fame Not only for incomparable Greatnes but much more for vnparalel'd worth. Not only a Perfect Example of all manner of vertue, but a Guide & Instructour for the Attainment of Happines to all Conditions of men. Why this makes vp all, that can be possibly required to the Complete Body of Humane Felicitie, Height, bredth, length, & depth. And was hee not then say you Happy? Nay what say you (replied the CHEIF smiling) Thats first to be known. You must tell mee your mind before you may heare mine.

You are perplexed, I see, in your Cogitations between the Euidencie of your own right & the Iealousie of my dissent. ⟨45⟩ Is it not so? Why take good heart. What need you doubt a Woman's Fancy, that are so strongly backed on all hands? Good men will not contradict you for the aboundance of Grace & goodnes, which was in him. The Aboundance of Good, that he was the Happy instrument of to so many & Especially to his own, will make those of Good and Louing Dispositions to take your part with Admiration.

The Braue Spirits though with Envy will follow for that Excellencie of Glory, which dazleth their Ambitious Eies. The Pomps, Pleasures, Honours, Riches & Authoritie, which attended & encompassed him in all fulnes & height will draw the whole world to giue their Vote That he must needs bee the Pattern of Happines.

It is not Enough I perceiue (sayd the GUARDIAN) that you haue Entangled vs, Except you also make your self merry with our Encumbrances. Your Encouragements doe more terrifie then your former affrightments: I like not this General Combination of Good & Bad, Wise & Fools. There is some greater danger then wee are aware of in this Extraordinarie appearance of safetie. There's some secret Ambush, sweet Companions, That our Politick Enemy Endeavours to traine [lure] vs into. ⟨46⟩ Why my Deare Father[1] (sayd the CHEERFULL) make no more adoe but with the great Alexander, if you cannot vnty this Gordian Knot, Cutt it.—How meane you, sayd the GUARDIAN? Cause our Cheif (said the AFFECTIONATE) to bring vs out of this Laberinth, that she hath lured vs into.

[1] See Introduction, p. xlii.

Indeed (sayd the PATIENT) worthy Cheif, That belongs to your place to be our Guide for the more ready discouerie of the Truth. And to this intent, I know, hath all this Art been vsed, that being puzled at the First wee might in the End be more clearly brought out.

You see (sayd the GUARDIAN) that all are against you. There's no excuse much less resistance to be made. Teach vs I pray, the solution of this Riddle, which you haue put. Why & how can it bee, that this man was not Happy? Because (sayd SHEE) If you will haue it in short & plaine termes, There's no happines at all in this World. So indeed (sayd the GUARDIAN) wee heare euery day told vs out of the Pulpit & wee beleiue it too, although our Practizes shew the Contrary. But thats not the point, which wee now aime at.—What then (sayd the CHEIF)?—Why this sayd the GUARDIAN, As skilfull Physicians think it not ⟨47⟩ Enough to lay the Cause of Death to mans Mortalitie in general, but tell vs the particular disease, & shew the working thereof in the body. So neither can it satisfie vs & discharge you to turn vs off so at randome with the Incompetencie of this Life & Happiness; but you must let vs see whereby & wherein the Perishment of this Stupendious Felicitie (for so to vs & to all the World it appeares) was caused. You, that haue so curiously anatomized euery part of it, must needs haue found, where the mortal Distemper lay.

Why doe you not perceiue it (sayd the CHEIF)? There's no soundnes in any part. All's Amisse.

What I perceiue (sayd the GUARDIAN) matters not. Doe you, I pray, so teach mee as though I neither knew nor saw aught at all.

Pardon (sayd SHEE) that I should goe about to teach you. I may not without Presumption heare, how much lesse vndertake, to performe. But if you be pleased to sett out one of my Companions here I shall endeauour with her Assistance to declare the thing in the same manner it was taught mee. Why here (sayd the GUARDIAN) taking her by the hand I consigne to you the Cheerful for this purpose. Not so much ⟨48⟩ for that more especial Interest, which by Adoption I haue in her, as for the Desire & in pursuite of making good that long agoe imposed Name of Scholler. The Perfect Answere wherevnto on her Behalf would farre more Endeare her to mee then the Latter of Daughter & proue to her of farre more Advantage.

It is the Affection of a Master & the Benefitt of Instruction, that I most prize (sayd the CHEERFULL) in your Fatherhood. & therefore cannot too much blame myself, that haue been so negligent in the making vse of that peculiar Advantage, which I had in my Master. But if the rather by your recommendation hee shall be pleased to continue his Fatherly Care & paines towards mee, I hope (God willing) to giue him & you better Comfort by my Proficiencie hereafter.

Though there can be no Addition made (sayd the GUARDIAN) to his Forwardnes,[1] which, I know, is in the height; yet for your better satisfaction I shall againe renew my desires to him by all the power & interest, that I haue in him. But now be content to become for the present your Worthy Cheifs Scholler, that I may by your teaching learn that, which I desire. ⟨49⟩

Neither shall you be my Scholler now (sayd the CHEIF) Sweet Cheerful. Nor is it from mee but from you that our Guardian must learne what hee needs wilbe taught for others rather then his own Information. Prepare your self therefore not to demande your own Questions, but to resolue mine.

Well (sayd the CHEERFULL) it will but proue your greater skill to draw the Knowledge of the Truth from my Ignorance. What euer way you transforme it, the Honour must be yours, if you can giue vs the satisfaction wee desire.

I pray (sayd the GUARDIAN) without any further Complements proceed to the Busines.

---

[1] Forwardnes—confidence. In this passage the Guardian seems to be speaking of himself in the third person in line with the distinction which the Patient had made between his functions of 'father' and 'master'.

CH. [Chief] Tell mee then what is requisite to make a man happy.

SC. [Scholar] The Aboundance of all these things, wherein Happines doth consist. CH. Doth the presence of them suffice?

SC. No. They must be both in Possession & Fruition too. He must haue them in his power & he must enioy them. For neither doth a man cease to be poore, that hath a Treasure in his House, if he know not of it, or cannot come by it. Nor though it be in his hands, if he make not vse of it, can he be rightly thought rich. ⟨50⟩

CH. What shall wee say then? Had Charles in his Possession & Fruition all those things, wherein Happines doth consist?

SC. In such manner, neither he nor any man can haue them in this World: For the most perfectest of them & the full measure belongs to that Other World which wee expect. But he had them in hope & in Assurance.

CH. But shall wee say, that he was Happy in Act [reality] for those things which he had but the hope of; or must we not say, that in regard of perfect & true Happines, he was but Happy in hope.

SC. Indeed wee can say no more, & hereby I perceiue the solution of that First Doubt, which so much troubled vs: That the good Estate of men in this Life to Godward is but Hapines in the way & in the Blossome (If so much) & not in the fruit & fulnes: But though he were not absolutely happy, yet why should wee not iudge him happy in part?

CH. In what part?

SC. In regard to the Great Aboundance of good things which hee had.

CH. But did you not at first say that there must be Aboundance of all things? ⟨51⟩

SC. I [Aye], to perfect happines. But now wee are fallen to Condition of Humane Felicitie, & to that ward wee cannot perceiue any defect in his Estate.

CH. But if there be no such thing, as Humane Felicitie in this world, can yours or others supposition make it?

SC. No such thing. How can that bee? Seeing that all mens Desires & Indeauours are & euer haue been for the Attainment thereof. It were surely a great & perhaps the very height of Miserie that could bee imposed on Mankind to be continually imployed with such sore Labour in the search of that, which cannot bee found.

CH. But were it not much better & more reasonable to conclude the Nullitie thereof by all men's failings in the Attainment, then the realtie by their pursuite & to say because it could neuer be found therefore it is not rather then that it must bee, because it is euer sought.

SC. Indeed wee so convince [prove wrong] the Vanitie of Alchymists. But they blowing all into Fume remaine in the end with nothing but Collow [coal dust] & soote on their hands & faces. But there's a Number of true substantial good things in the World whereon to found Happines. ⟨52⟩

CH. What are those I pray? SC. Honour, wealth, pleasure, & the like.

CH. Alas doe not they likewise vanish in the end like a Morning dew. The Proud are robbed, they haue slept their sleep & all the men, whose hands were mighty haue found nothing. They are not only smoak but shaddow & farre more besmeare their Owners souls, & perplex their minds in the very enioyment then the smoak doth the Foolish Alchymists, whom you deride.

SC. It is their own fault perhaps, not of the things.

CH. How so? SC. Because they cannot be contented. They loose the Benefitt of what they haue, & become miserable by want in their desires, that might otherwise be most Happy in that they Enioy.

CH. Then Content is necessarie to Happines as well as those things, wherein Happines consisteth.

SC. Most Necessarie: For though there be some contented without Happiness, yet none can be happy without content.

CH. How can any be content without Happines?

SC. Ignorance of better good makes many rest satisfied in that which is of no worth. Distemper of mind makes some contented euen in miserie. So wee see not only mad men, but carnal minded men, wallowing in their Filthines with all manner of ⟨53⟩ Contentednes, saue that they feare the depriuement of them; yet are not they nor those others therefore Happy, because they think themselues happy, to which is requisite the Enioyment of those things, which are truly good, which they, that haue, ought to rest content, & then they should be happy indeed.

CH. Why then I perceiue, there is a double sort of happy miserable people. The First Those, that are Happy in their own Conceits, but truly miserable. The others, that are truly happy in the matter of Happiness, But miserable by their own Conceits only.

SC. So it seemes.

CH. And which of them think you to be in the more wretched Case?

SC. Both of them are farre from happines, which is neither in the things alone, nor in a mans Conceit alone, but in both. He is neither a Happy man, that only thinks himself so. Nor he that others only think so: But he, that both himself & others think & know to be so. He is the Happy man indeed.

CH. Why then if our Charles be of this latter sort, that did not think himself happy, you will cancell him out of the Roll?

SC. Verily he must needs be struck out. And now I perceiue ⟨54⟩ your Determination of the Question. But after such a manner as Hydra like it hath multiplied our Perplexities in the solution of one, raysing vp many new & inextricable Doubts. CH. What are these many & inextricable doubts?

SC. It will be hard to make the proofs so cleare & full, as is necessarie, that he did so farre otherwise Conceiue of his estate then all other men did, that he alone should find miserie, wherein all others saw such transcendent Happines. But perhaps you are prepared for this. But why hee should be so affected & opinionated, or how it can stand with reason or sence, that he should be so, is past my Apprehension.

CH. For the first there will be little difficultie. If you will beleiue himself you shall haue it vndeniably evinced. But the Two latter points are not indeed so easy not in regard of themselues, but of you.

SC. It's my Ignorance then or obstinacie, that will put you to trouble?

CH. I say not so Deare Cheerfull. God hath giuen you an vnderstanding capable of deeper poynts then these, & he hath seconded it with a Heart, that dares not, I know, be against the truth. But you haue been so long rooted & fortified in the Common Errour of the world, that I see you haue taken it vp ⟨55⟩ for a maine Principal of truth, so as you are loth to admitt any Question about it. Which would you doe, I doubt not but that wee should soone grow to Composition [agreement], That there is a Certaine measure of Happines in this world to be obtained, & that it lieth in these things, which you haue formerly mentioned, & Charles did so amply enioy, is an vndeniable Truth in your Conceit.

SC. So Ancient, so Vniversal, so Constant an opinion of all Mankind, as, mee thinks, ought not at all to be questioned, nor ought the Dissent of some Few Melancholy persons empeach the Creditt there of.

CH. Will you put it to Iudgement?

SC. What Tryal will you haue? Whether by the Peeres, or by the Bench, or by the County, you will be certainly Cast [defeated]. Except your Charles be the Foreman & all the rest of the Jury of your own Choise.

CH. It is a matter, that in regard both of the high Consequence, & the great Difficultie requires the skill of some one excellent man as Iudge, rather then the surmises of many weaker minds to make a right Decision. The smallest matters of Conscience are, you see, referred euen by our Law to the Determination of one impartial Brest. How then would you ⟨56⟩ haue the most important of all others Questions to bee tryed by Number of voices, rather then by weight of reason.

s c. But wee shall neuer agree in any one man.

c h. Why is there no sufficient iudge to be found touching this matter?

s c. Enough. But such as you will not, I doubt, approue.

c h. Approue you them but Competent, & I will promise to stand their Awarde. Tell mee then what doe you require to make a iudge aboue Exception?

s c. First Freedome: That he bee not [by] Controll of outward respects either ouerawed or misguided, that he dare not boldly follow his own iudgement or declare it.

Next Integritie, that he bee not corrupted by the Partialitie of Inward Affections, Loue, Hate, Hope, or Feare. Any little mixture whereof like dead flies in Costly Oyntments poyson the vnderstanding.

The Third thing is a deepnes of Apprehension ioyned with a full Experience of the Particular in Question.

For iudgement without Experience is like a quick Eie in an vncertaine light. & Experience without iudgement is like a strong Arme in shooting without a good Aime, most Comonly missing the white itself by too steddily [obseruing] that, which is next it. ⟨57⟩ They must therefore goe both together. And in whom wee so find them protected by Freedome & accompanied with Integritie, wee may giue that man the Power of Giuing sentence without Libertie of Appeal in my opinion.

c h. And in mine too. But doe you think those Most, those All of mankind, that you haue so much boasted of, are thus qualified?

s c. Will you deny, that many are not?

c h. If I should I shall not I am perswaded be found a slanderer. Tell mee, how many of the better iudgements & spirits of men are there, whom the Ancient Traditions of their Forefathers, the present Examples of their betters, & the Common Practize of their Equals hath not in this & most other weighty matters so fettered, that they dare not dissent from that, which they cannot approue.

sc. But a Few, that are not thus ouerawed.

ch. But how many lesse can you produce, whom desires & Hopes of finding Content in this World hath not so forestalled their minds before they came to the Examination of the matters as no worse News can sound in their Eares, then that it is Labour in vaine to seek for any Happines here on Earth.

sc. You pose mee I confesse. ⟨58⟩

ch. But of Excellent Vnderstandings, that haue had perfect Tryal of the Condition of those things, wherein you conceit Happines to ly, & haue giuen Testimonie on your behalf, bring me only one.

sc. I cannot. They are all as the Proverb is, Wishers & Woulders, as my self am That speak & think out of strong Presumption of some sufficiencie in those things wee see before vs rather then out of the Proof of those things, wee haue attained vnto. Wee are all like Children, that seeing the moone rise behind some steep Hill clyme vp with great paine, hoping to shake hands therewith. But they, that are gott as high as wee desire, complaine, that they are neuer a whitt the nearer.

ch. But if I shall now produce a iudge euery way answerable to your Description will you stand to his Determination. Oh now mee thinks: you are in the wrong to make any demurre at all, the Case is so plaine.

sc. It is your Charles.

ch. Vnlesse you can find iust ground of Refusal according to your own Rules.

sc. Let's see, I pray. His Soueraignitie avoyds all Exception of being ouerswaied by others Authoritie. Hee must needs ⟨59⟩ bee free from all Awe, that was able to Commande All & could not be forced to take his Opinion from any, that had the power of Giuing Laws to euery man.

CH. Hee then stands free in his Libertie. But perhaps you haue better ground for Partialitie.

SC. It were sencelesse to lay any imputation that way vpon him. To what purpose? It is Advantage & Hope of Bettering their own Conditions, that makes men giue wrong iudgement. No man will goe against right, where hee gaines nothing. How much lesse to his preiudice? Why it marred all, that he should think them nothing. He only misseth of Happines, because he could not think he had it. Why it cannot be, that his Affections corrupted him, which by this meanes were all to be extinguished.

CH. Hee then comes out cleare likewise for Integritie. But he was of weak & shallow Vnderstanding.

SC. Oh no. The Prince of men. More Excellent by the Emenencie of Wisedome then of Dignitie. And for Experience hee indeed had full proof by Actual Enioyment of euery thing in its greatest perfection. Other men may talk of these things as Novellists[1] doe of farre remoued Countries ⟨60⟩ by pervsal of Maps made by Hearsay: but he can speak as a Travailer, that hath with his Eies & with his Feet measured euery inch of this Earthly Paradise, which wee dreame of, which we long after.

CH. Why then you see by your own Examination he comes forth an Absolute iudge in this Case.

The Cheerful not making so ready answere as was expected, ONE OF THE COMPANY[2] rising vp with a sober Countenance almost neere vnto sadnes spake thus to the Cheif. Let down your nett, Good Fisher, without longer delay. Though the Game, that you haue so long beaten make shy to enter, yet there is Certaintie of a Draught. If you cannot catch what you desire, yet refuse not

---

[1] Novellists—an early use of the word in the sense of those who tell strange and novel tales as if they were true.

[2] ONE OF THE COMPANY—Since this person is later addressed by the Chief as 'Sir' (p. 60) but is not identified here as the Guardian (John Ferrar), the only male participant in the discussion, I suggest that the speaker is Nicholas Ferrar, whose intention to retire completely from the world of affairs in London was already known. The words of the Chief on page 61 substantiate this identification. See above, p. 23 n. 1.

what offers it self. It is the Nature of this Fisherie to make that, which it takes of highest worth, howeuer meane it be in itself. Let down your nett therefore freely. I am perswaded there's more in this good Companie. I promise for my self, that if you make it good by Charles the Fift his Testimonie, that That Vnparaleld Degree of Happines, which he attained, was not indeed Happines & that this Worlds Honour, Wealth, Pleasure, Dignitie & Power are not the True ingredients of Content, I will neuer, God willing, loose ⟨61⟩ further time or paines in the pursuite of them, but steere directly the Course, that he ran as much as my weaknes shall giue Leaue. If you can bring his Affidauit, that this world deceiued him, you shall by God's Assistance haue my Defiance of it. I will neuer be a servant to those things, which he being Master of, could not be satisfied with. Why the Best of my hopes fall shorter of his Enioyments then the Ethiopians of the Highest Elevation of the Pole.

My largest Desires reach not to the Confines of that Felicitie, which he had passed many thousand Leagues into.

Record my Protestation, I pray, & if euer you see mee goe against it, lay it before mee freely.

'Here is a Fool of Foure & Twenty Carrats, that thinks out of the 'Gleanings of some few Clusters in a petty Fortune to Extract 'that wine of Gladnes & Content, which Charles the Fift could 'not doe out of the whole Vintage of Humane Felicitie.

Ah Sir (sayd the CHEIF sighing) As wee all know you need not my Declaration to be informed of that, which you much better know then I can tell you. So are wee perswaded, that this Resolution is not now to be made on your part, though it be now to bee ⟨62⟩ published. Not for the Confirmation of your own purposes, which are enrolled in a higher Court, but for our Invitation to the like. So the kind Physician to allure his wayward Patient, begins himself the Potion. This is your meaning, I am sure, to all. But for my Particular I vnderstand it yet further intended to admonish mee, that I should doubly fail if I should not follow you in the way, which you pretend by my Direction & Encouragement the rather to haue entered.

The Cheerfull smiles, & I confesse, she hath reason to remember my late Earnestnes in pressing her to enter that passage, wherein I myself am so soone come to a stand. You see: I am not more Couragious but she more wise to forecast the Event.

Well. Good Luck haue you in the Name of the Lord in this happy Voyage, wherein you are bound. Strongly may you beare vp through the waues, & safely may you steere through all dangers, swiftly may you run, & with Triumph may you attaine your wished port. Assoone as we can gett cleare & soone may it bee wee purpose to follow. There's no desire of your stay for Consortship. Wee are not so unequall [jealous] for our own good to wish your hinderance. Only this doe for our sakes, Beare ⟨63⟩ your Lantern as high as may bee, that wee may the better know & follow the Course, when God shall send the right wind & tide to bring vs off these shelues [sandbanks], whereon wee now ly grounded. Some thing you may hope of our safetie because you may perceiue vs apprehensive of our Danger. Hee that now giues the Desires shall in the end I hope perfect the Abilities. Amen replied THE WHOLE COMPANY. And doe you Deare Cheif, for the present without further interruption goe on with your Discourse, sayd the GUARDIAN, Limming out the Reuerse of this accomplished Pourtraicture of Happines, which you haue presented vnto vs so Real & Liuely, that wee shall euer after distrust our own eiesight, if you can substantially make the Contrarie to appeare. Wherein for our Clearer Discerning wee intreat you to draw the Representation by those proportions, Colours, & Connexures [connecting lines], which the Cheerfull prescribed.

Wee must haue his Testimonie in plaine words that he was not Happy.

Wee must know why & on what ground he so thought. And how it can stand with reason being so contrary to all others Iudgements.

Part V

The Chief at last reveals that Charles at the height of his career and for no apparent reason renounced all his titles and imperial responsibilities to devote himself to a monastic life. Because men in general have been seduced into the world's camp and have forgotten their duty to God, Charles was sent as a captain and guide to those who have the desire but lack the strength to follow in the service of Christ. Charles is hailed as a new and greater Solomon in his contempt for the world, a man so blessed by material riches that his denial of them is an unquestionable witness of their worthlessness. The Chief justifies her preamble by pointing out that its length is congruent with the long time that it took Charles to make his decision to forgo earthly advantages.

She proceeds to explain the divine plan of the Almighty in reserving 'the discovery and subjection of the New-found World' for the lifetime of Charles so that by his example the inhabitants of the New World might be corrected in their reverence for the material things of the Old. This message to the New World is balanced by the realization on the part of the Old that another Eden does not exist in the Americas; the reports of explorers only emphasize the fact that 'this world is but a vale of misery and our whole lives a continual exercise of afflictions and anguish'. Loathsome tobacco is the only novelty that the New World has to offer, and its pernicious effects on both body and soul are so great as to make it an emblem of the corrupting influence of all sensual and material pleasures.

It is little, that you require of mee (sayd the CHEIF) in respect ⟨64⟩ of what I hope to performe. You shall haue his Testimonie not only in Words but in deeds also, visible to the Eie, palpable to the hand, & manifesting it self to euery sence & apprehension. You shall haue it enforced by such a Companie of invincible Arguments, as I doubt not but your selues shall with him conclude, That it could not stand with reason, that he should haue done or sayd otherwise then he did. Renouncing all these great & glorious

things, which haue been reckoned vp, Not only as things vn-
necessarie but preiudicial to the attainment of true Happines, &
as the world conceiteth & vseth them the very Essential parts of
Real Miserie. And this Determination made not by way of
inference, as in the Great French Henry's[1] Example, Nor Liable
to tax of suddaine Passion, or natural weaknes, with which
perhaps though slanderously those Two Famous Popes[2] Decrees
(for lesse I accompt not their iudgements in this point) might be
blurred, Nor of Necessitie as may Cauillingly be objected to
Empeach the Validitie of the Mighty Phillips[3] irrefragable
sentence, As though he then dispised, when he could no longer
enioy the Happines of this World. But Charles after a serious
debatement some yeares with ⟨65⟩ himself & others, hauing
thereby as it were giuen Publick Summons to the whole World
to be spectatours & wittnesses solemly proceeds to a free resignation of All. At that Age, in that Temper of mind & body, & vpon
those occasions, which make other men most desirous to gett &
carefull to retaine those Trifles, that they haue in this kind for so
the greatest Enioyments euen of the highest may iustly seeme
being compared with that, which hee relinquished, & so relinquished, as if to that intent only, at least principally he had
receiued All, that you haue heard, that you can imagine, that he
might vpon perfect Tryal in the End reiect it as nothing to him,
as nothing in it self.

Oh the Riches of the Diuine Grace & Wisedome in this Admirable Contriuement shining out more bright & Comfortable to
the observant Eie then the sun it self.

The Loue of this World, the Confidence in the things thereof,
& the greedy pursuite after them, hauing not only mortally
benummed the desires & hopes of things aboue, but vtterly
casheered all seruice of God further then may tend to the readier

---

[1] Great French Henry—see above, pp. 20–1.
[2] Two Famous Popes—see above, pp. 22–3.
[3] Mighty Phillip—see above, pp. 18–19.

Compassing & freer Enioyment of the good things (as they are termed) of this Life & World: Least in so ⟨66⟩ strong & General an infection euen the Elect might perish. For whilest on one side the Mockers[1] foretold of by the Apostles of our Lord Jesus Christ taking advantage by the protracted delay of those things, which were long agoe threatened, as then imminently approaching, with their derisions weakening the Beleif of this worlds beginning & feare of its Consummation, quicken the Affections & Esteeme to the things thereof, as of Longer durance & better worth, then the scriptures make them.

And on the other side the false Apostles of Satan, transfiguring themselues into Angels of Light, by swelling words of vanitie, Extolling these things on Earth as Gods Blessings & Extending the Libertie, wherewith our Sauiour hath made vs free to Carnal Licentiousnes, haue made a composition between God & the World.

There's growen an Vniversal Revolt from Christs Royall standard. Euery man either by open Apostasie, or secret Transaction, passing into the worlds Campe, as doth vndeniably appeare by the Tender of these Affections, by the putting of that Trust, & by the performance of that seruice, which is only Due to God. ⟨67⟩

Least I say in so total a Falling away the Feare of Lonelines finding themselues like Beacons in a Desart left for gaze and wonderment, might perswade those very souls, that are sett apart for better things, to goe along in the Errour of the Wicked, God setts them forth a Captaine & a guide vnder the shelter of whose Authoritie they may boldly Contemne the world, that Contemneth them. & with vndaunted Courage retorting those Dispightfull Taxes, which are giuen them of Povertie of spirit & simplicitie of vnderstanding, with true imputation of madnes & basenes to all the worlds Followers, keep on that path of Deuotion & Religion, which this incomparable Prince, that he might run

---

[1] II Peter iii, 3; Jude v. 18.

the Freer in, stripped himself of all, which they admire, & cast them away, as Toys & Gauds in Comparison of that better Treasure & those richer Iewels, that he had discouered in the faithfull & continual seruice of God.

By the seriousness of your Attentions, I perceiue the Greatness of your Expectation. & yet is not the string wound vp to the height.

There's more then the Encouragement of good men in the right way, there's the Condemnation of all perverse Worldlings, ⟨68⟩ that was by God's Providence intended & accomplished in this Wonderfull passage.

The Malignitie of the disease had made that, which was ordained for the Medicine to be an occasion of further Distemper. The salues themselues wrought to the encrease of Festering.

The Survey and Censure of Solomon[1] is by the witty Atheist turned into merriment. If there were such a thing at all, yet because he sayd & did not, they hold it wisedome rather to follow his Practize then his Preaching.

Whilest hee kept still what he declaimed against, they can not beleiue that he sayd what he thought.

They are desirous, that others should follow this Advise, that they with greater hopes & Freedome amongst Fewer Competitours may follow after that, which he had attained vnto. In a word Solomons Mark of Vanitie & Vexation, which he stamped on all these Earthly things is become an Argument of greater Esteeme & Loue to the vnbeleiuing Worldling. But the Cunning Hypocrite hath another help. since Solomon writt his Book there is a Greater then Solomon come into the world, A true & Absolute Peace maker indeed; ⟨69⟩ that hauing reconciled vs, that were Enemies & the Principal hath together with vs made a reconcile-

---

[1] The Book of Ecclesiastes was ascribed to Solomon and the reference here seems to be to Chapter I. The passage referred to a few lines below is Ecclesiastes i, 14: 'I have seen all the works which are done under the sun; and, behold, all is vanity and vexation of spirit.'

ment with God of the World & all the Appurtenances thereof
being but the Accessories to our guilt. And now through the
appearing of Grace things haue receiued a better nature & worth,
then before. They hold now the full starling [sterling, purity] of
true Goodnes. They cannot be too highly prized, they cannot bee
too carefully sought, being in themselues All perfect & excellent.
The danger is only in the ill vsage.[1]

Thus is the very Balme of Gilead by this pysonous craft of the
old serpent turned into venome both to the Vnbeleiuer & to
the Hypocrite.

But that beguiling themselues without any Colour [reason]
they may be punished without any mercy God strips them of
these Figleaues by a New & a forceable reunitement of that
Ancient Enquest, taking away all those friuolous exceptions,
whereby they cauillously goe about to infringe the former.

A New say master[2] is sent in this last Age to make a second
proof of those things, which the world so boastingly Advanceth.
And he finds them on the touch to be still the ⟨70⟩ same as
formerly, altogether Counterfeit, & if in any respect altered so
much baser in the substance, by how much through subtle
Alchymistry they seeme in these later times to bee more refined.

And this hee giues not vnder his hand only, as the First did, but
he puts his seal too That there may be no pretence left for the
waving of the sinceretie of his iudgement. Hee breaks in peices
that, which he had in his own possession though it seemed
inestimably rich in the worlds valuation. That no man should
hence forward be deceiued by the Faire stampe & Colour, that
these beare of Good & perfect, he did by a seuere Abrenunciation

---

[1] Since Solomon—the lack of punctuation makes this passage obscure although
the tone is clearly sarcastic. The 'true peace maker' seems to assert that things in
themselves are good and therefore must be sought after; it is only the ill use of
riches that makes 'the World and all the appurtenances thereof' to be 'but the
Accessories of our guilt'. The proper use of riches under the direction of Grace
will reconcile us not only with Solomon's principle but also with God.

[2] New say master—a new assayist or one who makes a trial or proof; in this case
a new Solomon; i.e. Charles V.

of the most splendid & delectable condition, that euer mortal man enioyed, leaue the imaginarie idol of Humane Felicitie, like a false peice of Gold through the rupture of some part thereof clearly betraying itself to be but Brasse.

I shall not need your Courtesie to Accept him now for a iudge whereunto you see he is deputed by Commission vnder the broade seal of Heauen it self.

Nor will it be requisite to vse any larger discourse for the Clearing of that doubt, which I perceiue by your often ⟨71⟩ Iterations hath so strongly perplexed your mind. To what intent all this wast of Good things was made, if it were not to make him happy. The Voluptuous Worldling can indeed find no other end of Gods bounty in the infinite vanitie & store of sweet & pleasant things, wherewith by Gods Tender pitty this present Life is seasoned, but his sensual glutting of himself by a delightfull Enioyment of them without feare or moderation.

But this great & glorious Example hath taught a farre other Lesson to the sons of the Wisedome,[1] That they are ordained only as those Antepasts, which serue for the quickening of the Appetite, that by a sober Tast of their pleasingnes to our mortal sences, our immortal souls might be drawn to the Loue & pursuite of those Celestial Blessings, whereof these are but the Earnests & Resemblances.

So accepted & vsed they may indeed proue Beneficial & Comfortable to their Possessours. But as diuers herbs being very fragrant in a short & lighter handling doe vpon harder griping yeeld a Noysome sent, So all the Pompous & delightfull things of this world vpon Exact & perfect Tryal, as baser mettals in the Finers pott resolue only ⟨72⟩ into vanitie & vexation of spirit. The making of the proof is that whereunto all this Concourse of Earthly Good in one mans person was intended, Not to make him

---

[1] Perhaps followers of the Apocryphal book, 'The Wisdom of Solomon', which in the second part includes warnings against the evils of materialism. See also Prov. i–ix, in which Wisdom is personified.

an Example of Happines in himself & a Subiect of Admiration or
Envy; But that vpon a diligent & full inspection of the case super
Totam materiam, as Lawyers speak, he might be able to giue a
final sentence of Decision, against which neither writt of Errour,
Traverse, nor Appeal could ly.

But as it was spoken of Epictetus, that he, which was not
bettered by his Doctrine, was not otherwise to be corrected then
in Hell, so verily I may boldly say, that whosoeuer he bee, that
is not moued & perswaded by the Authoritie of this mans iudgement to beleiue & hold all the Excellencies of this world, as hee
pronounced, is not otherwise to be satisfied, then by his own
wofull experiment [experience] in & after death.

I Nothing feare your distast at the length of these Preambles,
though I know your desires Earnest to vnderstand the matter
itself: Strong medicines are not to be administered with out
Preparatiues, Nor Great Mysteries rashly revealed. I should
wrong both the Action & you to introduce that suddenly, which
was of many yeares contriuement in his mind, that performed it.
⟨73⟩ That's one thing, which euen the Diuine Providence it self
by the coniunction of many strange & admirable Passages hath
seemed as with the Finger of obseruation to mark out vnto vs, as
matter of deepest study & vse.

Tell mee I pray, what the full discouerie & subiection of the
New-found world reserued not only to his times but to his hands
can lesse import, then that he was appointed to conioyne them not
only by an intercourse of Ciuil Commerce, but by the farre more
perfect Bond of Christian Religion, so he was to cleare those
scruples, which had or might on either part disquiet.

What strange Conceits & preiudicial to the Entertainment of
Christian Faith the Luster & Magnificence of this old world sett
forth by lying Amplifications did breed in the Fancies of those
ignorant creatures, whereby the strength & vigour of Affections,
which was to be carried vp to Heauen, was turned to the Adora-
tion & longing after these glorious things, which were reported to

be here, is easy to be gathered out of the Histories of those Conquests.

Wherein as wee shall find the subtle Spaniard for his own Advantage to begett the greater Terrour & Reuerence to himself ⟨74⟩ impiously advancing the Power, Maiestie, Pleasures & Excellencies of those parts euen to the measure of Diuinitie so wee shall perceiue the simple Indian euery way offering vp that Tribute of Deuotion, which is only due to God, to that imaginarie All-sufficiencie, which was so gloriously represented vnto him from these vnknown parts of the world.

That this Poyson should not irrecouerably ceaze the heart, God immediately compounds & ministers the Antidote. Whilest they vnderstand, that Charles, whom they are taught to admire as a God, acknowledging him self as a wretched man, & for the better attainment of those heauenly matters, which by the preaching of the Gospel are tendered vnto them, voluntarily abandoning all that surpassing Happiness, wherewith he was sett forth vnto them furnished & adorned Cap a pie; They haue no reason to doubt of the Excellencie of those better matters, which were promised to them hereafter, or of the Vanitie & Wretchednes of all that, which this present world affords.

What could there bee either more necessarie or beneficial to them, then the right information of these two points & ⟨75⟩ What meanes so forceable could haue been deuised by mans wisedome, as was by the Diuine Providence contriued in the Admirable Resignation on Charles his part. That by his Example vnder whose Authoritie they were first subiected they might for euer be established in the contempt of things below on Earth, & in the Desire & Esteeme of things aboue in Heauen.

Thus doth he become like Solomon[1] a Royal & Euerlasting Preacher to these younger Sons of Nature. Vanity of Vanities all is Vanitie,[2] shall for euer be as often proclaimed as the Name of Charles repeated in the Newfound World. But this is but the

---

[1] See above, p. 66 n. 2. [2] Ecclesiastes i, 2.

outward Voyage & belongs to them. You would know the return of his Adventure: What he brought thence for our behoof? Why surely that, which highly imported.

The Remembrance of Eden, wherein our First Parents were sett, being propagated not only by sacred Historie, but by continued Tradition hath in all Ages brought forth a strong & rauishing conceit; That there was yet remaining in the world a place of Perfect Happines. Which because it appeared euidently false by the discouerie of ⟨76⟩ that Portion, which wee inhabite, The Mainteners of this Fancie haue alwaies cunningly described it to ly hid in farre remoued Coasts & accessible only to the Possessours thereof. You shall not find any of the wise Naturalists, that haue recorded to Posteritie their knowledge of the seuerall parts & conditions of this world, but haue withall expressed the common report & beleif (wherein you shall easily perceiue their own credence implied) of certain people liuing alwaies in an vninterrupted Course of Felicitie, & vnder the influence of a benigne Heauen, which some of them haue pointed out to be vnder the Poles, other farre in the West in certaine Ilands of the Atlantique Sea, on which they haue imposed the Names of Happy & Fortunate. And herein for the better satisfaction of the Curious & the more formal resemblance of truth, they haue boldly proceeded particularly to designe the very Climate, wherein they should ly.

That the Vanitie of these delightful Surmises & the pernicious inferences, which the Atheist & Vnbeleiuing Christian gathered to strengthen his diffidence of the souls immortall Happines in another Life & World, which they were perswaded was by some more fortunate part of mankind completely ⟨77⟩ enioyed here on Earth, & they depriued of only by the malignitie of some disastrous Planets, which till a prefixed revolution of some Certaine Ages are to Tyrannize ouer vs, God sends forth not the simple Doue, as Noah out of the Ark, but a Royal Eagle (for Charles his Armes[1] were the true Embleme of his Disposition) who hauing

[1] Charles his Armes—the Imperial eagle with his personal escutcheon in its claws.

with a swift wing & peircing Eie compassed the whole Circumference of this Earthly Globe, & ransacked euery obscure & hidden
corner thereof by the curious survey & discouerie of his Ministers,
brings back in his mouth not a greene oliue branch of Comfort
& hope, but the Confutation of all those idle dreames, Assuring
by the Experiment [experience] of Ten Thousand Eie Wittnesses,
That those Fortunate Ilands, which haue been so long boasted of
by Antiquitie are but a few petty barren rocks yeelding a scanty
maintenance to their short-liued inhabitants.

That those happy Kingdomes & Commonwealths, which the
world hath been deluded with the report of are but vnorderly
Associations of miserable Barbarians.

That the Pacifique Sea (For euen thereunto hath Fabulous
Tradition streigned our Expectations, giuing securitie and ⟨78⟩
quiet to the vnstable Element of water, that they might the
Easilier introduce the hope of Alteration in all other things) is a
furious Gulf euer combated with Stormes & Tempests. What shall
I say more, that so farre it is from finding any Paradise here on
Earth, as that by more full & curious search wee shalbe the better
& more invincibly confirmed in the truth of that, which God's
Eternal Word doth vncessantly preach vnto vs. That this world
is but a vale of miserie & our whole liues a Continual exercize of
Afflictions & Anguish.

This is the Proceed of that Voyage, the Cargazon of that
fraight, with which this Kingly Merchant returnes from the
Traffique of the New found World.

The Ancient & iterated Advises [reports] of Happines residing
in those parts are manifested to be but Cunning deuised Fables,
that haue gotten the Esteeme of Currant only by their long
passage from hand to hand; otherwise there cannot be found any
trace of such things as was expected. Solomon's Commodities
Apes & Peacocks[1] proue the return of this Adventure. Wee
receiue only strange shaped beasts & glorious feathered Birds

---

[1] I Kings x, 22.

from whence wee were ⟨79⟩ perswaded should haue been brought vs the Certaine Intelligence of their Happines & an Addition to ours. There's no man, I suppose, wilbe so mad as to value that Abundance of Gold & siluer, which hath been imported from the Indians into Spaine any improuement of Europes Felicitie. Hee, that rightly weighs the inumerable Euills, that haue been thence deriued, will execrate the very Name of it & almost the place itself, whence it came, as a new Pandoras Box. Besides those things are not theirs properly; wee had them before & more then Enough. They are the ioynt Commodities or rather Calamities to both parts: What is properly theirs are but indeed Gaudes & Trifles rather then good things tending to the Benefitt of Man's Life.

Dies & Perfumes & the like things only of appearance & shew & not of substance, of vaine pleasure, not of real worth. In a word all proportionably answering & suiting to that prime & vniversally accepted Commoditie there of Tobacco. A true & Liuely Embleme of this world's Happinesse, Though most loathsomly noysome in the Tast, vnbeseeming in the vse, & preiudicial in the operation, yet bewitching ⟨80⟩ all that meddle there with, & violently retaining them, that haue begun to take it with a kind of Absolute Necessitie, as though Life & Liuelines were depending thereon. Whereby in truth with the dulling of the spirits & increase of vitious humours, by the wast & drying vp of the radical moysture the very life itself is abridged.

How doe sober wise men smile, when to the mistake of this poysonous weed as of a Diuine Medicine they obserue a strange perversion euen of the Natural faculties in the Louers thereof. Whilest they heare them talk of violent smells in the stench of a filthie smother & see them boast of gracefull suckings in & whiffings out of Fire & smoak, so monstrous a spectacle, as I cannot think the invention of man can streigne higher to repre-sent the dreadfull visages of the infernal spirits in their invasions on mens souls then by Coppying out the Postures & Countenances of a Gallant Tobacconist.

But what's the Absurditie or dammage in this lighter matter answerable to that, which the spiritual man discouers in the wisest worldling whilest hee seeth him melting in the deliciousnes of those Pleasures, which St Paul counted ⟨81⟩ but dung,[1] Whilest he heares him glorying in those Pomps & Practizes, which the Regenerate is ashamed to mention, Whilest he beholds him night & day heaping vp those things for good & Excellent, wherein the sanctified Person discouers the Tast & sauour of Death, & wherein (to speak truly) the very natural iudgement till it be corrupted finds the Rellish of Loathsome Bitternes. Oh what an Exact Type [symbol] of this world's felicitie both in the Nature & Manner of Deceitfull working on the minds of men is Tobacco: Which being originally brought vnto us from the Newfound world, & so matching our present discourse I haue been bold to make this Digression. If happily by the Consideration thereof in the Abstract, wee might make a good vse of that, which generally in the vsage is of so hurtfull Consequences both to soul & body. It is indeed indeed[2] of much later importation then Charles his time, but being as it were the Complement of that Goodly Gaine, which wee haue reaped from the West Indies towards the better-ing of our Earthly Happines, I haue thought fitt to giue it his due honour after the common fashion, that makes it the vsher of euery serious matter, ⟨82⟩ introducing it the Prologue of that last & principal Act, which is yet to be presented to your veiw: Charles his particular survey & vaiuation of all those things, which the world giues vp, as those Termes & Numbers, whence the Product of Happines ariseth.

[1] Philippians iii, 8.   [2] Indeed indeed—so the MS.

Part VI

The Chief again emphasizes that her delay in coming to the point is justified because it parallels Charles's delay in postponing his retirement. His final decision was hastened by ill health, but infirmity of body and failure of policy were not principal causes of his action, as some detractors would maintain; it was by this means that God saw fit only to hasten Charles not to force him to take the final step. The Chief goes on to detail the events which led to Charles's resignation. His mother's death, preceded by long years of madness, having brought him to a realization of human frailties, he first announced his intention of establishing Philip, his ambitious son, upon the Imperial throne. Opposition to this choice forced Charles eventually to prefer his brother Ferdinand; but Philip, although denied the empire (which as the Chief remarked was 'of more glorious appearance than solid worth'), was amply rewarded by Charles's gift of the Italian States, Spain, and the New World. Mary of Hungary, Charles's sister, resigned as regent so that Philip might be absolute sovereign, a further proof of the contention of the Visitor, Nicholas Ferrar, that women have a part in every excellent event. Because Charles's other sister, Eleanora, of France, also retired at the same time, the Chief finds excuse for a paean on 'woman's excellency'. This section concludes with the Chief's description of Charles's formal and public abdication in Brussels on 25 October 1555, and with her spirited defence of simple living as exemplified by Charles's removal from the palace to live in a small and ordinary house nearby.

In the Entrance whereunto by how much through this longsome delay I haue perhaps the lesse Contented the sharpnes of your desires, that required a speedy satisfaction, by so much haue I kept the better & truer time with the Action itself, which proceeded by slow & sober Measures, & had not (it may bee) so soone been brought on the stage, had it not been hastened by the gentle putting forward of the Great Composer aboue in Heauen. Who finding the weaker part in Charles not so ready to follow the better & more Noble, by the touch of some Lighter infirmities in his own bodie & the vnexpected disappointment of some hopes & desires, though in things of no great moment, recalls him to his part, which he might iustly seeme a little backward vnto.

That you may the more regardfully prize the action I haue thought it necessarie to discouer vnto you the Finger of God working therein, ⟨83⟩ that you may not think, as some fondly surmize, that he did it out of weaknes or discontent. I may not forbeare to acquaint you, that all those troubles of Warre, which may be supposed to haue affrighted him, were either actually appeased by a firme peace, as those of the Protestants, or els in his own power to compound, as those with the French. Whose furious Encounters hauing been so often abated by his Armes, & now the strength of their Attempts defeated by his reconciliation with the Germane Princes, on whose Assistance & seconding the French mens confidence & hopes were cheifly built.

How sencelesse were it to imagine Charles his vndoubted Courage should now fail, especially being the Assailant too.

As for his indisposition of body, which himself indeed alledged as a motiue, I shall so farre accept it as to engraue it in the Frontispiece of this Admirable Action, as an Euerlasting President [precedent] to all Conditions of men to teach them freely & of themselues to surrender weighty charges, when their Abilities of exact performance of them decay. So farre I say wee may with applause admitt ⟨84⟩ his bodily weaknes, as an inducement to his resignation in part, to witt of that, which concerned the troublesome imployments of his Estate, but further it cannot be streigned. For naturally the infirmities & paines of the Flesh kindle a greater & more violent affection to Honour, Riches & delicacies, that so by the supply of Ease & Comfort, which they outwardly minister & that inward Content, which they promise to afford the mind, The greifs & sufferings of the body may be in part abated or recompenced.

So by how much for indisposition of Body he might bee perswaded to relinquish that which was painfull & troublesome, by how so much more strongly should he haue been induced to haue kept that which was glorious, pleasant, & powerfull in his fortunes, which being ten times the more & greater portion of that, which he abandoned, his total relinquishment of the world cannot be attributed to haue proceeded either from deiection of mind or impotencie of Enioying the Pleasures & good things of this Life, which you to most mens iudgements[1] would seeme, if not more seasonable, yet more necessarie, But must needs be in general acknowledged to haue been the sober Resolution of an Impartial iudgement following the Diuine ⟨85⟩ appointment & direction, Which hauing by a long & vniversal Commerce with the world giuen him the certaine knowledge & experiment [experience] of all the Commodities thereof, in the end calls him as in a publick Auditt to giue vp the Accompt of that infinite Stock, which had passed through his hands. Wherein finding him not so forward as was meet, Processe is awarded against him. The Distempers of his health and Affaires, though but in a weak measure being sent forth to summon him. So you may say, & truly (for so himself did) interpret them, The messengers of his appearance, no ways the makers vp of the Accompt. That was drawn vp only by sound reason & good Conscience. The Evidencie of whose firmnes you shall see not only in the Ballance, but vnder euery parcel [item] thereof. Wherein that with more Ease & suretie you may consider & carry away all things, giue mee leaue to proceed in my discourse from point to point according to that succession of order, which was in the Passage of the things themselues.

The Death of his Mother,[2] though full of Age & Infirmitie of mind was obserued much to affect him. She was a woman of

---

1 Which you to most mens iudgements—so the MS. Perhaps the passage should read 'which to you and to most mens iudgements. . .'.

2 His Mother—Queen Joanna. See above, p. 27.

admirable indowments of Nature & those ⟨86⟩ perfected by Learned Education to a strange height, which whilest she too well knew & prized, not able to broak [bear] some neglect & remissenes in her Husband Phillips Esteeme & Affections to her, she grew by giuing way to discontented Passions to a sore distemper of her mind, which in the end vpon the death of her husband & other Crosse Accidents turned into an open & settled Frenzy. Wherevpon her son was in his Childhood crowned by the States of Spain. And she remoued from all Societie spent almost Fiftie yeares locked vp with the Catts, the Delights & Companions of her Afflicted Life. Yet notwithstanding did her son continually to the very last by the ioynt Expression of her Name & Authoritie in all Publicke Affaires giue her the Honour of a Queen & the World a Testimonie of an Vnparaleld Duty & Affection to his Mother. Hee was Foure & Fiftie years old, when he lost her & that to so great Advantage of her own Happines, & yet it makes a breach in his heart through the tendernes of his Loue. But [*in*] all the end settles to the improuement & Exercize of his Wisedome. In her death he reads his own frailtie, in the consideration of her miserie, the wretchedness of this worlds Glorie & Greatnes. Hee takes it as a warning, that ⟨87⟩ hee bee not ouertaken in his better designes to bid adieu to the world, before it dismisse him.

Her end hastens the beginning of this great work, that he is to performe. & now he consults more solemnly of a comely discharge of all Earthly Affaires & References, then euer hee did for their Attainment. The matter was so well digested [arranged] by former preparations, that it grows speedily to an Issue. Since hee cannot find a perfect Example in this way, he meanes to make one passing all others as much in the manner of relinquishment, as he did in the Enioyment. That you may see how all things were guided by true iudgement & good Conscience he distributes all by Iustice & Equitie & not by Affection.

The vast Ambition of his son Phillip striuing to inherit all his Fathers Honours setts Charles vpon a serious Indeauour to install him in the Imperial Throne. But finding a iust opposition thereof by the Princes of Germanie, his Fatherly Affections being quickly reduced within their bounds, giues place to reason, & he preferres his Brother Ferdinando's meritts before his own Affections or his sons Importunitie, Which growing more strong by ⟨88⟩ disappointment put his Father againe vpon a second Attempt That Ferdinand should promise to make him Lieutenant General of the Empire of Italy. And herein wonne all his Father's Servants & Counsellours to be of his party. He very strongly engage [urged] him in that, which by all is approued as a thing, by reason of the great importance thereof, iustly desired by Phillip: so most necessarie for Charles a wise & indulgent Father to procure.

But when he vnderstands from Ferdinand & his sons, that they hold it the height of sacriledge to subdiuide by further fractions the too much dismembred Power & Dignitie of the Empire & that it would be a Transcendent kind of Simonie on both parts so to conferre or receiue, the Noble and Pious mind of Charles remaines so convicted [convinced], as without further Adoe he resolues absolutely & intirely to bestow this supreme Dignitie on his most worthy brother. As Happy a Gift for Christendome as Honourable to the Authour.

And this being the first in purpose & Contriuement, though not in Execution I haue thought good to make shew first of it especially considering, that as it is the most eminent in the Rank of this Worlds Excellencies, so it may be reputed the most ⟨89⟩ admirable part of this Action. But as in truth the Empire is of more glorious appearance then solid worth so the Cession thereof was farre lesse & more Easie then that which was made at Brussels first of the Dutchie of Burgundie & all the members thereof together with all those scattered states in Italy & a month after in the self same place of Spaine it self and all the Newfound world annexed thereunto.

An Action, that, I am perswaded, could St Austine haue foreseen hee would much more haue wished to haue been spectatour of, then of the mightiest Triumph, that euer Rome sett forth. For what Admiration or delight could the Pompous Boastings of a Proud Conquerour to haue subdued the whole world had answered to that, which this mans humble Contempt thereof did iustly deserue?

How much more incomparably Magnificent was it to be the Giuer away, then the Possessour of the mightiest Estate, that euer was on the Earth in one mans hand?

This was indeed so singular, so supreme a straine [height of accomplishment] & thereby he hath so much advanced his glorie aboue all other Potentates whatsoeuer, as I should almost doubt of Charles his sinceretie, whether to this intent he did it not, but that himself ⟨90⟩ hath caused a Premuniri facias, to be sent out against all such suspicions, When he appointed ouer the Chaire of Estate, wherein the performance of these things was made, St Pauls Protestation to bee Engrauen: God forbid that I should glorie saue in the Lord.[1] Let no man dare to think, that in a Politick Contriuement he sought to double by the Refusal that Glorie, which he had formerly by the Enioyment of these things. Whether he kept them or whether he left them, All was directed to Gods Honour not his own. And hereby according to that great Canon of our Sauiour himself, Hee, that seeketh his Glorie, that sent him, the same is true & there is no vnrighteousnes in him.[2] You may infallibly know & beleiue, that whateuer you shall vnderstand Charles did or sayd in this matter was really meant & performed by him. Hauing therefore caused Letters Patents of Resignation to be drawn, which hee signed with his hand & seal & summoned an Assembly of all the States of those Provinces vpon the 25th of October 1555 he comes into the Great Hall[3] of the Pallace, & first in the morning, taking from his own neck the Golden Fleece he puts it on his sons & then ⟨91⟩ creates him Cheif and Head of that Royal Order. In the Afternoone he returns

---

[1] Galatians vi, 14.   [2] John vii, 18.
[3] Great Hall—the Hall of the Golden Fleece in Brussels.

accompanied with all the Embassadours of Forraigne Kings & Commonwealths, his Two Sister Queens & a mighty Traine of Princes & great Estates. In the midst of whom hee sitts him down between his son & Sister Mary[1] the Widdow Queen of Hungarie, who hauing been the Faithfull & prudent Regent of those Countries for 33 yeares space comes now to be a partner in this Act, That aswell by the surrender of her deputed, as of his Principal right, Phillip may receiue a free & absolute investiture.

You see our weaker sex had their part euen in the Principal of this Admirable Action. A Happy instance of that Honourable Proposition, which our Visitor[2] hath so often engaged himself to maintain.

That there was neuer Excellent Person nor Action, wherein womans vertue had not a share.

Its but a slight relation may some think rather belonging to the Forme, then to the substance, that this Action of hers had to his. Bee it so. But they, that shall vnderstand how both she and her sister Leonora[3] the Widdow Queen of France ⟨92⟩ became likewise the imitatours & Companions of their Brothers heauenly Designes Retyring themselues & with him finishing their Daies in the Exercize of Pietie & Deuotion, cannot but attribute to them a greater part & interest then of Spectatours only in this Heroical Action. & giue vs leaue to inferre out of her necessarie partnership in this solemnitie, That neither Forme nor Substance of Mans Vertue is complete without the Consortship of Womans Excellencie.

But I returne to our Charles, who commands that surrender to be publickly read by the Lord Chancelour. The substance whereof was

That finding himself by Age, Indisposition of Body & other inconveniencies not fitt to take those long voyages & to endure

---

[1] Mary—widow of Louis II of Hungary. See above, p. 27 n. 2 and p. 30.

[2] Visitor—Nicholas Ferrar. See Introduction, pp. xxxiv–xxxv.

[3] Leonora—widow of Francis I of France. See above, p. 30.

those Labours & Troubles, which he had continually vndergone in the discharge of his place. He had resolutely determined immediately to sail for Spaine, & there to spend the Remainder of his Life, whatsoeuer it were, in quiet, Rest & Peace, Transferring the Dominion and Right of all those parts vnto his Dearest son, Now by age & all other Abilities sufficient for the Gouernment of them, ⟨93⟩ willing all his subiects of these Provinces to yeild due obedience & sweare Fealtie vnto him, as to their soueraigne Lord. To which intent he himself did there free & acquitt them of whatsoeuer Alleagiances they ought him with this Condition on his sons part: That he should truly & fully pay all those Debts, which had been made either by himself, or his Ministers in his Name, & so intirely discharge his Creditt & Faith.

This Instrument being come to an End Charles himself begins his own speech. Which for the help of his memorie, hee had brought in writing, & for the more vniversal vnderstanding of his Auditours was made in the French Tongue. Therein largely discoursing of his former Life, he manifested by the recompting of the seueral Passages thereof That his whole Age from his childhood had been spent in an vndefatigable course of serious Imployments for the Common good of Christendome, which he had sett vp for the fruit & End of his Life; & in the Prosecution thereof had been so continually Exercized with the Dayly Encounter of many sufferings & Difficulties, as he neuer had the least space of time nor opportunitie to take his Personal content ⟨94⟩ or Ease. But now his yeares declining apace & hauing sett all things in order by a General Securitie both within & without, he had firmely determined to withdraw himself apart from the Affaires of this World, & to liue the surplus of his daies to God & himself. And therefore did require & commande them, that they should hence forward yeeld that Homage, Faithfull honour & Obedience to his son now his Successour as they had performed vnto himself.

Then Phillip rose & with the putting off his hatt hauing giuen a Curteous Salutation to the Assembly, stepping to his Father with lowest Reuerence falling on his knees took & kissed his hand.

The Father with great tendernes of Affection Embraced him, & laying his hands on Phillips bare head declared him aloud to be the Prince of Belgia.

And hauing first a Crosse, did, in the Name of the Father, the Son & the Holy Ghost, giue him the seizin [possession] of his Royal Dignitie by a short Prayer to God for his happy Successe. Which ended addressing himself to his son he enioyned him in few but powerfull words. ⟨95⟩

That hee should aboue all things beware of falling away himself from the diligent seruice & reuerent Feare of the Diuine Maiestie.

That he should make it his principal Care to improue the Faithfull Exercize of Religion in others.

And that he should inviolably maintaine the power and Authoritie of Common Rights & Laws. For these (sayd hee) are the waies & this is the true skill of right and happy Gouernment.

Which hauing spoken, & Phillip in a submisse manner promised by the help of God to be mindfull & observant both of his Example & Precepts, the Good old Emperour was perceiued to weep, Whereof when the silence & amazement of the standers seemed to craue the reason he told them frankly.

That it was out of Compassion to his most beloued son, whose estate he could not but much commiserate through the imposition of so heauy a burthen on his shoulders. These words verified by his Teares left no dry Eies in the Assembly, all amazed & sighing at their own & the common mistake of the world touching places of supreme Dignitie & ⟨96⟩ Commande, which by the relation of his own past Life & the prediction of his sons Fortunes appeared nothing lesse then what they seeme. Nothing els indeed but Sorrow, Paine, & Danger in the pompous dresses of Power, Comfort & Pleasures, Breeding Envious Admiration to the Beholders of the outward, but like Hercules, his poysoned shirt, cruelly tormenting the inward parts of the Wearers. Lo Charles his Censure of this prime & Master peice of Humane Felicitie.

Dignities are but golden Fetters of Libertie and Command a busy restlesse Labour of the mind & body. Authoritie itself, that seemes to carry vp so high, a heauy burthen, that depresseth the soul. All but Vanitie and Vexation.

In a word, to giue you the weight & worth of this First draught, as this great Say master hath sett it down.

As the seruice of God is perfect Freedome: so the Rule & Gouernment ouer men is perfect Seruice.[1]

There's no other subiect, I am sure, can haue willing Admittance into your thoughts, but that, which concerneth this matter and Man. What euer els was there done by others, you little regard to knowe. Let it therefore sleep in silence, & goe wee on to Charles ⟨97⟩. Who vpon the finishment of the solemnitie choosing out William Prince of Orange[2] (wherein you may perceiue the Excellencie of his Iudgement in discerning & that I may say presaging the Admirable Worth of this most Famous Personage) Leaning on his shoulders passed softly through the Assembly & Pallace into a small & meane neat house which he had commanded to be prepared for him a good distance from the Court.

You will not wonder at this action, if you call to mind That often recompted passage with the Duke of Venice Who to quicken our Charles his Admiration, which he thought too remisse in the Commendation of that sumptuous Pallace, which he had shewed him, demanding how his Maiestie liked it, had for answere from him only:

These Earthly Vanities are they which make vs loth to dy.

[1] The say master is, in this case Charles V, who now seeks peace (see the Collect for Peace in the Book of Common Prayer) by giving up service to men for service to God. See also above, p. 66 n. 2.

[2] William Prince of Orange—William the Silent (1533–84) made a public profession of the Calvinist religion in 1573 and rescued the Netherlands from the power of Spain. He was a commander of the Imperial Army in 1555, but later fought against Philip II in defence of the Protestants, a fact which may have endeared him to the Little Academy.

What he then passed by word of mouth, hee now setts his seal to. That Stately Mansions are neither good for the improuement of Heauenly thoughts nor of Earthly Quiet.

Think not, that it was for the Tumult of the Court only, that he thus fled from the Pallace. No. But to giue a ⟨98⟩ direct Check to that Erroneous Loue & prize, which men haue sett on Glorious & vast Structures, as though the inhabitants souls were more Elevated to Noble thoughts & desires by the outward Magnificence & Largenes or their bodies dwelt more at ease in them. Charles, that had made as great proof as euer any did, resolues it now by his own Example. That a little & homely Dwelling (for so was that, which he chose) better fitts & serues to his purpose, that Aspires to Heauen & seeks for quiet on Earth, then the stately built & Royally furnished Pallaces of Princes doe. The son of Man, as himself professeth, had no place to Lay his head on. & the sons of God find their hearts doe quickly loose their quiet & themselues in the maze of a great & Pompous Habitation.

Is it not enough to haue our spirits groaning vnder the Tabernacle of our Flesh, but wee must putt a further surcharge on both by the weight of our own inventions, with the rearing vp of massy Piles ouer vs, burdening our souls with Cares, & Feares, & Dangers, & by the Enlargement of our Prisons further immuring vp our Diuiner part from the free and ready Prospect of Heauen, wherevnto as ⟨99⟩ it is appointed by Creation, so it can no where els find satisfaction then in the hope & looking after.

As for the Body, though it were thereby accommodated, as indeed it receiues extreme preiudice, yet what childish simplicitie is it to bestow so much Cost & paines in dressing vp a curious Roome[1] for an houres Entertainment (for what is the longest Life more then so short a space) of that wretched Carcase, that must in the end take vp its long abode with wormes in the dust & obscurity of the Earth.

[1] This passage finds a parallel in Shakespeare's Sonnet CXLVI, 'Poor soul, and centre of my sinful earth'.

But I am valiant, where there is no encounter & beare downe all, where there is no opposition.

The worth of this part of Happines lieth not in the benefitt, that it affords, but in the honour. It's a glorious thing to be the master of a goodly Frame.

How much pitty rather then Envy doth the Povertie of that Soul meritt, whose worth is inhaunced by the skilfull Composure of Wood & Stone, & grows it self more conspicuous by the Luster of goodly ornaments.

Hee, that is graced by a faire House disgraceth all the beauty thereof & is but like a Bristol stone[1] sett in gold. ⟨100⟩ Hee, that is Honourable indeed makes a Cottage Glorious. So did our Charles.

When the late Archduke had shown Ambitious Byroone[2] all the rauishing Excellencies of his own Pallace he leads him out into the Park where this poore house stands whereunto Charles retyred himself in the view thereof to behold the Noblest spectacle, that this Country yeelds. Oh the Certaintie of our Blessed Sauiour's Promise: That none shall loose by that, which he leaues for his sake.[3] Charles quitts his Pallace to become more Conformable to Christ, & dwells meanly the better to please him, that's best pleased with Humilitie.

He waues his own Honour to derision of vaine minds, that layd dotage to his charge, but God restores it a hundred fold: The proudest spirits on Earth shall doe honour to this Poore Building.

What shall I say something answerable to the thing it self? The Escurial built by his son with the Expence of Eleuen Millions is not gazed on by Noble minds with so much wonderment. Nor half that Reuerend Honour giuen Phillip for the Building thereof, as to his Father Charles for dwelling in ⟨101⟩ this simple Habita-

---

[1] Bristol stone—a quartz stone of little value found near Bristol.
[2] Byroone—Armand de Gontaut, Baron de Biron (c. 1524–92), was a Marshal of France.   [3] Matthew x, 39.

tion. To shutt vp all touching this point. The Stately Pallaces of this World are strong Diversions from the Attainment of the Heauenly. & though they seeme the fruits of Paradise, yet doe they proue but the Apples of Sodome, goodly delightfull in appearance, but adding Care & Anguish to their Owners minds.[1]

In one word: For what belongs to Earthly Mansions, he is the most happy, that had need of least, & he is the most worthy, that can be content with the meanest. This is the weight, that Charles sett vpon this second peice of Happiness.

[1] *The Voiage and Travaile of Sir John Maundeville* refers to the apples of Sodom and describes their interior as being composed of coal and ashes. For a full discussion of the history of the 'Apples of Sodom', see the article by J. Penrose Harland, 'Sodom and Gomorrah' in *The Biblical Archaeologist*, Vol. VI, number 3 (Sept. 1943), pp. 49–52.

Part VII

Charles's intention to retire immediately to Spain was providentially delayed until he brought about a truce between his son Philip and his old enemy, Henry II of France, an action in which he put the future good of the state ahead of his own present and personal desires. On 6 March a comet appeared, which Charles took as a sign of his approaching death, but which the Chief interprets in a different fashion. Charles hastened preparations for his departure, but he could not conclude his affairs until 10 October 1556, when he sailed for Spain with his two sisters.

Upon landing he kissed the earth and greeted it as his mother, thereby symbolizing his contempt for pride in pedigree or high place and his belief in the supremacy of the soul. The Chief, interrupting her paraphrase of de Thou, now takes occasion to trace the materialism and immorality of the English gentry to the desire to be thought superior to others and as the source of gluttony, envy, idleness, lust, anger, covetousness and pride. These Seven Deadly Sins as they appear among the gentry lead to contempt for 'the good honest man'. Charles by putting aside all titles and possessions and by acknowledging his kinship with all men (as did Christ when he became man) shows us the proper value to be put upon pride in place. In order to publicize his decision to retire, Charles arranged for heralds to announce his abdication in favour of Philip throughout Spain both by words and pantomime. As did Christ when tempted by Satan, so also did Charles cast aside the glories of the world that he might better serve God. The Chief comments movingly on the example of Charles and on God's intention that all should profit by it.

You haue seen him now withdrawn aswell in Body as mind from the Affaires of this world. Which, that hee may the more constantly perseuere in he makes hast of his return in to Spaine, That there in a settled Course & place hee might perfect what he had begun, A quiet & continual seruice of God.

But God that had yet more for him to performe touching this

World by the impediments of sickliness in his own person &
vnseasonable weather for Nauigation detaines him for the Conclusion of a Truce between his son & the ⟨102⟩ French King,
which by Charles his Wisedome & Authoritie is in the end agreed
vnto for the Terme of Fiue yeares, & solemly sworn to on Either
part, bred much Reioycing & would vndoubtedly haue produced
singular good to all Christendome, had it been as Religiously
obserued. But the perfidiousness of the breach in others afterwards makes not the indeauours & performance herein lesse
honourable & happy on Charles his part.

Who refusing not in this Management & others of the like
Nature for the Confirmation of his sons Royal Affaires & Dispositions of mind in a right way to bestow a large part of his time
& paines that Winter, thereby giues vs the true Estimate of our
own Particular satisfaction euen in the best kinds.

That there is nothing so Excellently pursued for our own as
interrupted for the Common good. Hee shall better please &
serue god, that condescends to serue & please his Neighbour in
things, that truly edifie, then he, that in an intire retirement, liues
to himself alone, though his Life be altogether in & vnto God.

Charles, that for himself would haue no more to doe with ⟨103⟩
the world, yet for others sake embathes himself therein againe &
willingly in a second rank imploys himself in those businesses,
which he had vtterly disclaimed to meddle with in a supreme
Condition & Qualitie.

Whether shall wee say was more Admirable, To relinquish
these things as inferiour to his own high sett Aime, or to reassume them againe as necessarie for the furtherance of others.
Lofty minds or Louers of their Ease might haue gone farre
towards the performance of the First. This second part could not
haue been Acted but out of the Aboundance of true Humilitie &
perfect Charitie. Charles, that had reserued nothing but Quiet &
deuotion, is content to waue them also for others peace & safetie
& to lessen his own portion of the best Good for the Procurement

of others Advantage in a Lower kind. Will you haue the summe of this Inference? Hee, that abandons Earthly Imployments for God is alwaies ready on Mans vrgent Necessitie to take them vp againe. & he, that for God's sake negotiates in the world is most forward, where there's least satisfaction to himself. The fairest Conclusion, that a man can make of this worlds ⟨104⟩ busines, & the best preparation to heauen is to leaue peace behind him.

This is that, which Charles his interchangeable Attendance of others Busines & his own Deuotion taught vs, whilest he stayd at Brussels & afterwards at Gaunt. Which, because the world was perhaps too negligently obseruant of, Heauen itself giues a watch word to quicken mens regard & Esteeme of these Diuine Acheiuments on Charles his part.

Upon the sixth of March a mighty blazing Comete like a kindled Beacon appeares flaming in the 8th degree of Libra. Which being the Constellation of iustice, & represented forth in the Celestial Globes by the Pictures of a Virgin with a Ballance in her hand, how fittly may wee interpret it to portend the Confirmation of that scrutinie and Ponderation of all Earthly things, which Charles was then about? That wee should both diligently attend & creditt his mark both for the weight and worth of euery Particular, as poysed all in equal scales with the hand of virgin Integritie.

Thus should I construe the meaning of this heauenly ⟨105⟩ signe. But Charles, whose Humilitie now admitts no conceit towards his own glorie, lookes vpon it as the summons of his instant dissolution. And therevpon with zeal & speed doubles his indeauours for departure into Spaine, Which yet he cannot effect till the 10th of October following; when hauing dismissed his son & the Duke of Sauoy an houre after sun sett he weighs Anchour from Sudebury[1] in Zealand & with Faire wind & good season in Companie of his Two Queen-Sisters[2] without the least

---

[1] Sudebury—Zuitberg, a town near Flushing in Zeeland.
[2] See above, p. 27 n. 2 and p. 80 n. 3.

offence of Sea-sicknes arriues in the end prosperously at ——[1] in Biscay.

Where he finds not only the Nobilitie but the Ambassadours of euery seueral Citty of Spaine expecting his Arrival with Affections of highest Loue & Veneration. But he, that comes not to receiue Honour but to exercize Humilitie, vpon his first setting foot on shore casteth himself down & in a prostrate manner kissing the Earth cryeth out:

Hail, thou most wished for Mother. Naked came I out of my mothers wombe, & naked doe I return to thee as to another mother. And in acknowledgement of those ⟨106⟩ many deserts [rewards] to mee ward I doe surrender & bequeath vnto thee All that, which is alone left mee. This wretched carcase & these Bones of mine.

The Lofty Saracens, that finding the most renowned Godfrey of Bullan[2] sett on the bare Earth, would not be perswaded that he was the man they sought for (For how can it be, sayd they, that so haughty a spirit, as hath subdued all Asia, can submitt it self to such Basenes) were by him smilingly answered: That no man ought to think himself so high as to forgett that both his beginning & his End were equal to the Lowest dust.

But Charles, that was ordained a Paragon in all respects from a farre higher pitch, then he was mounted, descends vnto a farre Lower Humiliation both in wordes & gestures. And clips the Earth his Mother with the most Expressiue Testimonies both of Respect & kindnes, that man's soul can invent. And thereby vndermining the Foundation bases euen with the ground [of] that sollem Vanitie, that high reared swelling of Gentry & Nobilitie.

Which the World fancying an Essential good rooted in the

---

[1] Blank in MS. Charles landed at Laredo.

[2] Godfrey of Bullan—Godfrey de Bouillon, Duke of Lorraine (1060–c. 1100), was a leader of the First Crusade. He is the hero of Tasso's *Jerusalem Delivered* (1575). The passage may be based on Book II, lines 457 ff. For the later opinion of the Ferrars on 'romances' and the determination of Nicholas to burn 'all these kinds of books', see Introduction, p. li n. 1.

Flesh & running in the Bloud & so entailed to the person ⟨107⟩ as neither Tyne nor Recouery[1] can possibly cutt off. Least happily [by chance] by the pretence of his Reseruation, the minds of vaine men might haue taken occasion to advance this matter of Nobilitie as a Iewel indeed, Charles finds this admirable invention to giue the world certaintie how much he despiseth it stripping himself in open view to avoyd all calumnie of secret retaining it.

And producing the Original of his own Pedigree, which incomparably passed all others, by the meannesse thereof disproues all those foolish Boastings of other men touching their high Descents.

If Charles be by his own Profession but the son of the Earth, who was born on the top of the mountaines; How are their braines crazed, that for the Advantage of a molehills eminency, whereon they were calued, ouerlook their Fellows with Disdaine as ignoble creatures of another kind, then themselues. Wherein lyeth the Betternes, if wee be all so neer akin as to haue one Common Mother, from whom wee receiue & to whom wee restore without manner of difference these Earthly Robes: ⟨108⟩ There's surely no Distinction of Nobilitie in the Bodie. They are all alike honourable, all alike contemptible, as they are all alike Perishable & frail, equally the Instruments of the soul.

In the Diuinitie thereof lieth the Preeminence & not in the mortalitie of the Flesh.

Hee, that by the Conformitie of his soul to Gods Image can call God his Father is the truly Noble.

Hee, that by the deprauation thereof is a stranger to God, though the extract of all earthly Nobilitie were infused into his veines, remaynes a Peazant of the basest Alloy. It's nothing at the most but Vanitie what euer can be made at the best of this Prerogatiue.

---

[1] Tyne nor Recouery—probably a legal phrase in line with 'entailed'. 'Tyne' is a variant form of 'teen', which meant harm inflicted or loss; 'recovery' had a legal meaning which implied the taking away of property belonging to one and the giving it to another.

But as the World setts it forth, & men Commonly accompt & inferre vpon it in their practize, I know not whether there be any more sinfull or preiudicial to be found amongst all those many things in this World, which they call good. Nor can I tell to what that most important Caueat of our Sauiour may more fittly be applied, That which is highly esteemed amongst men is abomination in the sight of God,[1] then to this Golden Idol of Nobilitie. Which as it swims ⟨109⟩ like oyle on the top of all other Humane Excellencies, so it makes greater hauock both of wisedome & Goodnes in the soules of men, then any other erring lust whateuer. There's no vice, that calls for the help of another, that makes any scruple to receiue it in his own Loathsomnesse. The Luxurious Person stands not of admitting Gluttonie in his own vnseemely Tyre; he grants it to be euill & yet he invites it to his Table because he is a furtherance of his wanton pleasures.

The Angry man offended giues present Entrance vnto Envy, though shee comes dressed with her snakes about her neck, & champing the Toad in her mouth. Hee embraceth her, though neuer so odious because she giues Assistance to his intended reuenge.

But the wretched soul, that hath been drenched with the Magic Cup of this conceited Excellencie grows now to such an impudencie, as after a little Fantastic disguisement producing to open veiw the most deformed Broode of Hell, it enforceth vs to accept them for the graces of Heauen themselues.

To this Eldest Daughter of Pride, the Conceit of being ⟨110⟩ Noble & gently born, doe wee owe that hatred & contempt of Laborious Imployments, which hath cutt the sinews of industry & brought in Idlenes as the Perfection of a braue spirit. So that theres no shame to them like to the Earning of a mans bread by the work of his hands.

To this are wee beholding for the keeping of those goodly Tables, which keep both soul & body in a continual surfett, haue

[1] Luke xvi, 15.

so vtterly casheered the remembrance of Temperance, as wee accompt the maintenance of Gluttonie in our selues & others the best expressions of a good nature.

To this must wee giue the prayse of those witty inventions to prosecute filthy Lust vnder the vaile of Worthy Loue. Are not all those wanton blindfold Choosings of their mates on St Valentines day? Those Adulterous Leagues of mistresship & seruice? Those Amorous Compositions of the Braine in loose Rimes, Those Artificial treadings of the foot in dancing measures, Those Prostitutions of the brests to open veiw. I can tarry no longer for blushing in this argument. What part of Furniture is there in all the wardrobe of Lust, that hath not been so perfumed & embroidered by this Excellent Master, Gentilitie, ⟨111⟩ As that now is necessarily required to euery well bred man in Christian Religion, that would haue been taken for an opprobie [sign of opprobrium] amongst the sober Heathen.

As for Anger it is so refined in the Limbeck of this Cursed Alchymist, that wilfull murther is grown an especial Argument of a mans worth. To haue slaine a man in the Field, as they terme it, both against Law & Conscience is a matter of Boasting in a Gentleman of Esteeme from others. Hee now shalbe farre more respectfull, that hath killed, then in old time he did, that had saued his Fellow Cittizens Life. As for Patience in Iniuries it's so beaten out of the schoole of valour, that he is shunned as a Monster, that is discouered to haue any Familiaritie therewith. I doe not bely them. Hee is a dastard, that will put vp any wrong. He is disgraced for euer, that taketh not double Reuenge.

An iniury in words must haue a blow for requital. A Blow requires Bloud for satisfaction. Bloud drawn can neuer be stopt but by Death.

These are the Laws of Complete Gentry deuised in Hell & enacted by Vniversal vote of all, that pretend the perfection of Nobilitie. ⟨112⟩

Envy is the next & that's the Quintessence of a Gallant, A

biting Tooth, a scoffing Witt, a poysonous Tongue, a Libellous pen, traducing Eies, & slanderous Gestures, carping not only at the best of men & Actions, but deriding euen the word & providence of God himself.

Why this is the Complete behauiour of a Gentleman in his Conversation with others.

As for Couetousnes, The most Wicked Practizes thereof: Oppression, Taking more of their own then they ought in Charitie, & not paying of what they owe in Iustice are the Two supporters of Nobilitie now adaies, & are made like serpents with their teeth knocked out to passe up & down in sport as Flashes of brauery of spirit. Which the Pagans censured worthy Giues [gyves] & brand-marks of Seruilitie.

So hee bee Noble it's neither sin nor shame not to pay debts. That's turned ouer to Merchants & Churchmen as a seely [harmless] peice of Necessarie Iustice or scrupulous Conscience. There's remaining only Pride, & that I dare boldly say, like morter in a building runs through euery part of Gentry & Nobilitie. Its in the Foundation & in the Roofe. ⟨113⟩ It's without & within. It ioynes all. It couers all. It's as vnseperable as the heat from the light of the sun. Only in the words & outward gestures it must put on the apparel of Humilitie. In all other regards by how much more open it appeares in its own Natiue swellings; it adds the greater grace to a Gentleman, & is all but that part of magnanimous Iustice, that confidently takes it own [on].

Thus are the seuen deadly sins by this imposture made free not only of the Corporation of Humane vertue, but of the household of God it self.

It scornes to entertaine vice as vice, so full of Excellency doth it prize itself, as whatsoeuer it approues is thereby made good.

Hee, that for the Defence of Gentry will abate of this Charge shalbe forced to abate as much in euery point from the opinions & Practizes of those, that boast themselues & are admired by others as the Grand Masters & Examples of this Profession.

Absolute Nobilitie straines [scruples] at none of these matters. He, that through Religion or Ciuil Wisedomes restraint dare not ⟨114⟩ passe on so farre, looseth as much of his Gentry in their Censure as he gaineth of the Precizian.

A good honest man he may be perhaps in their Accompt & that's all they afford him, & that's the most direct opposition, that they can imagine to Gentilitie. And wheneuer the world commends any in this Phraze they intend as much.

But howeuer this matter of Nobilitie & Gentry may be perhaps by cunning handling reduced into much better Compasse, yet I dare boldly say that there is no possible Composition to be made between it & Christian Religion.

The Challenge of Excellencie ouer others being the Foundation, & the Exacting of Honour therevpon being the Roof of this building, howeuer glorious it appeare to mortal Eies, yet is it too vile for God's spirit to inhabite. Whose delight being altogether in an humble & Louing spirit, the least Contradiction in either of the Dispositions keeps God further off then the strongest Barracados that Publicans & Sinners make by their Notorious Crimes. Wittnesse the Pharisee, who departed from the Temple more guilty by the Esteeme of his own goodnes then the other did by all the offences, which hee had committed. An humble sinner finds easier Accesse, sayd one & truly, ⟨115⟩ then a proud Innocent.[1] If the spiritual Priuiledges are forfeited, when they Exalt the heart: how dangerous must that Exaltation be, which ariseth from Fleshly & False Respects? Will God accept him, that thinks himself better for that, which is not his own vertue, & his Neighbour the worse for that, which is not his own fault (if it be a fault to be meanly born) that sent him away condemned, that lifted vp himself but a little in that, which was truly good, & depressed his Neighbour only in that, which was really Euill & altogether his own? Shall the Perfections of the soul, if they be stood on [put forward] in Comparison, hinder our approach to God; & shall

[1] Luke xviii, 9–14.

not much more the standing on Perfections of the body cast vs further from his grace & favour?

Hee cannot abide a goodman, that claimes any Priuiledge of Honour for his vertue; & shall he allow a Gentleman to doe it for his birth? Is Noble Bloud better then grace? Is it lesse abominable to be exalted in our shame then to be proud in our Glorie? Or lesse greiuous to be iniurious in contempt of our Brother without a Cause then vpon desert? But true Gentry avoydes both those. And what's the worth or Benefitt then of it? ⟨116⟩

Let vs not deceiue our selues. Theres no man makes pretence thereunto but because he thinks himself thereby & would be thought of others somewhat more then ordinarie. And the lightest of these thoughts or desires like fetters on the Leg doe so encumber the soul, that it cannot keep within ken of the son of God, howeuer busily it seemes to labour to follow him who can neuer be ouertaken but with the constant paces of Humilitie & Charitie: Which are the Reuerse of that Coate & Armes, which worldly Gentry & Nobilitie beares. This Charles vnderstood & this he meant to teach vs by his strange proceeding in this matter.

Hee quitts himself of all other things by Diuorce, but to the admired Excellencie of Nobilitie he sends a Defiance. He disclaimes them as impediments, but this he publisheth for an Enemie.

Of all kind of wares, that this world offers, theres none so much contraband for Traffique to Heauenly, as this Fume of Nobilitie.

This is the mark, that Charles stamped by his Fact [deed, action], & the weight that by acknowledging the Earth his Mother he sett on this soueraigne peice of Humane Glorie. By how much more ⟨117⟩ necessarie & excellent it seemes for the Perfection of Earthly Happines, by so much more pernicious it will be found for the attainment of the Heauenly. Whereunto our Grand Capitan Christ Jesus hauing entered by the Gate of Humilitie (For therefore was he so highly Exalted, because he had so lowly abased himself, As being the son of God to become the son of man) This good Souldier, that he might be made more conformable to his General, descending from the vnparaleld Eminencies of his Birth, whereby he might iustly haue claimed the principalitie amongst the sons of Adam, passeth by voluntarie Adoption into that most abiect Family of the Earth. Thereby admitting vnto an equalitie of Brotherhood not only the lowest of the sons of men, but the silliest [most insignificant] wormes of the dust it self; & now riseth more naked then he came into the world.

That you may know that none can claim any interest in him, but Christ Jesus his Lord, you see he strips himself of all other Additions, then that, which he receiued at his Baptisme. You cannot put a title more to his name then Charles, by which hee was at first presented here on Earth to God. And with it only he now prepares himself to appeare before him in heauen. ⟨118⟩ As if he doubted to haue been lesse known to God, by how much he should remaine more known to men by other glorious Surnames of this worlds Honour.

Which least that magnifique Reception of his by all the states of Spaine, of which you haue heard, should againe kindle the desire of in his own brest, or maintaine the expressions of it so liuely & working from others. To giue a Testimonie of the Constancie of his Resolutions, that he came to dy a Priuate man, & to take away all occasions of being esteemed or vsed as a Prince, He doth immediately giue order for an vniversal Publication of his former Surrender & that not in words only but by a sollem Act performed in euery of those Citties of Spaine, which haue priuiledge of sending Counsellours to their Parliament. Wherein vpon a sett day Two Heraulds apparelled in Coates of Armes, mounting on a scaffold purposely built & furnished the one representing Charles gaue vnto the other as vnto Phillip, A scepter, a sworde, and an Helmet with these formal words.

God grant, that it may proue Happy & Prosperous to Spaine & to all the seueral Provinces thereof. ⟨119⟩

The Emperour Charles the Fift made King of Spaine by Lawfull right freely & with a willing mind disposesseth himself of all Authoritie & ordaines Phillip his son to be his Heire & King in his stead. So that all the rights of supreme Gouerning, Possessing, & Conferring vpon others, shall be hereby transferred vpon him according to Ancient Law & Custome, & after the best manner of Translation, whereby all Publick & priuate Interesses can be Transferred.

The first hauing thus spoken departed the place, & the other taking vp the forementioned Armes & the scepter in his hand promised in the person & behalf of Phillip so to order all things, as should most conduce to the safetie & common good of the Kingdome & people.

The Intertainment of this passage with highest Acclamations of wonderment & approbation from the Beholders made mee think it could not but be acceptable to you to heare the Relation thereof & profitable to refresh the serious consideration of Charles his resignement of his surpassing Power & Glorie, so strong an attractiue of mans heart, as by the tender thereof in its complete height & measure ⟨120⟩ the Deuill conceiued hope to haue ouerthrown the son of God himself; whilest he had conceit, that he might be but a man.[1] It cannot therefore but be acknowledged a participation of that self same Diuine vertue & strength vnto Charles, which enabled him to so happy an Imitation, that he should for the better seruice of God leaue the fairest portion of Glorie & Greatnes, that euer fell to any one mans Lot in this world.

You may perceiue by their often recourse to this subject how strangely mine own thoughts are moued with the remembrance thereof. & I cannot deny the eagernes of mine own desires to enstamp on yours the self-same prints of Reuerend admiration & Loue to it As to an example aboue all worth, that prayse can expresse, fitt to be euer in our remembrance, till it may be in some part matched in our Actions. And herein, mee thinks, I doe but

[1] Luke iv, 5–7.

follow the plaine footsteps of Diuine Providence. Which by the contriuement of so often repeated Publication of this matter in such a solemne manner, & in so many seueral places, as you haue heard, hath as it were texted it out in Red Letters, as a Passage of Publick & euerlasting record for euery mans behoof & instruction. ⟨121⟩

This vndoubtedly to mee seemes the intendment of that supreme Cause & Authour, whose working in euery part of this Action being so conspicuous, how much more ought wee to attribute to him the disposal & ordering of this renowned Conclusion. Wherein besides the figure of our Life sett forth as in a glasse [mirror] to be but the Acting of a part on Earth, as on a Theater, wee haue a true Exemplication of that shallow hold & slight interest, which wee haue in this world & all the things thereof: Whereof the most Excellent & those, which wee count most inherent [essential] are so easily receiued & passed from vs euen by others words & Actions.

That as all things of this world are in themselues of no worth, so neither is our Right vnto them but imaginarie. That there is a double Falsitie in their own Nature & in our pretence vnto them. That they are nothing in themselues, nor haue wee the proprietie of them. That they are neither good nor can bee ours. This is that, which Charles, as it were, vnder his Royal seal by his so-often represented surrender hath left verified vnto vs. And now hauing finished his part he quitts the stage ⟨122⟩ no more to return again by intermedling with the Affaires of this world.

Part VIII

Charles, by stopping on his way to his place of retirement to super-
intend the education of his grandson Don Carlos, son of Philip II,
serves as a reproach to modern parents who turn over their children's
education to the parson and the teacher. At the end of this digression
on the parents' responsibility for the education of children the Chief
feels that she has lost the attention of her auditors, but the Guardian
(John Ferrar), after praising her strength of memory and voice,
explains that the silence did not stem from weariness but rather from
the profound thoughts her discourse had inspired in all the company.
The Resolved (John Collett) adds his own earnest request that the
Chief continue, but first he asks the Guardian to reveal the thoughts
which the narrative had inspired.

When the Guardian desires help in giving birth to his reactions, the
Resolved offers his services as midwife. The Moderator (Mrs Collett)
hastily volunteers her aid, but first allows her husband to suggest that
the Guardian is worried about his financial reverses in the plantations
of the New World. The Guardian denies this suggestion and maintains that he is far happier despite his private losses because of his
devotion to public affairs than he would have been had he put selfish
interests completely ahead of service to others. His real distractions, he
says, stem from problems much nearer home. He agrees to the Resolved's suggestion that the story of Charles's abandoning his palace in
favour of a humble abode has renewed his own worry about his
'longsome buildings' and he regrets the pride and desire for luxury
that motivated him in their erection. By humbly devoting such misguided ostentation to God's work, the family may in part justify such
unwarranted expense although the fear will always remain that others
may imitate their foolishness.

When the Guardian himself then ingeniously suggests that 'Plantation' and 'Building' are merely symbols employed by him, the
Moderator hastens to point out that even a blind man could tell that
the Guardian's son Nicholas is the building and his daughter Virginia
the plantation about which he is truly concerned. He admits the truth
of her deduction, scolds her for complaining about her lack of his
worldly means in maintaining her own 'sevenfold charge', and goes

on to say that he envies her her much larger family and that he is as much concerned with the welfare of her children as with that of his own. The example of Charles V, who considered the education of his grandson more important than the gratification of his private desires, leads the Guardian to determine to educate his children himself and to outline the daily lessons that he proposes to give his son. The Chief urges that he also accept her 'son' as a pupil and he reluctantly agrees. As a penalty, however, he jokingly requires that the Chief continue with the story of Charles as, he says, her well-earned rest has not only increased his burden but must be paid for by the completion of the history.

———◆———

It is the deep of Winter & his body not a little indisposed. But strong desires know no Impediments. As an ouer wearied Actour longing to disrobe himself of his combersome ornaments leaps into the Tyring House, So doth Charles hasten on to the designed place of his retyrement. And not being able to ride causeth himself to bee carried in a Litter. Yet was there an occasion that both stayed a while & somewhat diuerted him out of the way. The visiting of his Little Nephew[1] bearing his Name, the only son of Phillip, which was brought vp at the famous Validolid.[2]

Thither Charles turnes in not for the satisfaction of his weaker affections to be filled with the Company & Embracements of so deare a Pledge of his Loue & hopes, But for the giuing order touching his vertuous Education. Which that he might advance the prize [value] of aboue all other things whatsoeuer, he doth spend the whole time, that he stayd there, in instructing the Child with goodly precepts touching Pietie, Vertue, & true Glorie. Nor doth he depart thence ⟨123⟩ till both in his own & others Iudgement he leaue him sufficiently informed in the knowledge & inflamed in the Loue of them.

Behold here the last work in reference to others performed by

---

[1] Nephew—grandson. The child referred to was the unfortunate Don Carlos (1545–68), the son of Philip II.

[2] Validolid—Valladolid, capital of Spain and seat of the royal palace until 1561

him, & see the Example of Solomon[1] reviued & confirmed in the close of his Princely Life. Hee turnes a Preacher & a Teacher euen of Babes.

There's none so great (Except his wretchednes ouerbalance his Dignitie) that setts not himself in the end to learn & Exercize this Profession. Mark but the words of dying men of what qualitie soeuer. The Conclusion is commonly a sermon: Feare God & flee from Euill, Are the last Bequests to Children, the last Farewell to Freinds, a Codicil annexed to euery mans will.

But that, which there's scarce any man so bad as studies not to performe at his death, there's scarce any man so good that's not ashamed to practize in his Life.

How doe the words of Holines in Common Esteeme misbeseeme the lips of great Personages eminent either in Nobilitie or Wisedome.

To find such a one seriously exhorting & instructing ⟨124⟩ though it were his own Children in matters of Religion or Learning would cause more merriment from their Equals then to be found as Ageselaus[2] sometimes was riding a Cock horse amongst his Little ones. And they, that out of their grauitie would not perhaps laugh, would much more by their seeming Pitty condemne the Practize.

To spend the whole day in managing of a horse, in trayning of a hound, or in manning [training] of a Hawk is a Noble Imployment both of time & mind.

But to spend the least minute in the direction of a godly Life, To take the least care touching their Consciences, or to bestow the least paines in the spiritual Culture of their Familie, why it sauours of the Pedant.

It is not only discharge of his own duty, but matter of merit in a Parent & Master to send his household to the Church, & his

---

[1] Example of Solomon—see Proverbs iv, 1. The remark is based on the assumption that Solomon wrote Proverbs for the edification of his children.

[2] Ageselaus—King of Sparta, died 360 B.C. The story can be found in Plutarch's *Lives of the Noble Grecians and Romans*, 'Agesilaus', xxv.

Children to the schools there to learn what belongs to the soul & mind. The information & Accompt [responsibility] touching matters of Religion & Learning are put ouer to the Parson & the schoolmaster as too meane & base for Excellent spirits & vnderstandings to descend vnto. For the refutation of so pernicious & grounded an Errour ⟨125⟩ by a contrary instance aboue all Exception Charles makes this work the Finishment of all the rest.

Between that great Confirmation of peace & safetie, which he had newly been the happy instrument of to so many Millions, & his own settlement in Deuotion & Quiet, which he was now in hand with [very close to], hee brings in as a gracefull & necessarie interlude the settling and confirming of his Grandchild's tender mind in right opinions & affections. As though neither the discharge of his duty to men-ward were complete, nor his Liuing henceforth to himself could be comfortable without perfect order taken in this matter.

That he left a proof to the world of his desires, & carried along with himself the Testimonie of his Indeauours to become the Father of his Childs mind as he was of his body, & made it his last & greatest care to furnish him with vertue & Pietie as the best inheritance & Portion, Is that which Charles by his Diuersion & stay in so pressing & hasty a iourney intended to lett vs know & with all by the Example of his own strange solicitousnes to lay the sentence of a heauy doome on all those Parents, ⟨126⟩ that out of all Foolish Pride or slothfull negligence put off to others mouths & Eares the instruction of Godlines, which of all other parts of Fatherhood is the most necessarie & honorable in Charles his Iudgement. Who makes the Catechizing of his Grandchild (for so it was) the Epilogue of all his Heroical Actions.

Here the CHEIF stayd & that in such a manner Composing herself both in Countenance & Gestures as if she purposely would giue intimation, that with the mention of Epilogue on Charles his part she was likewise come to the Conclusion of her intended

Discourse. But perceiuing a Continued Expectation in the Auditours no way seconding her desires, After two or three Attempts, as if she were vncertaine herself how to proceed.

The Confirmation (sayd SHEE) of your Profound silence, Honoured Societie, so much passing the Degree of Attention to others, as it plainly declares the busy working of your meditations, giues an Euident Remonstrance, That either the impertinencie of my Narrations hath ouerwearied, or the interposition of your own better thoughts haue taken vp your minds or perhaps both together. Howeuer surely it will proue ⟨127⟩ matter of Content to you aswell as to mee here to break off my tedious discourse.

The Euidencie of Dislike, which the Faces & Behauiour of the Auditours discouered to this Close made a suddaine stop to the Cheifs speech, whilest a modest bashfulnes seemed to intercept the words, that were further intended to this purpose.

Which the GUARDIAN obseruing through the suddaine change of her blushing red into a wan pale to be not without some Alteration in her mind, Least further thoughts might increase perturbation in a Cheerfull manner thus made answere.

By what meanes soeuer you indeauour to carry it, wee cannot deny, Worthy Cheif, but that you haue great reason to seek the Release of this present Burthensome task, which wee haue enforced you vnto. Which were not all things in you answerable to your Name must needs haue sunk you down ere this time both in mind & body.

But since Heauen hath endued you with such indefatigable Abilities both of Memorie & Voice, as wee see you proceed with greater Vigour then you began, Howeuer sore the ⟨128⟩ Labour may be to your self, wee shall entreat you not to cease till you haue giuen the vttermost finishment to this Noble Historie, which hath kindled such restlesse desires in vs, as no other Necessitie of Busines much lesse pleasure can haue any Admittance into our thoughts till our Longing Appetite bee herein satisfied.

As for the pensiue silence, which you obserued in vs it grew not as you suppose from wearines, but rather from the weightnes of your Discourse.

Of your self since your modestie comports not the least prayse I will forbeare what is most due. But surely the things themselues cannot be heard without wonderment, & as you haue put them on without perplexitie, whilest by the representation of this goodly Model wee are more sensibly made aware of our own Deformities. So as snail-like wee are forced to pull in our hornes, where wee most thrust them out, perceiuing that wee haue had most Cause to be ashamed, wherein wee haue perhaps most gloried. I speak mine own thoughts.

And haue diuined all ours, replied the COMPANIE together. I am glad (sayd the RESOLUED) that this matter works on ⟨129⟩ others as well as it doth on mee. You see, Sweet Cheif, there's likely to be a better draught then you did imagine. It were foul shame therefore now to ply [steer towards] shore, when the game comes in so faire. Wherefore, Launch out againe Cheerfully & whilest you prepare your Netts & trimme the sailes, which you began to strike, Giue mee leaue by the force of mine own & all this good Companies Earnest Intreaties (who, I know, are partners with mee in the same desires) to draw from your Guardian the particular Declaration of those worthy thoughts, which he acknowledgeth his mind to be in travail with through your Discourses.

Which besides the manifold Good, that will accrue to vs through the Confirmation of his good Iudgement & Example, will perhaps also proue of especial Benefitt to himself, whilest reducing the vertuous inclinations of his soul from the largenes & varietie of Contemplation, which your Discourse hath ministered, to some determinate subiect, he may perhaps bring the fruitfulnes of his own & our minds into Act. For these good notions, that are begott in our minds by the proposal of vertues in general as ⟨130⟩ they spring out very fervent hott like the Bath waters, so they immediately freeze, except by this instant application of them to our selues not only by way of speculation but also of Practize, as by a new kindled fire they haue a continual supply of warmth ministred vnto them. Wherefore in this regard I shall advise you, Worthy Guardian, who I know, haue a desire to doe all for the best, to giue Life & birth to some of your good Conceptions. Whereby as you shall certainly gaine them, so you shall further the preseruation of the rest: For it happens most what [both] in the fruit of the mind as in the wombe, That Good Affections & Resolutions through their multiplicitie stifling each other all proue Abortiue.

Verily (sayd the GUARDIAN) the Confused striuing of many thoughts in my heart, as they sensibly bare witnes to the truth of what you affirme touching their present manner of affecting the soul, so they doe likewise breed iust feare of the danger, that you threaten which I feel already working apace whilest the mutual combate for precedencie of Expression giues a full proof that like those men ⟨131⟩ of Cadmus sowing they will destroy each other before they can be brought forth for seruice; Except some better skill then I my self am master of afford a helping hand.

A wise midwife (answered the RESOLUED) would easily bring you safe abed. And though I am no such yet because, where Necessitie exacts Charitable Aide, there runs no hazard of Presumption in the offer of weak Abilities, I shall indeauour if yourself please to deliuer you of this Burthen, by helping forth those Conceptions of yours, which haue attained their iust perfection, & by a quiet return of those other, that are not yet perhaps fully shapen to the womb of your further Meditation, That in their due time they may receiue a happy Birth. For hence, as I suppose, ariseth that Conflict, which your Countenance testifieth aswell as your words to be in your mind through the pressure of many Cogitations strugling for passage out, as though they doubted in being left behind to be quite lost. Whereas indeed there is no such danger. For that, which is most rare in the Corporal bearings of the wombe is most ordinary in the spiritual breedings of the mind to bring forth its fruit by way of superfetation. Wherefore take no thought ⟨132⟩ for the miscarriage of what you shalbe now forced to reserue. But let vs haue the speedy deliuerie of that which hath receiued its full perfection.

Here the Resolued stayd a while Expecting the Answere of the GUARDIAN, who shaking his head with a graue smile made answere

Your Earnestnes of Dispatch is nothing so Eager as mine. But the Remembrance of the old Proverb,

> The Hasty Bitch brings forth blind Whelps,

makes mee loth to outrun good speed by ouer much forwardnes.

Perhaps (sayd the MODERATOR) our Guardians mind is of the Nature of those Instruments, which vpon any short disvse must first haue a little water powred into them before they will draw vp & deliuer that, which is in the Well, though neuer so brim full.

Your opinion carrieth great shew of Probabilitie, sayd the RESOLUED & therefore I will adventure the Experiment. By the vncertainitie of mine guessings as by the Rule of Falshood I may bring him to the right singling out of his own intentions. ⟨133⟩

Is it peradventure the Discourse of the Newfound World, which hauing wafted ouer your mind to that Continent, the readines of the Passage hath drawn you to make a visitation vnto those most beloued Plantations of our English Nation?

What? Is it the Compassion of [grief for] what you find there euery way vnprosperous? Or is it the indignation against the Disturbers of so flourishing a Course, as it began with? Or is it rather the Greif of your lost time, Empayred Estate & fruitlesse toyle that doth so much perplex your mind?[1]

Ah say not so, Replied the GUARDIAN, very passionately. How-euer I know you doe it but by Artificial Dissimulation to quicken my zeal in bearing witnesse, yet such is my Tendernes in this matter, as I can no ways comport the opposition of the truth,

---

[1] For the Ferrars' connection with the Virginia Company see Maycock, Chapter IV, and for John's personal difficulties see also pp. 107-9.

though it be intended to the Clearer Confirmation thereof. It's neither lost time, paines, nor money, that hath been this way imployed by mee.

But my work is with the Lord, & his reward hath been with mee Tenfold. If not in the Age of this ⟨134⟩ worlds Honour [those things honoured by the present age], Wealth & Delights, yet in the Compensation of all those in a farre more Excellent manner. And yet euen in these things themselues, that I may not vngratefully abridge the riches of his Goodnes, I must acknowledge a larger measure & fairer Portion to haue befallen mee then otherwise I might haue euer expected.

Let no man stumble at my Appearing Misfortunes, which I professe haue led to a farre higher pitch of this Lifes Felicitie then I did my self conceiue, much lesse hope. I had vtterly lost all but for my shipwrack on this Coast. The damage of this Adventure hath more enriched mee then all the gaine, that I euer made otherwise.

And since the Emmetts [ants] well shapen Actiue members serue a proof of their Creatours Wisedome aswell as the many powerfull Limbes of the mighty Elephants, Let mee by solemne acknowledgement of my Excesse of Happines in a weak & priuate Fortune adde a Ball to [vote for] the Confirmation of that vndeniable Inference, which our Cheif made vpon the Transcendent Prosperitie of our Charles & his Royal Family. That there is no surer way to multipy a mans own, then by the promotion of many others good. ⟨135⟩ Nor more fruitfull seed for this Worlds Happines (if it be desired) then the Faithfull seruice of God in Publick Employments, Being by his Direction appointed thereunto; Wherein the more losse at first the larger Gaine will be in the end, & the longer it may seeme deferred of the greater durance will it proue.

This with my Tongue now with my hand, if need require, shall I euer be ready to Testifie, yeelding to that Estimate of my Condition, which by General Assessment you & other Absent Freinds haue made, That in outward respects I haue little Cause to envy any others happines. & all this cheifly springing in mine own apprehension from the ouerthrow of my Private in the too much following of Publicke Affaires. God of his infinite Bountie being pleased to reward the Effects of his own grace in a hearty & diligent performance of the business he had committed vnto mee. That's all I dare pretend vnto. And if so little haue so largely fructified to my profitt, what had it done if in euery respect I had discharged the place & person, that I bore. It is my Negligence not my Paines, the Houres I took to myself, not those ⟨136⟩ I spent; The thrift, that I vsed, not the wast, that I made of my Estate in this busines, that when it comes to remembrance, troubleth & perplexeth my Thoughts. As hauing been altogether wanting in Zeal, in Paines, in Cost both to the worth of the Busines & mine own Profession. And so hauing enough & ouermeasure of Guilt in my self I haue little reason, & I thank God, little Temptation of indignation against others, Who either haue, or I hope will advize themselues of their Errours, & obtaining Gods Pardon they shall most freely haue mine.

As for the present Distresse of the Plantations, though it often deeply affect my soul, yet it was not that, which you now obserued to haue distracted my thoughts, which are drawn much neerer home in the circumference of these Walls.

According as it works on all hands (sayd the RESOLUED) this myne of our Cheifs storie giues hopes of passing Potesy[1] it self. Why euen the days oare proues gold vpon the first melting. I haue not lost my shott, howeuer I haue missed the Aime. Since therefore there is such Certaintie of gaine I will by your Good Leaue, Sweet Company, adventure a second Arrow if happily I may strike the white. Which by the Leuel of these walls, which you haue taken, makes mee think ⟨137⟩ may be the ouerlarge Expense of Cost & Care, which your longsome Buildings haue stood in.

---

[1] Potesy—Potosí, in Bolivia, was, for fifty years after its founding in 1545, the richest source of silver in the world.

Your silence Confirmes my Suspicion.

You haue touched a sore indeed, replied the GUARDIAN, which Charles Abandoning of his Pallace made smart amaine.

I acknowledge for myself it hath been a manifold Errour euery way in the thing & in the manner.

Nay, I pray, sayd the RESOLUED, since you are in so good a way of repaying the Fault, as the beginning of Confession promiseth, Take mee. And vs all, sayd the COMPANIE. Why be it so, sayd the RESOLUED. Take vs all as ioynt Partners & mee as Principal in the Confession of this Guilt.

Why then (replied the GUARDIAN) since it is your Desire to haue the perfect Cure I must lanche [lance] it yet a little deeper by the Protestation of Great Folly in the Lauish disbursements of those incombs, which should haue been applied to more necessarie vse.

Of Ambitious Vanitie in seeking to match the Pompe & state of Great Personages. And ⟨138⟩

Of many Wanton Appetites & desires touching Ease & pleasure, howeuer valed under the pretence of Conueniency & Comelynes. It is no small Broode, nor or Petty Vermin, that haunts the building, but such as might iustly haue driuen out, if not deuoured vs vp, had not the mercy of God been more soueraigne.

That Wast should be repayd with Necessitie.

That Pride should haue a fall. And

Vaine Delights bee closed vp with bitter sufferings, were but the iust recompense & fruits of this misdoing. This is the doome, that mine own heart giues against it self, when I consider Iustice on God's part, & Desert on mine. And this I could wish euen grauen on the Frontispice of the House for a Caueat, that none of weak & troubled states should by our Errours be encouraged to the like Prodigal Excesse. The strength of Venome, that ill Presidents [precedents] in this kind infused into our minds, makes mee feare the danger of others, impoysoning themselues by our Example. Wherefore let vs be diligent seuerely to Condemne in our selues, what we would haue others carefully to avoyd the imitation of. ⟨139⟩

And since it must stand (for to pull it down againe would perhaps be the rearing vp of Madnes on the Ruines of Folly) let it stand a monument of the weaknes of our minds, not of the Abilities of Estate.

Let it be in the worlds Eie an Honour but in our own an Argument of Humiliation.

The Cost is I doubt not forgiuen if wee can keep from the Taint of Pride, which like a Dampe strikes vp from the ground of all faire Buildings & dizying the Braine makes all the sences to mistake in their seueral apprehensions.

Wee shall by God's Blessing, I hope, make that good in the end & vse, which in the Contriuement & performance was not so.

The Commodiousnes, the Beauty, the Pleasures, both within & without are our own for a sober Enioyment both in busines & delight. But the Honour whateuer fashion it comes dressed after belongs only to God.

Let vs with gladsome Thankfulnes acknowledge to haue receiued much more, then the most, but let vs not think our selues any more then the meanest for that, which hath ⟨140⟩ been freely Conferred by Gods Grace & is not good neither except it be vsed with Humilitie.

There's nothing tending to Esteeme & Exaltation, that wee may take to our selues or accept from others.

There's nothing but that, which wee may now freely take, though many things perhaps, that wee ought to haue forborn the procuring of, the Vnseasonablenes & Vnorderlines whereof corrupted our affections, but not the Blessings of God: they remaine pure, if the mind, that enioyeth them, be not defiled.

It's the solicitousnes therefore of my Thoughts in this matter only how to prevent others dammage by vnwary Imitation of our Errours. And for our selues to improue it to the vttermost benefitt that may be, Avoyding Carefully the vndermining of Ingratitude to prize lesse, or lesse to reioyce in God's Blessings through the remembrance of mine own failings.

Which since God's Grace hath passed by, why should I not remember either to Feare or Greif for Humiliation to my self & Caution to others. I hope I shall neuer forgett them. You haue my settled Resolution of this matter. ⟨141⟩

And wee accompt it no small gaine (sayd the RESOLUED) in so important a matter by the prescript of yours to be taught how to guide our own affections & iudgements. Wherefore though I perceiue this second Rouer [arrow] to haue gone wide, yet hauing hitt perhaps more luckily, then if it had gone to the mark itself: I cannot but boast of my good Fortune, howeuer my skill comes short.

It is ouermuch skill perhaps (sayd the GUARDIAN) or rather ouermuch strength, which carrieth you beyond the Butts [target]. If you had mett with a large heart[1] you had done best to Angle in the Deep of these Publick Considerations. But my thoughts as smaller Fishes haunt the shore & dare not adventure out of the shallow of mine own peculiar [personal affairs]. And yet verily you could not perhaps haue reduced them to any other heads more fittly by way of Comparison, then those Two of Building & Plantation, which you haue light vpon.

A Blind man (sayd the MODERATOR vpon the Resolued's Longsome Pause) may feel day at the light of this Crany, And therefore our Resolued thinks it not worth his discouery. ⟨142⟩ Since you are so Confident, Gentle Moderator, (sayd the RESOLUED) I shall gladly leaue it to your hands.

And by my hands (sayd SHE) & not by my Tongue shall I performe it.

Wherevpon laying her hand on the Guardians only Son,[2] That

---

[1] Heart—the metaphors shift from those based on archery to new ones based on fishing. 'Heart' could be modern 'hart', but such a reading seems inconsistent with 'angle in the deep'. The copyist may have mistakenly written 'heart' for 'beast'.

[2] Guardians only Son—Nicholas Ferrar, the third of that name.

stood close by & with smiling Cheere turning her Eies to the Father, How can you longer (sayd SHEE) vpon so manifest a Confrontment dissemble the matter?

You haue indeed half found it, sayd the GUARDIAN.

In this Case (replied SHE) the half will be as good as the whole. Grant mee but this is the House, that you speak of, & your little Daughter[1] must be the Plantation, aswell in your present intention, as in her Name. But if the Care of these but Two & so hopeful Children so ouerloade you, how would you vndergoe my seuenfold charge,[2] & that with all those disadvantages of present meanes or future hopes, with which your Estate abounds.

Alas (sayd the GUARDIAN) how strangely mishapen must the inward features of our minds needs bee, When the richer & better proportioned the Garment is of Gods Cutting out, the worse it fitts & lesse becomes vs in our own Fancies. ⟨143⟩ Why, verily it was the Emulation of your Happines in this Kind, that most of all other thoughts or Affections was all this while so seriously on work in mee. And were it not that in yours I haue as great an Interest, I will not say as you, but as in yourself, My Dear Sister, I doubt not whether it might not passe on to Envy, According to my great weaknes in vertue & that great height & Excellencie thereof, wherevnto some of yours doe truly aspire, & I haue Confidence by Gods help reaching out his powerfull hand, shall in the end attaine.

You know mine but you know not your own farre greater Happines in the forward growth of some of your Childrens souls in true wisedome like fruit come to its ripening, in the hopefull knitting [formation of fruit] of others & in the faire blooming of the youngest. If sharp frosts of wrong grounded opinions nip them not, or boysterous winds of ill examples in Superiours doe not quite blow away the hopefull fruit.

[1] Little Daughter—Virginia Ferrar.
[2] Seuenfold charge—Susanna Ferrar Collett (the Moderator) is known to have had at least twelve children.

Because our Adventures by both freight in the same bottome [are carried in the same ship] I cannot seuer the Consideration of mine own from yours, & in this warning of what imports you to look well to prevent, & in this remembrance of what you ought aboue ⟨144⟩ all other things to reioyce in & thank God for, haue told you the summe of my Desires, & the maine issue of those Cogitations, which the last related passage of Charles his shutting vp all [excluding all other interests] in the Catechizing of his little Nephew (as our Cheif hath well stiled it) raised in mee.

It is the making of that kind of Provision for my children, which he endeauoured to leaue to his Heire, as the best portion. It is the Acting of that part for my self, which Charles thought the most gracefull for him to depart the stage with, that puts my mind to that sore Travail, which you perceiue it labour in. Wherein that I may not by longer delay hinder you from more worthy subiects of your thoughts, This is the substance. That I haue resolued it the only true proof of my Fatherly Loue to my Children, & the only sure ground of their Happines euen in this world to giue them a good Education, not according to the vaine Traditions of the world, nor after the retchlesse [reckless] manner of Parents nowadaise, shifting all the Paines & Care from themselues; But according to the eternal Precepts of Gods word & after the manner of truly wisemen, who haue euer accompted the Forming of their Childrens minds to a perfect Disposition, & the ⟨145⟩ ordering of their Actions in a right manner euen from the very cradle, to be the Principal charge of the Father.

In the pursuite whereof, till I may euery way come to the exact knowledge & Practize of what herein is required to the vttermost, I haue firmly established it in mine own determination, God assisting mee, To lett no day passe, when my son is with mee, till his own Abilities haue ouertaken mine (which I pray God they may speedily doe) without an Equal Provision of Nourishment for his mind as for his Body, That he may not grow vp only well clothed & fed in the outward, but much better filled & adorned in the inward man by good Instructions in all kinds according to that Talent, which God shall bestow on mee.

And herein that by telling all, as you desire, I may receiue either the Approbation or Correction of your better iudgements, I haue designed my Performance after this Model.

To begin in the Morning with the Precepts of Religion towards God. To proceed at Noone with Rules touching vpright & mercifull Conversation amongst Men, And To conclude at Night with Directions of Ciuil Wisedome touching his deportment in publick & priuate Affaires. ⟨146⟩ You haue now the full of what I can say in this matter.

The Pangs of Bearing are past, sayd the RESOLUED, & you haue reason to triumph in such a manlike Infant, But the Nursing vp will not be brought about with so little Toyle & Cost as you perhaps imagine.

Well (sayd the GUARDIAN) since it is born, it must be kept, as sayth the Proverb.

And therefore to begin with that, which is alwaies first, The Invitation of Godsibs.[1] I pray you & all the rest of this good Companie to become witnesses thereunto. And as they, that vndertake such Charges are bound to haue a Care of its welldoing, & wherein you see mee wanting freely to admonish, & if need require to make supply for my failings.

There was no other Answere returned then by smiles from the whole Companie, except the Cheif, who retaining the former sobrietie of her Countenance,

I know not (sayd the GUARDIAN) Faire Cheif whether from your pensive silence I may conclude the Grant of this Desired Fauour, which by the Cheerfull Behauiour of the rest I presume to haue attained. ⟨147⟩

It is not the Denial of this Seruice to you (replied the CHEIF)

---

[1] Godsibs—witnesses, godparents. The Resolved has consistently carried out his metaphor based on his role as midwife assisting at a birth; the Guardian continues it by saying that since his conceptions are now brought to life, godparents are necessary.

but the feare of your Denial of a greater Fauour to mee, Worthy Guardian, that keeps mee sad.

Verily (sayd the GUARDIAN) whateuer it be, you wrong your self by needlesse doubts & mee by vndue suspicions. Since there is nothing great, that I can giue to you, nor any thing difficult, that you shall commande mee. Whereof now make the proof: If you please.

Vpon any termes (sayd the CHEIF) I am content to gaine the satisfaction of my Longings. And therefore though with the preiudice of mine own Modestie I am resolued to take it, as you offer it. Least if I should straine in good manners to receiue it by way of Curtesy, I might perhaps loose it. Wherevpon beckoning to her son,[1] that stood next to the Guardians, a Child of the same Age, when he was come to her rising vp she led him to the Guardian, & with a low Reuerence making Tender of his hand, I recommend (sayd SHEE) Honoured Guardian, in the most Affectionate & Powerfull kind that I may, this restlesse Care of mine to your hands, That he may by your Loue be admitted to a free & constant participation ⟨148⟩ of that singular Benefitt, which you haue promised your own, of dayly instructions & Teachings.

Ah (sayd the GUARDIAN) this is a matter, the Exercize whereof belongs only to a mans own.

Why then (sayd the RESOLUED) since you cannot goe back from what you haue promised, That you may the better & more Easily performe it, you shall doe well to take him for your own. For I dare assure you this Course will in the end make you so accompt [consider] him.

You see how truly & deeply her Loue & maintenance hath engrafted him into the Cheifs heart, That she perswades herself not only vs, that she is indeed his Mother.

---

[1] Son—not, of course, her own son, as the words of the Resolved later attest. The boy may possibly have been Ralph Woodnoth, 'who seems to have been brought up and educated. . .as one of the family' (Maycock, p. 165). His father, Arthur Woodnoth, a cousin, was a close friend and counsellor to the family and, like Nicholas and John, a member of the Virginia Company.

Well (sayd the GUARDIAN) for her sake I will doe what she hath enioyned mee. I pray God it may proue as successful as she hopes.[1]

Nothing doubt it (answered SHE) & therefore with all humble Thanks I Accept what you haue promised. Herevpon making a signe to the Child he kissed the Guardians hand, as he had formerly seen his own son doe. And the Chief retyred to her place; Wherein, she was scarce well settled, when the GUARDIAN with a pleasant Earnestnes began: ⟨149⟩

The Respite, that wee granted, Faire Cheif, was intended to your own Ease for a while, not to sett others on Endlesse work. There's no reason therefore you should longer enjoy what you haue so misemployed. Besides your own Busines I doubt not is ouer-ready els you could not haue intended the Discomposing of mine. & to speak, as you perhaps will imagine, since my Pitty of your wearines proues so burthensome to my self, I shall be wary of vsing it any more in this kind. And now in Reuenge aswell as Desire shall without intermission vrge your Prosecution of your Admirable Historie. The Loue whereunto is no whitt abated through the Relatours Vnkindness.

Since there's no hope (replied SHE) either of Mercy or Compassion, Lets know how much is already told out, & I will see to make vp the full summe of this Payment, as I may. Where did I leaue him?

Why vpon Departure (sayd the PATIENT) from his Little Nephew. And because you told vs at the first, hee made such hast, wee suppose he is by this time come to the end of his Iourney & now settled in his long desired rest, wherewith I pray proceed. ⟨150⟩

[1] For details of the school at Little Gidding see Maycock, pp. 164-5.

Part IX

The Chief upbraids the Patient for her impatient attempt to have the narrative resume with an account of Charles's life in retirement. To do so, she asserts, would omit consideration of the great simplicity of his journey, which contrasted so dramatically with his former royal progresses. Charles now travelled on horseback and denied himself all but the most necessary bodily comforts, thereby presenting a great contrast to the luxurious coaches of our 'dainty-limbed sybarites' and especially to the great assembly of coaches and lackeys which now barricade even the church doors. The Chief goes on to criticize contemporary ostentation in the keeping of servants: by the hiring of many servants men follow the corrupt examples of Esau, Abimelech, and Absalom in their attempts to rival the glory of God and his hosts of angels. God is jealous of the honour accorded him; and men, except for His appointed regents and their ministers, sin in trying to emulate it. Charles, who formerly was waited upon by princes, now kept only four servants in his retirement; his practice clearly demonstrates that servants should be hired only for need, never for ostentation. The Patient, although right in her original misgivings about the progress of the narrative, praises the Chief's diatribe against servant-keeping and concludes with her personal renunciation of all 'glorious sinfull vanities', a declaration which is hailed by the Chief.

◆

Ah, Dearest Patient (sayd the CHEIF & Laying hand on hers) how doth the vnwonted impotencie of Desires transporte you to the preiudice of themselues & all here, Whilest too impatiently you require Accompt of his Retyrement & Quiet, A subiect best suiting your own Disposition, that haue almost lost one of the most rare and worthy sights, that euer any mans Eie in this Age much lesse yours beheld.

That in euery thing our Charles might become an Example of the True Condition of our Mortal Life, that is but a wearisome Pilgrimage euen in the highest. And that none might pretend they had any reserued Portion of Good things towards Happines, which had not been known & tasted by him, He is by the Diuine Providence led about continually in a restlesse Travail throughout all the choysest Parts of the Earth.

Fourty & three Seueral Expeditions, Two into Africk, Nine into Germanie, Seuen into Italy, Ten into Neather Lands, Foure into France, Seuen into Spaine, & Two into England did this man performe, yet in none of all these Royall Progresses should you haue encountered that True ground of Admiration, which this short iourney would haue raysed had you mett him in it. Now without any Guard at all, whom formerly you should haue ⟨151⟩ seldome mett vnattended by an Armie, Neuer without a Troupe of Princes waiting on him, that now rides accompanied only with Twelue seruitours & had but one single Horse, & that neither for Ease nor Honour, but for Necessitie. The infirmitie of his Body answered not the Desire of his mind, els you had seen him measuring the way with his own feet, that now is carried on Horseback for weaknes sake, sayth the Judicious Historian.[1]

Oh that I could by one Call bring all the mistaken Gallants of this world to the Consideration of this spectacle, that in the veiw thereof they might read the Fond & Feeble Errour of their souls in the Affectation of Pompes & Delicacies touching their own Persons.

Neither Age nor sicknes, though either of them might haue seemed iustly to claime it, can prevail with Charles to any further ease or tendernes of his body then is absolutely needfull to make it hold out for the full accomplishment of the minds seruice.

Hee forsakes the Litter assoone as he can sitt the horse not for change of Pleasure but for the Exercize of Patience by the induring of Labour. & holds it a shame by the vse of any Easy ⟨152⟩ manner of travailing, to seeme delicate in the Evidencie of double Infirmitie both of yeares & Indisposition, Whereas the adle [empty, vain] Iudgements of these times haue resolued it a meane proof of their

---

[1] Judicious Historian—this passage is based on de Thou, Book XVII, p. 74.

Noble spirits aswell as of their Gentle Bloud to make wanton provision for sloth & Ease, & esteeme themselues so much the more Respectable in others Eies, by how much they appeare lesse able to vndergoe any kind of Labour or suffering. They dare not adventure themselues either to summers heat or winters cold without a house ouer their heads. A trotting Horse leaues them more toyled [exhausted] then the Iustings [joustings] of old time did their Forefathers.

The very stones wound their feet in treading, that they cannot passe the streets but in a Coach, & that Bedded & Bolstered for feare of Bruising: & all these too must be hung by sloues[1] & cunning Deuises to avoyde the shaking of our daintie Limbed Sybarites. But Ile leaue them to the deserued punishment of their own Folly. A Common Prey to Cheating Flatterers, & the Derision of Braue & Actiue spirits. Whose minds I see are much more perplexed in this equal contempt of Ease & Honour, which Charles made Remonstrance of in his being contented (for so the Noble Thuanus setts it down) with such ⟨153⟩ a sorry Retinue & one single Horse. This say they, as little to his Honour, might haue been more discreetly passed ouer in silence both by the First Relatours & mee. So manifest a Forgetfulnes of himself as this Action speaks, moues a doubt, whether hee be now worth any more remembrance from others.

The proof of so great Hardines of mind in so great weaknes of body deserues the highest Commendation. But what was gloriously neglected for Ease would haue been iudiciously taken along for Honour: A Litter & a Coache & spare Horses led by, ought to haue been prouided, though not ment to be vsed. Why these & a large Traine of Attendants richly clothed & Nobly furnished are the necessarie ornaments of Nobilitie & Greatnes. And to descend proportionably, There's nothing more speaks a Gentleman, then his Loue to Horses & his Carefull looking to be well attended. Oh that I might here leaue this matter. But the

---

1 Sloues—slivers, leather straps used to suspend the body of a carriage.

Obseruation of the Church doores themselues euery way barri-
cadoed with Coaches & Horses, Coachmen & Lackeys draws mee
on to a weeping pursuit of this Pestilent Vanitie euen into the very
Entrails of Christianitie, Whilest ⟨154⟩ I see the most zealous
Professours [professing Christians] of this Age no lesse engulfed
in the solicitous Provision & Boasting Practize of these kind of
vainglorious Pompes, then the most debauched worldlings themselues. Footmen & Pages, Vshers & Groomes, I [aye], & Gentlemen
too for Attendants, Wayting Mayds & Gentle women & Women,
which is now of more Grace (though I know not why, except
perhaps that in our Natural Abilities without any other Addition
wee best serue for Instruments of Pride & Folly) are all, & many
other not worth Naming, become in this Age not only needfull
members but ornaments of a Christian Familie.

And it goes currant for a vertue, not only for a point of Libertie,
To make the vttermost show, that not only our meanes but our
witts can reach vnto in Horses & Coaches & Liueries & all the rest
of such like glorious furniture. There's nothing better spent in
Midling Fortunes, then that which is layd out to gaine creditt.
There's nothing more necessary to bee prouided in higher Ranks,
then that, which is to the maintenance of Honour in this kind
& way. Howeuer other Dispositions receiue Variation [other attitudes may vary], yet to be the master of many men, & those kept
like men too, ⟨155⟩ though there be no good imployment for
them, To exact much Honour in little seruice & lesse worth of
their own is in all Estates & Conditions without exception Resolued
An high point of vertue & a maine part of Happines. And yet haue
they no better warrantie for it in all the Scriptures, that I remember, then Esau's meeting Iacob with 400 men,[1] Abimileck's hyring
of vaine & Light Persons to follow him,[2] And Absalon's Preparing
Chairets [chariots] and Horses & Fifty men to run before him.[3]

If these single Irregularities stand Branded in God's book with
the Note of highest Infamie by instancing the Practize of them in

---

[1] Genesis xxxii, 6.   [2] Judges ix, 4.   [3] II Samuel xv, 1.

such Reprobate persons as these are, Shall the Composition of them altogether into one Body of Pride & Vanitie in these our Last [present] times be iustifiable?

Haue the Children of God now gott a Priuiledge for the Exercize of that altogether, which these wicked men acting but by peice-meals scaped not without seuerest punishment? I know not whence they can hope of better acceptation in these courses, then those other found with God. The things themselues are no whitt bettered & the Attendants Condition surely grown much worse. ⟨156⟩

Could wee lay no fouler imputations to great mens Retinues, then Abimilechs Followers are charged with, wee should giue them occasion to think their Families so many Households of Saints. Why then all the Help lieth in the Masters vertue. And that's a new discouered Alchimistry, that bad Actions should be transmuted into good by the Doers Holines. It should rather seem to Adde then to take away Guilt from Euill Practizes. By how much better the man himself is, by so much more heynous is euery vicious Action, that proceeds from him.

But I goe vpon what is not granted, That the Thing is simply Euill. The fault of those condemned wretches lay in their bad intentions. Our Good makes it turn to a Blessing in vs, which in them was the Fruit of sin & Mother of a Curse. And what think you might their intentions be, that thus Corrupted all, Reuenge & other Euill designes? Indeed to such purpose they made it serue (& who in these daies on like occasion shall wee find innocent of the like Abuse). But these neither were, nor could be the Principal Ends of these things. It was the Honour of their own Persons from the Admiring multitude, that they sought by the ostentation of all ⟨157⟩ this might & Brauery. And this I am sure, which was in them the worst, is the very best, that now can be pretended in the Continuance & Improuement of these Practizes amongst vs.

I haue rather I see perplexed in the shaking of the old then any waies persuaded you to that, which seemes altogether new. There's no Pedigree on Earth so Noble but if it be traced vp to the original, returnes with Blemish.

And if the Personal Wickednes of them, that first begun things, be sufficient to condemne them, wee shalbe forced perhaps to quitt the most excellent & beneficial Arts, that God hath made vs masters of.

But if rightly distinguishing in these matters between the skill & the inventours wee doe neither with Lesse thanks accept, nor with lesse comfort make vse of Gods good Guifts for the perversenes of the Instruments, by whom he made the Prime Conveyance, Why should wee by any whitt discouraged for the Deriuation of this Practize from any Authours whatsoeuer, be they as irregular as they may be & in all other courses vnimitable, yet this hauing descended through the succession of all times not only with approbation but ⟨158⟩ applause of the best & wisest. Why should there be any Question but that it is in truth, as it appears, A Soueraigne peice of Excellencie & Happines, & rather branded with the mark of infamie in the Practizers for their own vnworthines, then for the Guilt of the thing itself. Which take it, which way you please, either in the desire or in the Enioyment, You shall find there's no Appetite so strong, nor Pleasure so satisfying, as those, which spring from this root. And how shall we think, that that, which seemes incorporated in to the very essence of euery Generous soul, should be an Aberration from Good, Or make a scruple to pursue with vttermost of all indeauours that, which amongst all other Prerogatiues seemes neerest to advance vs to the Resemblance of God himself; Whose Glorious Maiestie being alwaies represented vnto vs with Millions of Angels Attending him not for Necessitie of seruice but Manifestation of Honour.

Why should wee not proportionably rate euery small participation, though but shaddow like of this Diuine Excellencie at the highest prize [price]. Which swelling vp to any conspicuous height doth so Deifie Greatnes, that it boldly laies ⟨159⟩ claime & takes the Seizin [possession] of one of those Peculiars [privileges], which the very Cherubines & Seraphins dare not accept.

TO BE LORD OF CREATURES

For by this Name now adaies doe Men enroll themselues into Great mens Families, I [aye], & Fauours too. That you may not think it's the Basenes of the Servants Disposition only to giue it, you shall easily obserue by the kind Acceptance, that it is the Masters Expectation too. But not in that sence, which I ouerstreignedly charge them with by too precize Enforcing the signification of the word from its first original, rather then from their intentions, which with common vse ought to be the Interpreter of Language.

I know well enough what faire Colours [excuses] they sett, what fitting abatements in the weights & scales, where with it is to be tryed, what necessary Allowances to the thing it self, they vrge, yet will not at all serue to make it passe for other then False & Trayterous Coyne minted by the late most Excellent Masters of Atheisme, & therefore no way currant amongst them, that professe the knowledge & Feare of God, Who with you & mee are forward I see to spitt at the tender of Honour & Seruice in such execrable Phrazes. ⟨160⟩ But alas it's not the word but the Action, Not the outward expression of the Mouth, but the inward Disposition of the heart, that the maine Danger lieth wrapped vp in.

What bootes it to abhorre as impious the plaine & open receite of that, which wee secretly canvas for as truly Excellent. Let none in so perilous a matter as this is desperately abvse himself with the Conceit of his own sinceritie, or with the Confidence of others Goodnes, that are his Examples: It's the very Throne of God itself, that this Affection aspireth vnto, by what euer turnings & windings it serues to creep along.

Of all those Forbidden Delicacies which God hath sett apart for himself, There is none, that he more choysely prizeth then that of Honour. Of all kinds of Honour he hath professed greatest Iealousie touching this, whereof wee seeme most Ambitious.

To make mans weaknes the foyle of our Glory; That our Power, our Wealth, our Excellencie, our Absolutenes may more fairely sett it self off by the remonstrance of others Inabilitie, Need, Basenes, & Dependancie is the Life & soul of that state & Pompe, which is Aimed at in the ⟨161⟩ maintenance of Large & Noble Retinues, & in the Loue of Honourable seruice & Attendance. Which desires & Practizes, howeuer in Princes & Magistrates they be allowable by reason of that Communication of Gods own Soueraigne right & Power, which he hath invested them with, yet are they no-waies tolerable in men of Private Condition. Who hauing nothing but their own in them cannot without highest sacriledge exact that Tribute, which is only due to God.

THAT MEN SHOULD SERUE TO HIS GLORIE

was that End, that God at first created Adam for, & to which the Continued Propagation of his seed is & euer shalbe directed in the Almighties intention. And how then must hee needs resent the Presumption of them that in so Reserued a Portion [restricted a position] will be forceable Partners & Sharers with him. As for those Publick Persons, who with the imprinted Character of the Diuine Power haue receiued a Participation of the very Name of God, It is not to be denyed but that with the grant of the Principal there's a Deriuation of all the Collateral Excellencies likewise. And that they who by God's appointment serue in his stead to men may, for the promotion of his Glorie in the ⟨162⟩ free Exercize of their Authoritie to Good, make vse of this Soueraigne Priuiledge it self. And so those Royal Provisions of Solomon & others in this kind recorded in the Scriptures are Lawfull warrants for supreme Princes & all that are in Commission vnder them proportionably to sett forth Maiestie & State by the multitude & Magnificence of all kinds of Attendants, On [through] their Ministers subiected Humilitie rearing vp the Prospect of their own Eminencie, Not of their Persons but of their Dignitie. In so narrow Bounds euen to them is this Priuiledge limited That the Exercize thereof may not passe the verge of their office without danger of a Praemuniri.

Witnesse Nabuchadnezzar,[1] who vpon the Appropriation of it to the Honour of his own Person made a Forfeiture of his Manhood not only of his Principalitie, being driuen out as a Monster amongst the Beasts of the Feild. The manner of the chastizement answering the Nature of the Crime. A Brutish ignorance & Mistake at the best of this Prerogatiue, Like Aesops Asse[2] interpreting the Prostrate Worship of the People, that was offered to the Golden Image on his back intended to his Beastliness. Which as amongst the Barbarians of all Ages aswell as now without exception, wee shall perceiue to work with all Excesse & Opennes. So amongst all ⟨163⟩ Ciuill Nations there hath euer been a great Restraint in the vse thereof, And where euen True wisedome & worth mett with Royal Dignitie in one mans Person, wee shall I dare say euidently discouer so spare & sober a Proceeding in this matter as wee may truly conclude It was not out of choise but Necessitie, For the maintenance of Due Reuerence to their Crownes not for the Arrogation of Excellencie to their owne Persons whateuer they haue in this kind either required or accepted.

No verily. The Depressing of Mens Souls & Bodies in the exacting of Pompous Seruice & Attendants to themselues is a unerring symptome of a Base & Degenerate mind, that hauing lost the Comforts of its own Excellencie seeks to regaine it in that vilification of Others.

It's impossible that he should know the Noblenes of Mans Nature in himself, that contemnes it in another.

Hee that truly valueth the vnparalleld worth of his own soul and body is alwaies so equal an Apprizer of the selfsame in others, That he rather inferres the Humilitie, then the Exaltation of his own Condition from the Advancement of his owne Honour &

---

[1] Daniel iv, 30–3.
[2] Aesops Asse—see the fable of 'The Jackass in Office', number 182 in *Aesopica*, Vol. I, edited by Ben Edwin Perry (Urbana, Ill., 1952).

Glory vpon other mens weaknes & Disgrace, whilest in the wretched Deiection of the selfsame Common Nature he reads the Frailnes & ⟨164⟩ Pouerty of all mortal men, Not only in all outward Respects, but euen of those things, which are most essential & wherein the eminency of our worth doth consist.

And perceiuing that in the Depredation of that ioynt Capital of Freedome & Lordship, which God hath bestowed on mankind there grows a Treble Dammage to him in the maine, he doth wisely forbeare the Acceptation of all Gaine & Advantage, that may seeme thus to accrue to him by the vnderhand Trade of his own proper stock. Thus doth the truly Generous & with Provident Forecast [foresight] to maintaine without infringement the Royall Prerogatiue of his own Natural Condition, To be Imployed only to Gods Honour & Glorie, Allows not though to himself the Tender of any others seruice in this kind & to this End further then must necessarily be required & may rightly be transferred to that expresse Representation of Gods Diuine Nature, which is euery way conspicuous in Royal Dignities & in all the Lawfull Deriuations from them.

An instance of this you haue (& one will suffice for all) in the Demeanour of this Incomparable Prince, a Perfect Epitome of the Vertues aswell as of the Happines of all other Princely minded men. ⟨165⟩

Who with the resignation of his Soueraigne rights & Power disrobes himself not only of the Ensignes belonging to Maiestie, but of all manner of Abilements [regalia] & furniture deuised for the setting forth of State & Greatnes. And riding now in this simple Equipage, that you haue heard, assoone as he comes to his settled Abode, casheeres Two Thirds of this small Retinue & liues Attended only by Foure Seruitours, whom Mighty Kings & Princes did formerly Esteeme a Grace to waite vpon. The Thought of this Spectacle brings the Graue Florentine[1] to a stand, & he closeth it vp with the seal of wonderment.

---

[1] Graue Florentine—see Introduction, p. xlvii.

Howeuer old the World is, yet this (sayth hee) was altogether New. To see this Person, who was wont to bee Excessiue Great & so surpassing Pompous, waited on with such Ambition & Accompanied with so many Armes, liue now in the Fashion of a Priuate man with a few Household servants & without any signes at all of Greatnes.

These are his words, And thus he Leaues it with Admiration, which wee must take vp for Example & Direction. Being a cleare & Perfect Determination of this weighty matter, which so solici-tously exerciseth the thoughts of all Noble ⟨166⟩ Personages & Brauer Spirits.

Would you know the Partition that God hath Bounded his owne Demeanes [desmesnes] with from that, which he passed ouer in any kind of occupancy to Men? Why thus 'tis marked out by Charles his Treading.

The Seruice that tends to Benefitt may be lawfully taken by men from their Fellows. But that which is directed to Glory is the reserued Portion of God himself.

All the Subiection of Mankind to their Brethren is only for the ministration of help not for the manifestation of Honour.

There's an allowance of Servants for euery Need.

There's no allowance at all for Ostentation.

Hee breaks into the Imperial Pale of the Creatorship itself that seekes worship & creditt (to vse the lightest termes) in & by mans Seruice & Attendance.

Thou madest him little Lower then the Angels, is the comon & equal immunity of all the sons of Adam. Which not with standing there's no disparagement in the mutual seruice Each of other, So it be but to supply of Need, or Assistance, & Help. To this Intent the Angels themselues disdaine not to tarry all the day long round about vs. Are they not all ministring ⟨167⟩ spirits sent forth to minister for them that shalbe Heires of Saluation? But when Seruice & Subiection passeth from the manifestation & Releif of Weaknes to the setting forth of Honour & Exaltation, The very

Highest of those Heauenly Orders are afrayd of the Tender not only of the Acceptation thereof from men.

See thou doe it not (sayth the Angel to John, when hee fell at his feet to worship him) for I am thy Fellow seruant.[1] What euer the mistake or Errour of this Blessed Apostle may bee thought to be touching the Person or the Action itself it no way Infringeth the Absolutenes & Vniversalitie of that Caution, which the Angels Answere doth necessarily inferre. That amongst Fellow seruants there's no Arrogation of Honour by seruice without highest note of Sacriledge against the Great & Common Master. Let the Great Ones of this world & especially those of our weaker sex, that hold themselues such, take good advise touching this point. And where they cannot plead a higher Communication of the Diuine Rights & Power in their superioritie ouer their Brethren then this mighty Angel (for such a one he was), how will they be able to make good those Pompous traines of seruants ordained only to the shew of their Magnificence & the exacting of their seruice in the self-same kind & manner, that the Angel durst ⟨168⟩ not presume to receiue it in. As for Nobilitie of Bloud or Abundance of Riches, be they neuer so Illustrious & Large & the Patents of them neuer so amply drawn to all manner of full Enioyment & free vse, yet is there no iust claime by vertue of them to be made to the exercize of this Royaltie without an euident proof of the concurrent Participation of the Diuine Power & Authoritie together with them.

It's a Soueraigne Prerogatiue & neuer granted to any vnder other words then these expresse termes. I haue sayd you are Gods. Hee that dare not accept this Title in its right sence, let him be afrayd with Charles to deck his head with any of these Flowers reserued for the Imperial Crowne of God himself. Whose Bloud is their [there] of so orient Nobilitie, that layd by Charles his, lookes not of a deadish hew, & falls more short in beauteous lustre then the Liuelesse stammell [coarse] cloth of the Richest scarlett.

---

[1] Revelation xix, 10.

And though wealth doe crown it with excesse yet shall they not thereby advance the Glosse of their Gentilitie to any proportionablenes of Comparison in this matter.

What Incomes are so large that may safely warrant the maintenance of state & Pompe, which Charles on the yearely reuenue of Thirty Thousand pounds (for so much he reserued) durst not keep? ⟨169⟩

As for all other Respects of Forepast Dignities, The worlds present Censures, & Freinds & Childrens future honour, who can by vertue of any of these without his own Blushing & others Laughter make pretence to more then Charles might Who Leauing on the Throne of Maiestie all the ornaments of Excellencie & Greatnes comes downe into his priuate fortune with no more nor Greater Attendance then was requisite for the supply of Necessitie; & thereby & in the curious Restraint of all Appearance of Greatnes hath sett an euerlasting Brand mark of Presumptuous Arrogancy vpon the vsurpers of it in any kind without the Euidence of Publick Authoritie, to which & not themselues the vse & Acceptation thereof must be by them referred.

Greatnes is the proper Attribute of God & proportioned out to men by no other measure then that Authoritie & Rule, which he giues them ouer their Brethren.

There's an Equal Ordination of Mankind to serue to Gods Glory onely & not to one another.

There's no Possibilitie of Liuing our selues to God's honour & making our Fellow servants liue to ours:

Is that which Charles his Lowly affections & Demeanour by ⟨170⟩ so narrow Contraction of his Retinue, and the vtter Exclusion of all State intends to teach us; In nothing that you haue yet heard soe great, as in this contemptuous ouerthrow of Worldly Greatness, Which Goliah like having with insolent Ostentation of its huge Vastness, & Power by the sworne Association of all manner of States and Conditions for the defence thereof, put to shamefull Retreat and Silence the Tongues of the Stoutest, who are sett to combatt Sin & Folly; God makes it fall, since words are soe feeble, by the hands of a Mighty Champion. Lett who soe dares build up again this razed Castle and reare up aloft a Landmarke for the Port of Felicity, which Charles hath cast downe as a Vaine Imagination, and only high in that it exalts it Selfe against the knowledge of God. But lett him be sure the laying of the Foundation, will in the loss of his Vnderstanding cost him the Eldest Borne; And the setting vp of the Gates bring Religion to the Graue, The Younger but farr more Noble Offspring of his Soule; He must forgett both himselfe and God, before he may take Greatness to his owne Person, or Exact Glory by others Seruice. This is the proper Inference, Which Charles by his Example intended to giue the World.

The Deliuery of this Last Passage with more then Vsual Vehemency both in Speech & Gesture, hauing drawne the Eys of the whole Company to a Stedfast obseruation of the Cheifs Countenance, as soone as vpon her Stay she perceiued what in the Currant of her Discourse she did not, turning her Face aside as if she craued Shelter from the lookes, and thoughts of the Beholders, The PATIENT bending the Selfe same way, as if she meant to receiue her into her Bosome, in the meeting of their Faces ioyning her mouth to the ⟨171⟩ Cheifes, Giue me Leave (saith she) to kiss those Lipps, which haue beene the happy Instrument of so great a Cure as Gods Grace hath begun, & I hope shall perfect in my Soule, by the true Discouery of this Counterfett Excellency; If the persuit thereof in greatest hight, & highest Ranke be but Sinfull Folly; What can the affected Offalls & Scrapps thereof in Lower Fortunes testify but shamefull Madness. What a Balme would this proue to all Sorts of Men, both in their Estates and mynds if rightly applyed. How would plenty, how would Peace run ouer there, where For the most part there is nothing but Complaynt of Pennury to be heard, and Sighs of Perplexity, and all for the iealous preseruation of this accursed Greatnes. The Maintenance of State & Honour in noble, of Creditt and Reputation in lower Conditions, is that which keeps the largest Meanes always at an Ebb, and the merriest Hearts on a continuall Rack, through Cares, through Feares, through Envy and a thousand otherlike tormenting Passions.

The great and reall Calamitys of this Lyfe, Deepe Poverty, & Distress, like the wild beasts by Gods tender Goodness, confined to the woods, and appoynted to range only in the dark, doe seldome fall vpon any that doe not wilfully run in vpon them. Their Names indeed not only their approaches are very frightfull, but few in Comparison are supprised by them, and their feare and danger hath its recourse to most mens Fancys but vpon certayne sollemn Tymes and Occasions. But those other Cares and desires touching Reputation, like flys and lesser Vermin in Fennish Countrys and sluttish houses, keepe mens mynds and bodys in a restless Vexation, euer buzzing in their Eares, euer biting on their Flesh & ⟨172⟩ gnawing their Estates, at home & abroad, in Bed & at Board, in our pleasures & in our businesses, they put vs to a restlesse shrugging, a Continuall Fencing, & an endlesse watchfull Carking [fretfulness] all the Day, I [aye], & greatest part of the Night too.

Let's take all the Necessities of this life one by one, & of all the paines & sorrow, that wee endure for the supply of them, wee shall know at least nine parts of ten to arise meerely from the sollicitousnesse of answearing others expectation, & our owne Ambition, touching the appearance [of] Greatnesse.

That, which Nature in euery kinde requires, is but a little & very easilie Compassed; But the superfluities belonging to Reputation are in number infinite, & full of intolerable difficulties, in the procuring, in the Enioyment, I [aye], & in the Dismission of them too.

It's not that, which is for warmth or Comelinesse, that wrackes our Mindes in the providing of apparrell; But that, which is for fashionableness & conformitie with the Best & highest. It's not that, which is for hunger, no; for Daintines neither that wasteth vs in our Diet; but that, which is for report of a ⟨173⟩ good table, for the fame of great Housekeeping. It's not that, which is for Convenience, no, nor for ornament neither, that setts vs so vncessantly at work in the building & Furniture of our Houses; But that, which is for the ostentation of state & Magnificence.

It's not that, which is for ease nor for vse neither, that consumes vs in the keeping of many officers & large retinues; but that, which is for Honour & Worship.

It's not that which is to Damage or trouble; but that, which is to shame & disgrace, that so impatiently offends vs either in their want, or in the ill-Attendance of our Servants.

Could wee bee but once content to bee thought by others, such as wee are indeede; there's very few, that might not finde Content enough touching Worldly matters in themselues, & in that they enioy. That, which ouerthrowes all & keepes vs in perpetuall distemper both of our mindes & Affaires, is the affectation of seeming more & greater then in truth wee are; Better then our Brethren in the flesh, then our fellow servants in the Lord.

And this, both by Invincible arguments & vncontrolled [indisputable] Examples you haue made, faire Cheife, appeare to bee ⟨174⟩ euery way Incompatible, either with true Reason or sound Religion.

In Gods Name then before you all I bid adue foreuer to those foolish desires of my misguided Affections, to those fond [silly] opinions of my erring Vnderstanding, which haue so long detained my soule in chaines in the Loue & Admiration of these glorious sinfull Vanities.

Henceforth by Gods Assistance my Cares, my desires, my endeauours shalbe more seriously bent to the dispising, then formerly they were to the longing pursuite of these seeming Excellencies. What euer offer it selfe with pretence of Adding Greatnes to my Condition, either in Apparrell, Diet, Dwelling, or Attendance shall find churlish refusall at my hands, as a deceitfull enemie of my peace, howeuer it put on the glozing vizor of

Freindship. As for others misprision, its but a Childish Bugbeare; & shall not make me start, I hope, howeuer frightfull it come dressed. What Neighbours talke, or the World censureth, If I striue not to make the best shew, shall no more trouble mee then, the Bo-ohs wherewith Nurses terrifie their little ones. ⟨175⟩

It's a shame indeede to beare a high mind in a meane fortune, & a true signe of a base spirit to subiect it selfe to others folly.

Henceforth my study shalbe to know what Wisedome & Good Conscience direct vnto, & my Practize, God willing, to follow it. As for others Approbation, that Men should speake good of mee for doeing well to my selfe, Ile not buy at the prize, either of the smallest Cost, or the lightest Care. In a word, it shalbe my Constant Labour, as it is my hearty desire, to make my loue & studie of aequalitie to passe the greatnes of my former wishes in advancing others in these things & this way.

Ah Dearest Patient (sayd the CHEIFE embracing her) how doth my soule more strictly enfold you, then myne Armes; & trebly returnes, not those kisses, which you gaue my lips for words; But that high prized loue & Honour, which your Noble Resolutions deserue. You haue serued up the Ripe Fruit, whereof I presented but the Buds & Flowers.

Part X

The Moderator promises to follow the Chief's good advice and fervently hopes that her daughter the Submisse (Joyce Collett) will be led to the same contempt for worldly ostentation. The Guardian feebly, perhaps insincerely, tries to defend the Submisse's humility by pointing out that she refuses to wear a habit, that she prefers mean company, and that she desires to become an attendant upon others. The Moderator charges her daughter with baseness of spirit in wishing to wait upon a great lady and challenges the Guardian's defence by asserting that the Submisse is moved only by worldly ambition. The Guardian admits his error in this respect and also in interpreting her preference for the company of servants and other inferiors and her dislike for monastic attire.

The Moderator proceeds to prove the baseness of service by the well born upon the nobility; and although the Resolved confesses himself puzzled at times and demands clarification of how servitude can be a token of ambition, her impassioned arguments about the equality of men convince him. The Cheerfull and the Affectionate urge the further discussion of the problem presented by the Submisse, much to the Guardian's annoyance. The Resolved warns of the danger and almost certain futility of trying to correct others, and the Guardian seems ready to drop the matter as not pertinent to 'the subject we are now upon'.

The discussion continues, however, and it is agreed that giving unnecessary service to others is as degrading as accepting it. The Guardian proposes that they investigate the subject in a platonic discourse in which, led by the Moderator, all take part. The group finds that accepting the position of attendant is unbefitting a Christian and an intelligent person since it fails to obtain the ends desired. An enquiry is made to discover a common name for this profession which includes both men and women, children and adults, serving men and gentlemen. The Moderator and Guardian conclude that all such fall under the general heading of servants and that gentility, for which liberty is essential, is not to be attained by any kind of servant. A gentleman-servant is a contradiction in terms and equivalent to a monster in nature. The dialogue ends abruptly as the Guardian and the Moderator seek to discover why all attendants are not essentially servants.

You haue both of you (sayd the MODERATOR) in this passage whereof much to reioice; & taught vs the spare of much sorrow wherewith our liues haue beene hitherto encumbered, ⟨176⟩ If wee shall well take out [follow] that good Counsell & example which you haue worthily giuen in this matter.

I shall endeauour it for myselfe, & blesse God, that in cheer-fullnes of all your faces I read as full & certaine a promise of the like intentions, as my words binde mee vnto.

But if the free & open profession of the Submisse[1] might testifie her faithfull assent to the truth of what wee are all agreed on, It would crowne this Daies Content, mee with a double wreath of happines, In the euidencie of Gods Grace directing your hearts to the search of wisedome & virtue, & in the assured hope that shee would henceforth begin to follow in the same path of humilitie.

Alas, then, (sayd the RESOLUED) I perceiue this Louely Name is not imposed on our Submisse for desert; but Instruction to teach her, what shee ought to bee, rather then to tell others what shee is.

Its not in this respect (sayd the MODERATOR) that she is lesse then others. There's none here perhaps answeares to their Names, as an expression of their Natures, or Conditions; but as a testi-monie of their desires & endeavours, that they would faine bee such as they are called. ⟨177⟩ But that, which troubles mee in the Submisse, is, that shee hath neither loue nor intentions conform-able to her title. I read in her countenance the Challenge both of vnkindenes & revenge for so publique an imputation in a matter wherein she thinketh herselfe perhaps most free.

But indeed (sayd the GUARDIAN) I should haue thought them quite mistaken had any other spake then yourselfe. Why? doe not both her words & deeds in the refusall of that habite, which her sisters weare, as too high; In the Choyse of meanest Companie, as

---

[1] Submisse—Judith Collett, one of the younger daughters of John and Susanna Ferrar Collett. The efforts to dissuade her from seeking service seem to have been successful; she later married the Rev. Solomon Mapletoft. See Maycock, p. 177n.

more sutable to her lowely disposition; & most of all in her desire
of becoming an Attendant to others, manifest an abiect minde
rather then an Ambitious.

Ah (sayd the MODERATOR deeply sighing) You haue touched
the very quicke, both of my greife & her sore: for so it is parted
betweene vs; she hath the infirmitie & feeles it not. I haue the
sorrow & cannot helpe it because the ground thereof lieth in her
disease.

I perceiue (sayd the GUARDIAN) that your Daughters inclination to liue abroad, as shee termes it, is that, which afflicts you.
But why should it doe so, I conceiue not, especially in so good
a fashion, as proposeth it not as a common servant ⟨178⟩ nor to
any of meane Ranke, but as a Gentlewoman vpon some person
of Honour.

Why doth it not imply (sayd the MODERATOR) a great basenes,
both of spirits & fortune, to descend to the choise of such a
Condition.

Oh (sayd the GUARDIAN smilingly) Its happy none but freinds
heare you, That knowing your mind by the experience of an
humble & moderate deportement in your Actions, know there
can bee no ill meaning, howeuer vnreasonable your words
sounde. Dare you, My Good Sister, professe the dislike of that as
too vile for one of Yours, which thousands of Parents, that euery
way twenty times exceed your worth in all outward respects, doe
sollicitously endeauour to obtaine for their Children. An Honourable Ladies service is the best match, that a Midling Gentleman can
make for his Daughter, next to a Good Husband, & perhaps the
fairest way of procuring that too.

Your erring aspersions will not reache to the disgrace of this
Course, so full of worship & Credit in all Mens Accompts, that
none can aspire therevnto without euidence of higher conceits of
themselues & pretence of better deserts then ordinarie. And how
then can it any way be suspect of Basenes? ⟨179⟩

Your well pleading (sayd the RESOLUED) hath put new life

into the Submisse, & her face testifieth, that the cause it selfe, & the Advocate haue her heart more then euer.

Why, if the persute of this Condition belongs not but to those of better spirits, & bee such a faire way to preferment as the Guardian makes it, You trouble both your selfe & your Daughter very vnadvisedly in the resistance of her desires thereaboutes.

But then (sayd the MODERATOR heavily smiling) Her choise of this estate, proceeding, as You both will haue it, from opinion of Worth, nourished with conceit of Honour, & tending to advancement, rather confirmes my Charge of an ouerhigh, then your hopes of a lowly mind in the Submisse.

Indeed (sayd the GUARDIAN) you haue handsomely brought mee to the Deniall of what I began to differ with you about at first. Its no necessarie proofe of more humble Affections in our Submisse, but rather of the Contrarie, whilst shee may, nay I see, can scarce be led to the desire of this Chaunge, but out of Ambitious fancies & hopes to better her estate in those things, wherein shee accounts Respect & Honour perhaps cheifely to lie, Fine cloathes, ⟨180⟩ Braue Company, Iolly conversation, & the like appurtenances & imployments of this kind of life. The conceited delights whereof make her loathe, I feare, the sobriety of that tyre, which her Sisters weare; howeuer it may bee she deceiue herself in the thought, not onely vs in the allegation, That a vayle is too stately a Couer for her head; which being full of Changeable phancies can no waies brooke so solemne a Dresse, & sitting so fast to her head, as it may not bee layd aside here amongst vs, but vpon alteration of that condition of the Wearers, either to a married or, which God forbid, to a meaner Estate.

As for familiaritie with servaunts, I like it in children, when it is suted with [accompanied by] respectiue freedome amongst their aequalls, & Loue of their Betters conversation, when it is allowed them.

But if affectation of preeminence in Company encline them to leaue the better for the worse, or if the liberty of vaine discourses keepe them more delighted amongst Inferiours, it's a signe of an ill tempered minde, either to Vertue or Wisedome.

How it fares with the Submisse Ile leaue to her owne ⟨181⟩ examination with this Addition onely,

If insolencie of behauiour to them, that are aboue in their worth, bee found in any of those, that prize themselues for lowly minded by reason of their gladsome conversation with those of lower Ranke, its a sure argument of incorrigible sottish Pride.

Hee, that stoupes out of true Humilitie to receiue into his Bosome that, which is beneath him, can neuer exalt himself against that, which is aequall. He, that in the willfull choise of a meaner degree in any kind beares himselfe lofty against his betters, doth carry printed in his forehead the markes of that arrogancie, which he most condemnes in them, & vnanswerably condemnes himself, To haue chose the Reare onely out of false humilitie, that hee might with true pride march in the head of a meaner troupe. Thus haue you not onely my recantation for what I sayd amisse, but the best amends, that I can make by declaration of the weakenes of those arguments, wherewith being deceiued my selfe, I went about to deceiue you. Wherein to haue rectified both mine owne & your vnderstanding is I assure you of so much comfort, as I feele not ⟨182⟩ at all the Batterie of that shame, wherevnto this suddaine retraction iustly seemes to haue exposed mee in the necessarie inferences of rashnes, ignorance, or vnconstancy.

These are men's imperfections (sayd the RESOLUED) that draw blood indeed, but are instantly healed without scarre by the vertue of that remedy, which you haue happily applied, & now stand fairer in your reputation touching your Loue of truth, & abilitie to discerne it, then you did before. The cheerfull redeeming of a mans Errors by ingenuous Confession being the best proofe, that can be giuen both of a good heart & of a sound head. Hee must needs loue & know truth well, thats ready to buy it at the price of his best Credit; & needs feare no shame for his weaknes, thats supported by the worth of such a disposition. The imitation whereof wee shall as aequally applaude, as wee doe expect from our iudicious Moderator.

From mee sayd SHEE halfe starting.

Howeuer strange you make it, I am sure (sayd the RESOLUED) your owne Iudgement testifieth it will bee necessarie to call back those Passionate disgraces, wherewith through the sides of feble waiting women you haue ⟨183⟩ contemptuously affronted the whole order of free & Gentlemen Attendants,[1] which compriseth a farre Greater Number, as I suppose, of well borne & well educated Persons of both sexes, then any other Profession whatsoeuer. Who making refuge hither cheifly to prevent disgrace & scorne, which through handy [manual] Labour or meaner Imployments they should incurre, must needs resent with sharpest indignation your iniurious tax of Basenes, though it seeme but glancingly performed.

Why the repaire of this errour (sayd the MODERATOR) is that, which keeps my thoughts buissied, to make vp by plaine affirmation, what I formerly passed but by way of question, touching this course of life; In the Intimation of degenerate Baseness in all the pretendants therevnto, adding the proofe of most Abiect Vilenes in the condition it selfe.

You take the errour & purpose the amends (sayd the RESOLUED) in a quite contrarie way, then I had hoped.

Instead of righting them in their owne Persons, ouerthrowing them in all the comforts of their liues, doubling the wounde, that you gaue in the imputation of meanenes of spirit ⟨184⟩ by the surcharge of folly in their vnderstandings. For it is an Infallible consequence of your proposition, that they must bee straungely defectiue in point of wisedome, that take Sanctuarie here to saue Credit, where there is such a Magazyne of shame & Infamie, as you would perswade.

---

[1] In reference to this conversation it is interesting to recall that Nicholas Ferrar (the Visitor) began his five years of Continental travel as a gentleman-in-waiting to the Princess Elizabeth on her wedding trip after her marriage to Elector Frederick V, Count Palatine of the Rhine.

Your collections [inferences] are true & Answearable to my intentions (replied SHEE). I say it in plaine termes & seriously; whether men or women, they are the poorest both in vnderstanding & spirit, the weakest minded & the basest hearted of all others, that hire themselues forth to waite for honour, & not to worke for service, for attendance on their Masters Persons to Advancement of Glorie, & not for performance of business to profit or Necessity.

The Contradiction of your discourses (sayd the RESOLUED) intangle my thoughts, as in a Laberinth; & though, mee thinkes, now & then I see light, yet it proues but like those foolish fires, that lead wandering passengers into further errours. The resemblance of what you now say to the Cheifes discourse makes me ready to accept it for a truth: But the euidency of opposition, that it beares to what by your enforcement the Guardian last deliuered, makes me suspect it for a Paradoxe. ⟨185⟩ For how shall the Submisse or any other bee charged with Pride for the affectation of that, which is so contemptible? Is not honour the marke, that a high minde shootes at? & Excellencie the prize, that Ambition reacheth after? Either let your Inditement fall as wrong Layd, or put the full value, that the law requires, to those things. To arraigne men of swelling desires in the prosecution of Base Designes is as Incongruous & Impossible, as to lay Petty Lassinie [larceny] to a Riche Mans charge.

The Mountaine hath at last brought forth a mouse (Replied the MODERATOR) Its not for yourself, I am sure, you thus dally in picking vp straws; you see others weakenes, & therefore will haue the way cleare without any colour of rubbe [trace of difficulty].

If pride thrust Men to this Course, it cannot bee base. If the course be base, it cannot bee Pride, that should induce them to the persute thereof. True, if it appeares so to them. But as the faire Guilding makes many a Couetous Wretch take a peece of Brasse in payment for a good Commoditie, & yet it would bee but a foolish argument to say, that such a one were a kinde hearted ⟨186⟩

Man, because hee gaue away his goods for nothing, seeing hee ment to bee payd to the full: so verily it's a weake proofe of humilitie to euince the thing meane & vile, which a Proud Man follows with conceit & opinion of Excellencie. His false Apprehension, though it alter not the Nature of the thing, yet truely inferres the ambition of his desires.

Its sufficient to pride, that there bee but an Appearance of Honour; that there bee by common esteeme matter of vaineglorious conceit in himselfe, & of applause from others is All, that an Ambitious man requires. Whether there bee truth & substance hee regards not, hauing his eie fixed not vpon the worth of the thing it selfe, but onely vpon the eminency of his owne Person in the boasting ostentation of what hee enioys more then ordinarie. Its no contradiction therefore to lay Pride to their charge, who follow or aime at this profession, howeuer Vile & Base it bee indeed, as long as in shew it appeares to them otherwise. It is the opinion, it is the appearance, it is the delight of Advancement aboue others, that draws them at First, and ⟨187⟩ maintaines them in the constant prosecution of this Course of Life.

There's no Doubte at all therefore to bee made, what the roote is, whence this fruit springs; nor any kind of slaunder to bee fixed in ioynt Censure of this whole generation, as Vainglorious Creatures full of ouerweening Conceits in themselues, & fondly ambitious of esteeme from others.

There's not a worse kinde of stone to bee chosen in all those Quarries of Hell (sayd the RESOLUED) then that, which you perswade vs the foundation of this estate is layd in.

Indeed (replied SHEE) the Groundwork of all those professions, which God calls men vnto, is the promotion of others good in the exercize of our owne abilities.

Loue to our Neighbours & Humilitie in our selues, by being profitably imploied to common benefitt & by painefull diligence kept low in our owne Appraizements, whilest wee see ourselues but fellow labourers with the meanest of Gods household, are those two maine ends, wherevnto in euery calling God cheifly directs vs. But the loue of preeminence is the Deuills condemnation ⟨188⟩ & whateuer Condition of life sets vp to vtter this sorte of ware, must doe it by Pattent from him. For no Vocation of God's ordinance hath any priuiledge of traffic therein. Aequalitie is Man's Vertue. To bee aboue belongs to God. & no Man may take this Honour to himselfe, but hee, that is called God.

By the Draught of the Pedigree (sayd the GUARDIAN) you haue made good that charge of Basenes, which you so resolutely gaue. There's no degree of vilenesse so bad, that you may not iustly fasten vpon that profession, whose descent you can truly carry vp to the Author of Euill.

This Argument alone would suffice to a right disposed Minde (sayd the MODERATOR); but because wee shall bee sure to meet with many Eager Opponents, it will perhaps bee requisite to fall to a more particular survey of this matter. That in the aboundance of reasons wee may bee able to convince errour on all hands, & to cleare the truth, when, either by ignorance, or by malice it shall be empeached in the Contradiction of this Proposition.

Your intent is so good (sayd the GUARDIAN), & the certainty of Profit so great, which the handling of this subiect, like a faire ⟨189⟩ & riche Coast makes ouerture of, that I should gladly giue content [satisfaction] to what you advise. But the longsome Voyage, which wee are bound on, makes mee loth to put into any other Harbour. As for the Submisse, let neither feare nor thought trouble you. The helpe already afforded will suffice by God's Grace to bring her cleare of [off]. Ile vnderwrite the policy of her Insurance. Keepe on then your course whilest tide serue, & winde setts faire.

Were the preiudice of our stay much greater, then any way appeares, yet I see not (sayd the CHEEREFULL) how should wee dare passe on without a warning Peice or two, first shot of [off]. If they, that come after should lay their miscarriage to our negligence, & pretend they would haue kept aloofe, if we had giuen notice of the perill, which in our owne striking wee discouered; Runne wee not great hazard of being found liable by iudgement of the Trinitie house[1] to the Repaire of those Damages, which wee might haue prevented. Diligence in our owne behalfe is good, but Charitie must goe along for others behoofe likewise, if wee deserve to grow riche by these kinds of Adventures.

Nay if wee meane not to loose all as the match is made (sayd ⟨190⟩ the AFFECTIONATE). For the saueing of our owne stake seemes much more doubtfull to me then our Guardian conceiues. Many a man for want of good play looseth the game, that faire Casting had certainly made him Master of.

It is not enough to haue prepared the Remedies, except they be applied. Hast makes Wast, is an Old sayd saw. And proofe of it likely to follow in this matter, if wee leaue it so soone. I shall therefore advise, to make all sure, to stay the administring of this Physicke to the Submisse, Wherevnto her owne disposition of Minde, & many opportunities so well serued at this present, as I doubt wee shall afterwards repent, If wee doe not at this time make vse of them.

If you please (sayd the GUARDIAN with a distastfull smile). Lets sett downe, & see the operation of all things till the cure bee quite wrought. Your Longings on all hands appeare so greate, that the miscarriage of your Patience will follow if you shalbe disappointed in your purposes. In which regard for your content, how euer cleane it seemes besides the subiect, wee are now vpon, I yeelde my self a willing Auditour of what you haue to say.

That will not suffice (sayd the MODERATOR) wee must haue you beare a part, & become an Actour with vs too, as need shalbe. ⟨191⟩

And need wilbe (sayd the RESOLUED), I dare assure you, before this adventure bee finished. It's a strong enchantment, that detaines these erring soules, & such as makes them feircely oppose their owne deliuerance.

---

[1] Trinitie house—a guild or fraternity in charge of lighthouses, buoys, etc.

They are in Loue with their misery & neither feare, nor hate anything more, then the meanes of their Release. Weigh well therefore not onely your strength, but your patience, whether it bee of proofe [strong enough] to beare the mortall Iniuries of them, whose safetie you endeauour with the hazard of your owne.

To suffer for welldoeing (sayd the PATIENT) is so infallible a Condition, as hee must needs haue small experience in the world, that hopes to bring any good busines to effect without his owne Preiudice. Hee must quitt all desires, not onely attempts of vertuous performances, that resolues not to part with his quiet, and Patiently vndergoe the ill will at least of those, whose Good hee cheifly endeauours.

Besides the slaunders & Censures of a Number of buisy Bodies, that haueing sett vp their Rests in the embracement of folly & Errour in their owne Courses, can by no meanes ⟨192⟩ brooke the manifestation of truth & vertue in any kinde. But as euill doers, that loue & need Darkenes for their owne workes, are iealous of any light, though it appeares neuer so remote, so these men, obstinately determined to perseuere in their owne euill waies, are vtter enemies to all others Reformation. Which they runne out feircely to oppose in their neighbours behalfe, onely to keepe aloofe the daunger (for so they esteeme it) from their owne homes. And haueing gotten a faire pretence in anothers quarrell to exercize their Malice, they arraigne, condemne, I [aye], & crucifie truth & vertue, not onely as disturbers of the inward peace of Men's Consciences, but as the stirrers vp of sedition, & Razers of those maine principalls wherevpon the wellfare of Mankind seemes cheifly founded.

This wee must looke to heare.

And provide to answeare (sayd the GUARDIAN) & that in a substantiall manner. As for making all men parties, that shall any way appeare against you in the cause, which our Patient aimes at; though perhaps it may haue much truth on its side, yet it will finde so little ⟨193⟩ beleife amongst indifferent men, as adds no incouragement at all for me to enter that League, which I see you haue all agreed vpon to the ouerthrow of this matter, which in mine eie seemes one of the most Impregnable, that amongst all the seuerall Conditions of Mens Liues you could haue vndertooke.

If you loose your Courage, wee shall quitt your title (sayd the RESOLUED) such faint-heartednes suiteth not with your Name; & is much greater, then the present occasion allows. That leuelling of state & greatnes aequall with the lowest dust, which your Cheifs Batterie hath wrought, hath left this matter like a dismantled Fort open to the Assault.

And easy to the sacke (sayd the CHEEREFULL).

You haue in truth (sayd the RESOLUED) so faire an advantage, as would invite a Coward to the Attempt: & therefore I cannot much blame your eagernes to take the opportunity, whilest it serues. The Garrison is indeed remoued from the defence. But yet there's daunger, & that not a little in the inhabitants obstinacy, rather to continue a Lazie servitude, then to gaine a ⟨194⟩ painefull freedome.

It were too much weakenes (sayd the AFFECTIONATE) for dreade of a little schorcheing [scorching] to neglect the pulling them out of the fire, now wee are come so neere. Wherefore I pray without more adoe, Let's sett about the Busines.

So neere (sayd the GUARDIAN)?

Yes verily (sayd the MODERATOR) The Braunche springs not more naturally from the Stocke, then that, which wee now propose, from the former discourses. For all, that I intend, is nothing els, but to take of [off] these prints of sinne, shame, & folly, which the Cheife hath engrauen vpon the backe, I [aye], & the forehead too of that vnlawfull vsurpation of state & greatnes by men of priuate Ranke & condition in the seeking to gaine honour to themselues by others Attendance on their Persons.

To take them of [off] (sayd the GUARDIAN)?

As men (sayd SHEE) take of [off] these devises & pourtraitures, that are wrought in seales, & print them vpon wax, whereby there's a Multiplication of the selfe same figures in ⟨195⟩ a new subiect yet without any Diminution at all of the first Modell.

At last I perceiue your interest & mine owne former Blindenes, sayd the GUARDIAN. It's very true & right that those three Monstrous figures, which are so liuely cast by our Cheifes hand in the essence & exercize of this kinde of profession, doe much more plainely appeare on the servants part in giuing, then in the Masters Acceptation of such kind of service, that is to & fore honour.

As much more plaine & conspicuous (sayd SHEE) as engravennes[1] doe vpon the outward stampe, then vpon the peice whereon they are inwardly graued.

It were therefore too much wast of time, & too little improuement of your skill, Iudicious Moderator, (sayd the GUARDIAN) to let you spend your paines this way. Euery Bunglers cunning with a little Care serues well enough to cast of [off] the figures according to the print already cutt by the Cheife; I meane those plaine conclusions, which doe necessarilie follow by application of the selfe same Rules to this other matter. Mastership & service are perfect Relatiues & whatsoeuer is proued on one part ⟨196⟩ doth euidently appeare true proportionably on the other. But because our Cheifes discourse seemes to mee either too short & narrow, as fitted to another purpose then what wee are now in hand with, or at least too Curious & subtilly couched for duller eies to take their directions, For the raysing of euery needfull proposition, that were fitt to be instructed of, & for the Resolution of those many doubtes, that will certainely bee obiected against this matter, I shall desire, that wee may proceed after a more easy & more ample manner, being our selues, & hauing to doe, not with Cunning Artists, but with Persons of meaner Capacitie. And besides the difficultie & newnes of the propositions doe exact all manner of helpe, that can be deuised both by orderlines and

---

[1] Engravennes—that which is engraved. The meaning here is that the stamping shows the likeness more clearly than the die.

explanation of all things, as wee goe along. To which intent the treating of them in a continued discourse, which you seeme to intend serues not so fitly in my iudgement.

What's the way then that you direct (sayd the MODERATOR)?

I am not so skilfull my selfe (sayd HEE) to set you on it. But it is the same, which our Cheife led vs in, or rather by which shee led vs out of that great Maze, wherein wee were ⟨197⟩ Intangled at the first vpon the seeming Contradiction of Charles his true want of Happines in the appearent possession of it. That kind of teaching did with such fullnes & facilitie informe my vnder-standing, & perswade it, that I could wish the same method, or that which comes neerest, if the same may not, should bee held in the handling of this subiect wee are entered vpon.

The paines & care, which the Learner makes spare of in this way, which you haue chosen (sayd the RESOLUED) returnes with double travaile on the Instructors head. Whilest therein hee takes on him not onely his owne, but the Burden of him, whom hee teacheth, by skillfull Art endeauouring, as well to induce the ready apprehension, as the right proposall of the matter, with much more difficultie of study perhaps fitting the truth to the Learners capacitie & affections, then he tooke on himselfe to finde or declare it.

The paines is not a litle but the skill much more (sayd the MODERATOR) that belonges to this methode, & more then I am Mistres of. Besides I know not how to goe ⟨198⟩ backe hand-somely the way wee are already so farre entered, & am afraid of loosing much, if wee leaue out any of those many, that offer themselues partners in this search & labour. I see euery bodys mindes full; & therefore cannot thinke, that any two mouthes should suffice for the performance of that, which hath sett so many thoughts on worke.

Vndoubtedly they cannot (sayd the GUARDIAN) & therefore my intendement was onely to reduce the discourse to the manner vsed in the former, not to the same number of speakers. Let euery one that will, nay, let euery one be bound to contribute their part; but let it all be put into one hand as of a Common Steward.

And who shall be the Steward, sayd the RESOLUED?

Who els, but our Moderator the Architect of all this busines, sayd the GUARDIAN.

I will not thanke you, sayd SHEE, for this office on so different Conditions from that, which I desired. But since I know there's no avoyding, Ile settle myselfe for the performance of it, if you will but sett mee in the way where to begin.

Why at the beginning (sayd the GUARDIAN).

You say well, sayd SHEE, for that, which hath beene formerly deliuered ⟨199⟩ like those tumultuarie [hasty, temporary] peices, that are often rayled before large Buildings may serue for matter & substance, but must needs receiue a new framing to make it fitt to our present intendement. Leauing therefore that, which is past, till in due time wee may reassume it for vse, let's make our enterance from the very first & so proceede.

From the egge to the apple, sayd the GUARDIAN.

But is not in all Actions the Consideration what is to bee done the first in order. If wee fall adoing, before we fully vnderstand ourselues, & others meaning, we shall make but bad worke in the end, besides much confusion in the performance. Wee must therefore state the question before wee goe about the proofe. Let euery one therefore orderly declare those seuerall points, which they conceiue necessarie to the making vp that full charge of guilt, which belonges to this Busines. If so be happily vpon the perfect discouery of the hidden euill we may perswade any to come out, or to forbeare entering into this Maze of Errour & Daunger.

Wherein sin & Wickednes seemes to keep court, (sayd the PATIENT) so presumptuously doth it reuell ⟨200⟩ in euery part and exercize of this profession. The first conclusion therefore, which I desire may bee well examined, & I am afrayd will be too easilie & fully proued:

That this profession is not onely in regard of the Licentious

Practizers, with which it is now adaies stained, but essentially vnlawfull in respect of its owne Nature, being contrarie to Gods word & ordinance. And therefore no ways competible with a true Christian Heart.

No nor with a Reasonable soule either (sayd the CHEERFULL) being altogether opposite to the Dignitie of man's nature.

That's the second Position [proposition], which I suppose will be made as plaine as the former.

That hee must needs bee an vnworthy Man, if worthy the name of Man at all, that prostitutes his soule & body to this Vile Exercize.

But the most part of the world now adaies (sayd the AFFEC-TIONATE) measure all things onely by profit. That which is advantagable for gaine either of Riches, Honour, or pleasure ⟨201⟩ shalbe good, holy & iust. Whateuer wee proue touching the Absurditie or sinfullnes of this matter will come to nothing, if wee make it not palpable, That it is contrarie to their owne designes as well as to Gods ordinance & Nature's direction, & this I conceiue the third proposition, & nothing hard at all to bee demonstrated.

That they doe vtterly faile in this Course of the Attainement of that, which they most endeauour after. So that it is most preiudiciall to them in their owne wayes & intentions, & therefore

A foolish hurtfull choise of life as well as a sinfull & vnworthy one.

The Accusation is plaine (sayd the GUARDIAN), if the proofe be as euident, There will not assuredly bee found amongst all the errours & Miseries of Mankind a more pernicious exorbitancy.

Its against Conscience, Its against reason, Its against their owne particular intentions. Why here the hight of all irregularities in all Respects. And the very extract of all vnhappines must needs follow in the losse of God, ⟨202⟩ of themselues, & that, which they most esteeme, though least worth, the losse & disappointment of their owne worldly & sensuall appetites.

But are wee not a little ouershott in the drawing vp of this Inditement, haueing runne out to the declaration of the crime without manifestation of the offender. Ought wee not first to haue specified what that profession is, which wee thus oppose? Our mutuall vnderstanding eache others meaning is no way sufficient to excuse this solecisme in Arte, that requires first the determination of the subiect in its proper bounds, before any further enquirie be made into it. Both the Particular kinde, vnder which it is ranked, & the proper name ought to haue beene first expressed. Els wee shall fight in the Aire. But the fault at present is the lesse, because it is so soone discouered & easy to bee remedied.

Nay rather your skill is the greater, that can so readily vnty this double knott. Tell me therefore first the Name: for that surely is best knowne, & may perhaps lead vs to the discouerie of the Nature it selfe of this profession. It hath perhaps not one but many according to the diversity ⟨203⟩ of the persons, & the seuerall exercizes of the practizes thereof. Those of Lowest degree are called serving Men & waiting Maydes. If they be of higher ranke, they are Gentlemen and Gentlewomen. Those of younger yeares are now adaies Pages. & those of your sex, that were about great Personages, had in old time the Name of Damzells. To which that of women answeareth at present as I suppose.

In respect of their different exercizes & imployment there's a great variation of their Names. Lacquies & Footmen, Vshers, Groomes, & Traynbearers; Yeomen, Squires & many more then I can reckon.

But shall wee say that any of these, or all of them together, are that profession, which we speake of, or rather that they are all of them braunches & members of that profession, Which is another thing, & hath a speciall being of it selfe. And wherin all these seuerall sorts, that differ thus amongst themselues, doe mutually agree.

Vndoubtedly these are not the profession it selfe, but seuerall parts thereof.

But if wee should enquire of that outward Earthly part ⟨204⟩ of Man, which is the instrument of his soule, would you tell me that it had different Names according to the different situation & vse of the seuerall parts thereof? & say that as it beares on the ground it is called Leggs. As it brancheth out from the body, it is called Armes. As it incloseth heat & Life, the Brest & so forth. Or would you not rather in one word answeare mee that the Name thereof was a body, & all these forereckoned members and many other more Parts thereof.

So I ought to answeare.

And in Manuall Trades, if I should enquire of them, that frame their workes by smiting on the Anvill, would you answeare me, that some of them were makers of lockes, others of gunnes, some working in Iron, others on better Mettalls & so forth?

No verrily, but I would say, that they are called Smiths & these seuerall Occupations Members & Branches of that Grand Trade. Wherefore I perceiue, that we must to a new search touching the Name of this Profession for those, which wee haue reckoned vp are, but the Names of the seuerall parts & different sorts thereof. ⟨205⟩

But the name of euery Profession ought to be euident, & if here it be concealed, it must be either, because there is no Name, or perhaps an ill one.

The granting of either of these would be a great preiudice to the Cause.

But a iustification of our former proceedings in omitting the Particular Name, which we could not at all, or at least not easilie finde. But though there be not any one Common Name perhaps to be found, yet there must bee one Common Nature, wherin all these seuerall things agree, els they cannot be things of one but of seuerall kinds.

That must needs be & in the expression of that we shall perhaps find the Name, that we seeke after, at least we shall attaine a good knowledge thereof: like as when we heare, that such a thing is an herbe, we haue presently a certaine generall apprehension of the nature thereof, & are able to inferre many particulars touching the Condition, Properties, and Power thereof. And so it is in Beasts & in all other sorts of things, that are reduced vnder one Common Head.

Then that, which wee seeke after is such a kind of Common Name wherin all these seuerall Practizes meete & are one as the many ⟨206⟩ one, as the many infinite sortes of lesser plants doe vnder the Common Name & Head of Herbs.

G[1] But what need wee seeke that, which is vnder our hands? Are not all these reduced vnder the Common Head of Servants? And their profession appeares plainely to be service.

M Bee it so. But then there can be nothing in any of these Practizes Contradictorie to Seruice.

G No verily, there may be Contrariety betweene themselues, amongst those things, that meete vnder one Common head & so Blacke & White are Contraries, & yet both of them immediately meet in Colour. But therin & therewith they must agree absolutely, otherwise they should not be Colours. And so likewise in this present Case there must be nothing essentially in any of these seuerall professions, that is contrarie to the true Nature & Condition of seruants.

M But is not Gentilitie contrarie to Service?

G Diametrically: for Gentilitie sure, either is, or at least cannot be without the Perfection of Liberty. And service & Liberty in the same person & respects can no more stand together, then Light & Darknes in the same visible obiect. ⟨207⟩

M But did not you in the list of this profession mention Gentlemen & Gentlewomen, as one of the cheife branches therof.

G I did. & so doth all the world besides, not meaning onely, that diuers of Gentle & noble Birth doe take vpon them this Profession, But that there is Certaine Degree of this Profession

---

[1] The letters 'G' and 'M' are used here for the first time in the manuscript to identify the Guardian and Moderator respectively.

wherevnto whosoeuer attaines doth therby become Gentle, though he were not so before. And the profession it selfe is euer Called & accepted for a Gentlemanlike Estate.

M Shall we say then, as they are Gentlemen, they pertake of freedome; but as they are bound to service, they are servants. And yet it is but one & the selfe same Condition of Gentlemen Servants.

G That verily is the proper Name, whereby they are knowne.

M But is there any such Example in the Generations or Productions of Nature, That any one thing is compounded of two Contrarie Common Natures, both of them remaining intire in the selfe same subiect.

G If it happens at any time, we call that thing a Monster. As when the humane & Brutish Natures meete together, ⟨208⟩ Whether the body be Manlike, & the soule onely sensitiue, or the soule bee reasonable, if it be put in the body of a beast, we call that Composition (& so it is indeed) a Monster. And the same Name & Censure must wee giue of euery other like Composition & Mixture of Contrarie Essences.

M Then we must say that either the Condition & Estate of Gentlemen-Servants is not a Naturall, but a Monstrous Profession; or els we must put out one of the two, & leaue them either absolute servants, or none at all.

G It cannot be denied but that this addition of Gentry is a mere Chimaera of the Braine. And howeuer by mistake of simple Vnderstandings & by the Collusion of the World they are puffed vp with a Conceit of some kind of participation of this Admired Excellencie, yet in very truth it's but like those feasts & Bankets, which the Deuill entertaines Witches & Sorcerers with, of stones or vilest excrements vnder the shew & Appearance of Dainty Cates.

There's no Glimps of the Brightnes of Gentilitie at all in this Profession, but onely a false shew therof, the better to hide the Basenes of their Slauerie, & the Greatnes of their Misery.

If the Beautie of this Profession (sayd the PATIENT) make it Monstrous ⟨209⟩ how will it appeare when the Deformities thereof shalbe produced to light.

Your turne comes shortly (sayd the MODERATOR) & all that wee are now about is but to cleare the place from encumbrances, that you may the more freely exercize your skill in [knowledge of] this miscreated profession. Which being vailed vnder many goodly appearances must needs first be stripped to its Originall Nakednes before it can be fitt for the Anatomizers hand.

Tell me then (sayd SHEE [the MODERATOR] continuing her discourse with the Guardian) since on all hands it is agreed, that this Profession is Seruice & the Practizers thereof are Servants, And that this Adiunct of Gentilitie, howeuer Faine they would haue it, cannot possibly be the prouen difference, whereby it is distinguished from those other degrees & Conditions, which are truely & properly termed Servants. What shall wee say is the reall difference, which doth constitute this Profession, & whereby it becomes an especiall sort & kind of service, & they servants of another Condition & Qualitie, then those, which ordinarilie & generally are accompted Servants.

G The Inward Differences of things are hard to bee perceiued by the eie of the vnderstanding, but much more difficult to bee ⟨210⟩ expressed by words.

M You mean the Internall Natures of them, but not the outward workings of them.

G So I meane indeed, for although to sett forth the inward Principle, wherein the Differences of Beasts from Birds, & of Fishes from them both, doth consist, is extreme difficultie, if at all to be performed by Man's Witts. Yet the outward working of them is most easy & plaine to bee discerned by the diversities of shape, Flesh, Motions, & other the like accidents. All which variety proceeds from the distinct Power & Nature of the Inward difference. Which not being able to apprehend, much lesse to expresse, wee sett forth by the outward effects thereof. And so wee say that

Birds differ from Beasts by feathers, Bills, flying, & other the like Distinct outward Qualities.

And if wee goe this way to worke in this Case, we may happily finde the manner, if not the nature of this Difference, which wee seeke after & be able to say how, & wherin to appearance & outward operation this profession differs from other kinds of service.

M But were it not perhaps best to searche out first wherein it agrees with them. ⟨211⟩

G You say well for that Comparison like matching things together will more euidently sett forth their mutual differences. ⟨212⟩

ON THE AUSTERE LIFE

Part I

At the request of the Cheerfull the Little Academy is called to an unexpected meeting some time between the third and fourth Sundays in Advent 1632. The Cheerfull expresses grave doubts that the great festival of Christmas is appropriately celebrated by special food and over-indulgence. When the Moderator protests mildly, the Cheerfull insists that true joy can be found only in the Lord and never in sensual pleasures. The Mother upholds the Cheerfull in her condemnation of taking food *for* delight as opposed to taking delight *in* food and points out that the motive determines the true goodness of an action. The Moderator agrees that those who would keep a spiritual and godly Christmas would be scorned by the world, but she does not join in a wholehearted acceptance of the Cheerfull's strictures. The Patient and the Mother make spirited attacks on the immorality of contemporary Christmas-keeping, and cite Biblical passages—especially the Propers for Advent and the holy days which follow Christmas—to emphasize the solemn nature of the great Christian festival. The Guardian cites Pico della Mirandola, and the Mother (relying on Foxe's *Book of Martyrs*) expresses her special admiration for Pico because of his contempt for worldly possessions and preferment. The Cheerfull, eager to get to her point, suggests that they cease examining holy examples and begin practising holy ways, and that they preach to the world by their actions rather than to themselves by their words. The Mother admits that they have no precedents to guide them, that there is 'A dearth of patterns in an exuberance of rules'. She is eager, nevertheless, that the Little Academy be persuaded of the beauties of abstinence and be won over to the practice of everlasting temperance.

———◆———

CHEERFULL. Pardon mee If I seeme importunate in occasioning this meeting so much before your expectation. Not onely the earnestnes of mine owne desires, but the Necessitie of the thing it self admitts no longer delay.

MOTHER. You say very true. For except you now giue vs the

better satisfaction wee may no longer forbeare the making of our Christmas provisions.

CHEERFUL. Call them as they bee, I pray, Carnal Excesses & spiritual preiudices, that corrupt the Body, defile the soul, & wast the Estate. All this is included in that good cheare, where-with the world generally solemnizeth this approaching Festiual. Iudge then with what reason it vsurps the Name of Christmas fare & provisions.

MOTHER. I dare not but recant what I sayd amisse. It must needs be some other Deitie; that they intend to honour by this meanes. Sure it cannot be Christ, whose Kingdome is not meat & drink; but Righteousness, & Peace, & Ioy in the Holy Ghost. And he, that in these things serueth Christ is acceptable to God & approued of men too sayth St Paul:[1] But he, that walks in Lasciuiousnes, Lust, Excesse of wine, Reuelling, & banquetting, the common entertainment of this Festival-season works the will of the Gentiles, sayth St Peter[2] ⟨2⟩ & will with them be found guilty of abominable Idolatrie euen to haue made his Belly his God.

AFFECTIONATE. Seeing wee know these things before, wee are bound doubly to beware, that neither the Errours of any example, howeuer authorized, misleads vs from our own stablenes. Nor the violence of any opposition, howeuer intended, cause vs to runne into the same excesse of Riot; Considering, that though it appeare very strange to men & they speak euill of vs, yet it will be much lesse hazard & danger to vndergoe the vttermost of that, which they can say or doe then to goe along with them to the triall of these practizes at that great Assize, which the Gospel, read the former sunday,[3] gaue vs warning of: The Church suited not things well if the worlds custome be right, to make the Remembrance of the Day of iudgement the Vsher to bring in Christmas was done, as if they ment purposely to ouerthrow all that, which commonly makes it to be prized as the best of all other Times.

---

[1] Romans xiv, 17–18.   [2] I Peter iv, 3.
[3] Gospel for the Second Sunday in Advent: Luke xxi, 25–33.

What Dainties can a man rellish; or what sports can he delight in, that hath the sound of that Trumpet in his Eares, Arise & come to iudgement?

PATIENT. Or what wast of Cost dare they make in any kind, though neuer so rich, if they think themselues to be but stewards & know, that it is required in stewards to be faithfull, as the ⟨2v⟩ Epistle read this last Sunday teacheth.[1] It was a very vnmeet consideration to be proposed so neere the Festival, if either Gluttonie or Gaming were to be priuileged therein. That wee spend & play away none but out own Money is the best defense, that I can heare any man make for this Licentiousnes in both these kinds. Now if that hold break, & all, that wee possesse, proue our Masters Estate & not our own, What censure shall wee fall vpon if our Accompts come in with great summes layd out & lost for our own honour, & pleasure, & very little, if any at all for his. Shall wee haue the praise of God, which the Epistle ends with, or rather the Condemnation of Diues,[2] whose sin wee imitate.

GUARDIAN. No man can say these are streightned collections [forced inferences], that heard the Epistle on Advent sunday,[3] the first summons, that our Church giues to this Festival. Let vs walk honestly as in the day time not in eating & drinking[4] so it was read: or if wee take the new translation, in Rioting & drunkenness.[5] It amounts vnto the same and inferres a plain contradiction to that, which the world vseth to doe at this time, especially driuing out the spirit of God & drowning his graces in their souls by these inundations of meat & drink, where with they surcharge their stomachs.

[1] The Epistle for the Third Sunday in Advent: I Corinthians iv, 1–5.
[2] Diues—a rich man; see Luke xvi, 19–31.
[3] The Epistle for Advent Sunday: Romans xiii, 8–14.
[4] Eating & drinking—this is the translation of Romans xiii, 13, in the Great Bible (1539) and the Geneva Bible (1560).
[5] Rioting & drunkenness—this is the equivalent phrase from the Bishop's Bible (1568) which was retained in the King James Version (1611) and in The Book of Common Prayer.

MODERATOR. They, that goe so farre by eating & drinking (And yet, ⟨3⟩ in truth, who doth not almost at Christmas) can by no meanes excuse themselues: But yet in a gladsome Festival a little Addition in Diet & some exchange for that, which is more daintie, seemes sutable to Natural reason[1] warranted by scripture & confirmed by the example of the best. Wee solemnize a benefitt, that tends to the happines not of the soul onely but of the Body also. And therefore it is euery way reason, that the Body should haue that likewise in all kinds ministred vnto it, whereby after its own proper manner it may become Partaker of ioy & gladnes aswell as the spirit. My heart & my Flesh reioyceth, sayth Dauid,[2] vpon this ground & a like occasion.

CHEERFUL. But take with it what follows, It is in the Liuing Lord that both their Mirths & Iubilees are founded & exercised in. My heart & my Flesh reioyceth in the Liuing God. This pretence, that you haue alledged, the Church foresaw & therefore to take away the occasion of abusing it giues in the Epistle of the sunday immediately preceding Christmas[3] a direction, which way the streames of ioy both of soul & body, which fitt the times & our selues, are to be deriued.—Reioice in the Lord alwaies & again I say reioyce.—Wee may eat Flesh & drink wine, that our Flesh may reioyce the more: But our reioycing must ⟨3 v⟩ not bee in the Flesh & in the wine but in the Lord. Wee may so cherrish our Bodies as they may truely beare a part with our spirits in their common ioy: But the ioy itself is to be onely in the Lord. That Mirth, which goes otherwaies is all lost, if not worse. Reioyce in the Lord alwaies, is the Churches Lesson. & her allowance of better cheare on Festival seasons onely so farre as may serue to the increase of this ascending ioy. But when wee bring down our

[1] Natural reason—by this phrase the Moderator seems to mean reason according to the nature of man as Aristotle described it in the *Nicomachean Ethics*. It seems very close to 'right reason', for a discussion of which see above, p. 4 n.

[2] Dauid—Psalm lxxxiv, 2, in the Great Bible, which is the source of the translation used for the Psalms in the Book of Common Prayer.

[3] The Epistle for the Fourth Sunday in Advent: Philippians iv, 4–7.

Reioycing to the meat; & the delight, that was begun in the spirit ends in the Flesh, wee fall so farre short of good Christians, as wee scarcely deserue the Name of Reasonable men. For to eat purposely for delight belongs not but to the Nature of Beasts. And whensoeuer wee stoop so brutishly with our affections wee rank our souls with theirs.

MODERATOR. Doe you exclude all delight from eating?

CHEERFULL. No verily. But I debarre all eating for Delight as vnworthy the Excellencie of mans condition. The difference betweene Temperance & Gluttonie lies not in the sence of the Palate; but in the setting of the heart vpon the meat. The Pleasure, that food brings with it, is no preiudice to holines, as long it passeth not the mouth. But if it sink down into the hart then it turnes to sin. ⟨4⟩ Not the taking of Delight with meat, Not the taking of Meat with delight: but the taking of meat for delight, & the seeking of delight in Meat is that, which defiles the soul & brings vs within the compasse of that Idolatrie, which setts vp the Belly in Gods stead.

MODERATOR. A Nice Distinction to make so great a difference in the present Qualitie of Men & in the future censure of God.

MOTHER. It was a light matter, that two & fourty thousand Ephramites lost their Liues for at the passage of Jordan, Shibboleth & Sibboleth carry so much resemblance,[1] as he, that knows it not before, would be scarce able to find, wherein the Difference lay.

The matter at the Day of iudgement (whereof that dreadfull Execution by Jepthe & the Giliadites was a figure)[2] wilbe carried much alike. The difference seemes so little touching the vse of all outward things betweene the Godly & the sinner, As you can by no meanes beat it into their heads, that there is any at all. But what

---

[1] Jephthah and the Gileadites said Shibboleth, but their enemies the Ephraimites were discovered by pronouncing the word as Sibboleth; see Judges xii, 4–6.

[2] The search for parallels between the Old and New Testaments is as old as the New Testament itself; see also Romans v, 14; Hebrews ix, 9; I Peter iii, 21. In this passage the Mother implies that there is only a minute difference between the godly and the sinful.

they will not now vnderstand they shall one day heauily feel, that a little difference in the intention makes a great one in the Action, & the putting in or leauing out of but a title [tittle], as they esteeme, so alters the case as that shalbe ground of condemnation to one, that shalbe occasion of Reward to another. Let vs not therefore goe hand ouer head & think our selues well because wee are neere the mark. Except wee hitt the ⟨4 v⟩ white, wee shall not attain the prize. If our meaning be not the same with that of Gods Children, the likenes of our outward demeanour touching things of this Life will not be able to beare vs out. He, that desires the office of a Bishop desires a good work, he that desires the preheminencie of a Bishop runs vpon Diotrephes[1] his guilt.

I begin too high lets come to our selues. The putting on of better apparrell seemes to be the same thing in all the commers to church on solemne daies; & yet in very truth, when it is done by one out of the honour that he beareth to the Exercise & to the congregation, & by another for the honour, that he desireth to his own person, it comes to be in these two seuerall persons, as different, as pride & humility can make a thing. The seeking by shew of kindnes to gain the good will of them, who are out of the right way seemes to be the same in all that exercise it. & yet in very truth, when it is done by one to make himself the better thought of, & by another to make him the better, that he makes much of, it hath in these two persons as different an issue, as the promotion of Gods Kingdome & the canvasing for the Deuills. For he, that sheweth Loue & freindship for his own sake to them, that doe amisse, confirmes them in their Errour & makes himself guilty of the same.

GUARDIAN. You may spare your labour in going to other particulars; wee perceiue by what you haue already instanced, that the difference between ⟨5⟩ good & euill lies in a point, which the bleare eies of Flesh & Bloud are as vnfitt to discern as duller eares to iudge between Shibboleth & Sibboleth. But is there no

[1] III John, 9.

other difference I pray of these two words, then that, which is in the sound of the Letters.

MOTHER. The one signifies an Eare of Corn, & the other Chaff or a Burden, as I have beene taught.

AFFECTIONATE. This verily suits right to make this passage a liuely Type[1] of the Day of Iudgement. The whole busines then will lie upon the right pronunciation of this self same word. I meane as touching Hypocrites & false Christians. Euery one pretends to be a freind to the great Jepthe our Lord & Sauiour Jesus Christ. Feasting seemes to releiue the poore, & fine Clothes to sett them awork. Going to Law is for defence of right, & heaping of Riches to doe good. And who dare say they are in the wrong, especially being so cleare in their own consciences, as themselues tell vs. But if you look well you shall find, that it is all but Sibboleth Chaffe & Vanitie, Sin & a Burden, that is included in their hearts & comes forth in their Actions, & they must not look for better speed, than the Ephramites did.

CHEERFUL. It then concerns vs to look well about, that wee perish not by the same mistake. And wee cannot haue a better occasion to ⟨5 v⟩ begin our provident circumspection in this kind, then at present, Indeauouring that both our Cost & our reioycing, which this approaching Festival requires may be so husbanded, & ordered, as wee may be found at the Passage of Jordan, the departure of our souls out of our Bodies, true pronouncer of Shibboleth, that is, that our Celebration of this Gladsome solemnitie may in all respects be performed, as it may not proue a Burthen to our Consciences, & be condemned for chaff in Gods iudgement; but become an Eare, I [aye], a sheaf of good corn to be carried into the granarie of Heauen. Which I hope vndoubtedly it shall doe if wee put in practize the churches counsell, which is to put on the Lord Jesus Christ by conforming our Actions & dispositions of mind answerable to that, which he requires, & gaue vs example of, & not by making provision for the Flesh to fulfill the lusts thereof.

[1] A liuely Type—see above, p. 163 n. 2.

MODERATOR. Thats indeed the close of the first summons that the Church giues on Advent sunday[1] to this great Festivall & is point-blank opposite to that, which the world both by word & deed invites vs vnto. All whose study & care now runs, that there may be nothing wanting to the vttermost of satisfaction for euery Lust & desire both of mind & body & there its sayd wee haue kept a good Christmas. As for putting on the Lord Jesus in our spirit, which is so admirably accommodated to this Festival, when wee solemnize the remembrance of his putting on ⟨6⟩ of our Flesh, it is a thing so little thought vpon by the most, & so much disliked by the greatest as he, that should really goe about the performance thereof, shall, I am perswaded, minister more occasion both of talk & mirth, then all the good cheare & Revels of the country besides.

PATIENT. It is better, if the will of God be so (sayth Snt Peter) that wee should suffer for welldoing then for euill doing.[2] Its better to run vpon the obloquie of the world for leauing of their companie in that, which is amisse, then vpon Gods censure for going along with them. The disgrace, that they threaten is nothing so heauie as the woe, that God pronounced by the mouth of Esay the same sunday, when the day of iudgement was brought to remembrance.[3] You can hardly I am perswaded single out a chapter in the whole Bible so vnseasonable to the time, If the fashion of the world be right. Pervse it well & you shall find the production of woe & guilt by God's accompt to come forth out of those selfsame parcels, which the world setts down & summes vp the vertue & happines of this time by. Wine & strong drink & mingled drink, good cheare & Musick are imputed to the Jews as great crimes & the ground of their calamities. & why think you? because they began & ended the day in following them ⟨6v⟩ till they were inflamed without regard of the work of the Lord or considering the operation of his hands. There's neither surfitting

---

[1] Romans xiii, 8–14.　　　　[2] I Peter iii, 17.
[3] Isaiah v, 8–30, a possible First Lesson at Morning Prayer on Advent Sunday.

nor drunkennes, but onely inflammation; Nor wantonnes nor
madnes in their Feasts, but onely Musick; Nor contempt of Gods
works, but forgetfulnes & Neglect, that is thus heinously layd to
their charge. And how then shall wee Christians escape, that haue
added so much to excesse & exorbitance in all kinds, As this,
which they are taxed for seemeth nothing. I appeal to your selues,
if wee haue not hitherto deemed our selues very innocent touching the keeping of this good time, because wee haue not gone as
farre, as our Neighbours, though much beyond that, which is
here condemned.

MOTHER. That, which you haue alledged is plaine. So those
other generalities in the self same chapter, which are marked with
a Woe, seeme to my apprehension so appliable to the euill
practizes of this good time especially, as I cannot think any mans
comment able to expresse them so liuely, as the bare veiw of a
great Christmas kept after that manner, that the world most
applaudes would doe to an observant eie. Tell mee where the
drawing of iniquitie with cords of vanitie & sin as it were with cart
ropes is to be more easily, more fully exemplified, then in ⟨7⟩ the
Reuels, sports, & gamings of this season. Tell mee where the plain
& open setting vp of euill deeds & works of darknes & bitter fruits
of Death for the debasing of that, which is good, belonging to the
light & yeelding true sweetnes is more euidently & more eminently
to be instanced then in the common solemnizing of this holy
Festival. I tremble to speak what I see done euery where. Euen the
most of those, that pretend to haue put on Christ all the yeare
before, are not ashamed at this time to make direct profession of
putting him of [off]. Theres no Lust of the Flesh, no Maliciousnes
of the mind, which they make not Christmas-Liberty to serue as
a cloke & an occasion vnto. All Religion is layd aside, all Laws are
silenced, I [aye], all Authoritie is dissolued, that impietie, vniustice,
& vncontrouled appetites may haue their full swinge. I need not
descend to particularities. Take it from the highest to the Lowest
That's allowed in publick, in priuate, to children, to servants too,

who wil make vse of it, which at all other times is strictly restrained & would be seuerely punished. Consider well & see whether wee may not truely apply the Prophets words to this time aboue all other. Hell hath enlarged her self & opened her mouth without measure.[1] ⟨7v⟩

CHEERFULL. As the Doctrine so the Examples which the Church now proposeth to our imitation inferres a flatt contradiction to all that, which the world commends as most seasonable for the time & occasion. John the Baptist, who came in a rayment of Camels Haire with a Leathern Girdle about his Loines neither eating nor drinking but Locusts & Wild honey & lost his head at a Feast & vpon a dancing, is twice brought to remembrance in the two preceding sundaies of this good Time.[2] What think you. Is this man a fitt Messenger to invite the guests, if fine Cloaths & Banquets be the complement of this Festival.

AFFECTIONATE. Nor will any of those other, whose memory wee now celebrate at this time better fitt the purpose.

For St Thomas[3] (I will say nothing because wee can say nothing of certaintie, but that, which wee haue heard related) is I am sure as opposite as may bee to the worlds mind. That he should enter into India to preach the Gospel in extreme Pouertie & Humilitie, his apparrel so meane, as it were not whole, his Body so leane as his face was pale, that he seemed nothing but a shaddow, is the Description, that wee haue heard made by an Ancient Author, that wrot his Life. But this I mention not to enforce your beleif in this particular but to take away occasion from them, that seek occasion for Errour ⟨8⟩ & would argue, that whosoeuer could be palpably brought against you were for them.

---

[1] Isaiah v, 14.

[2] Third Sunday in Advent: Matthew xi, 2–10; Fourth Sunday in Advent: John i, 19–28.

[3] St Thomas, also known as Didymus, was the apostle who according to legend carried the Gospel to India. His feast day is celebrated on 21 December. The ancient author referred to a few lines later may have been Eusebius Pamphili (260–340), Bishop of Caesarea, whose *Historia Ecclesiastica* was available in several editions.

MOTHER. Let's come to that, which is infallible Steuens Martyrdome, Johns Doctrine, the Innocents Massacring, Christs shedding his bloud in circumcision, & his manifestation to the Gentiles. These are the attendant Festivals to this great Solemnitie.[1] In which of them can wee adventure to make vse of that Libertie & those pleasures, which the world allows, without an open Defiance both of Reason & Conscience. It's a double incongruitie, & such as I haue heard cannot be parralleld by any erring superstition of the Heathen. Who neuer so mismated things, like that foolish Orator, crying out, Oh Heauens, & pointing to the earth, As to celebrate sad accidents with Mirth & Laughter, & to honour sober Deities with Mirth & Wantonnes. There was a Flora picked out on purpose, A Bacchus or a Venus sett vp for Presidents [precedents], when they ment to exercize these practizes, which wee haue sorted out for the honour of Christmas & the intertainment of the Saints.

GUARDIAN. I haue heard it should be the saying of Picus Mirandula;[2] That it cannot but be extreme obstinacie to doubt any thing of the truth of Christian Religion, which hath beene ⟨8 v⟩ so notably preached & so wonderfully confirmed by miracles through the whole world. But to beleiue it & not to liue accordingly could not be but extreme madness. But to sett out solemne daies for the praises of them, that have excelled in it, & to goe to Church, & with Reuerence & admiration to attend to the Remembrance of their vertues, & to come home, & to fall a doing all the day after, I [aye] & most part of the Night too cleane contrarie must needs be a peice of Transcendent Frenzy.

[1] Holy days which follow Christmas: St Stephen, deacon and martyr (26 December); St John, apostle and evangelist (27 December); Holy Innocents (28 December); Circumcision of Christ (1 January) and Epiphany (6 January).

[2] Giovanni Pico della Mirandola (1463–94) was an Italian nobleman and scholar who had an especial attraction for the Ferrars because of his intention, forestalled by his early death, to give away all his worldly possessions and to wander about preaching the Gospel. The Guardian's source seems to be Foxe's *Book of Martyrs*. See below, p. 170 n. 3.

MODERATOR. But Men doe not perhaps conceiue them so different as you doe.

MOTHER. Let them put them together & the matter wilbe plain: Take the instance in St Steuen.[1] He full of the Holy Ghost wee of Lust. He full of Faith wisdome & power, wee of wine & good cheare. He ministring to widdows, & wee attended vpon with much pompe & many servants. He disputing with the Jews wee shufling cards. He repeating the Scriptures, we singing Catches & behoulding interludes. He rebuking sin & wee encouraging it. He praying for his Murtherers & we cursing ill luck. Hee kneeling & wee dancing. If wee goe the right way to that Blessednes, which he hath attained, then wee may boldly say, wee are much more in Gods Favour then he, that find a Paradise here on earth more then he did. ⟨9⟩

AFFECTIONATE. There's no conformitie with St Steuen on any one point in all, that the world delights to passe his day with & euident it is, if comparison be made; the same contradiction will be found between all the rest.

Snt Johns Doctrine, which on his day wee pray to be enlightened with,[2] beares no more proportion then St Steuens example to those courses, which the world takes to please and honour themselues, & neither God, nor the Saints without any warrantie as wee see either from the word of God or from the practize of the Church.

MOTHER. But I pray before wee goe any further. Is that Picus Mirandula, whom you cited that miracle of Nature, that Mr Fox writes of,[3] so skild in all Languages, & so exact in all sciences as coming to Rome booted & spurred (that's his phrase) he sett up Ninety conclusions to dispute vpon against all commers.

---

[1] St Stephen, the Church's first martyr, whose feast day is celebrated on 26 December, appears only in chapters vi and vii of the Acts of the Apostles.

[2] St John, apostle and evangelist, is honoured on 27 December. The reference is to the Collect for that day.

[3] John Foxe (1516–87) first published his *Book of Martyrs* in 1559 in Latin. A corrected English version appeared in 1563 and a second corrected edition in 1570.

GUARDIAN. The very same, being a great Prince both in bloud & estate as well as in Learning. But why seeme you so affected with the remembrance of him?

MOTHER. Neither for his Excellencie of witt & knowledge aboue all others in many Ages before or after him ioyned with such Eminencie of Dignitie, nor for the vnparalelld honour, that he hath obtained in the world. ⟨9v⟩

GUARDIAN. For what then?

MOTHER. Why for his own notable contempt of these things, which others so admire him for. It was his Resolution at last (& yet that was very early in him: for it was before he was two and thirty yeares old) to giue all away & to take a coul, & to goe about & preach. But the Lord permitted him not, saith Mr Fox. He died shortly after.

PATIENT. In a happy houre no doubt being grown to so holy a Determination.

CHEERFULL. But shall wee be recommending good examples every day, I may say, almost all the day long & neuer goe about to follow them. Why should wee not euen from this Houre proportionably sett in hand with the performance of that, which we so magnifie in him, Not putting on a Friers coul, which this Prince of men & learning would haue done for Christ Jesus his sake, but putting on Christ Jesus himself. Christ was made of God vnto vs Wisedome, & Righteousnes, & Sanctification, & Redemption, sayth St Paul.[1] In putting on these wee shall become so cloathed & apparrelled with Christ, as wee shall euen in God the Fathers eies appeare all one with his beloued son, Christ Jesus, who is blessed for euermore. Amen. ⟨10⟩

MOTHER. And though wee may not preach by words, which was his desire, yet wee may preach by our Actions, as he still doth by his. His Resolution encourageth vs, Our example may perhaps hearten on some others. Let vs not blame either our sex or condition, as disabled for the advancement of Gods Kingdome. Wee

[1] I Corinthians i, 30.

haue a Talent & a great one committed to vs, if wee bee carefull
to imploy it, Not in the Tongue, No, that belongs to the Ministry
but in the hands & in the feet, that's common to all Christians.
Wee may tread out the way to heauen & wee may lead on by good
works, though wee cannot teach by words. & perhaps that Real
kind of Instruction hath in all Ages beene the most forcible, is in
this the most Necessarie. Where there are many Masters but few
guides. A Dearth of Patterns in an exuberance of Rules. Wee need
not goe abroad for instances. The want of Presidents [precedents],
the lack of seconds, is that, which gravels vs both in this & all other
the like matters. If wee had Authoritie, if wee might hope of
companie, we would run where wee now goe creeping, wee
should it may be reach that height, which wee now stand pointing
onely at with our fingers.

AFFECTIONATE. Our Iudgements & our Consciences approue,
that it is Right, Beneficial, & Necessarie for vs. Why come wee
not ⟨10v⟩ then to the Execution? Wee are afraid to goe alone.
Let vs not think so. There are others of our minds, if they had an
Example to alledge for their opinion. Wee shall haue them, that
will follow in the way assoone as they know there's any gone
before. But we are loth to be the foremost. Why that's advantage,
if wee well mark it. Wee shall thereby haue a double Benefitt, Not
onely our own but others welldoing in Imitation of vs shall run to
our Accompt. Wee want an Example, let's make one, wee shall
runne some hazard at first. Wee shall certainly reap more honour,
more Reward from God & goodmen at the last. & yet perhaps the
danger, that affrights vs, is nothing so bad, as it makes shew of.
The wounds, that wee expect, are but words; the Sufferings, that
wee shall feel but in conceit. When one told Aristotle, that he was
illspoken of abroad, That no more troubles mee sayd hee, then
the beating of my Clothes, when they are of [off] my Back. What
euer the meaning be, if the blame be iust it is a Benefitt to vs to
beare it, wee shall come to know our Errours & I hope by Gods
grace goe on to mend them. If the Blame be vniust, wee haue no

cause, saith St Peter, either of Feare or Trouble.[1] The Errour lies
not in our doing that, which wee ought, but in their speaking
euill of that, which they vnderstand not. And the gain or losse
will ⟨11⟩ fall accordingly. If they repent not they shall perish in
their own corruption, & wee, if wee faint not, shall receiue
a crowne of Glorie, that fadeth not away, in which euery reproach, that wee suffer for Righteousnes sake shall shine as a
precious stone.

MOTHER. Let vs goe on then perfecting holines in the feare of
God, Euery one bringing what they think meet for the building
vp our selues in the most holy Faith, obseruing in euery thing
St Pauls caution, That wee be ready alwaies to giue an Accompt
to euery one, that asketh vs a reason, with meeknes & feare.[2]
Touching what wee are not to doe this Christmas there needs no
more to be spoken, If now that, which you propounded to bee
done shalbe well as proued good, as that, which the World
practizes, hath beene convinced to be euill. I hope wee shall as
cheerfully goe on to the performance of the one, as wee doe
carefully draw back from the continuance of the other.

CHEERFULL. The disproportionablenes of Excesse hath bred a
loathing in your minds. I hope the Deformitie & danger, which
vpon further inspection will appeare shall cause an vtter expulsion
of it from amongst vs, Not onely for this ensuing solemnitie but
for euer. & the Laws of Temperance, which is so beautifull in it
self, so beneficial in all kinds of good ⟨11 v⟩ & so sutable to our
ends & profession, shall haue their free & full course in this Family,
& in all those others (& many may they bee) that like grafts shall
spring from it.

GUARDIAN. You shall deserue an honour & attaine a peice of
happines, which the best of your sex may envie, If you shall proue
the instruments of this work.

CHEERFULL. The honour belongs to God alone, & the happines,
which I cheifly desire, is that I may proue my self a faithfull

---

[1] I Peter iii, 14. [2] I Peter iii, 15, wrongly attributed by the Mother to St Paul.

obseruer of that, which I endeauour to perswade you vnto & if Reason and Gods word may sway, I hope I shall prevail.

GUARDIAN. If you can make good those grounds, which you haue layd of Louelines, profitablenes, & proportionablenes there will be no resistance.

CHEERFUL. I doubt not by Gods grace, where shall I begin?

Part II

The Guardian urges the Cheerfull to 'make that agreeableness of Temperance . . . as evident as it hath been often inculcated', and she promises not only to do that but also to prove that Temperance increases 'the enjoyment of all the good things of this Life'. The Moderator suggests that they agree that 'the increase in God's grace be the chief of our desires and ends'. When the Patient, the Affectionate, and the Guardian (in especially fervent and homely language) readily assent, the Mother rejoices in their intention: 'This day . . . shall every year with me henceforth . . . be kept Festival.' The Cheerfull, in her praise of the beauties of Temperance, works out an elaborate simile in which she compares the soul burdened with the sins of gluttony to a ship weighed down with its cargo. The Mother cites St Cyprian (in words found in Foxe's *Book of Martyrs*) and the Patient quotes from St Basil on gluttony. The Affectionate, Moderator and Cheerfull work out the 'resemblance of gluttony to Judas', proposed first by the Affectionate, who then applies the abstinence practised by John the Baptist to all those who would be ministers and followers of Christ. Although the wise men of the past (Galen and Cicero are cited) have advocated abstinence for all who search for truth and goodness, modern man pays no attention either to heathen or Christian pronouncements. The Affectionate agrees that intemperance is accepted as a fault, but that great concern for good food and drink is a universal practice. The Cheerfull, however, counters with quotations from a recent sermon on fasting and hopes that her words may prevail at least with members of her family to bring about abstinence and moderation. The Guardian concludes this section with the hope that the force of their words and examples may spread abroad outside their walls.

———◆———

GUARDIAN. Why, with that last part of your diuision; but whereon you first took the occasion for the proposall of this matter. Make that agreablenes of Temperance to this Euening Festival & our maine ends as euident, as it hath beene often inculcated.

175

CHEERFULL. Why surely, if Christ was so angry, as he could not forbeare blows, when the Temple, that was ordeined for praier was made a house of Marchandize, he cannot be well pleased to see this Festival ⟨12⟩ sett aside for Thanksgiving imploy'd all in vanitie; Nor the mouths, that should be opened wide with prayses stopped up with good cheare. But I will enter no further on this point because it falls in with that other of our own ends, If our ends be as right as I hope. The Glorie of God, The increase in his Grace. & the attainment of euerlasting happines.

MODERATOR. To these things indeed Christmas serues, if it be right vsed & if wee deceiue not our selues, all our meanings & desires are to that effect onely perhaps wee wish somewhat more asmuch content on Earth as can well stand without losse of heauen, & as many of Gods Temporal Blessings as may possibly be enioyed with his good will.

CHEERFULL. This surely is a great Alloy to the perfection of the former desires. But since wee are no better & wiser, Let this likewise be put into the bargain, & if Temperance come not forth absolutely compleat to our furtherance for the enioyment of all the good things of this Life, accept it not for your gouernour in your Diet.

GUARDIAN. These are great Prayses & large things, that you promise.

CHEERFULL. They may be lesse then the subiect deserues & short of what by Gods Assistance the Effect shall approue, if my ⟨12v⟩ companions will ioyn with mee: For alone the burden would be too heauie.

MOTHER. Your motion prevents ours. Wee were about to entreat you, that wee might not be excluded from the seruice, although your self alone are able to goe through with it. Doubt you not therefore, but you shall haue help, more then perhaps you would and in proof hereof giue mee leaue not to mend (for that perhaps cannot be done) but to limmit somewhat that large Expression which you made of your ends. That so reducing the matter to a more narrow point, we may be the better able to discerne & iudge of that Necessitie & sutablenes, which you haue vndertaken to demonstrate between Temperance & our ends, which I would for as much as concerns this present Busines restrain to the middlemost of these three things, which you mentioned, that is, The Increase of grace.

MODERATOR. You say very well. These two others, the Glorie of God, & the Salvation of our souls are such generalities, as not onely all things are equally directed, but all men doe vnanimously pretend vnto. And therefore like great & publick scales hung vp in town-houses vnmeet for weighing of smaller parcels will not so properly serue to either part of this Busines, that is, either to distinguish our particular ends or to make ⟨13⟩ the comparison vpon between them & Temperance. But the Increase of Grace (if that be agreed vpon to be our end) as it will seuer vs & our ends & intentions from all those persons & things, from which wee ought to be seperated: so it will proue a iust square & Last to make our Tryal by not onely in this, but in most of those other good designes, which wee haue in agitation. I would therefore desire, that it may be first personally voted, whether the Encrease in Gods grace be the cheif of our desires & ends. Not that I feare any Bodies dissent, but that I hold it Necessarie, that euery one, whom it concernes, should actually expresse their Agreements in the Foundation, before wee goe foreward with the Building.

PATIENT. You say very well. A Explicite assent will in this case be needfull like the subscription of hands in publick attempts to bind men the firmer to the performance of what they vndertake. I for my part make profession, that the Encreasing in Gods Grace & Christian Vertue is the cheif & main of my end & desires. Not hereby excluding or falling short of those two forementioned ends, Gods Glorie & mine own Eternal happines, but intending them absolutely in their right order primarily & necessarily included in this end & desire of Grace. ⟨13 v⟩

AFFECTIONATE. Questionlesse He, that really aimes at Grace

must needs fully & eminently intend Gods Glorie & his own Happines, & therefore you doe very rightly, & therein I ioyn with you making proficiencie in Gods grace the main & cheif of my ends & desires likewise, to which I subiect all inferiour wishes & designes of my mind so as whatsoeuer shall appeare contrarie therevnto, shall by Gods assistance find refusal from mee & that, which doth euidently conduce therevnto, shall by the same merci-full Assistance, I hope, find submission from mee in iudgement & Acceptance in my Affections.

GUARDIAN. Grace being the onely stock, that they, that pro-fesse to traffique for Gods Glorie in this world must sett vp with, & the onely earnest, which they, that desire to haue assurance of their salvation must rely vpon, It seemes to mee wee cannot pitch our ends vpon any other thing more conveniently, then this, which onely giues a cleare proof of the Sinceritie & Sufficiencie of our desires in the other two points. For he, that pretends to haue sett vp Gods glorie for his cheif end & yet makes small accompt of proficiencie in Gods grace, shows that he doth but dissemble & tells indeed that what he sayth in words is but for fashion sake, because he would keep the Reputation of a good Christian ⟨14⟩ amongst men, though his own conscience tell him he haue lost his Creditt with God. And though the desire of salvation be neuer so vnfained, yet if the Loue of Grace & good works be vnsound, It will proue as insufficient to compasse what it aimes at, as those Eggs, which hens lay without the cock are for producing of Chickens. The desire of salvation is but the womb, the Zeal of grace & good works is the Masculine seed, that giues Life to these happy conceptions of Eternal happines in our minds, which other-wise proues alwaies like those moles & Lumps of Flesh, which women sometimes goe with child of, Consuming away like a snail, & neuer comming to see the sun of Righteousnes. I therefore giue my Ball to [vote for] the advancement of this self same end, which you haue all agreed vpon, setting vp by resolution for my self & humble prayers for all the rest of this Familie, the Growth in Grace & in the knowledge of our Lord & Sauiour Jesus Christ, to whom be glorie both now & for euer, for the main End, sole Rule, sure Guide, & ouerruling Mistresse of all our Opinions, Desires, & Actions in this World & tending to our selues. As for the glorie of God that is aboue all & the Salvation of our souls is to be hereafter, & both of them will necessarily follow & be fully perfected in their due season vpon our good attainment & accomplishment of this other preceding & preparative End. ⟨14v⟩

MOTHER. This Day merrits a Red Letter in our Calendar & shall euery yeare with mee henceforth, God willing, be kept Festival. If wee be enioyned so many holydaies for the contemplation of the fruits of holines in others, wee may I doubt not be allowed to make one in Remembrance of our laying the Foundation of it in our selues.

PATIENT. Mee thinks, It were very meet, that as in these Additions of Structure & Ornament, which haue been made to the material Church there was none of our Familie, that had not their share, & they, that through Age or Absence could not doe it themselues, had a Brick layd by some other hands:[1] So much more in this building vp our selues a Spiritual house & Temple vnto God euery one from the first to the Last should be invited to a ioynt participation therein.

MOTHER. You aime at a particular declaration like these, that haue beene now made, from the rest of our Familie in this way.

PATIENT. And a profession in their behalf, that cannot doe it themselues by those, that haue the Cheif interest in them.

MOTHER. Why surely the Attempt cannot but be euery way of marveilous advantage. But because the matter is so weighty ⟨15⟩ & ought to be altogether voluntarie, I shall advize the deferring it for the present. & that in the end the performance may bee made in writing, which will more solemly oblige them, who agree & more seriously & plainly represent their true condition and Estate to them, who shall refuse this subscription. If any

[1] See Maycock, p. 130.

179

shall be found so vnwise & vnhappy as to depart not only from God and his Freinds, but from his own happines: For questionlesse the increase in Grace, & in the Knowledge of our Lord & Sauiour Jesus Christ is not the Foundation of holines & eternall happines only but of the best prosperitie & happines, which this World can afford, & this Life is capable of.

GUARDIAN. Wee haue reason to belieue no lesse, that in those imperfect & insincere Indeauours, which our own Consciences beare witnesse of, find such abundance of reward, as iustly breeds Admiration in all others. But since this matter is not now to be gone through with, Let vs I pray reseruing it to further opportunitie proceed with that wee are vpon.

You see Beloued Cheerfull, our ends, Let vs now see your skill in applying your discourse. So as wee, who desire it, may be made Capable, & they who perhaps desire it not may bee convinced touching that Necessitie, Comelines & advantage which ⟨15v⟩ you so often haue alledged in the behalf of Temperance touching the attainment of this end.

CHEERFULL. I may not arrogate to mine owne skill in this case more then the Remonstrance [evidence] of anothers skill & Art, from whom I haue learned & receiued what I shall teach you, That you may neither prize mee the better, nor the matter it self the worse. Know, that I am but a repeater.

MOTHER. What not a Belieuer too?

CHEERFULL. Yes verily in the highest degree.

MOTHER. Why then I know no reason coming fairly by it, why you should not think your self the owner of what you haue Learned. Since you haue made it trebly your own by vnderstanding, by Assent, & by so Learning it, as you are able to communicate it to others.

CHEERFULL. As much as pertaines to Benefitt I esteeme it mine own in euery way. But if there be happily honour like to follow in any respect I disclaime it in all.

AFFECTIONATE. I commend your wariness to keep your own

the surer. You are scrupulous of being offered that, which is not yours. You refuse the prayse, because you would not diminish the reward.

CHEERFULL. You guesse right in part, but there is yet more. ⟨16⟩ Its Iustice aswell as Couetousnes, that makes mee thus timorous: For I could not but with double wrong seek respect to myself in this Busines, When he, from whom I haue receiued it, makes profession, that there is nothing but the Errour & imperfection in it, that is his. For good is altogether Gods. From him it comes to us by Guift & to him must be returned again by Thanksgiuing & Acknowledgement. & that it may like good seed in good ground be now receiued & hereafter fructifie needs his special help & Fauour.

GUARDIAN. To him therefore with you wee lift vp our harts, humbly beseeching the guidance & assistance of his holy spirit, that by the Light & vertue thereof wee may be lead on to the knowledge & Practize of this Diuine grace. Amen.

CHEERFULL. To begin therefore with that last description of our End taken out of St Peters concluding argument in his second Epistle,[1] & observing the same Method, which you haue made choise of, transposing the parts, & setting that first which Snt Peter setts last the better to accommodate it to our present vse I say, that without Temperance wee can neither come to the knowledge of Christ Jesus as Our Sauiour, nor continue in grace as his servants & so no way able either to advance his glorie in this world ⟨16v⟩ or to attaine our happines in that, which is to come. Spiritual truth can no way enter into that vnderstanding, which is cloyd vp by intemperance, Nor spiritual good be held by those affections, which are infeebled by disorder of Eating & Drinking. It is the expression of truth & Wisedome it self: & therefore neither to be denied nor bettered. That Surfetting & Drunkennes ouercharge the heart: Now that, which is ouercharged, you know, can neither admitt any new addition, nor conserue itself long in its former

---

[1] II Peter iii, 18.

being. A iust weight layd vpon the summers [supporting beams] within poyseth the Building & makes it stronger; but that, which is ouerheauie, makes it fall & Ruine. Proportionable Ballast carries on the ship with more speed & more stedines in her course, but ouerlading sinks it vnder water. And though it be not so much as to breed such danger; yet if it be any whitt at all more then ought, it breeds impediment: Food moderately taken makes the Vessels of our Bodies more strong & apt for the Wafting of our souls vnto the port of euerlasting Happines: But that which is ouer-measure any way breeds trouble & encumbrance in our sayling, though it be but a little. But if it come to great Excesse it hazards, or rather without hazard certainly enforceth the drowning of the soul in the waues of ignorance & in the mire of wicked appetites. The apprehension ⟨17⟩ of Celestial Truth & Loue of Vertue sinks in the mind proportionable to the rise & swelling of Intemperance in the Body & vpon the great ouerflowing thereof are quite swallowed vp.

MOTHER. That Passage of St Cyprian, which Mr Fox hath registred in his Book of Acts & Moniments, will notably confirme one part of this Doctrine.[1] Snt Cyprian, sayth hee, as himself writes, Had a Reuelation from God, wherein he was admonished to be spare in his feeding & sober in his drink, least his mind giuen to heauenly meditations might be carried away with worldly allurements, or oppressed with much surfet of meats & drinks, should be lesse apt or able to Prayer & spiritual Exercize.

PATIENT. Admirable in mine eares did that sound, which I lately heard read out of St Basil touching that second part of this Doctrine, The necessarie Corruption of the Affections through intemperance.[2] And because it fitts so well to the present, & serues

---

[1] The passage quoted is found *verbatim* in Foxe's *Book of Martyrs*, in which the life of St Cyprian is recounted under the heading 'The Eighth Persecution of the Church, Anno 259'.

[2] The passage to which reference is made is in *Sermo De Renuntiatione Saeculi*, 208 A. St Basil was the brother of Macrina, an anchorite who, after the death of a suitor, vowed to remain unmarried. She founded a monastic community, which her mother joined, on the family property and established a sisterhood of virgins devoted to a simple, communal life. Basil's brother, St Gregory of

for continual vse I shall, if you please, now relate it. As it is the Nature of Water, sayth hee, being drawn out into many Trenches to make all those places flourish, which it encompasseth, So likewise Gluttonie being digested in the heart and issuing out through the senses causeth a wood of Euill to spring vp in a Mans Soul, & turnes it to a Den of wild Beasts. I haue ⟨17v⟩ seene, sayth hee, many recouered, that were tainted with vices, but a closse [secret] Deuourer or a Glutton I neuer saw, but either fallen away from a continent Life & become polluted in the world, or els indeauouring to shrowd themselues amongst the Continent, yet in truth warring for & with the Deuill. They, that are such, are Lyars, common swearers, & forswearers, seditious, contentious, Loud brawlers, opposers of Liberalitie, Daintie, peeuish, such as delight in darknes, and such as willingly make head against euery vertuous action. For to hide the Vice of Gluttonie they fall into a sworm [swarm] of wickednes. These in outward habit appeare amongst those, that are to be saued, but in very truth they are amongst the Reprobates. This saith Basil, & after the Allegation of some particular examples for proof thereof concludes to this purpose, If thou gett the Masterie of thy Belly thou mayst dwell in Paradise; but if thy Belly gett the Masterie of thee, thou art giuen ouer as a prey to Death, or adiudged therunto, as Costs & Damages are to him, that gaines a Tryal at Law.

AFFECTIONATE. Gluttonie therefore was very aptly in my opinion resembled to Judas. For as he went before the Band of Souldiers to betray Christ: so doth Gluttonie lead the way to all vice & by the selfsame watch-word as he did, whom I kisse, whose lips I ⟨18⟩ ceaze upon, doth to This Day betray Christ Jesus, that is, As much as it finds of him in any mans soul to be mocked, crucified, slaine & buried. There is not any one Right Notion of Christ, nor true peice of Affection towards him, but is vtterly

Nyssa, has left an account of the way of life adopted by his mother and sister, whose thought and action were similar to those of Mrs Ferrar senior and her maiden daughters.

extinct & kild in that mind & heart, which Gluttonie hath gott the masterie of. And that there may be a perfect imitation of this spiritual crucifying him to that, which he formerly suffered in the Flesh, we shall alwaies find, if wee rightly obserue this wicked vice accompanied with such a perfect scorn & contempt of Christianitie, as the cheifest of its solace & delight seemes to be placed in the derision of sacred Mysteries & iesting vpon the sincere professours & Practizers of them.

MODERATOR. The Reproaches of them, that reproached thee, fell vpon mee, sayth Christ.[1] The affronts & skornes put vpon the Members are principally intended against the Head & he as actually resents them now in heauen, as he did here vpon Earth. You may well therefore say, that Gluttonie deliuereth Christ to mockage as well as to Death & Burial by quickning Lust in the sensitiue & bringing a Lethargie vpon the intellectual parts of a mans soule. And if you put to this, which hath been sayd, that hardheartednes & oppression, which alwaies attends gluttonie, ⟨18v⟩ as a steward or Maiordomo, you shall in the Cruell Exactions, which it euer exercizeth on the poore, find in a Gluttonous heart as plain & painfull a Crucifying of Christ Jesus in his members, as was by the Iews on Mount-Calvarie in his own Person.

CHEERFULL. The Resemblance of Iudas & Gluttonie will appeare the more liuely, & sett out the truth itself the more clearly, if wee take into consideration that proportion & exact practize of Temperance with which Snt John Baptist came preparing the way of our Lord and Sauiour Iesus Christ. It cannot questionlesse be without great Mysterie, that he should be forbidden Wine & strong drink, before he receiued his own being; Nor that his sober & strict Diet should be so particularly sett down, when he came to reueal Christ Iesus to the World, but euen intended to signifie what wee now are vpon. That the Purifications of the Body by Temperance are necessarie to precede the entertainment of Christ Iesus in our souls or the conveyance of him to others.

[1] Romans xv, 3; Psalm lxix, 9.

Wee shall neither be fitted to embrace him our selues by beleif; nor
fitt instruments to propagate the Loue & knowledge of him vnto
others, vnlesse wee bee, as Snt Paul sayth, Temperate in all things &
in particular in our Diet, so as wee may keep vnder the Body from
opportunitie of exercizing its Lusts, & bringing it in subiection
for ⟨19⟩ the ready acceptance of Grace, els as he sayth, there runs
hazard of becomming castawaies our selues,[1] & there can be little
hope of perswading others by our words to become Christians.

GUARDIAN. True. For mee thinks, by what euer I haue heard
or read, I find Temperance in all Ages & amongst all Nations to
haue beene so absolutely, so vniversally, & so perpetually required
from all those, who professe the instructing in Diuine Mysteries,
as it seemes to mee to haue gained the Authoritie of a Principle in
Reason to be granted not onely without contestation, but without
consideration, as being euident in it self, & needing no other arguments then the bare proposal of it to obtaine assent, That Neither
heauenly Wisedome, nor true holines can possibly be retained in
that mind, whose Body is euer charged with excesse & riott.

CHEERFULL. If you had put in humane Wisedome & Moral
vertue likewise you had not exceeded at all either the bounds of
truth or the Expression of Natural Wise-men themselues. That
great Philosopher & Physician Galen hath left written, That they,
who being giuen ouer as a prey to sensualitie & Voluptuousnes
studie to fill their Bellies can by no meanes either liue long or
healthfully & that their souls being drowned ⟨19v⟩ in fatt & redun-
dancie of Bloud are not able to lift vp them selues to the Contemplation & Speculation of high & heauenly matters, but are always
intent to think on Base & earthly affaires. Such as are Flesh, meat
& drink, & other things of the like nature. All tending to the Belly.
And Tullie [Cicero] the great Romane Scholler & Statesman hath,
as I haue been told, left it written, That too much Eating & drinking doth disturbe the Counsell, ouerthrow Reason, blind the eies
of the mind, & is an enemy to vertue. Ile tell you his very words.

[1] I Corinthians ix, 25-7.

Voluptuousnes hinders Counsell, is an Enemie to Reason, &, as I may so speak, dazels the eies of the mind, & maintaines no commerce with Vertue.—And againe, They, who be replenished with much meat & drink cannot enioy or vse aright their minds.

GUARDIAN. These are home-Testimonies & to the purpose.

AFFECTIONATE. And harsh, except you giue them a more fauourable interpretation, then the words seeme at first to carry.

CHEERFULL. How so?

AFFECTIONATE. Why, To speak plainly. As long as you declaime against Intemperance in generall, it may well be borne. There's no Body, that professeth Ciuilitie much more Christianitie, that professeth not Enmity to it. And that they may giue the better proof of it, are content to ioyne in the prosecution of Gods & Mans Law to the vttermost against Gluttonie ⟨20⟩ & Drunkennes, surfetting & Excesse. They be Abominations, that defile a sober mans mouth to name them almost. Marry. If you come so low as Repletion with much meat & Drink, & make the desire and Care for good meat such a heinous matter & the filling of a mans belly such a beastly practize, as it shuts a man off from the societie of good & wise-men, I know not what to say considering, that the opinion & Custome of the best & Wisest men in the world appeares clean otherwise.—Why the Keeping of a good Table, though it require not onely much care but much Cost to maintaine & a Mans taking part of it himself, aswell as his free imparting it to others is not onely by the common vote of our Nation, but by the warrantie of the greatest, Wisest, & in a word the Best, recommended as an especial peice of honour & Vertue, aswell as of Earthly Happines. Look therefore before you lay this cornerstone & consider, whether it were not better & safer to reiect these Heathen mens Authoritie then to condemne the Christian World in this sort guiltie of foul intemperance & consequently incurring those forfeitures of Wisedome & Vertue, which necessarily follow vpon it.

CHEERFULL. That, which the rather animates mee to produce

those Witnesses, that speak so plainly, was that, which I lately read out of that Famous Sermon preached to the King, the sunday before the ⟨20v⟩ Fast appointed & kept by the last Assembly Parliament. Think not, that you can climbe vp to heauen with full panches, euer reaking of Indian smoak, & the surfetts of your gluttonous Crammings & Quaffings. Oh easy & pleasant way to Glorie. And a little after.

Ve saturis. Woe to the full, sayth our Sauiour.[1] But euen Nature it self could abominate, Bis de die saturum, one, that is full twice a day. One of the sins of our Sodome is fulnes of Bread.[2] All the rest (& much you shall find to this purpose) is worthy your reading. I onely cite what is proper to the answere of the Affectionates scruples, that none should esteeme the lesse of that, which was alledged, because it was first spoken by Heathen-men, when they heare it confirmed in such a serious manner & vpon such a solemne occasion by a Christian Prelate great in Learning, & in the Eminencie of all other vertues belonging to this place. I will conclude as he doth there in words, but I pray God it may proue more successfull in deeds amongst vs.

Oh that my words could prevail so farre with you as to bring Austere Abstinence, & sober Moderation into Fashion, sayth hee. I must contract it into this Familie: for further then the bounds thereof I may not presume, that my weak voice should be heard.

GUARDIAN. Though your modesty limit the matter according to your own part in it, yet I trust God (whose busines & work it is) shall en⟨21⟩large it according to his own power and grace abundantly, & that it shall proue like the flinging of a stone into the water, one Circle still begetting another & a greater. You shall see the accomplishment of your wishes very speedily in some of this Familie I doubt not. In due time, I hope all the rest. & the substance of your Arguments & the force of the Example will, I am very confident, in the end spred abroad, howeuer the sound of your words bee confined within the Walls of this House.

---

[1] Luke vi, 25.   [2] Luke xvii, 28.

Part III

All having agreed that gluttony is a sin, temperance—not over-indulgence—is the subject which now occupies their minds as the discussion becomes more personal than it was. The Mother promises the Cheerfull that 'upon full proof of what you have undertaken', she will become a faithful practitioner of 'what you desire' and confesses that she personally has already experienced many of the blessings of temperance. Next the Patient makes an unconditional surrender to the wishes of the Cheerfull. The Guardian praises temperance as proof of one's love for God and points out that the Mother's surrender was conditional only in order that by further discussion the doubts of the unconvinced might be dispelled. The Guardian proposes both himself and the Resolved as confirmed followers of temperance.

The Cheerfull, a bit impatient with these personal digressions, is eager to set about persuading all the others. To help her, the Affectionate will voice some well-known doubts of the value of temperance in order that they may be refuted. The Affectionate is forced to agree that although the great, the wealthy and the wise may indulge themselves with no apparent harm, waste of body and estate will inevitably follow. The Cheerfull's proposition that 'Satiety and delicacy in food are irreconcilable enemies of wisdom and virtue' is upheld in a dialogue in which the Affectionate generalizes from her own experience. As tobacco distempers most men at first but 'upon frequent use gives help unto all other operations of mind and body', so it is conceded that by custom a man may force himself to overcome the effects of indulgence. The disadvantages, however, are still present, and whatever he forces himself to do is done poorly. 'Daily glutting . . . brings a man in the end to stupidity', and all efforts, whether intellectual or physical, made when suffering from satiety are injurious to the health. Galen and Cicero are again cited as confirming authorities by the Cheerfull.

MOTHER. That by an Earnest giuen you may be more bound & better encouraged to goe on with your work, Beloued Cheerfull, I pray take my promise before hand vpon full proof of what you haue vndertaken to become thorough Gods assistance a faithfull practizer of what you wish. The choyse of my iudgement & the desires of my heart, howeuer the weaknes of my Flesh draw back, are to vndergoe the Refinings of the fire it self, If they serue best to make mee Louely in the eies of my Lord and Sauiour Iesus Christ: And how then should I not gladly submitt to the vttermost of that, which Temperance shall enioyn by way of Necessarie preparation for the Entertainment & increase of his Loue & Knowledge in my heart. If the Maiestie of Ahashuerus required such a length of time & Excesse of Cost & aboundance ⟨21 v⟩ of prouisions for the purification of her body, whom he ment to ioyn vnto himself by corporal wedlock:[1] Vndoubtedly there can bee no thought of passing on to the spiritual Embracement of that glorious Lord & spouse of our souls Christ Jesus without a diligent forecleaning of our selues from all filthines of the Flesh & spirit. I am therefore come to a resolution, God willing, cheerfully to vndergoe whateuer in this kind shalbe needfull, & so much the rather, as I find by that little Esay, which through God's mercy I haue made of this vertue, There is no likelyhood of disadvantage or Losse any way. For howeuer Sober & Austere, as you term them, the first greetings of Temperance appeare, yet vpon better acquaintance shee proues so free & pleasant an Intertainer of her Guests as Gluttonie it self with all her skill & cost comes short of her euen in point of making good cheare. For to beare witnesse to the truth I solemnly protest, that howeuer I haue cast away through Gods enabling mee, not onely the appetites, but the thoughts of Dainties, as the world calls them, yet I enioy the sweetnes of them to the full euery day. There is scarce one Meal in the weak, that Bread it self relisheth not more pleasant in my Tast, then formerly the greatest Delicacies, that Art or Nature could afford. And I find it most true, that I heard of old but could not belieue. That the pleasantnes of meats lies not in ⟨22⟩ the costly steeme of a daintie cooked dish but in the pure keenenes of a well ordered appetite.

[1] Esther ii, 8–13.

PATIENT. That Temperance extracts more pleasure out of the most ordinarie, then Gluttonie can adde to the daintiest Cates, that can be imagined, is too euident to be denied: But that by eating little according to her precepts a man should come in the end to eat the more seemes a mysterie, yet is vndoubtedly most true. And in part I can say to haue found the experiment in my self. In both these regards therefore, that there is no feare of any losse, & that there is assurance of so much advantage in Temperance, I for my part without taking any respite for fuller information or further advice doe offer my self in Gods Holy Name an Apprentize, Beloued Cheerful, to that Austere Temperance, which you speak of, Desiring to vnderstand her Laws & Ordinances, that I going instantly to the obseruance of them, I may goe on the faster to the enioyment of my Happines. For other happines I accompt not of, then that alone, which consisteth in the knowledge, Loue, & faithfull service of our Blessed Lord & Sauiour Iesus Christ.

GUARDIAN. I am very well assured, that this desire & hope is that, which leads both you & the others, so zealously forward in their Resolutions & that those other reasons, which you haue mentioned, haue been cast in the Scale rather to help others then your selues. ⟨22v⟩ Though Temperance were as Cruell & uniust as the World conceits neuer affording a God [good] morsell & euer defrauding the Belly of its due measure: yet am I confident that would no way diswade perhaps the more encourage you to the Acceptance & Submission of her gouernance. True & ardent Love delights in suffering, & esteemes it gaine to be at much Cost & pleasure to vndergoe sore trauel for the proof of its own Loyaltie, & the more abundant ingratiating it self in the heart of its Beloued. Its for others sakes therefore that you alledge these second arguments. That main & Royal advantage, which Temperance brings with it for the attainment of your end, the increase in Grace & in the Knowledge of our Lord & Sauiour Iesus Christ is onely [all] that, I know, which swaies with you. And though you, Deare

Patient, bee fully satisfied both in knowledge & Conscience touching this Excellent Benefitt of Temperance. So as there needs no further information in regard of you. Yet in respect of many others not so well grounded it will be found a matter perhaps not onely of great Vse but of absolute Necessitie. With a iudicious eie therefore & to this intent I am perswaded did the Mother make her capitulation with the Cheerful on such conditional termes. That vpon pretense of her own vncertaintie she might giue occasion for the clearing of others doubtfulnes, & draw on the more to ioyn with her in that sur⟨23⟩render, when they should perceiue it enforced by Necessitie of safety, aswell as by hope of Advantage. Wherefore I desire that our beloued Cheerfull will proceed in this Remonstrance [demonstration] & the rather to procure your good will herevnto, Deare Patient, knowing that the Assurance of more company in the iourney will make your present stay with lesse tediousnes, I haue a Warrantie from the Resolued to subscribe his Name vnto the self same Articles, which the Mother hath propounded. & that it may be a full messe[1] I beseech you to accept mee for the fourth in this Agreement.

CHEERFULL. Howeuer little in truth my part be in it, yet shall I euer reioyce without measure, that any waies I haue beene the occasion of bringing to Light these concealed Treasures of holy & happy Resolutions. And to the intent that by full accomplishment they may come the sooner forth to common Benefitt, Since as you affirme my remonstrance is first to proceed, I shall desire earnestly, that you would sett me in the way, which you would haue mee keep, & giue mee leaue to continue therein without any more digressions, although these haue beene so profitable & so much to purpose as Nothing, that you could haue heard from mee is able to equalize.

AFFECTIONATE. That, which wee haue heard & that, which wee expect to heare from you, shall I doubt not work more

---

[1] Messe—a group of four persons sitting together and eating from the same dishes; a common division of guests at a large dinner.

effectually in the ⟨23 v⟩ end through these diversions. Wee cannot therefore but accompt them gaine to vs aswell as they euidently appeare advantage vnto you. For Resolued Auditours are easy to be perswaded. But that you may not through too much Confidence of prevailing, because you know you speak to your own partie, vse lesse diligence or care, then the weightines of the busines requires, giue mee Leaue, I pray, to become your Antagonist by proposall of some doubts, & opposition of some such arguments as I haue often heard alledged against that, which you intend, & neuer yet heard so fully answered as were needfull.

CHEERFULL. That, which you offer, will be a double pleasure to mee. Inasmuch as besides a necessary quickning of my mind it setts mee into the same way, wherein I was taught my self, What I now goe about to declare vnto you.[1]

AFFECTIONATE. Why then to begin where wee left. Since by your own choyce you are come down so low, I shall not willingly giue consent, howeuer the Eleuated desires of others may perhaps wish otherwise, that you should proceed to higher points, till you haue first made good that bold challenge, which you made to convince [convict] all those, that follow Dainties & fulnes, as Runawaies from the camps of humane Wisedome & Moral vertue. The Authorities indeed, that you alledged are great & euident. But Experiment [experience] a more infallible ar⟨24⟩gument proues the Contrarie. The Wisest in all kinds & the best disposed euery where will vpon suruay taken be found the most Liberal & Delicate in their Fare of all others. And how then can it be, that there should be such an opposition & ouerthrow of Wisedome & vertue by Satietie & good Cheare, as you would perswade vs.

CHEERFULL. Tell mee I pray you. Doe you not find likewise in these selfsame houses & Families, where you find Wisedome & good Cheare coupled together oftimes great wealth & much wast in expence.

---

[1] This passage, introducing a kind of Socratic dialogue, might imply an oral source for the Cheerfull's opinions.

Cheerfull. Pardon mee, If J seeme importunate in occasioning this meeting so much before yoʳ expectation. Not onely yᵉ earnestnes of mine owne desires, but the necessitie of yᵉ thing it self, admitts no longer delay. —

Mother. You say very true. For except you now giue vs tᵉⁱ better satisfaction wee may no longer forbeare tᵉ making of our Christmas-provisions —

Cheerfull. Call tʰᵉⁱ m as tʰᵉⁱ bee, J pray. Carnal Excesses & spiritual prejudices, yᵗ corrupt tᵉ Body, defile the soul, & wast tᵉ Estate. All this is included in that good cheare, wherewith the world generally solemnizeth this approaching Festival. Judge tʰᵉⁿ with what reason it vsurps yᵉ Name of Christmas-fare & provisions. —

Mother. J dare not but recant what J sayd amisse. It must needs be some other Dietie, yᵗ they intend to honor by this meanes. — Sure it cannot be Christ, whose Kingdome is not meat & drink: but Righteousnes, & Peace, & Joy in tᵉ Holy Ghost. And he yᵗ in tᵉˢᵉ things serueth Christ is acceptable to God & approoued of men too, sayᵗʰ Sᵗ Paul: But he, yᵗ walks in lasciuiousnes, lust, excesse of wine, Reuelling, & banquetting, tᵉ common entertainment of this Festival-season workes yᵉ will of tᵉ Gentiles, saytᵉ Sᵗ Peter,

& will

Cheerfull. Vpon what occasion?

Affectionate: The Filling of the Belly with good cheare.

Cheerfull: Why though it be well done to be shy in taxing others yet the more free you shalbe in shriuing of yo:rselfe it will be carry way the better for yo:rselfe & vs. I pray therefore let mee become yo:r Confessor.

Affectionate. What is it you would know?

Cheerfull. How you find yo:rself affected & disposed of sea good cheare.

Affectionate. Why good for nothing.

Cheerfull. For nothing?

Affectionate. For nothing, y:t good is. For play, for reading, for Folly. (& in a word for any euill) I find such an aptnes That with great Difficultie I can restrain my selfe from seeking opportunities, when they be not offered for these exercizes. But for all good affaires I am like a Dore of the hinges, y:t turns not but by maine force

Cheerfull. How meane you?

Affectionate. Why vtterly vnable except vpon pure necessitie for any Busines (& then, howeuer I sett my selfe by constraint, altogether vnfitt for the accomplishment of it?

Cheer: How

AFFECTIONATE. Yes verily.

CHEERFULL. And in the selfsame persons, which you intend [cite as examples], doe you not sometimes obserue abundance of ill humours in their Bodies. & yet no appearing abatement either in health or strength.

AFFECTIONATE. Nor can this well be denied.

CHEERFULL. And yet shall wee make any scruple to affirme That Prodigalitie & Wast doe necessarily bring on a consumption in the Estate & that ill humours breed sicknes & hasten Death.

AFFECTIONATE. The greatnes of a stock provided before hand & the strength of a good Constitution may for a while beare out the vnderminings of Riotous expences & ill humours. But because the ouerthrow of Estate & Health doe vnavoydably follow in the end vpon continuance of such disorders, wee may absolutely conclude ⟨24v⟩ that they are necessarie causes of Pouertie & Sicknes, & vtterly opposite to Health & Riches, which by this meanes goe on to certain Ruine, though it be not instantly perceiued, & by infallible degrees, howeuer not sensible perhaps, but to them, that are of better then ordinarie apprehension.

CHEERFULL. Why then if it shall appeare likewise, that the Care of Dainties doth in the end bring on a contempt of all better things & the Filling of the Belly at last foils the vnderstanding, Wee may safely conclude, that Satietie & Delicacie in Food are irreconcilable Enemies of Wisedome & Vertue. Nor will the remonstrance [evidence] of their seeming League or Freindship for a while in any one subiect proue the contrarie, as long as there may be discouered a continuall supplanting of each other, whilest they doe stay together, & in the end an vtter ouerthrow & Expulsion of the one or the other. For either Wisedome & Vertue driue out excesse in the Body, or Excesse in Eating & Drinking driue out Wisedome & Vertue out of the soul.

AFFECTIONATE. That, which you say, if I rightly conceiue it, is, First, that the Constant Followers of good Cheare should bee or appeare wise & well minded is by vertue of provision formerly made in these kinds. Next, that they doe dayly empaire & in the end come to a plaine Losse of Wisedome & Vertue by these meanes. ⟨25⟩ These things I desire to see a little better explained & proued.

CHEERFUL. Why did you euer know any, that stock of [gain in] Wisedome in any kind, or true Vertue in the vse of a full & wanton Diet.

AFFECTIONATE. Neuer.

CHEERFULL. Doe you know any, that when he came to the keeping of good Cheare for himself, I meane aswell as for others, did keep what he had formerly gotten for Wisedome or Learning?

AFFECTIONATE. Hardly.

CHEERFULL. And for Vertue?

AFFECTIONATE. Much lesse. But my Experience falls too short for proof of this matter.

CHEERFULL. The particular instances, which you can alledge, are perhaps but a few. & yet your Experience [is] large enough to make a general inference. Tell mee, I pray, Hath not meat & drink the same manner of working in your self & all others?

AFFECTIONATE. I see no difference in any, that I know.

CHEERFULL. And why should you expect to find any in them, that you doe not know?

AFFECTIONATE. Because I would be necessitated to condemne them for those euill Effects, which I find in my self and obserue in all, that I doe know, vpon this occasion. ⟨25v⟩

CHEERFULL. Vpon what occasion?

AFFECTIONATE. The Filling of the Belly with good cheare.

CHEERFULL. Why. though it be well done to be shy in taxing others, yet the more free you shalbe in shriuing of your self, it will be euery way the better for your self & vs. I pray therefore let mee become your Confessour.

AFFECTIONATE. What is it You would know?

CHEERFULL. How you find your self affected & disposed after good Cheare.

AFFECTIONATE. Why good for nothing.

CHEERFULL. For Nothing?

AFFECTIONATE. For Nothing, that good is. For play, for prating, for Folly, & in a word for any euill I find such an aptnes That with great Difficultie I can restrain my self from seeking opportunities, when they be not offered for these exercises. But for all good affaires I am like a Dore of [off] the hinges, that turns not but by maine force.

CHEERFULL. How meane you?

AFFECTIONATE. Why vtterly unable except vpon pure necessitie for any Business & then, howeuer I sett my self by constraint, altogether vnfitt for the accomplishment of it. ⟨26⟩

CHEERFULL. How comes this to passe?

AFFECTIONATE. Why principally through a certain kind of Dulnes & Sloth, that instantly vpon good cheare seazeth the head & afterwards diffuseth it self through all the other faculties both of mind & Body, leauing them feeble & disioynted for any painfull or serious imploiment.

CHEERFULL. Indeed the old Proverb is. When the Belly is full the bones would be at rest. But shall wee say, that this comes alwaies thus to passe. Or rather that as wee find it in matter of Tobacco, howsoeuer at first taking it much distempers most men, yet vpon frequent vs [use] it giues help vnto all operations both of mind and body: So likewise the Satietie & Fulnes, which wee speak of, may perhaps to them, which are accustomed therevnto, be of no such impediment as it is to you or others, that seldome light vpon it.

AFFECTIONATE. I haue too often run vpon it, the more is my guilt & greater hath beene my dammage continually.

CHEERFULL. But suppose it might be granted (Although I confesse I haue not found it in my self or any, that I know) that not vpon custome of a mans filling himself, for that cannot be; but of forcing a mans self to doe busines vpon a full stomack a man should come ⟨26v⟩ lesse to feele this vnaptnes for seriousnes

& paines taking. Yet must wee not say, that the vnaptness it self is not by Custome taken away but onely they by Custome made more expedite to doe what they desire, though it be with this vnaptnes.

AFFECTIONATE. So it seemes. And that herein it fares as it doth with men accustomed to fetters & Manacles. They goe much quicker, & vse their hands better vpon long vse. And so in regard of what it was to themselues at first, & in regard to what it would be to others, it seemes that Custome makes the impediment lighter, yet in very truth it is the selfsame as it was in the beginning, an vtter disabling of them for all seruices of worth & moment.

CHEERFULL. Very well then. The fulnes of the Body is alwaies of impediment to the operations of the mind, howeuer it appeare not so euident, nor be so much felt perhaps vpon Custome of doing busines after such fulnes. But what shall wee say touching that dulnes & darknes of the vnderstanding, which euidently appeares vpon Satietie? Is this euill effect any whit abated or otherwise mitigated by Custome & vsage? So that, although it cannot be denied, but that naturally vpon satietie there ariseth a great Difficultie in the vnderstanding for the apprehension of truth & Right then there was before. Yet euen this Difficultie by vse and ⟨27⟩ Custome is remoued & they, that are continually vsed to it, are as able after a Feast to iudge & discerne of what is good, true & right, & fitt, as others or themselues would be vpon Fasting or after a sober meale.

AFFECTIONATE. Not onely the general consent of all men, but the whole contriuement of all businesses & affaires in the world shews this to be otherwise. That the Filling of the Belly at any time doth not onely difficult [render difficult], as you say, but endanger the right apprehension of things for that present: & that this dayly glutting a mans self with meat & drink brings a man in the end to stupiditie are such manifest truths confirmed by vniversal vote & verified by vniforme practize of all Nations, as it would be much easier to pluck the club out of Hercules his hand then to maintain the contrarie.

CHEERFULL. Why then Custome in this matter helps not at all?

AFFECTIONATE. No verily. But as by how much more frequent the offences of Fire & smoak are, the greater emperishing follows in the ey-sight: So the more often & continued the Gluttings and Satietie be in the Body, the more is the weaknes & Dulnes of the vnderstanding encreased thereby, till in the end (as all often iterated Actions turn into habit) it comes to plaine stupiditie.

CHEERFULL. You meane comparatively to that quicknes & excellencie ⟨27v⟩ of vnderstanding, which themselues had before, or might haue had, but through these disorders.

AFFECTIONATE. You interpret mee & the common opinion & Proverb right, That Continual Cramming makes a man become a Sott: is to be vnderstood in respect of what he was by Natural abilities or former Condition. And so taken I think it neuer fails, & but seldome in the largest sence of all.

CHEERFULL. But it will not be amisse before wee goe any further to summe vp what wee are already agreed vpon, least afterwards you should more vnseasonably perhaps come vpon any additions or Subtractions.

AFFECTIONATE. You say well. Let heare I pray what you take for granted.

CHEERFULL. Why First that vpon Satietie in Meat & Drink there doth immediately follow a Lazy Sloth & vnaptnes in all the powers & faculties both of mind & body for serious & painfull employments.

AFFECTIONATE. I know not how this can be denied.

CHEERFULL. Next That there ariseth a confusion & Darknesse in the vnderstanding, that disables it for easy apprehension or Right iudgement of that, which comes then to consideration. ⟨28⟩

AFFECTIONATE. This must needs be granted.

CHEERFULL. Why then wee haue found two present euill

effects of Satietie, Sloth & Stupiditie. and this last goes alwaies encreasing remedilesse vpon the continuance of this kind of excesse.

AFFECTIONATE. So it seemes.

CHEERFULL. But for the other there may be some kind of help found. by Force & Constancie men may vpon Satietie bring themselues to dispatch busines of weight & Worth.

AFFECTIONATE. To doe them?

CHEERFULL. You say well. It is but a slubbering performance indeed, that must follow, when the vnderstanding is either away or lamely & blindly present. But doe them, they may, if they will.

AFFECTIONATE. After a while though not at first perhaps some may bring themselues vpon Satietie to a kind of outward seriousnes & painfulnes of mind & body but to little purpose.

CHEERFULL. You meane touching the perfect accomplishment of things of moment. But let vs consider, whether it can long last or be without further Dammage.

AFFECTIONATE. I see no dammage in any kind.

CHEERFULL. No, not in Health? ⟨28v⟩

AFFECTIONATE. Yes verily for matter of health there is nothing more preiudicial then to intend the mind seriously after a full repast of the Body, Distempers, Sicknesses, & Diseases in Extremitie doe immediately & vnavoydably follow vpon such vnorderly courses. He, that hath filled himself with good Cheare must first take his ease & afterwards goe to his Exercize, or els he shalbe sure to fall into the physitians hands & hardly all that can be done will keep him from tumbling into the graue.

CHEERFULL. Why then wee haue found three preiudices of satietie touching those businesses, which require serious & painfull intentions of the mind. That a man cannot vpon a full stomach with out great difficultie sett about the performance of them. That he can by no meanes performe them as he ought. And that his Endeauour & performance such as it is, cannot be without certain ouerthrow of health. And so wee find that third euill consequence of satietie mentioned by Galen, manifestly & euidently verified especially in those, that would striue to confute him by their owne Example equally pursuing the Filling of their Belly with good cheare & the furnishing of their minds with wisedome & knowledge. They, that doe this, besides that it is all but Labour in vain, can by no meanes liue either long or healthfully. And if for the preservation ⟨29⟩ of Life & Health they giue ouer Seriousnes & painfull intentions of the mind, must they not necessarily incurre the forfiture both of Wisedome & Vertue.

AFFECTIONATE. Vndoubtedly Wisedome can be neither gott nor kept with out serious intention & much studie of the mind, & the giuing ouer of painfull imployments must needs make a man proue Bankrupt with Vertue. Stupiditie & Sloth are the two main fountaines of Errour & Vice. And those minds, which these streames water can yeeld no better fruit than Ignorance & Lust.

CHEERFULL. Then was not Tullie to blame in saying, that they, that are replenished with much meat & Drink can neither vse their minds aright, nor maintaine any commerce with Vertue.

Part IV

The Affectionate now attempts new attacks on the virtue of Temperance and points out that commercial arrangements are best made by the German races when the discussions are accompanied by wine-drinking. Her opponents cite the contradictory custom of the ancients, who observed strict abstinence before and during important negotiations. After a long Socratic dialogue, the Cheerfull admits that wine does not increase the wisdom of men in making bargains, but benefits the conduct of such affairs only by the removal of shame and conscience.

The Affectionate next brings up the possible benefit of wine to poetry and the poets; but as the dialogue progresses, she is forced to admit that sacred and serious poetry (e.g., the work of David and Vergil) cannot be written under its influence. Ballads, sonnets and satires, however, which rely heavily on scurrility, ribaldry, and blaspheming, are usually improved by over-indulgence. The Guardian asserts that many popular poets have closed their works, as did Sir Philip Sidney, with a recantation and a confession of the wrong use of wit, and the Mother condemns love poetry as an instigator of lust and blasphemy, confusing as it sometimes does mistresses with angels. The Cheerfull concludes the discussion by stating that the excess of wine makes both tradesmen and scholars less understanding and skilful in those things wherein properly the wisdom of merchants and scholars consists.

----◆----

AFFECTIONATE. That I may not seeme a Prevaricatour in yeelding before I haue sayd & done the vttermost, you must giue mee leaue to try once more the force of some obiections, which like fresh supplies to a Beseiged Castle offer to make good the breach.

CHEERFULL. Let's see these bold Champions I pray, that diswade your surrender vpon so manifest a Necessitie.

AFFECTIONATE. You haue to deal with more & those of another condition then you are aware of. There's a generation ⟨29v⟩ of men you know amongst vs & a whole Nation abroad, as they tell vs & that one of the most renouned in the World, who are wisest

200

as they terme it in their Cups, who Negotiate busines of importance most willingly in a Taverne & dispatch them best after they
haue drunk well.

MOTHER. These Folk whoeuer they bee, are of a cleane other
mind then Romulus the Founder of the greatest Empire that euer
was. He being one Night rather present at a Banquet, then a
partaker of it, being demanded in the end, why he had drunk so
little, because too morrow, sayd hee, I am to treat of very weighty
affaires.

PATIENT. The answere of Theontichides[1] was to the same effect,
when one asked him vpon obseruation it seemes of his Abstemi-
ousnes, why the Lacedemonians vsed to drink so sparingly.
Because, replied Theontichides the Lacedemonians should be able
to giue Counsell at all times & haue no need at any time to ask it
of others.

MODERATOR. The Carthaginians Law was more universall &
more streight in this point. They absolutely forbad the vse of
Wine to all sorts of Magistrates during the time of their gouernment & quite banished it their camps, whilest the warre ⟨30⟩
lasted. And in this last point they were seconded by the Cretians
& Lacedemonians clean contrarie to the opinion of our Age, who
think the vse of Wine most necessary for military men & the
excesse of it least misbeseeming them of all others.

GUARDIAN. The proper issue of Excesse in Wine are Madnes
& Lust, was neuer enough praysed Alphonsus[2] wont to say &
therefore howeuer the Common Vsage of all princes was often
enforced by his Freinds as an Argument. Yet would he seldome

---

[1] Theontichides—the same name occurs in the Magdalene College manuscript
volume (see Bibliography, p. 317), but a crabbed hand, writing in brownish ink,
has corrected it to a form of Leonidas, a king of Sparta.

[2] Alphonsus—I have not been able to make a positive identification. There are
four interesting possibilities: Alfonso X of Castile (1221–84), patron of literature,
author of *Las Siete Partidas*, and known as 'The Wise'; his successor, Alfonso XI
(1311–50), about whom the Guardian told a laudatory story (Sharland, pp.
34–5); Alfonso V of Aragon (?1385–1458), benefactor of many humanists at
his court in Naples and known as 'The Magnanimous'; or Alfonso V of
Portugal (1432–81), who retired to a monastery at Cintra.

be perswaded to drink any Wine at all & neuer then but so allayed as it differed very little from sheere water. & his Answere or his Apothegme (for so it deserues to bee stiled) was, that Wine did darken Wisedome. Whether their Authoritie, who hold it a furtherance & help to Wisedome bee of like Creditt to these, which you haue heard alledged to the contrarie, wee shall then be able to iudge when we know who they bee.

AFFECTIONATE. I see not now how all the German power, though Netherland & the Suitzers should afford the vttermost of their Ayd to boot is able to withstand the force of this Charge. But let mee see, you take my words too large. I meane not, that store [abundance] of wine makes these people the more able ⟨30v⟩ for the great actions either of Warre or Peace, but for the better dispatch of some priuate & ordinarie affaires, such as are buying & selling, making of bargains & the like.

CHEERFULL. But these Buyings & Sellings & Bargaines & other the like matters, which are better done by the help of Wine then without, are they such things, as either tend directly to vertue or are alwaies accompanied at the least with Vertue.

AFFECTIONATE. They tend onely to profitt & that being the end the obtaining thereof is onely to be considered in this Case. As for Vertue, whether it be an ingredient or no, is not, as I suppose at all material.

CHEERFULL. But can Wisedome stand possibly without vertue, or can that by any meanes be wisely done, that is not well done?

AFFECTIONATE. If Wisedome be the ordering of the meanes to the end, shall not that be accounted a help to wisedome, which helps to the attainment of the end & shall not they be termed wise men, that effect what they aime at.

CHEERFULL. Wisedome is not the ordering of euery meanes to euery end, but of the right meanes in euery kind to a right end, that is proposed. & he is onely to be counted wise, that brings good matters to passe by good meanes. For tell mee, I pray, did

⟨31⟩ not Alexander as fully vnloose the Gordian knot by cutting it with his sword as any other could haue done by skill.

AFFECTIONATE. What then?

CHEERFULL. And yet you will not say he did it by Wisedome.

AFFECTIONATE. No but by force.

CHEERFULL. And did not Jezable as fully invest Ahab in Naboth Vinyard, as any faire purchase could haue done.[1] And will you say, that Jezable brought that to passe by Wisedome?

AFFECTIONATE. No but by fraud & false accusations.

CHEERFULL. Why then as the Proverb is, There being more waies to the wood then one, wee are not to say, that euery one, that attains his end is wise.

AFFECTIONATE. No. Except he doth it by the right meanes. For he, that by fraud or force, or any other indirect meanes compasseth that, which he aimes at, is not to be called wise, but strong or powerfull, or deceitfull, & the like.

CHEERFULL. Why then before wee giue these people, whom you speak of, the prize of Wisedome, because they attain their ends, wee must examine whether they be effected by the help of wisedome or some other meanes.

AFFECTIONATE. By what other meanes can it be then wisedome? ⟨31 v⟩

CHEERFULL. Let vs put an instance, & wee shall better perceiue the matter. That, which you say, is that these people sell dearer & buy cheaper, hold their own faster & gett from others more freely, when they are well filled with wine then when they are altogether sober.

AFFECTIONATE. And are they not then to be thought the wiser?

CHEERFULL. They, who make getting of money to be a Vertue and Happiness cannot well think otherwise.

AFFECTIONATE. Well. Suppose they be not to be termed wise-

[1] I Kings xxi, 15–16.

men, yet that they be not wiser Marchants in this disposition and by this meanes no man can deny.

CHEERFULL. But how shall wee say this is brought to passe? Haue they, when they are thus heated with wine better skill to discern & iudge of the Nature & Worth of those commodities, which they deal in?

AFFECTIONATE. Nay verily. Neither eies, nor any other sence or apprehension of the mind, but is perverted rather than improued, when men are in this Case. It were madnes then to goe about to iudge either of Colour or any other qualities in Ware of what kind soeuer.

CHEERFULL. But it may be thus disposed they better vnderstand the opportunities of venting their commodities. ⟨32⟩

AFFECTIONATE. They scarce know where themselues be, or what they doe, & how then can they be able to calculate the Necessities or guesse at the Dispositions of farre remoued Persons or Places?

CHEERFUL. Why but doth not the Wisedome of a Marchant cheifly consist in these things?

AFFECTIONATE. Yes verily. And he, that is ignorant or unskilfull in the worth & Nature of his commodities & in the opportunities of venting them is but a fool for a Marchant, as the Marchants Phraze is. & yet on the other side how making better bargains in this Case they should not be allowed the title of more Wisedome I cannot see.

CHEERFULL. Why doe you call those, that be thus made better bargaines, because they are more iust or more Equall?

AFFECTIONATE. No. But because they proue more gainfull.

CHEERFULL. Why to this intent Vnreasonableness perhaps may oftimes serue as well & better then reason or wisedome.

AFFECTIONATE. The Italian Proverb indeed makes little witt one of those three littles, which are necessarie for a man, that intends to grow quickly rich.

CHEERFULL. And what are the other two I pray? ⟨32v⟩

AFFECTIONATE. Little Shame & little Conscience.

CHEERFULL. Why then. It may be after the manner it is, that Excesse of wine helps men in their Bargains & other like affaires not by addition of Wisedome, but by taking away Shame & Conscience.

AFFECTIONATE. You haue verily hitt vpon the right. That little scruple, which men of whom Wine hath gott masterie, haue of Lying, Swearing, Defrauding, & oppressing, the little respect they haue to Freindship, Christianitie, or any thing but their own interest & the sencelesse Wranglings, Facings, Importunities, & Obstinacies, are those prevalent meanes, whereby they come still in the disposition to gett advantage of others.—But howeuer you haue routed these Mechanick Bands, yet put not off your Armour nor proclaime the Victorie. There's yet behind a mighty Troop that's ready to assault you. & see they come directly from the camps of Wisedome & Vertue itself.

CHEERFULL. They must needs come from them: For sure they can by no means stay there.

AFFECTIONATE. Why you will not I am sure deny but Poetrie & Poets merrit a cheif place amongst the Professours of knowledge and goodnes. ⟨33⟩

CHEERFULL. No verily. It being plain, that the First seeds of wisedome & vertue haue been planted by their hands throughout the whole world.

AFFECTIONATE. And it is much more plaine as well by their own Confession, as by dayly Experience, That Wine taken in good measure serues notably to help them in their Compositions. As on the contrarie it is a common by-word, that, Water-drinkers neuer make good Verses.

CHEERFULL. But if Dauids were good Poetry, this Rule is false. He drank more teares then wine, when he composed the most excellent peices of his work.

AFFECTIONATE. I speak not of sacred compositions.

CHEERFULL. And Virgils verses should be nought too, for sure he wrot them by force of much studie & not of much wine.

AFFECTIONATE. Nor doe I tend these, nor any other such kind of serious Poems.

CHEERFULL. Why but these sacred & serious compositions are those onely, whereby the conveyance of Wisedome & Vertue haue been made by Poets vnto the world.

AFFECTIONATE. But there are other kinds of Poems besides these, though not of such solid Benefitt perhaps, yet of singular ⟨33 v⟩ delight: & that witt of the Composers of them, if you will not allow it to be called wisedome, is much advanced by good Wine without all contradiction.

CHEERFULL. Oh now I vnderstand it. You meane Ballate-makers, Epigrammatists, & such as write Sonnets of & to their Mistresses, Satirs, Comoedies & the like.

AFFECTIONATE. I meane these indeed though I cannot allow the first a place at all, much lesse the Cheif in this Rank.

CHEERFULL. Indeed a good Ballet is a peice of better stuff then to match with most of the other. But tell mee I pray are these kinds of things approued by wise & good men?

AFFECTIONATE. Not as wise & good things perhaps, but that they be witty no man can deny.

CHEERFULL. Are there not of them, who terme that Scurrilitie & bitternes & Libelling & Ribauldry, I [aye], & Blasphemie too, which the world most admires, as the quintessence of Witt in Playes, Satirs, Epigrams, & Loue sonnets.

AFFECTIONATE. There be a great many, that goe so farre & not without iust cause perhaps in most kinds of these composi-tions.

CHEERFULL. But what say they, that giue the mildest censure?

AFFECTIONATE. That the best of them are but pernicious vanities. ⟨34⟩

GUARDIAN. They cannot well say lesse. Sir Phillip Sidney

closeth vp his works with a sonnet of Recantation, & seals it with splendidis longum vale dico Nugis.[1] I bid a longsome Farewell vnto splendid Trifles or Bables. And I am very confident, that the like Palenodie will vpon Examination be found to haue in the end been made by most of those, who haue excelled amongst vs in any of these forementioned kinds. I could instance in a great Number if need were.

MODERATOR. There is no need at all. There's very few either amongst vs or any where els, as I haue heard, that euer came to their right witts at last, but made open confession, I may say proclamation, that all the witt, that they had shewed in these matters, was quite wrong & nothing but sin & folly disguized with a superficial varnish of Art & Eloquence.

CHEERFULL. That wine should giue furtherance to the working of such Master-pieces as these are like to proue at best were no great commendation. But let vs see I pray which way it comes to passe, that these kinds of good fellows come to doe these works such as they be better then others or themselues otherwise could doe. Doe they by well-tipling themselues grow to a better apprehension of the nature, issue & consequence of those things they goe about. ⟨34v⟩

AFFECTIONATE. No verily. But they are better or rather more fitted to make significatiue expression of their own passions. They vent their amorousnes, their spleen & all other such like humours more freely & sett them off more liuely & conspicuously, when they are heated with wine then before. Otherwise there is no question but their iudgements & all other faculties are much impaired for the right discerning of such obiects as then fall vnder Consideration. For the powring in of wine vpon the ouerflowing of any passion is such a help to the vnderstanding, as the tying of

---

[1] The sonnet referred to is 'Leave me, O Love which reachest but to dust', to which Sidney gave the postscript, 'Splendidis longum valedico nugis'. See *Poems of Sir Philip Sidney*, edited by William A. Ringles Jr (Oxford, 1962). This sonnet, number 32, was the last of the group called 'Certain Sonnets', which was appended to the 1598 folio. The Latin phrase is original with Sidney.

a Bend [band] vpon the eies after they had been dazled in the sun would be for the distinguishing of Colours.

GUARDIAN. Indeed if passions blind the mind, that which increaseth the passions must needs adde to the blindnes. But shall wee think that Amourousnes is one of these.

MODERATOR. Why not, since Cupid the Poets God of Loue for this reason cheifly is by them alwaies brought on the stage either blind, or at least blind-fold.

GUARDIAN. That is to signifie as I haue heard the blindnes of Louers Affections in the choise & first setting on but not after-wards in the prosecution of them, their [there] being no one thing in the work perhaps, that so much quickens the witt as Loue doth. ⟨35⟩ Why Experience shows, that a little of this Ingredient sublimates the dullest Capacitie to such a height of Finenes & quicknes as no Art nor Studie can reach vnto; how much more then when it comes vpon a Rich foundation of Natural Abilities perfected by Learning & Art shall it not eleuate the vnderstanding, Affections & conceits to the loftiest pitch, that humane Nature can sore vnto.

MOTHER. And aboue too: For had not your amorous Poets gott by this meanes some other knowledge & apprehension of good & Euill, of God & Pan, of Happines & Misery, then either Reason or Religion teacheth, they durst neuer think in their hearts what they sing & publish to the world in their sonnets & Madrigalls.

GUARDIAN. What is that I pray, that you take so offensive?

MOTHER. Why wee silly Christians hold the least taint of Lust such a defilement as cannot be washed cleane without hott water of hearty teares. & these eleuated spirits esteeme it a Gallantrie to sett their Lasciuiousnes out in prospective to Men & Angels & to propagate as much as they possibly can the remembrance of it to after Ages. But this is nothing in regard of that transcendent boldnes, which they vse with God, investing their Mistresses ⟨35v⟩ with those diuine Attributes, which wee tremblingly lift vp our eies to look vpon.[1] As for their souls, because they be their own, they think they may dispose of them as they please. But truely they prize them not as Christian men ought to doe, when they offer them vp in Vassalage to filth & Rottennes; For no better is the Beauty & the Pleasures they professedly adore, & aime at in & by their Compositions.

CHEERFULL. And of what Condition shall wee say that is, which rellisheth so much in Epigrams, Satyrs, & Comoedies.

AFFECTIONATE. Much of the same Nature. The Girdings [sneerings] & Scoffings at mens persons vnder a pretence of correcting Vice, The Rayling on Authoritie & the traducing of vertue vpon some friuolous Colours [excuses] of inconveniencie, that follow vpon great & good mens Actions & opinions, or at least vpon some incongruitie they obserue in themselues.

GUARDIAN. Indeed this is that sauce, that hath alwaies made this trash goe for Dainties. Wittnes the Athenians, that were so taken with Aristophanes, his Clouds purposely made for the abuse of Socrates.

MODERATOR. I haue heard, that Socrates himself was present at the Act. ⟨36⟩

GUARDIAN. It is very true. & when he saw many strangers look about to see the man, that caused such mirth, he stood vp in the place where he formerly satt, that euery one might haue a full view & take their fill of Laughter at him.

MOTHER. It was nobly done of him & would turn mainly to our Reproof, if wee should be lesse confident in much better things then Socrates knew or made profession of.

MODERATOR. You doe well to arm your self timely. Without all question you shall fall proportionably on the like trials of others scorn & your own patience, if you keep on the way you haue begun.

MOTHER. I hope by Gods grace they shall still passe as easily

---

[1] As in many metaphysical poems of which Donne's 'The Dream' is an obvious example, not published, however, until 1633.

with mee as they come & I shall alwaies haue the heart to contemne their mocks, that haue the heart to mock at vertue.

CHEERFULL. But if this be so (& I see not well how it can bee denied) that the perfections of these compositions according to the Worlds iudgement lyeth in that, which in truth is Atheisme & in humanitie shall wee allow excesse of wine the honour of sharpening the witt because it makes men more apt & more impudent for deuising, penning, & publishing these things.

AFFECTIONATE. No, but the honour or rather infamie of increasing Malignitie against God & Man. ⟨36v⟩

CHEERFULL. Why then all, that you haue gained by these fresh supplies is but a further Confirmation of that, against which they were first brought into the Feild.

AFFECTIONATE. So mee thinks.

CHEERFULL. Why it is plaine, That Excesse of Wine makes both these Trades-men & Schollars lesse vnderstanding & skilfull in those things, wherein properly the Wisedome of merchants & Scholars doth consist.

AFFECTIONATE. True. For Vertue is the commodititie, that all Learning trafficks for. & therefore they, that take or vtter vice instead thereof, as these Poets doe in their verses fail as much as those Merchants (if any such were to be found) that should professe dealing in rotten & infectious wares.

CHEERFULL. Well then. That last Censure of Alphonsus must be granted true & deserued, That Wine at least much of it obscures Wisedome.[1]

AFFECTIONATE. It cannot possibly be denied.

[1] See above, p. 201 n. 2.

Part V

To conclude the discussion of the evils of wine-drinking, the Cheerfull
again quotes St Basil's condemnation of gluttony and remarks 'if the
filling with wine be such an overthrow to wisdom and such an introduction to all manner of evil . . . it cannot be but the repletion of more
solid stuff, as meat, should be more operative to the same effects'. The
Guardian takes the Affectionate's place in the ensuing dialogue with
the Cheerfull and is forced to admit that even slight excesses in food
produce lethargy in both mind and body, whereas slight excesses in
wine breed nimbleness of the same. Because fasting encourages fresh-
ness of the wits, the morning is the time for the conduct of important
affairs, says the Moderator, who claims that work of any sort after
eating impairs the health, for nature cannot attend efficiently to both
mental and physical activity. The Affectionate points out that Eve was
deluded by the Serpent's appeal to eat and thereby become wise, and
that all defence of food as a benefit to the understanding comes from
the Devil. Drinking 'cool and small liquors' which have no nourishing
qualities is not at this time considered detrimental to the smooth
functioning of the mind and body, yet it is agreed that any drinking
breaks a religious fast, as the practice of the Turks and Moors indicates.
The Guardian, moreover, feels that excess of wine and strong drinks is
more detrimental to the functioning of the mind and body than excess
of food.

———————◆———————

CHEERFUL. And shall wee not say, that St Basils iudgement
against Gluttonie[1] not onely in the general, when he layeth to its
charge, that it makes a whole wood of euill to spring vp in that
hart, which it waters, & that followers thereof, whateuer ⟨37⟩
semblance they make, warre indeed directly for & with the
Deuill; but in euery particular, that he mentions, is made good to
a haire.

AFFECTIONATE. With advantage.

GUARDIAN. With advantage truly euery way, whilest much

[1] See above, pp. 182-3.

more then hee expresseth, is verified in these, that fall vpon the lighter part & practize of it.

CHEERFULL. You say well, if the filling with wine be such an ouerthrow to Wisedome & such an introduction to all manner of euill, as appeares in them, that came in to giue Euidence[1] of that Benefitt, which it pretends to afford to some kind of people & professions, It cannot be but the repletion of more solid stuff, as meat, should be more operatiue to the same effects.

GUARDIAN. I see the Affectionate agrees not to this, though I perceiue she intend not to oppose whether out of wearines or out of doubt of being foiled I know not. Giue mee leaue therefore I pray to enter the list vpon this point, wherein verily, mee thinks, you haue the wrong.

CHEERFUL. Belieue it what euer you think. Excesse of meat and Excesse of drink are but two branches of one & the same Root or stock of Gluttonie & proportionably work the same effect both in mind & Bodie. ⟨37v⟩

GUARDIAN. You meane that aequal surcharges in each kind are as dammageable one as the other to the peruerting of the Vnderstanding and the Debauchery of the affections.

CHEERFULL. I [aye], and to the corruption of the body & vtter ouerthrow of the health.

GUARDIAN. Touching this last you haue the right on your side; For though the Distempers of Drink work more forceably for the present, yet surely the disorders of eating doe in the end work more violently & malignantly. Great Drinkers rub out [contrive to get on] longer & with lesse adoe then great Deuourers. And so it holds proportionably in euery degree as I suppose in this case of bodily health. But shall wee think it is after the same manner in the health & temper of the mind.

CHEERFULL. Why not. Dry Gluttonie & Wett Gluttonie differ no more as a most worthy Authour[2] of our times writes, then the

---

1 Them, that came in to giue Euidence—see above, p. 200.
2 Most worthy Authour—see Introduction, p. lxxxiv.

Land & the Water ratt. & his Resolution is (howeuer not the world onely but many good men perhaps think it a Paradox), that our Land groanes more vnder the Burden of Surfetting by meat then by Drink.

MOTHER. You will not think this so improbable, Worthy Guardian, howeuer strange it seemes at first, if you call to mind that Fulnes of bread is layd to Sodomes Charge[1] as one of the three main parts of her guilt & necessarie inducements of her punishments.

GUARDIAN. In very deed you stumble [puzzle] mee: For although all other ⟨38⟩ sorts of Dainties & Excesse be perhaps included hereunder, yet that they should be specified by no other Name then Fulnes nor in no daintier a kind then bread giues a marveilous Blow to all kind of Repletion & truely a deadly Wound to that, which is vpon varietie of Choise Delicacies.

CHEERFULL. If wee follow the Clue, which you are now light vpon, it will guid [guide] you out of this maze very speedily.

GUARDIAN. I am not aware of that Light, which you seeme to discouer in this busines vpon that, which I haue sayd.

CHEERFUL. Yes verily it cannot be but you, that haue found the dore, should show the way out. But for others better instruction you will haue it sett wide open. The Question between vs is, Whether the Excesse & other disorders of Eating be as preiudicial to Wisedome & Vertue as those of drinking, or Whether Gluttonie & Surfetting, as wee vse to restraine these termes to solid food be causes of as many euill Effects in a mans soul, as Drunkennes, which wee appropriate to Liquours.

GUARDIAN. You say very well. I see wee must come in the end to a triall vpon the whole. But I pray first let vs goe on with that, whence the Difference between vs had his rise. That is the point of Satietie, which mee thinks, can by no meanes ⟨38v⟩ bee made as damnable in dry meates, as it appeares in Liquours.

CHEERFULL. Suppose the Question made whether Cloth of

---

[1] Luke xvii, 28.

wool or Silken Stuff were more Costly how should wee cometo a certaine decision of this matter.

GUARDIAN. Why wee must calculate the Difference of prizes [prices] between the same quantities as between an ell or a pound of each. & that, which wee find highest rated wee are to accompt Dearest.

CHEERFULL. But is not a yard of some Cloth more worth then a yard of some Silken Stuff.

GUARDIAN. There hath been verily Cloth made amongst vs, that in it [its] own natural condition, I meane without any enrichment of Dy or Art hath been more worth then many sorts of veluet & that not onely Ell for Ell, but pound for pound likewise, if they had been weighed together. Wee must therefore, make the tryall in this case not between the quantities onely, but by all other manner of equalities, that is, wee must set the best of each of these commodities against the best of the other & the worst against the worst & so successiuely going vpward & downward, still making the tryal between the same degrees or sorts in each kind. And because so doing wee find ⟨39⟩ the meanest sort of wollen Cloth to be much cheeper then the meanest kind of silken stuff, & the best kind of silken stuff to be much more worth then the best sort of wollen Cloth & so answerable [proportional] through the whole progresse of this matter, the silk stuff still advancing the Cloth in prize, we must necessarily conclude, that Silk stuff, is dearer & more costly then wollen.

CHEERFULL. Why then wee must not likewise, except wee mean to deceiue our selues make the comparison between Satietie of meat & drink vpon the proportion of quantitie onely but of qualitie also, setting out, as I may say, & matching Liquours & food, that, which is highest in each kind with the highest in the other & that, which is lowest with the lowest & so through euery degree. And so doing I suppose wee shall find, that not bread & ordinarie victual, but that, which is daintie & licorish to the appetite is to be sett against wine, as it seemed to mee, you intimated.

GUARDIAN. You say very well. As for bread that in this tryall is to answere [correspond] to water & ordinarie food to small and weaker sorts of Liquour. And now I begin to see already that wee shall in part find the satieties of Food to be worse then ⟨39v⟩ those of Drink: For vndoubtedly the Repletion or ouercharging of water & small Beere or the like, are not to Body or Mind so dammageable in any respect, as the proportionable Excesses of Bread or ordinarie victuals.

MOTHER. The Satietie of Bread or the surfett of it is the worst of all others, as I haue often heard from Physicians. & then it will not perhaps hold the lowest place in this comparison.

CHEERFULL. It may be so, that a full surfett, as wee call it, of Bread should be the worst of all others for bodily health not in regard of its own working perhaps more perniciously in the Body, but in regard that those surfets, which come vpon varietie of meats are through the mutual contestation of them each with other the easier to be wrought out of the stomach by the force of Nature & Help of Art: But that otherwise Repletion of Bread should generally be more pernicious to health then that of Flesh or Dainties is in experience euidently false. Inasmuch as wee see poore people, that liue vpon nothing els but Bread almost, howeuer undoubtedly they much exceed in the Quantitie of what they ought to doe, yet farre lesse subiect to diseases then they, who exceed in abundance of Flesh or other the like sorts of more rellishing Food. As for the excesse of Dainties besides a continual torment ⟨40⟩ through many noysome infirmities, as Gout, Stone, Wind, Collick, & the like wee see the issue is plain Rottennes & that in a very instant almost. But of this wee shalbe necessitated to speak more, when wee come to the Consideration of these Benefitts, which Temperance affords towards a long & pleasant Life. Now this may suffice to take away that doubt, which may arise touching our opposing Bread amongst Food against water amongst Drinks, which is no waies preiudiced in that Physitians hold that the surfett of Bread is generally the worst of all surfets, which is to be vnderstood of a full down surfet. & that it is the worst is by accident in regard that matter through the vniformity thereof is not so easy perhaps to bee remoued. But whether it be thus as I haue been taught or otherwise it is not much to our purpose, who are now vpon Examination, not of the preiudice, that follows in bodily health but of those, that follow in the mind vpon satietie in which regard I suppose there is little question to be made touching that, which wee are agreed vpon.

GUARDIAN. You say well, That proportionable excesses in bread and ordinarie food should not be more dammageable to the mind, then in water or small Liquours, there is no contraversie. But that excesse in any sort of food should be of so much dammage to the mind, as wine & other strong Liquours seeme to mee, I confesse no way to be made good. ⟨40v⟩

CHEERFULL. No way? Not for the ouerthrow of Wisedome? Consider well I pray, whether the Satietie of great good cheare, as they term it doth not bring on as equall a Lethargie & confusion in the vnderstanding & all intellectual faculties as the fulnes of wine doth.

GUARDIAN. Yes verily. A little excesse of Wine seemes to make the greater part of men more Nimble & Actiue in their conceits words & Actions whereas the other Excesse breeds euident dulnes. As for the right discerning & iudging of things, I hold the case to be much alike. The ones witt runs at wast by his mouth, the others soul is carried down into the stomack, & can by no meanes like a spring cloyed with mud, rise vp till it be cleared. And to this purpose I remember to haue heard it out of St Hierome [Jerome], That obliuion comes alwaies along with satietie thrusting the Abilitie of apprehension out of the mind, till Hunger hauing recalled Memory brings it back again.

MODERATOR. How preiudicial Fulnes of meat must needs be to the operations of the mind is most vndeniably to be evinced by that prize, that all the World giues to Fasting for the Dispatch of all such matters as require strength of intention or depth of vnderstanding. Wise men will not put a bitt into their mouths when they goe about such matters, till the Difficulties in both these kinds be ouerpassed. ⟨41⟩

MOTHER. A proof hereof, I haue heard in that, which Busbequius writes of himself;[1] howeuer a man of Rare Abilities in Nature and very exquisite Learning ioyned with great Experience in state affaires, yet (as he himself tells of himself) Most what but Fasting he durst not adventure to treat with Haly Bassa a man of choise parts amongst the Turks, that I might, sayd hee, with more Freedome of my witts better attend the Discourse of that sharp vnderstanding man, although it being commonly afternoone, that the Bashaw sent for him. He confesseth, that hunger did not a little torment him but eat before he durst not for feare of befooling himself.

PATIENT. The Freshnes of the Witts, which Fasting brings with it, is as I suppose one of the Cheif of those Reasons, which giue the morning the priuiledge aboue all other times of the Day for the contriuement & dispatch of those businesses, which are to be done by the head. As on the other side for the selfsame Reason perhaps in old time the Repast of the Body was deferred till Night especially amongst scholars & all those other, the Exercize of whose profession lieth in the vnderstanding according to Socrates his precept, Rise with the Sun to Counsell & at the going down thereof sitt down to eat.

MODERATOR. It was questionles a wise Rule: For Eating being ⟨41v⟩ ordained to the maintenance of Corporal Life & Strength must needs be of impediment to the spiritual operation of the mind, whiles it necessarily calls away not onely the spirits, which are the instruments of such operations, but as I may so speak the

---

[1] Busbequius (Busbecq, 1522–92) was ambassador (1554–62) of the Emperor Ferdinand I to the sultan in Constantinople. He is the author of *Legatione: Turcical Epistolae Quatuor*, a volume of letters written from Turkey and published in 1581 in Antwerp and in 1589 in Paris. The book was most recently translated by Edward S. Forster under the title *The Turkish Letters of Ogier Ghuselin de Busbecq* (Oxford, 1927). The passage cited is in Letter IV, p. 193. The man referred to below as 'Haly Bassa' is Ali Pasha.

whole Course of Nature to a New & painfull work, for the Digesting of meat & partitioning it out afterwards for nutriment to euery seueral member & vse is, wee see, a busines of such importance as requires the whole Attention of Nature to doe it rightly as it ought. And therefore Physitians alwaies enioyn them, who are carefull of health & strength either Sleep or such Exercize as onely may serue to this purpose euen after the most moderate Repast that may be. & wee see it plain by dayly Experience, that they, who transgresse their Rules in this kind setting vpon any serious Labour, especially of the mind, how temperate soeuer their meals be, yet vnavoydably fall vpon indigestion & the euill consequences thereof. And this surely is the main ground of that weaknes of stomack & other infirmities, which alwaies afflicts great students. For Nature being but one, whilest it is at once put vpon the two principal operations both of mind & body, is constrained to be wanting to the good performance of both. And so it comes to passe, that they profitt but little by studie after meals & quite marre their digestions. He, that would ⟨42⟩ doe both rightly, must doe both in their orders & alone by it self: & therefore Socrates his rule was vndoubtedly a very Oracle. That men should sett about digestions of the mind (for so is study to be accompted) when Nature is freed from the Attendance of Bodily Digestion. And when they sett about study of the Body (for so Digestions are to be accompted) they should giue Nature a vacancie from the studie of the mind, at least from all those, which require serious & painfull intentions.

AFFECTIONATE. You know, Wee heard it lately out of a graue Authour as St Augustines obseruation, if I mistake not, that as all the rest of the Discourse, which the serpent had with Eue was Deceit & Lies, so the Argument, whereby he ouerwrought her, was most absurd, Eat & you shall be more Wise is such an apparent Falsehood, as had not her iudgement been corrupted by her Appetite, she could not haue but known him to be a Deceiuer and suspected his intention to be naught, howeuer faire his words

sounded. It is cleane contrarie sayth St Augustine, Eating especially eating too much, or any waies disorderly, as it was in this
Case, offends the vnderstanding. & either not Eating or Eating
very sparingly, is that, which quickens the mind & whereby a man
becomes wise. ⟨42v⟩

CHEERFULL. You then see, out of whose schools all these allur-
ing sophismes to draw down dainties, come. That helps the
memorie, That comforts the braine. Another furthers the Apprehension & generally fine Cates [delicacies] & Daintie Fare breed
good Witt. They are all but new Enforcements of that first
imposture, which wrought our Woe. All Eating is in its own
Nature of impediment to the vnderstanding though some be
Necessarie, whilest the soul is confined in the Body.

GUARDIAN. But is not drink so too especially of Wine?

CHEERFULL. Drinking to speak generally is immediately ordained [related] to Eating, that by the Fluentnes of the Liquid
substance the solid Food may be more easily & aptly conveyed
& distributed through the whole Body. & therefore is not
properly & primarily intended to Bodily strength, so perhaps
consequently of much lesse Diuersion to the operation of the
mind. The concoctions & distributions of these Liquours, which
are rightly called Drinks, being an easy peice of work & such as
Nature is able to dispatch as Actiue men oftimes passe through
many by-matters [trivial affairs] with out any great disaccom-
modation to the businesses, wherevpon they are intent.

PATIENT. I begin now to discouer some kind of Reason in their
behalf, (& many they be for the opinion & practize is spread
almost ⟨43⟩ through all the Western parts of the World) who
hold drinking to be no breach of Fast itself: For suppose the end
of Fasting (as it is generally held); to be the humbling of the Body
by abating of Food, & the Exaltation of the mind by giuing it a
free disposal of all the Faculties of the soul, it seemes there doth
not follow any reall, at least any great contradiction between
Fasting & Drinking, which breeds perhaps but a light calling away

of Nature or any ministring faculties thereof from the seruice of the mind, & yeelding no nourishment at all (as is plaine in water), doth not preiudice that Humiliation of the Body, which is cheifly aimed at in Fasting.

GUARDIAN. But this perhaps is to be accompted not onely an Errour in Religion, but an Absurditie in Reason, the light whereof hath taught all the rest of the world besides [except for] the Papists to hold any drinking much more of Wine or such other prepared & mingled Cups as they vse, to be an absolute breach of Fast. The same Busbequius,[1] whom you lately spoke of writes, The Turks scrupulositie to be so great in this point as they dare not wash their mouths in Cold Water on their Fast days before the starres appeare in the sky, at least the time of their appearance, which in the Dark Night is proclaimed by their Mouden (as they call the Sexton) from ⟨43 v⟩ the top of the Steeples. Such is the strictnes of their Fast. Although when these Fasting seasons, as euery sixth year they doe, fall in the beginning of summer they be oftimes miserably tormented with drought through the length of the Day & the Excesse of the heat, yet will they not willingly break their Fast for feare of transgressing their Law. In the time of Warre no, nor at the Day of Battell it self neither, but after many perswasions of their Learned men & vpon the Example of their Prince, who in such Exigents comes forth & publickly eats himself before the whole Armie to giue them the better warrantie for doing the like.

AFFECTIONATE. So strict are the Moores, sayth the Historie of Barbarie in keeping their Lent, which is of thirty daies continuance & immediately preceeds their Feast called Rumedam answering to our Easter, as many grow faint with Fasting. And mine Author, sayth the story, reports to haue seene diuers layd before the Church doores ready to giue vp the Ghost for Drought, & some haue died holding it no question something meritorious to dy in seeking to fulfill their Law. But that, which followeth is marveilous strange. Once, sayth the Storie, the same gentleman

---

[1] See above, p. 217. The passage is found in Letter III, p. 152.

travailing to Moracko with certaine Moores in his company in that time of Lent. One of the Moores oppressed with heat & travell went & drank a little water at one of the Conduits in the open streets ⟨44⟩ of Meruecco, whereat the people made such wonderment & fell to so bitter reuiling, Crying out, that he know not God for breaking in publick their Law (though it doth admitt that one may break the Fast for great Neccessitie a day or two in his Trauell, so he take vpon his Conscience to fast as many daies as he hath missed before the next Rumedan come againe) that the poore wretch seeing himself condemned of his own people & dishonoured before the Christian Travailers in a desperate mind (which may be counted Zeal, sayth the Storie) killed himself with his own Dagger.

MOTHER. Vndoubtedly the great Conscience (as appeares by so many admirable Examples in sundry kinds) which those miscreants haue of breaking in the least title their vnprofitable & painfull superstition, will one day come in a sore informer against that stupid wretchlesnes [recklessness], which the best of vs vse touching the obseruation of the most easy, necessarie, & beneficial precepts of our Holy Christian Faith.

CHEERFULL. Howeuer Drinking in any kind proues a breach of a Religious Fast, which requires perhaps besides the increase of the minds vigour by abating the Liuelines of the Body, an Actual restraynt of all sensual appetites from their proper satisfactions as wee of the reformed Churches are taught & reason perswades the Mahamitans ⟨44 v⟩ & all other kind of infidels. Yet if it proue either none at all or but of Little impediment to that Fasting, which is naturally intended to the better performance of the operations of the mind, wee haue then gained the full proof of what wee desired. That is, that Drinking to speak in generall is not naturally of such impediment to the Exercizes & Works of vnderstanding, as eating is & consequently much more the satietie of Drinking not so preiudicial, as of Eating.

GUARDIAN. Indeed limitting Drinking & Drinks so precizely as

you doe to cool & small Liquours it seemes to be true & euident
what you say: But in the case of Wine it will perhaps be found
otherwise. Wine & strong drinks cannot be denied to haue some
kind of Nourishment in them. & such as though it be of little
continuance, yet for the present adds much strength & vigour to
the Body, & therefore they must needs break that Fast, which is
ordained to bodily Humiliation. & though in regard of their
Natural heat they digest not themselues onely, but help digestion
of all other things in the stomack & so in their regard perhaps may
be thought not to call away Nature nor any other faculties, that
are needfull for the service of the mind as Concoction of solid
food necessarily doth, yet by the selfsame qualitie of heat ascending themselues & carrying vp with them much other euill matter
into the head, which is the workhouse & shop of the ⟨45⟩ vnderstanding. They doe by their actiue vnrulines cause much more
disorder, distraction & impediment to the mind in all her operations then any substantial food in the stomack can doe by withdrawing Nature & the other faculties from the attendance & seruice
of the mind.

MOTHER. That, which you haue obserued in the excesse of
wine is vndoubtedly proportionable in the use of it in all lesser
quantities. It euer causeth more Alteration in the operation of the
mind by its own working there, then Food doth by calling down
the help to the stomack.

AFFECTIONATE. They, that study best after a morning draught,
as a number professe they can doe, will hold that these Alterations
are for the better & help, if not the vnderstanding in its proper work,
yet the other subordinate apprehensions as Fancie & Memory.

MODERATOR. This Benefitt, if it be so in any, must be by
accident: In regard that some crudities, that oppresse the stomack,
are either by the heat of the strong Liquour immediately digested
or els by force thereof, As wee see in suddaine inundations, carried
down into the Lower parts. & so Nature being disburthened hath
the more freedome to attend the seruice of the mind. ⟨45v⟩

Part VI

The Cheerfull proposes the question of whether wine is drink, food, or medicine. The Guardian finds it 'a pleasant medicine, if it be a medicine' and cites Scripture in its defence as an alleviator of the pains and sorrows of life. The Mother adds that wine may have its special use as a medicine but is not to be considered a common substitute for water. The Guardian insists that each man be allowed his own practice and judgement as long as he avoids the excesses forbidden by St Paul: 'taking too much in quantity or setting the heart too much upon it'. The Mother agrees that God's word is the only rule and that in the passages cited abundant use of wine cannot be imputed a sin; nevertheless riotous practice is condemned in other sections of Scripture.

After apologies for unscholarly digressions, the Cheerfull encourages the Mother to interrogate the Guardian on the meaning of the phrases 'too much' and 'given to wine'. The Mother enters a long Socratic dialogue with the Guardian in an attempt to define the latter phrase. She shows wide and intimate knowledge of various translations of the Bible in English and other vernacular tongues as well as in Greek and Latin; however, she does not prove that wine is anywhere forbidden. When she re-emphasizes that Christians must be wary of over-indulgence, the Guardian reiterates that the words of the Bible must not be extended 'to a stricter sense than the lawgiver intended'.

The Guardian and the Mother now undertake the definition of 'much'. What is too much wine for one man or for one occasion may be the equivalent of none for another or for the same man on a different occasion. The Guardian suggests that much wine begets much mirth and appetite, both good things, whereas little wine produces only little of these pleasures. The Mother again upholds great moderation. The Cheerfull points out that without wine the digestion of an excessive amount of food is impossible and that the effects of gluttony can be relieved by wine: temperance in solid food is necessary if the use of wine is restricted or prohibited. The Mother says that tobacco also effects the same office and is joined by the Patient in vehement condemnation of that 'loathsome remedy'. The Patient suggests that the censure of wine was also intended to include an injunction against being given to rich foods and perhaps was made so that temperance in the

223

use of wine resulted in temperance in the eating of food. The Guardian again objects and says that only those dainties such as dried grapes and others related to wine are forbidden and that it is wrong to extend the condemnation to all dainties.

———————◆———————

CHEERFULL. Well. Be it as it will, either by Nature or by accident, wee haue found, that some Excesse of wine (for no man can denie but, these morning draughts are excesses) may help some men in some kind of manner towards the better performance of those operations, which belong to the mind. A Condition, which I suppose wilbe hardly found belonging to any Excesse in that, which is properly & simply food. But letting this ly in store to make vse of vpon occasion, Let vs, I pray, consider before wee goe any further whether wine be rightly to be accompted amongst Drinks. For if all kind of water, that serues naturally for drink be cold & without any nourishment, & those waters, which fail in any of those conditions are excluded from amongst Natural Drinks, such as Sea-waters, Bath & other mineral waters, how wine, that is nutritiue & hott; & so both in substance & qualitie directly opposite should be properly accompted amongst drinks I see not: For the liquidnes, wherein it agrees with water will not more serue to make wine drink, then it doth milk, which sometimes perhaps may be taken instead of Drink, but is alwaies truely & really Food.

GUARDIAN. But if wine be not properly drink much lesse is it to be accompted food: In regard the nourishment it af⟨46⟩fords, is not properly to the encrease or maintenance of that, wherein Life & strength consists, but onely to the encrease & quickning of those spirits, which serue as instruments to the soul for the performance of all actions both of mind & body.

CHEERFULL. Why but if wee cannot rightly place [*it*] amongst either meats or Drinks, wee shalbe forced, it may be, to rank it amongst Medicines, for that is the onely remaining head, vnder

Mother. And how will you exclude him from being Given to wine, y't makes it y'e Prologue & Epilogue of all his mirth and solace.

Guardian. Wee say likewise y't a man is given to y'e Eat, w'ch hath such Mastery over him, as to cause him for Love or any other respect thereunto, to transgresse y'e bounds of higher obligation. & so wee say a man is given to his pleasure, when for the enioyment thereof he neglects serious Busines. To his quiet, when he is content rather to vndergoe losse, then Trouble. To Ambition & Honour, when for y'e attainment thereof he regards not Conscience or Friendship.

Mother. And how shall wee free them from being given to wine, y't are so subiect to it, as they can any way run vpon neglect of busines, wast of Estate, minishing of Credit; or wounding of their Conscience for y'e Love & delight they take in good wine.

Guardian. Wee may well free them because themselves I am sure desire to be free from this Charge.

Mother. But if there were a Prize sett vpon being Given to wine by S't Paul, as there have been by many great Princess of y'e world, would any of these y't wee have reckoned vp take it well to be debarred from their claime thereunto.

Guardian. No surely. Hee y't could bring proof of his vsing to
drink

a exterior

b interior

4 The Chapel at Little Gidding

which wee can bring those things, that being neither Food nor drink properly, are yet good at sometimes & vpon some occasions to be eaten & drunken.

GUARDIAN. It is a pleasant Medicine, if it be a Medicine.

CHEERFULL. That it should be a pleasant Medicine, is agreable to the incomprehensible Excellencie of the Physitian both for wisedome & Bountie & sutable to the Nature of the disease for which it is prescribed: For Pleasure is the proper Remedie of Greife.

GUARDIAN. You say well. The scripture euery where makes the end of wine by Gods institutions to be the Asswaging of greif, the Releif of cares & the increase of right sett joy. Hee brings forth grasse for the Cattel, sayth Dauid, & green herbs for the vse of man, that he may bring food out of the earth, and ⟨46v⟩ wine, that maketh glad the Heart of man & oile to make him a cheerful countenance & bread to strengthen mans heart.[1] As for quenching thirst & all other vse, which drink is needfull vnto, it seemes water is appropriated in the same place & euery where els in scripture & wee directed vnto the vse thereof alone.

MOTHER. If to this vertue of wine, which the old Testament so often mentions you put that other, which St Paul intimates to be in it, when he adviseth Timothie to vse a little wine for his stomack & often infirmities sake,[2] wee may then conclude, that as Wine is properly to be accompted a Medicine being ordained to the cure of the most proper & principal infirmities both of mind & body: so the turning it to an ordinarie drink must needs be a perverting of that, wherevnto it was at first ordained, & beyond the bounds of any priuiledge, that wee find recorded in scripture. For surely according to Solomons manner of arguing, that it belongs not vnto Kings nor Princes, that haue great Authoritie & are at much ease, to drink wine, because wine is for them, that are oppressed, heauie minded, & in miserie,[3] Wee should conclude

[1] Psalm civ, 14–15.   [2] I Timothy v, 23.
[3] Proverbs xxxi, 4–7. See p. 102 n. 1.

from St Paul's iniunction of it as a necessarie medicine vpon infirmitie & indisposition of Body, that it ought by no means to be vsed out of wantonnes by them, who are strong & in health.

PATIENT. They then, that stretch this text to the patronage of that ⟨47⟩ riotous excesse, which this Age is guiltie of, & from St Pauls iniunction of a little wine for an ill stomack through abstinence & Fasting inferre the Libertie of drinking a great deal for the better help of disordered eating must needs be thought to argue rather out of the strength of wine, which they are full of, then out of the force of reason, which [it] is to be suspected they are destitute of, at least in this case making vpon one & the same ground inferences clean contrarie to those, which Solomon the wisest of all men did. Either he was a bad Logician, or els surely they are not so good Diuines as they boast themselues for.

GUARDIAN. But though this place to Timothie serue not it may be either for any larger vse of wine then of a little onely & that but vpon Necessitie through indispostion of stomack, yet in regard St Paul condemnes not the vse but onely of too much wine in Deacons and Aged women, euen when he appoints them to be Gods Vshers, as I may say in the school of Vertue, or the immoderatenes of the Affections towards it, when he sayth they must not be giuen to wine.[1] It seemes these two excesses auoyded, in taking too much in quantitie, or setting the heart too much vpon it, there is no other sin or danger in this matter. & therefore howeuer the Allowance to Timothie bee too scant perhaps to warrant men like him in tendernes of conscience, ⟨47v⟩ that ordinarie abundance of wine, which is now generally vsed, yet if it fall not in compasse of that prohibition, which St Paul hath sett down, no man ought to be restrained from his Libertie either of iudgement or practize in this Case.

MOTHER. Vndoubtedly Gods Word is the onely rule, whereby the moral streightnes or crookednes of all things is to be proued, & all enlargements or abatements of Christian Libertie ought to

---

[1] Titus ii, 2–3.

haue plaine warrantie from thence.[1] If therefore this ordinarie abundance of wine, which is now adaies vsed, making it serue in great part for drink it self, & altogether for the Digestion of meat or more daintie meats haue not a plain check in scripture, it ought not to be imputed as a sin, nor they, that think fitt to make vse thereof depriued of their Libertie. But as it is without question, as I suppose, that there is store of plain & vndeniable arguments to be brought from diuers other places of scripture against this riotous practize: So I haue heard those very places of restraint & prohibition like a two-edged sword beaten back to the wounding of that Head, for the defence whereof it was held vp, enforced very strongly as I conceiue to the ouerthrow & condemnation thereof, as if it were not for diverting you from that, which our beloued Cheerfull is vpon, I should now tell you. ⟨48⟩

CHEERFULL. Wee are neuer out of the way, whilest wee come to learne or further that, which is good & vsefull. Though our often digressions therefore in scholars methodes be compted errours, yet returning with such advantage to the maine of our intents, as they alwaies haue done, I esteeme them rather perfections & by no meanes to be waued, when they opportunely offer themselues, as this doth. For in very truth a great part of the Busines both touching Wett & Dry Gluttonie lies vpon the Clearing of those two words, that is, what is ment by, too much, & what by being Giuen to a thing. Both which all men will yeeld, as well in wine, as in all other manner of Dainties, to be vitious. But how farre these words are to be extended, will not perhaps be so easily accorded & yet it will be necessarie to come to agreement herein, before wee can come to that particular application of things, which will be needfull both for ourselues & others. I therefore earnestly beseech you to proceed in this matter to the vttermost.

MOTHER. Well then. To giue you accompt not onely in sub-

---

[1] The Mother's reluctance to extend the injunctions against wine without Biblical authority parallels the Guardian's words on p. 235 below.

stance of that, which you require, but after the same manner, that I learned it: I desire first to know, Worthy Guardian, what you vnderstand by that Phraze of being Giuen to wine, which St ⟨48 v⟩ Paul in his Epistle both to Timothie[1] & Titus[2] seemes to allow the full Authoritie of a legall exception against a Bishops consecration.

GUARDIAN. What els should be ment then that, which is sett down in the marginal Note of the Geneua Translation, A Common Tipler & One, that will sitt by it.

MOTHER. Such as these may be truly sayd to be Giuen vnto it with a wittnes, as the proverb is. But if nothing els be ment, why did they not put these words in the text, rather then those other, which are more general & lesse plaine to be vnderstood, as appeareth by the Necessitie of this comment.

GUARDIAN. Giuen to wine answeares perhaps best to the original & therefore is put into the Text. & those other better exemplifie the thing intended & therefore are added by way of explanation.

MOTHER. But shall wee not say then that expression, which best setts out this thing intended, most answears vnto the Original, as wee count that Glosse the truest, which most liuely represents the image rather then that, which represents more substantially.

GUARDIAN. Well let it be granted, which I see you aime at. Giuen to wine will compasse in a greater circuit then these general words reach vnto. ⟨49⟩

MOTHER. Why then wee haue not yet found any more then some part of that, which Snt Paul condemnes.

GUARDIAN. Wee haue found the principal.

MOTHER. Bee it so. But must wee not goe on to the search of all the rest, that is included vnder that phraze. & take it not onely those soakers, which you haue apprehended, but all those other, whoeuer they be, that any way fall in Compasse of being rightly & truely sayd Giuen to Wine.

[1] I Timothy iii, 3.   [2] Titus i, 7.

GUARDIAN. Will you then extend the sence of this phraze in the particular of Wine, as farre as it goes currant in other things?

MOTHER. Why should you make any abatement here rather then elswhere. & think that Being giuen to Wine, meanes lesse than being Giuen to other things?

GUARDIAN. Why wee may say men are giuen to that, which they doe often, whether it be in morall or Natural Actions. And so wee say he is giuen to sweat; another giuen to Ly, a third is giuen to play.

MOTHER. And how shall wee exempt him from being giuen to wine, that drinks wine often vpon what occasion soeuer it bee.

GUARDIAN. And wee say, that a man is giuen to that, which he takes delight or pleasure in, as in walking, Gaming, study, or the like. ⟨49v⟩

MOTHER. And how will you exclude him from being Giuen to wine, that makes it the Prologue & Epilogue of all his mirth and solace.

GUARDIAN. Wee say likewise, that a man is giuen to that, which hath such Mastery ouer him, as to cause him for Loue or any other respect therevnto, to transgresse the bounds of higher obligation. & so wee say a man is giuen to his pleasure, when for the enioyment thereof he neglects serious Busines. To his Quiet when he is content rather to vndergoe losse, then Trouble. To Ambition & Honour, when for the attainment thereof he regards not Conscience or Freindship.

MOTHER. And how shall wee free them from being giuen to wine, that are so subiect to it, as they can any way run vpon neglect of busines, wast of Estate, Minishing of Creditt; or wounding of their Conscience for the Loue & delight they haue in good Wine.

GUARDIAN. Wee may well free them because themselues I am sure desire to be free from this Charge.

MOTHER. But if there were a Prize sett vpon being Giuen to wine by St Paul, as there beene by many great Princes of the

world, would any of these that wee haue reckoned vp take it well
to be debarred from their Claime thereunto.

GUARDIAN. No surely. Hee, that could bring proof of his vsing
to ⟨50⟩ drink oft, would hold himself abundantly qualified for any
reward belonging to them, that were giuen to Wine, howeuer it
may be wine itself were no way so delightfull, but the Contrarie to
his pallate. And he, that could make his delight in wine apparent,
would hold himself questionlesse much wronged, if any should
put in a Caueat against him, as being but seldome times or a small
drinker through want of wine or any kind of restrayning Necessitie, as health, or any other the like. As for the third sort I am sure
they would plead, as well they might, Not to bee giuen to wine
onely, but to be giuen ouer to it.

MOTHER. What new allegation shall wee then find for their
excuse, when on Gods behalf they are endited on the selfsame
ground as Giuen to Wine.

GUARDIAN. Why wee must interpret Giuen to Wine in Snt
Pauls Language is to meane all those three together, a Common,
delightfull, & subiected following of wine. & so I perceiue all the
rest but the common Tiplers, which wee first light vpon, wilbe
acquitted, & a great part of them will put faire to escape too.
Whilest either they will demurre vpon Commonnes, Extenuate
their delight in the wine, or absolutely deny their subiection to it.
But this seems very vnprobable considering that Negatiue precepts in Diuinitie as ⟨50v⟩ I haue bin taught, reach not onely all
the seueral kinds & degrees of that, which is forbidden, but extends
their restraining force to all those other necessarie Actions & dispositions whatsoeuer they bee, which directly & necessarily tend
to the effecting & accomplishing of that, which is principally
forbidden. And so wee see not onely all kind of vnlawfull
Coniunctions, but all manner of Lusts. & not onely all kind of
open wrong, but all manner of deceit restrained vnder the prohibition of Adulterie & Theft in the Decalogue. It must needs
therefore be according to this Rule, That not onely the being

Giuen ouer to wine iointly, & in all kinds & manners, as common Tiplers be, but the being Giuen to it in any one kind or after any other manner whatsoeuer is here intended to be forbidden.

PATIENT. After any manner whatsoeuer, trencheth very farre vpon [cuts deeply into] the priuiledge, that wine hath gott in this Age. Doth not the constant sollicitousnes of mind about any thing make a man rightly termed Giuen to that thing?

GUARDIAN. Yes verily. And so wee say men, that are careful to get money, are giuen to the world. & they, that are carefull about Books & matter of Learning, are giuen to Learning.

PATIENT. Why then it will follow, that they which are carefully sollicitous to haue choise wines & abundance in store should [fall] within ⟨51⟩ Compasse of being Giuen to Wine.

MOTHER. If so be they doe it not, as Vintners or Wine Marchants, but for their own Drinking, I see not how it can be avoided, but that they will be found not onely giuen to wine, but giuen to much wine, which St Paul forbids Deacons to bee.[1] & as it hath been interpreted to mee by a word properly signifying such kind of sollicitousnes, as they make shew of, who listen earnesly to a thing.

GUARDIAN. A very fitting expression. There being no one sensual appetite whatsoeuer, I suppose, that setts the faculties of his soul more often & more busily awork then the Loue of good wine & Dainties doth the Eare to hearken after them. But, I pray, is the selfsame word vsed likewise in the restraint of much wine to Aged Women?[2]

MOTHER. No verily as I am told; but another which signifies seruing vnto Wine, which the Geneua Translation does interpret subiect. & so read it not, as the New Translation, Not giuen, but, Not subiect to much wine.[3]

---

[1] I Timothy iii, 8.   [2] Titus ii, 3.

[3] Geneua Translation—Wyclif reads Titus ii, 3, as 'not given much to wine'; but the Geneva translation reads, not as the Mother quotes, but 'not given to much wine'. The 'new translation' to which reference is made is the King James version.

GUARDIAN. Why they, that are thus subiect or seruing to Wine are plainly Likewise to be termed, Giuen to wine. & in this sence it is wee say many are giuen to Tobacco, when they cannot free themselues from the taking of it. And therefore I perceiue our new ⟨51 v⟩ Translation hath aptly enough rendred these seuerall words by this one Phraze of being Giuen to Wine, which indeed includes them both. But, I pray which of these two Phrazes is it in the Original, whereby Bishops are forbidden to be Giuen to Wine.

MOTHER. It is by neither of them but by a third single word,[1] which extending as it seemes, in Common vse amongst the old Grecians to more then one kind of Dispostion hath receiued very different interpretation too in sundry Languages & oftimes in the selfsame Language by seuerall interpreters.

GUARDIAN. The Geneua Translation agrees with our New, but the Old English reads the place to Timothie, Not giuen to ouermuch wine, & that in Titus, Not giuen to much wine.[2] But it seemes belike, that this, much, is too much, & the ouermuch, indeed ouermuch. But how I pray you is it in the Moderne Languages, as you haue heard.

MOTHER. Why the Elder Translations straine the meaning of the word high, & the latter bring it down. & so the old Italians read it plaine Drunkards in the first Place &, great Drinkers, in that touching Deacons, & Drinkers of much wine, where it is forbidden in Aged women. The New Italian Translation read it iust as wee doe, in our new English, in the two first places, ⟨52⟩ but in the third it hath it, Not servants of much wine.

GUARDIAN. But how doe the Dutch read it I pray?

MOTHER. Both high Dutch & Flemish Translation vse the self same words in all three places without any variations.

GUARDIAN. What. Doe they not put in the much, which the Original hath in the two last places?

---

1 Original—μὴ πάροινον, I Timothy iii, 1-3.
2 Cranmer's readings.

MOTHER. No verily. As I am told the Germaine Testament hath it euery where Wine Sauffers & the Netherlandish Wine Suppers without any addition. & these two words, because they run so much vpon Sipping & Tipling, mee thinks, I vnderstood the meaning, & could not forgett the words themselues.

GUARDIAN. Here is great Diuersitie I perceiue in these latter Translations. But how goes it in the more Ancient Language and particularly in the Latine?

MOTHER. Why for the Latine Translation most of them it seemes agree in these places touching Deacons & Aged Women, rendering them Giuen or addicted to much Wine. But for that of Bishops there is belike great Difference: some Translate it followers of wine, & others put a word deriued from wine signifying little lesse then plain Drunkenness. But some later interpreters of great skill in Languages, as is generally held, vse ⟨52 v⟩ another word deriued likewise from wine, signifying in his prime & Latine value no more then a man desirous of wine & purposely found out & appropriated to men, as was proued by the Authoritie of Plinie, because onely men of all other Liuing Creatures drink though they be not athirst.[1]

GUARDIAN. Why but this is hardest of all the rest perhaps, if so by accepting this interpretation wee shall be forced either to take in those, that vse to drink wine, when they are not dry into the Number of those, that are Giuen to wine, or exclude them out of the Number of those, whom St Paul accompts worthy to be made Bishops.

MOTHER. He that shall rightly weigh those many prohibitions of wine in the old Law to the Preists, when they went into the Tabernacle of the Congregation, enacted for a statute for euer through their generations, & that vnder the penaltie of Death.[2] To the Nazarites all the Daies of their separation,[3] to diuers Women a long time for the better bringing forth & rearing up an holy

---

[1] The remark seems to be based on Pliny's *Natural History*, chapter xxviii.
[2] Leviticus x, 9.   [3] Numbers vi, 2–4.

seed, Elect & sett apart to great Seruices[1] & to these prohibitions shall adde the many sore Complaints, that he shall find made on Gods behalf for the transgression of these Laws & the Mischeifs specified to follow therevpon, As in particular the Preists erring from the ⟨53⟩ right way both of Learning themselues & teaching the people.[2] & shall on the other side well ponder Solomons Resolution of withdrawing himself from wine, when he sett himself to the studie of Wisedome,[3] & Daniel & his Companions their Refusal of it, when it was pressed on them,[4] the better to keep themselues pure & vndefiled both in vnderstanding & Affections. Hee, that shall, I say in the Ballance of the Sanctuarie weigh all those things, will vndoubtedly grant, that since the Office of a Bishop is not of any Lower Carrat then that of the Preists, nor the Mysteries of the Gospell of a lesse spiritual Nature then those of the Law were, & that the strength of wine & the Weaknes of man is the same now adaies, if not more then of old, that there is a marveilous deal of warines to be had by Bishops & all such, as are and ought to be equally eminent with them for point of holines in & about the vse of wine. & howeuer they will not perhaps restraine euery man out of these words of St Paul so precisely, yet will they not condemne him, that restraines himself according to all the seuerall interpretations, & thinks himself bound both in St Pauls & our Churches meaning, that hath authorized these Translations, neither to drink wine Commonly, nor to seek delight in it, nor to be any way carefull thereabout, or in any manner ⟨53 v⟩ subiect therevnto so as to run vpon the least indecorum of a perfect Christian for the Loue or vse thereof; Nor lastly to drink it without thirst, except for Charities sake, Nor indeed vpon any occasion, but that end, to which it was ordained,

---

[1] Divers women—as in the case of Samson's mother (Judges xiii, 4–5) and of Samuel's mother (I Samuel i, 13–14).

[2] Isaiah xxviii, 7.

[3] There is no confirmation of this statement in the Bible. It may be based on a free interpretation of Proverbs xx, 1: 'Wine is a mocker, strong drink is raging: and whoever is deceived thereby is not wise.'

[4] Daniel i, 8.

the moderate cheering vp of the heart, or the Cure of the infirmities of the body & then neither but according to St Pauls precept to Timothie in small quantitie. I haue told you the substance of what I haue heard & the winding vp of all by way of particular application to himself so to think & so doe in this matter, till he shall be better informed, if so be, he bee not right. As for others, what weight these arguments beare with them, he leaues it to the enforcement of their own Consciences, not minding to Censure any Frequencie, delight, sollicitousnes, or subiectednes vnto or touching wine, but that which is apparently intangled with sin & necessarily ends in some remarkable inconveniency.

GUARDIAN. How sin or inconveniencie at least to Christian Decorum should possibly be seperated from those practizes & Affections to Wine I doe not well see. & therefore I doubt not an absolute Condemnation of them must needs follow. But in the meane while till the business may come to a further scanning his modestie is to be commended & his opinion ⟨54⟩ & practize for himself, in our iudgements to be approued, it being, as it seemes to mee the safest Course in all Negatiue precepts in Diuinitie to keep a mans self from becomming liable to the breach of them in any true or reasonable sence whatsoeuer. It being a very hard matter to beleiue, that the world should mainly to their own Preiudice extend in common vse any word to a stricter sence then the Lawgiuer intended it.[1]

CHEERFULL. Well the Clearing of this first part seemes much better then I could haue thought to our purpose. Dainties & Wine are so neere akin as what wee find in the one, we may boldly expect in the other. If, Giuen to wine, meane what hath been shewed, wee shall hardly be able to make giuen to Dainties meane lesse or otherwise. Since this therefore hath proued so well, I beseech you worthy Mother to goe on with the rest & let vs know what you further heard vpon that second Prohibition of St Paul to Deacons & Aged Women, that they should not be giuen either

---

[1] See above, p. 227 n.

by sollicitousnes or by subiectednes to much wine. Let vs know both the interpretation of these words much[1] & the inferences that were made therevpon.

MOTHER. Why that, which was first obserued, was, that St Paul did not say, as the False Eccho of the world commonly reports ⟨54v⟩ these words, either Too much Giuen to wine or Giuen to too much Wine: but simply Giuen to much wine.

GUARDIAN. Why but. Shall wee not think, hee doth meane these Excesses both these Excesses in the Affection & in the Quantitie?

MOTHER. Vndoubtedly. They must needs be both intended, as euery great Transgression is necessarily forbidden in the restraining of the Lesser. But not so intended as the world conceiues, that he, that is freed from the heinous Enormities ought to be acquitted as it were by proclmation from all guilt or penaltie in this matter. No doubt he shall incurre the danger of both who euer he be in either of these Ranks, that shalbe found Giuen to much Wine.

GUARDIAN. Why then it seemes this much Wine forbidden in the case of Deacons & Aged Women should be but as it were the Crosse-hedge[2] answering to that other Little Wine, which is prescribed in the Case of infirmities. & so the vse of wine but [by] St Pauls Doctrine should stand bounded between the Libertie of a little for Necessities sake & the prohibition of much vpon any ground or occasion whatsoeuer.

MOTHER. You haue found it out of your self better then I could haue related it.

GUARDIAN. But now the Difficultie grows to find out the true weights ⟨55⟩ & measures, whereby this much is to be tryed: seeing that perhaps is much to one, which is little to another. The Opinion of mens minds, the Constitution of their Bodies, & the Effects of wine are so different in seuerall Persons that that perhaps will be accompted too much in one in this Case, which is so little

---

1 That is, what the word 'much' means in these different contexts.
2 Crosse-hedge—a hedge that meets or crosses another and so forms a boundary.

as wilbe thought and termed Nothing at all in another. & how then shall wee come to any certaintie in the particular application of that word, touching the full & true sence whereof there is so much varietie? You know the old Fable, when the Moone desired a Coat, it was answered, She must then resolue to keep one shape alwaies, otherwise being euery day on the Change it would be impossible to fitt any thing to her back. The same exception wilbe against any thing, that any waies partakes of the inconstant variation of this great Embleme of Mutabilitie. If wee cannot determine the measure of Much & Little wine as mee thinks it will be hard to doe when these Notably vary not onely in Different, but oftimes in the selfsame persons vpon different Tempers & Dispositions of mind & body, how shall wee come to iudge of the obseruancie or breach of this iniunction of being Giuen to much Wine.

MOTHER. But shall wee not find it after the same manner ⟨55 v⟩ in all other things, whereof Much & Little are predicated?

GUARDIAN. Yes verily. That, which may be truely said much & ouermuch Riches in a subiects Estate would be but Pouertie in a kings. & that measure of Learning, which deserues the Name of much in a Gentleman would in a professed Scholar hardly perhaps deserue the Name of Tolerable. & that wee accompt no Wisedome at all in a States-man, which would goe currant for much Wisedome in a Father of a Familie or some inferiour Magistrate.

MOTHER. Why but then it seemes wee haue found that wee seek for, that is, the Measure of much & little.

GUARDIAN. Wee haue found it indeed, but not where wee sought it in the quantitie of the things themselues, but in the qualitie and Condition of the subiects, wherein these things are, & in respect of the vse & ends, wherevnto they are properly ordained. & so wee may iustly say, that is much in euery man & in euery kind, which serues to an ample effecting & performing of that, wherevnto it is ordained & intended. & that little, which produceth more weak & remisse Effects. & so that is much Wealth

or Riches, which serues to notable Exercize of vertue. For Riches
are well defined by the Philosopher to be the instruments of vertue.
And that is much Wisedome in euery man, which serues notably
to the attainment of his ⟨56⟩ proper end in a high degree, as I may
speak & so in euery other thing.

MOTHER. Why then since wee haue found Wine to be ordained
in the Authours intention a Medicine for the care of the lower
parts of the soul & of the higher faculties of the Body and asswage-
ment of the greif of the mind, & a remedie for the infirmitie of the
stomack, why shall wee not in the vse of wine call that much,
which produceth more abundant Cheerfulnes & Vigour in the
Affections & appetites. & that little, which onely serues to a modest
& remisse accomplishment of these effects. & so that to be accompted Much wine, which breeds much mirth & causeth much
& strong digestion & that but a little wine, which helps & setts
forward Cheerfulnes & digestion in a lighter measure & degree.

GUARDIAN. So doing wee shall easily passe ouer that stumbling
block, which most men fall at in the very Enterance of their
consideration & disputes touching this matter. It is the first obiec-
tion alwaies by them, which mean not to be limitted in this Case
but by their own appetites, that no man can say iustly what is
Much or Little seeing mens minds & Complections differ so much
as one is ouertaken by that quantitie of wine, which stirres not
another ⟨56v⟩ at all. Marry if much & little bee thus to be determined not in comparatiue proportion to others, but in respect of
these effects in a mans self; there will alwaies be an easy resolution
to be had in the Case, whilest the outward working of these
effects will giue vndeniable proof of the inward measure and
degree of them. For much Cheerfulnes will cause much mirth and
iollitie & much appetite & digestion will draw down the more
meat. But since both Meat & Mirth are really good, why the more
of them should not be accompted the better, as long I meane as
they grow not to excesse I see no reason, & I am sure I haue the
greatest part of the world on my side.

MOTHER. But not the Best, as I conceiue. St Paul, that giues in Charge the keeping vnder of the Body & so moderates carnal reioycing, as it should scarce by his Rule appeare at all, & they, that reioyce, sayth hee, speaking of wordly matters, as though they reioyced not,[1] will not perhaps allow that progresse in that argument, which you make, that euery more, of that, which is good, is still better then that, which is lesse in the same kind. A little cheerfulnes of heart is sometimes requisite perhaps to help the soul in her spiritual reioycing, as [a] gentle Gaill of wind speeds the birds flight, whereas a stronger blast would hinder or it may be quite ⟨57⟩ diuert her in her course & a moderate health & vigour of the stomack may best fitt them, it may be, who are to ioyne Action to contemplation; whereas much appetite & strong digestion would be of dammage & impediment whilest either in the satisfaction of them by supply of much Nutriment there would euery way arise inconveniencie, or els in the resistance & tempering of them a continual strife & pain would ensue both to mind & body. & therefore on this very ground, for which the world is moued to reiect this Interpretation should wee perhaps be the rather induced to accept it as most agreeable to St Pauls Meaning & intention. & inferre, that he therefore so strictly moderates the vse of wine not onely to prevent the danger of Slipping from Much to Too much; but because he would haue both the Carnal Mirth & Bodily Nourishment of them, who are to attend spiritual Mysteries to be very remisse [restrained] & moderate euen when the largest participation of them is most intended.

This was the substance of what I heard touching the second point & the particular application of it to his own practize was, that he would esteeme that to bee much Wine in himself, which puts him forward either to the showing of more mirth & freedome then other sober iudgement would approue in him or to the taking ⟨57v⟩ of more or other kind of meat, then according to solid iudgement hee durst otherwise haue adventured vpon.

[1] I Corinthians vii, 30.

CHEERFULL. He is not onely gott into the great Road-way of temperance, but makes speed in it, whosoeuer he be, that is come to this Resolution. He, that makes a scruple to make vse of this Benefitt, which wine & strong liquours afford for the digestion of much meat, puts himself vpon the Necessitie of a spare & single Diet. For Fulnes & varietie of Food & especially of Dainties doe expect, or to say better doe so peremptorily exact the Assistance of Wine, or that, which is Equivalent, That Whosoeuer shall without their help adventure the satisfaction of his appetite in these two kinds shall quickly be brought in to better order by compulsion of Necessitie. Paine & Infirmities will multiplie so fast, as hee shall be made wise, whether he will or no touching the measure & qualitie of his Diet. I know I shall pay for it, puts the knife to most disordered appetites, that can be. As on the contrarie a Cup of Wine will digest it, draw on oftimes the most stayd & moderate to the committing of many perilous excesses in these Cases.

AFFECTIONATE. Verily. He that at a great Feast should take away the wine might I am perswaded on this ground well saue ⟨58⟩ two thirds of the meat, at least of that, which were most Daintie.

PATIENT. If so be the Case of strong waters at home likewise were shutt vp [supply of strong beverages were cut off], these Guests, that would not of themselues make spare of the Good Cheare, would vndoubtedly be putt to no lesse hazard then the Toad Combating with the spider ranne into, when the Plantin Root was taken away. There wilbee almost a Necessitie of Bursting, if they haue not the Liberty of disgorging themselues.

MOTHER. Nay there's a third help besides, which this Age exuberantly fruitfull aboue all, that haue gone before, in the deuizing both of provocations to Gluttonie & Remedies for Allaying the present inconveniencies, that follow vpon it, hath found out.

PATIENT. What may that be?

MOTHER. Why Tobacco.

PATIENT. Oh were not Gluttonie a most Deformed Beast in its own opinion aswell as others, It would be ashamed to haue recourse to this hidious, Loathsome Remedie. For as a man cannot well fancie perhaps a more infernal spectacle then the manner of taking it: So verily I think he cannot feel a more odious smell then it leaues behind not in the Roomes, but in the stomack & mouths of them, that vse it to this intent. ⟨58 v⟩ What a wonderment was made, when the sauage Diet of the Blacks at Cape-vert was read? Oh how did it almost turne our stomacks at that supper to heare, that Beasts vncleansed Gutts & Flesh putrified to Carrion should be dainties to them! But what is the sauour of the worst odour of any wholesome Beast to the Fasting steeme of a gallant Tobbacconist his breath, when it hath been well incorporated with wine & other good cheare ouer night.

MOTHER. There is no one thing perhaps to be found, where, by the general & absolute soueraignitie of Gluttonie ouer this Age is better to be exemplified & proued then by the Creditt & Reputation, which not onely against all Religion and Conscience, but euen against common Reason & sence it hath obtained to this abominable weed, if the matter were as fully anatomized by a skilful hand as the weightines thereof requires. In which regard I should wish the surcease of any further prosecution thereof at this time least by an vnwary or imperfect handling thereof wee should giue advantage to them, that are blinded or besotted in the Loue thereof. And to return where the matter began in confirmation of what our beloued Cheerfull obserued, I shall tell you, that it was se⟨59⟩riously propounded by way of Quare [question], when I learned what I haue already acquainted you with, whether wee ought not to vnderstand an Exact Temperance for matter of sollid Food as purposely intended, as it seemes necessarily included in the absolute restraint of wine & strong Liquour from the Nazarites & others.

PATIENT. Vndoubtedly there was something more in the matter, then Drunkennes or an hazard of it, that was intended in the strict prohibition of wine to the Nazarites & Sampsons Mother, els the exception of moist and dryed grapes, or of anything that commeth of [off] the vine, needed not in both places to haue been so particularly specified. All the daies of his separation shall he eat nothing, that is made of the vinetree from the kernel ot the husk, sayeth the Law of the Nazarites.[1] Why this addition makes it sound in mine eares, as though it were rather for mortification of Delicacie then prevention of Drunkennes, that wine should be so strictly forbidden to these sanctified persons. There is no danger at all, as I conceiue, of intoxicating the braine from the husks & kernels. No. Nor from dryed grapes themselues. Or if there be, it must needs be by some such excessiue or disordinate vse of them as mee thinks there ought ⟨59v⟩ to be little suspicion that such holy persons as the Nazarites and Manoahs wife were, should be likely to be guilty of.

MOTHER. Put to this Daniels and his Companions[2] refusing the Kings Delicate Food as well as his Wine & all the like passages (& many agreable herevnto will I suppose be easily gathered out of scripture) & wee shall happily be induced to think, as you say, that wine it self should be forbidden not only for greater securitie against that accidental Euill, which the Excesse breeds, but euen for that very pleasure & Deliciousnes, which is essentially incorporated in the very Nature thereof.

GUARDIAN. And so in the Addition of Dainties in the same clause you will inferre the restraint of wine to be not onely in respect of its own proper Nature, but in respect of common agreement it hath with Dainties: But doe you not see, that not all kinds of Dainties are here forbidden, but onely those which come of wine. & therefore the Argument will not hold, that because

---

[1] Samson's mother was the wife of Manoah (see below). The references are to Numbers vi, 2–4, and Judges xiii, 4–5.
[2] Daniel i, 8.

some dainties, which are made of wine, ought to be forborn, where wine itself is forbidden. & so the wine is not at all taken away in respect of the Daintines, but these Dainties are remoued in regard of that Affinitie, which they haue with wine.

MOTHER. I should wrong the Cause to goe any further ⟨60⟩ in this point, wherein the Cheerfull is, I know, much better provided to giue satisfaction, then I can doe.

Part VII

The Cheerfull and the Guardian agree that dainties are really dry wine, and wine but wet dainties; and that surfeiting is dry drunkenness, drunkenness but wet surfeiting. Some dainties, such as spices, are more akin to wine (because of their 'natural virtue and outward operation') than those such as raisins, which are related to wine only by taste and smell. The Guardian maintains that wine is 'properly never to be accounted drink' because the best wine is the poorest quencher of thirst just as spices, dainties, and heavily seasoned dishes do not satisfy hunger, but rather nourish the choler; hence the Catholics are in error when they permit eating of stimulating dainties during periods of fast. The discussion now shifts to the classification of 'Fat and Dainties appertaining thereunto'. The Guardian and the Cheerfull assert that fat, butter and oil do not appease hunger but rather arouse choler just as do the other dainties discussed earlier. Wine, too, as it heats the blood and causes bad feeling, must be numbered with dainties; even Mahomet, that 'impure beast', forbade its use to his followers, as the Affectionate's story makes clear. The Guardian and the Mother both agree that Mahomet and his followers err greatly in absolutely forbidding the use of wine to everyone for fear of the excesses of a few.

———◆———

CHEERFUL. Indeed you haue brought mee to the place, which I aimed at, & more readily & handsomely then I could haue told how my self to haue gott to it. To Loose no further time therefore giue mee leaue knitting my new thrid [thread] to this Bottome [skein], which our worthy Mother hath begun to wind of [off], to demand of you, worthy Guardian, what affinitie you find between Raisons, Currants, & the like fruit, & Wine, more then between wine & other Dainties.

GUARDIAN. What more say you? Why the fruits of the vine-tree & the iuice thereof are the very same in substance. So that wee may not vnfitly say that Raisons are dryed Wine & wine Liquid Raisons.

CHEERFULL. And why may wee not affirme the same of all Dainties & say that Dainties generally are but dry wine & wine but wett Dainties.

GUARDIAN. Such termes & such opinions will suit indeed with that, which you layd for foundation in the beginning of this Discourse & as it seemes vpon great Authoritie. That surfetting in meats is onely but dry Drunkennes & Drunkennes ⟨60v⟩ in Liquour nothing but wett surfetting. & both Natural branches springing from one & the same stock of Gluttonie. But how this should be possibly made good I see not, there being such an Euidencie of Difference between wine & all other Dainties, as a man cannot alwaies tell where to find any likenes between them.

CHEERFULL. You mean by the eie or by the touch. But neither by these senses can you discern, I am sure, any kinred between Raisons & Wine.

GUARDIAN. That's true; but the smell & the tast & the vertue, & the effects of Raisons agree euidently with wine.

CHEERFULL. Not of all Raisons with all wine?

GUARDIAN. No, but of euery kind & sort of Raisons with the same kind & sort of wine.

CHEERFUL. Why but. Doe you not think, that most kind of Dainties wilbe likewise found to agree either in all, or at least the cheifest of those properties with some kind of Wine.

GUARDIAN. Yes verily. There be some kind of Dainties, which perhaps agree in all these properties with that wine, which comes from the vine-tree.

CHEERFULL. Why these then will not be much further akin, then the grapes themselues. And these dainties that agree with wine in the ⟨61⟩ effects & vertue, though they should not agree so much in smell & Tast, yet ought not perhaps to be accomped [accompted] much further of [off] from wine.

GUARDIAN. The Differences of wine in these two regards, that is of smell & Tast are almost infinite so as perhaps there wilbe hardly any kind of Dainties to be found so different from others in these qualities but that there wilbe found some kind of wine answerable therevnto. But suppose that there were, yet in very truth considering that the extreme opposition of wines betweene themselues not onely in these two sensible qualities of Tast & smell but also of Colour doe not yet make any such partition, but that they all agree in the common Denomination of wine and claime the neernes of affinitie each with other not from the likenes of their outward accidents, but from the strict sympathizing in vertue & Effects & so harsh Sacks [white wines] in regard of their strengths are more neere muscadine then smaller wines though neuer so pleasant. I see no reason to deny but those dainties, which most agree with wine in the two substantial matters, that is in Natural vertue and outward operation, should be accompted more neerer to wine then these, which agreeing lesse in the maine qualities agree more perhaps in those other sensible properties ⟨61 v⟩ of tast & smell. And in this regard I should esteeme these Dainties, which wee call spices, more neere of kin then dryed raisons are to wine speaking of wine in generall, as wee agreed, as it is indeed to be vnderstood not onely of Liquours, which come from the vine-tree, but of all those other strong liquours, which are aequivalent therevnto & which are ordained for the cure of the infirmities of the stomack & of the chearing vp of the heart. And so wee haue found indeed another cheif sort of Dainties answering to another principal sort of Wine as fitly & proportionably as Dainties doe to the Wine of the Vine-tree. & may as well and fittly terme these two kinds, the one Liquid spices & the other Dry wine. But though the matter stands thus in these kinds of Dainties, which serue naturally to making of Wine yet surely it cannot be so in those dainties, which are altogether Food.

CHEERFULL. Why. Is there any Food that is properly to be called Dainties, or any kind of Dainties, that are properly to be called Food?

GUARDIAN. The proof of this Opinion will Cost you more, I

am afrayd, then that other did, that wine is properly neuer to be accompted Drink.

CHEERFULL. You are then satisfied touching that point.

GUARDIAN. Yes verily. Not onely in regard of that, which I ⟨62⟩ heard from you, but of that, which hath since come to my mind.

CHEERFULL. Let's heare it, I pray: For it cannot accord to that strict Relation, which you see is between wine & Dainties, but be vsefull to the question wee are vpon.

GUARDIAN. Why. It is vpon obseruation That the best wines serues worst for Drink, which ought not to be so in case wine were properly ordained to be drink, for the perfectest in euery kind is the measure & Rule of all, that is inferiour in the same kind. Inasmuch then as those wines, such are the strongest & hottest, are the worst for Drinks: for they so little quench thirst, which is the end of drink, as they rather inflame it more, it must needs follow, that they are not properly ordained to this intent.

CHEERFULL. It must needs follow, that these strong hott wines are not properly ordained for drink but smaller wines perhaps quench Thirst well enough.

GUARDIAN. Why that is a further confirmation of the matter. That, which is worst in the kind & most imperfect seruing better for the producing of any effect then that, which is more perfect, shows plainly, that that Effect is wrought by some accidental propertie & not by that which is essential. & so it ⟨62v⟩ being manifest, that the best Wine seruing worst & the worst wine seruing best for drink & quenching of thirst, It cannot be denied but that this end & Effect, that is of being drink & quenching thirst is so improper to Wine, as it belongs not to wine, but onely perhaps as it is not wine, that is altogether for the watery substance of the wine.

CHEERFULL. Why but, Shall wee not vpon Examination find it after the same manner in those other particulars, that wee are vpon? Can you find any richer or perfecter kind of Dainties then spices are?

GUARDIAN. No verily in my iudgement they ought to be accounted the prime & cheif of all Dainties in regard that generally & absolutely they serue to Dainties more then all other kinds of dainties whatsoeuer. I meane amongst vs. For there is not any kind of food no nor of Drink neither, that I can think vpon, which is not made daintie by spices. Nay there is no kind of daintie whatsoeuer, as I suppose, which by the Addition of spices becomes not more daintie.

AFFECTIONATE. Verily That which makes dainties must needs be daintie. For nothing can giue that which it hath not in it self. Spices must needs be daintie. And if they giue more Daintines ⟨63⟩ then any other, they must needs be the Cheif in their Kinds. And to speak plainly, as farre as my skill in Cookery, or in any of those other subordinate or supreme Arts of Confectionarie or the like reaches vnto, that, which you say touching this matter, is right. All other kinds of dainties seeme to haue bounds & limits. The sauoury, the sweet, the Fatt though they serue for many, yet none of them serue without Exception for all sorts of food & dainties to make them more daintie as spices doe. And therefore in regard of this vniversal and Eminent participation of Daintines must surely be themselues the Cheif of all Dainties.

CHEERFULL. Why such spices, that thus carry the prize amongst Dainties haue no place at all amongst Food.

GUARDIAN. That [is] euident without all question. There is no manner of Nourishment, wherevnto Food is ordained, bred by spices, at least by those, which are the proper & most principall among spices, such as are Cinnamon, Cloues, Nutmegs Pepper & the like.

MODERATOR. The contradiction, that spices haue to nourishment haue made the Indians, as wee heard read, to belieue that wee & the Hollanders carried them away in such abundance ⟨63 v⟩ for some other end & vse then for food, as wee pretended, & to be half perswaded as it was merrily told them, That wee made the walls of our Houses with pepper instead of morter.

That Spices should be the Cheif of all Dainties & serue so ill to Food is a sore shake to the Busines.

GUARDIAN. They agree with Food in solidnes of the matter but differ vtterly in the qualitie of their forme, being dry & hott in Extreeme, whereas the Nature of Food ought to be Temperate & rather inclining to Cool and moyst.

CHEERFULL. But let vs goe on to the next sort of Dainties, as the Affectionate hath quartered them out, that is to the consideration of the sauoury.

MODERATOR. There might some question perhaps be raysed, if wee had to doe with Curious Artists whether these spices ought not to be reduced vnder the head of Sauoury, or whether many of these other Dainties, which you are likely to bring vnder the head of Sauoury ought not to be Reckoned among Spices. But since the end of our inquisition is not for Artificial making of these things for a Philosophical speculation, but for a moral Application, it will be sufficient for vs to make the sorting & partition of them, & generally to proceed to the handling of them according to ⟨64⟩ common opinion & apprehension. And so vnder this kind of sauoury I suppose you meane to include not onely salt it self, which for its Principalitie in this Rank seems either to haue giuen the name of Sauoury to all the rest, or like Elder Brothers, that carry away cheif of the Estate & honour, to haue inherited the title alone, but also all other tart & sharp Dainties, such as are Vinegar, Vargis, Lemons, Oringes & the like.

AFFECTIONATE. I [aye]. And those keen herbs, Onions, Garlick & all that kind, & in a word all those other kinds of saucie dainties, which is a pleasant biting in the mouth, seemes to quicken & rouze vp all the dull appetite for the seeking of Food. In which regard they all agree, & therefore seeme not vnconveniently placed vnder one & the same head.

GUARDIAN. But doe not spices & the like?

AFFECTIONATE. No, as I suppose. They more properly comfort the stomack by addition of heat. They quicken the appetites

by their keennes & serue principally for the digestion of the meat
after it is receiued. Whereas these salt, tart rellishing dainties
seeme to be ordained purposely, if not almost altogether for the
drawing down of meat. & therefore for this great difference in the
end & operation are not vnfittly distinguished from spice. ⟨64v⟩

CHEERFULL. Well then. What shall wee say of this second kind
& head of Dainties? Are they properly to be termed food or no?

GUARDIAN. No verily. None of these things, which wee haue
reckoned, can be sayd to be food at all.

CHEERFULL. Yet these are of the principal in this kind.

GUARDIAN. True. And those other whatsoeuer they be vnder
this head, which may sometimes passe for food must not doe it by
vertue of their Sauourines but by their abatement of it rather. &
so wee see perhaps sweet Onions, & sweet Lemons, & Oringes
now & then help to make a repast. But this appears to be plain in
this regard, that they are neither Onions, nor Oringes indeed at
least not of that sort & kind, which serues for & to Dainties. I must
therefore giue the right in this second matter like-wise, acknowledging that Sauoury Dainties are not at all Food. But for the
sweet it seemes otherwise.

MODERATOR. The plumes [raisins] are not yet, I perceiue, out
of your mind.

GUARDIAN. In very truth there is so much tacke [solidity] in
them as it will seeme great iniustice to debarre them the priuiledge ⟨65⟩ of food. Here is a great Number present I am sure,
that would not wish for better meat.

CHEERFULL. For a meal or two.

GUARDIAN. So I meane.

CHEERFULL. Why but this instant Cloying of the stomack
after two or three repasts made on them shew, that they are not
properly food. But neither are these the principal vnder the head
of sweetnes.

GUARDIAN. No. Sugar & honey, & other the like hauing much
more lusciousnes in themselues & proportionably much more

sweetning other things, then Raisons doe, are & ought to be accompted the Cheifest in this kind. & they in very truth are so farre from being Food themselues, that when in composition of meats they gett the superioritie, they make that, which otherwise is most Natural Food to become no Food at all. For wee see that no body will allow preserued & candid [candied] Fruits & the like iunkets, no, nor Marchpan it self; though the substance be flower of wheat or some other equiualent to that in Nourishment, to be properly Food.

MOTHER. And good reason, because the Nourishment which they yeeld is not to the increase of the Radical moisture wherein the ⟨65v⟩ Life consisteth & whereunto Food is properly ordained.

GUARDIAN. Of what then?

MOTHER. Why of Choler.

GUARDIAN. Indeed euery mans particular Experience of this truth hath made it become a general Proverb, that sweet meats turn to Choler. & this giues a better Colour [reason, excuse] then I was till now aware of, for the Papists opinion, that their Abstinencie in Lent & other such like solemnities is not much, if at all infringed by their glutting themselues in this kind.

PATIENT. The mortification of the Appetite being aswell intended by the Churches iniunction of these Religious Fasts as the abatement of the ouermuch vigorousnes of the Bodie & their being more danger for the commotions of Euil Lusts from these dainties then from real Food it self, there must needs be as in all the rest of their Religion a double Errour and a notable peice of Hypocrisie in this Opinion & practize of theirs mainly canvasing for the delight of the sensualitie, when they seeme most to restraine it, & Arme their Lusts secretly whiles they openly proclaime Warre against them.

GUARDIAN. In very truth the abundance of colour [choler] in the bodie is perhaps much more perilous then any height & fulness ⟨66⟩ of stength [strength] can be for the breeding both of spiritual & corporal diseases. The substraction therefore of real

Food & the supply of these Dainties in their roome is a matter of high folly, if they vnderstand it not. If they doe vnderstand it & find these effects, as hardly they can doe otherwise, clean contrarie to that, which they make shew to aime at: It tells them plainly there must needs be a great heap of Falshoud both in their own hearts & in their Abettours.

MOTHER. Well. Howeuer these are mistaken in point of that Religion, which belongs to God, I am sure the world plaies her game handsomely enough for the promotion of that Religion, which belongs to the Belly, taking occasion, as I suppose, of bringing in their iunkets as interludes between euery Act of Gluttonie, because these are not properly meat nor serue directly for food. It were too great a shame for the Sibarites themselues much more those, that professe Christ to heap Food vpon Fulnes & to ioyn meal to meal. & therefore these things must come in vnder the Name of a Banquet & in the Nature of Gallantrie & not of Victual, but by no meanes allowed to serue for any part a meals-meat. But howeuer they be not proper Food to strength, yet are they proper and strong Food to Lust. & by how much the Necessitie ⟨66v⟩ and Benefitt of them is lesse, the Excesses about them are much worse euery way then those, which are committed in & about that, which is real Food.

CHEERFULL. Well. Howeuer they be not properly Food, yet that Gluttonie is & may be more properly & most Enormiously exercized in them wee shall perhaps hereafter more conveniently take into Consideration. At present this publick Testimonie of the world serues notably to the proof of that, which wee are now vpon. That sweet Dainties are not properly to be termed Food, wherein certainly the world is in the right, howeuer wrong the application & vse be, which they make of this truth. There remaines only now the Fatt & Dainties appertaining therevnto. Let's here I pray, what can be sayd on their behalf.

GUARDIAN. Nay verily the Casting of their Fellows is such a conviction of them, as they will not dare I am sure, to bring the cause to triall. The Principal amongst them Butter, Oile, and Suit, by their easy melting shew the want of that Firmnes & Soliditie, which belongs to the Nature of Food. They slip out of the stomack, as they doe out of the hand before the Fire, & leaue no thing of substantial Nutriment behind them for Nature to work vpon. But as for Colour [choler] they agree with, if not exceed all the ⟨67⟩ rest of these forenamed dainties nourishing & increasing that humour in abundance. And therefore in this respect likewise they are together with their Fellows I see to be put out of the companie of Food & Victual.

CHEERFULL. They are to bee put out of the Liuerie indeed, to keep your own similitude, but not out of the company. they remaine free of the corporation, though excluded from bearing office amongst Food & Victual.[1]

GUARDIAN. I vnderstand your meaning. You hold not these Dainties to be properly Food, not in their own proper Nature of dainties to serue for food: But accidentally & together with Food they may & doe serue to nourishment; if not of that, which tends principally to the conseruation of being yet of that, whereby the Life & being are bettered.

CHEERFULL. True. For besides the manifold helps, that Food it self receiues from them for the better accomplishment of its own office & work, euen the maintenance of these humours & particularly of Colour [Choler], wherevnto Dainties seeme properly & principally ordained, is very necessarie & expedient for the well being of the Bodies constitution & the better performance of all humane Actions. ⟨67v⟩

GUARDIAN. The Necessitie & benefitts of the humours in the Bodie is euidently to be seene by the Notable disabilitie, that instantly follows in the principal operations both in mind & Body vpon the great remissenes or defect in any of them. The Conseruation therefore of them in their due proportion is vndoubtedly

---

[1] Liuery, company, corporation, office—all terms connected with membership in a guild.

one of the prime businesses, which belongs to that part or facultie of the soul, wherevnto God hath giuen the Regiment of the Body in charge. & consequently the supply of fitt & Convenient Food to this intent is necessarily appointed from the Diuine wisedome & Loue. Now what the proper Nourishment of other humours may be, is not at all to our purpose to make enquirie of. But touching Choler, which as you well obserue, seemes the principal of all the rest I meane for matter of Action I think it not so lightly to be passed ouer.

CHEERFULL. No verily. The whole issue of the Busines lies vpon this point almost, as you in the end shall perceiue. & therefore you shall doe well to follow this trace a little further. Wee haue found Two kinds of Dainties alwaies breed Colour [Choler]. Now if this effect arise from them essentially and Naturally as dainties it will likewise be found to arise and follow vpon all other Dainties. ⟨68⟩

GUARDIAN. Why so questionles it doth. For howeuer the fluent Liquidnes of that Colour [Choler], which is bred by the Fatt & the Sweet, makes it perhaps the more sensibly felt in the body & more apparently discerned by others in the outward actions, whether Moral or Natural, yet it is not in truth any whitt more, nor perhaps perfectly Colour [Choler], as that other kind of adust humours,[1] which is bred by spices & salt meats, which vndoubtedly is euery way more powerfull & more operative, Although the manner of working in the stomack & other parts of the Bodie be more secret & insensible for the present then of that other kind of Fluent Colour [choler[.[2]

CHEERFULL. Why but if all dainties breed Colour [Choler] then either wee must find this effect bred from wine likewise or els wee must exclude it from the Number of Dainties.

---

1 Adust humours—those humours which cause dryness of the body resulting in heat and thirst. See Burton's *Anatomy of Melancholy*, Partition I, Section III, Member I, Subsection III.
2 See Burton, *Anatomy of Melancholy*, Partition I, Section I, Member II, Subsection II.

GUARDIAN. Little search will serue the turn to discouer the truth in this matter, howeuer good fellows pretend, that it is good blood, that wine breeds. & in proof alledge the scarlet dy in their faces, & the sweetning of affections one towards another vpon their first Cups. Yet Wine itself shews the contrarie & by producing fiery pimples, sower breath, & other the like brand-marks in open veiw & by shutting vp all merry meetings in ⟨68v⟩ this kind for the most part with Clamours & quarrels, proclaimes aloud, that it is not good bloud but bitter Choler, that is the natural fruit & issue of wine.

AFFECTIONATE. The breeding of ill bloud & oftentimes the shedding of the hart bloud it self amongst the best freinds, is I am sure, & euer hath beene an ordinarie effect of wine. & the obseruation of this as the Turks themselues tell the storie, was the onely Cause of all Mahomets seuere inhibiting the vse thereof to his Followers.[1]

GUARDIAN. The story cannot but be much to purpose. I pray lets heare it & know the Reason, how this impure Beast seeming studiously to advance Carnal Lusts both by his Doctrine & Practize came to depriue his Musulmen of this Liquor, which so much tends to the furtherance of that, wherein he makes a great part of his Felicitie to consist.

AFFECTIONATE. As Mahomet travailed one day, I know not whither, he turned aside into his friends house now in the way. Where vpon occasion of a Bridal Feast he found much good cheare & store of Companie mett together, being invited he satt down with the rest & obseruing besides much mirth a marveilous deal of aimablenes in the guests both amongst themselues ⟨69⟩ and towards him expressed by often embracements, kisses, Claspings of the hands together, faire words, sweet termes, & large profers of Freindship, he Called his Host aside & seriously demanded the resolution of this Mysterie seeing such a wonder, that true Loue, which grew so starvingly euery where els in the

[1] Busbecq; see above, p. 217 n. The story is told in Letter III, p. 154.

world, as it could hardly be kept aliue amongst neerest kinred should so strangely flourish in this place, as strangers, that neuer saw each other, in one houres space contracted solid Frendship of foure & twentie Carrats. His freind made answere, The good Wine, that they drink, was the cause of this good will, & these wonderfull effects. Wherevpon say they Mahomet gaue wine his blessing & bid his Freind make accompt of it as well it deserued aboue all earthly things whatsoeuer.

This done he kept his iourney & next day at his returne calling at the selfsame place he saw such another face & appearance of things, as made him at the first veiw, horribly agast. Here lay one Arme dismembred from the Body, there a leg, here a Corps without a head, & there one head by cleauing made two. The Floor swomme with bloud & the Aire was filled with groanes & outcries of dying men. Assoone as he had recouered himself he asks the reason of this change. His Host answeres, It ⟨69 v⟩ was the selfsame wine, which yesterday breeding good bloud brought forth so much kindnes, as hee then saw, Afterwards kindling Choler hath wrought all this slaughter. Wherevpon, say they Mahomet revoking his former blessing & giuing Wine his euerlasting Curse vtterly forbad the vse thereof to all his Followers vpon penaltie of Cruell torments to be certainly vndergone by the Transgressours of this Law in the world to come, howeuer they escape in this Life.

GUARDIAN. Whether this was not a true passage, but a moral tale coyned by Mahomet himself or his ministers, since his time, it seemes to lead vs to the discouerie of that, which is worth knowing, that is, the first ground of his strict restraining & their constant forbearing Wine, that it should be begun and continued amongst them not out of Loue to Chastitie, which they sett little prize vpon, nor out of feare to enflame Lust, which they desire rather to kindle; but onely, at least mainly for the prevention of disorder & the better preservation of Loue and vnitie amongst themselues. And surely howeuer they goe too farre in absolutely restraining this excellent benefitt of God for the perril, that the Excesse brings, yet they shew both more Wisedome & more Religion in this ensuing restraint ⟨70⟩ of Wine, which they make on this ground, then many amongst vs Christians doe, that defend Alehouses & Tauerns fitt to be sett vp & frequented for the maintenance & increase of mutual Loue & Freindship amongst Neighbours.

MOTHER. That Wine should serue in its own nature to the propagation of any higher or more spiritual kind of Loue, then that, which is really to be termed Lust, or to the promotion of any other Freindship, then that which ends in Carnalitie, is, as I haue heard, a conclusion proper to the Art of drinking & no way to bee made good by any ground of Philosophy, Phisick, or Diuinitie, which all agree in this, that the progresse of wine is not from mirth to Loue, from delectation of the heart to the exercize of charitie, from good fellowship to perfect Freindship, from pleasure to happines, as the bone [boon] Companions of ours & most other Ages it may be haue perswaded themselues & sought to make others beleiue; But from mirth to madnes, from freedome to Insolencie, from iollitie to injurie, & from Delight to anguish & affliction. After this manner I am sure, the Wise Solomon guided by the holy Ghost setts down the Pests of wine, making Woe & Sorrow, Bablings & wounds without cause the proper return of those, that bestow ⟨70v⟩ their time & affections in this kind of trade & Marchandize seeking out the good Wine, as they terme it, with great diligence, & setting down to it with much Content, when they found it. In stead of pleasure & good blood, wherewith they think to store their hearts & fill their veines sucking in, as he makes it, deadly poison both to their vnderstandings & affections, in the end sayd he it will bite like a serpent and sting like a Cockatrice. Thine eies shall behold strange women, there's the Loue. & thine heart shall vtter perverse things, there's the Wisedome, that wine begetts & furthers, when it comes to the Helme & proues Steerman in the Body.[1] The Turks

---

[1] Proverbs xxiii, 29–33.

therefore haue the right on their sides, touching matter of Opinion I meane, & seeme (as our Resolued vse to speak) in this point the better Christians of the twaine Erring lesse, although they erre much, in absolutely restraining the vse of Wine, then they, that enlarge it vpon a false ground & euidently contradictorie to scripture: because it naturally cheares vp the heart it ought not to be generally restrained in this Vale of Misery, nor any depriued but those, that voluntarily depriue themselues of the priuiledge, that God hath granted to all that need through infirmitie of body or indisposition of mind to make vse thereof. But to extend it to the Patronage ⟨71⟩ of such Excesse, as is now adaies vsed vpon pretence, that it's proper not onely for sodering of natural affections but to the Cementing of Charitie it self is vndoubtedly a vaine Errour & the ground to infinite more mischeifs & inconveniencies, then the Turks vtter banishing of it is or can be.

Part VIII

The Affectionate points out that if wine, because of its similarity to dainties, acts like them 'to the prejudice of solemn feasts', then the world's esteem for it as a creator of good will and friendship must be quite wrong. The Mother raises the question of whether that which defiles the body can promote virtue and charity, and maintains that the love inspired by good cheer is short-lived at best. The Moderator, however, defends good cheer as the creator of good will, but the company agrees that, in truth, backbiting and malice are the inevitable results of feasting. The Mother and Moderator discuss the relationships between the sensitive and reasonable parts of the soul, and the Patient explains how 'reasonable' arguments for self-indulgence can corrupt the reason. By worldly minded men, good cheer is defended as necessary to the welfare of the body and spirit; that it is largely attractive because it also produces pleasure, excites lust, and leads to malicious gossip and backbiting is never acknowledged. When the Moderator suggests that lust is the ultimate result of indulging the appetite, the Mother, by claiming inability to understand, forces her to elaborate her argument, in which attempt she is aided by the Patient. They point out that God has clearly made the preservation of the body by food and of the race by propagation attractive to mankind, but that the reason is deceived and by its attempts to increase these pleasures allows the entrance of gluttony and lust. It is agreed by all that the pleasures of the senses delude the reason.

AFFECTIONATE. Though I see not any faire Colour [reason] for denial of what you say in the particular of wine, yet considering according to the strict Relation, that appeares between it & dainties, that it might turn much to the preiudice of solemne Feasts, I hold it necessarie to vse great circumspection on the admittance of What you perswade vs, & to speak plainly from the euident observation of that great force & vertue, which good cheare hath for the maintenance & increase of mutual Loue &

Freindship, am induced to beleiue, that there is rather some errour in your Arguing, though I know not how to find it, then so great a mistake, as otherwise must needs follow in the opinion & practize of the world, which generally holds Wine & that in a Tavern, is in its own proper Spheare of Soueraigne vertue for the sure knitting of Loue & Freindship & the better Composing of all quarrels and Enmities.

GUARDIAN. You are afraid, that if merry meetings at wine ⟨71 v⟩ should be made vncapable of promoting Loue & Freindship, there would necessarily ensue an abatement of this effect from solid Feasting. & that's one of the maine points, which wee intend to inferre [make conclusions] vpon.

MODERATOR. So doing wee shall pull an old house vpon our heads, as the Proverb is, & burie our selues, I am afraid, in the ruines before wee are aware. Fourty yeares haue I heard this good qualitie & Effect, to witt, that Loue & Freindship is bred by good Cheare, made a Cloak for all other Enormities (though they cannot well be denied to be many & great) that are committed in & by Feasting. But Charitie couers a multitude of sins,[1] was in this matter not according to the Apostles meaning, but surely in the worlds application manifestly verified. Because good cheare breeds good will, & great Feasting greatly tended to the encrease of amitie, It hath been alwaies thought not onely fitt, but necessarie by the iudgement of the best, that I haue euer been acquainted with, that they should be kept on Foot & as often put in practize as opportunitie serued by all those, that were of abilitie, howeuer otherwise perhaps many iust exceptions lay against them in regard of Excesse & wast their vnseparable Attendance & consequencies. ⟨72⟩

MOTHER. You say well. There is no accompt at all to be had either of Dammage in Estate or disorder in bodily health nor of any other inconvenience whatsoeuer for the advancement of true & perfect Charitie. The purchase of this Iewell is cheap with the

---

[1] I Peter iv, 8.

losse of all other things. But shall wee beleiue, that Dainties and good Cheare, which haue not as Christ tells vs any power of defiling a man in their own Nature (for Nothing, that goes down the belly, sayth hee, defiles the man)[1] should haue the vertue of perfecting a man in the height of vertue, & perfection & by an incussion [inspiration to] & participation of Charitie become instances to Cleanse & purifie the soul, whilest they corrupt the body. Why this surely is a mysterie, that till this last Age hath beene vtterly kept hid from the saints of God, or els they would not without doubt haue bin generally of so different opinions from vs, most of them proclaiming Emnitie, all of them professing great suspicion & ielouzie in this matter of Feasting tending rather to the ouerthrow, then the building vp of Christianitie.

GUARDIAN. You ouermatch the subiect with the weight of these arguments. It is too much honour, that you giue to this fond Errour to quell it with the sword of Gods word. Let vs take ⟨72v⟩ it I pray into consideration that way, which the Italian proverb leads vs. Quel che si dona, luce; Quel che si mangia, puza. That, which a man giues shines. That, which a man bestows in good cheare, in a few howers turns to such Euill sauour as no man can abide the smell thereof. Can the Loue, thats built vpon this Foundation be of any longer continuance in the heart, then the meat is in the body? & must it not needs in the end together with the groundwork be resolued into the draft purging all meats?

PATIENT. Euery mans Experience, that hath had any experience in the world, will afford him, as I suppose, store of instances for proof of this conclusion. The Fools Lamentation in Ecclesiasticus, That they, which haue deuoured a man in his prosperitie should turn away from him & oftimes against him in distresse & Calamitie,[2] is as Common now adaies, as the stones in the street. A man can hardly sett foot any where, but he shall haue his eares filled with complaints in this kind.

MOTHER. That Freindship & Loue contracted by good cheare

---

[1] Mark vii, 15, 18–19.   [2] Ecclesiasticus xx, 16.

is of no great durance for length of time, nor of that solidnes as
to abide the Test of adversitie is as euident as the sun at Nooneday.
& wee in this Familie serue as good examples, as any perhaps can
be brought, to verify the truth thereof, being able to ⟨73⟩ say
vpon triall made in great Necessitie, That the yeeld in this kind
is not so much as after the Rate of a dramme of Loue vpon a
hundred pounds worth of good cheare. For the shame of the
world, as the phraze is, & through importunities & other by-
reasons, it may be there wilbe found of them, who now and then
make some kind of sorry retribution this way. But that euer good
cheare begatt true Loue or gained requital of kindnes for its own
sake, is a thing I neuer saw or heard of.

    MODERATOR. Well. Bee it so. That the Loue, that's bred, dies
without continual watering in the same kind, & can by no means
abide any chill blasts, yet whilest its kept fresh & flourishing, it
seemes with the beautie & redolencie thereof to adorn and make
glad not onely earth but heauen it self. Consider I pray the
obseruancie of inferiours, the affabilitie of superiours, the Curtesies
amongst aequalls, the many services & mutual kindnesses, that
arise vpon these occasions &, mee thinks, you should not gainsay
the common opinion, that nothing keeps Loue & freindship more
aliue & flourishing in the world, then this practize doth.

    GUARDIAN. You say well. But take withall the vnseparable
condiment & garnish of all Feasts & Meetings in this kind, ⟨73 v⟩
that is, the backbitings, Slanders, & Traducing of high & Low
Freinds & Enemies, & all, that come in the way, & mee thinks it
will bee hard for you to perswade yourself, that the Loue & good
will, that seemes by this meanes kindled amongst them, that meet
ᵗogether, should be real or any mutual effect or consequence of
good cheare, which seemes to sett their tongues & harts so
malitiously awork against all, that are absent.

    PATIENT. Vndoubtedly. True Charitie moues & works always
to vniversal & vnfained Loue of the Brethren, as St Peter speaks.[1]

        [1] I Peter i, 22.

& therefore this partial kindnes & Affectionatenes to the present only can be no branch of this Diuine stock, but onely some fruitlesse succour [sucker] of corrupt Nature, If so be it be not altogather Flatterie & dissimulation.

AFFECTIONATE. He, that shall well mark the Censures, scoffs, merriments, & misprisions after solemne farwells in publick, that Guest vse to passe on vpon the other in private, will scarce be induced to beleiue otherwise, then as you say, that the interchangeable good esteem & good will, which receiues such notable abatement vpon parting, was meere Hypocrisie in presence.

MODERATOR. I confesse these are sore preiudices to the cause, & as I know not how to deny, that this Affectionatenes, which behaues ⟨74⟩ it self so contradictorily at the same time, embracing some and without iust reason persecuting others, cannot be Charitie, which alwaies works vniformly both to the absent & present. So neither can I well tell what to say for excuse of this vnfaithfull dealing, which wee are all too subiect vnto vpon turning our backs to whisper in the eares of those, with whome wee are confident the disgraces of those selfsame persons, which wee haue immediately before magnified to their own faces, & to whom wee haue perhaps vowed Loue & seruice to the vuttermost.

GUARDIAN. The Commonnes of this fault & the qualitie of the offenders (the greatest & best of all sorts of professions being for the most part the most guilty in this kind) breeds shinesse I perceiue Worthy Moderator, in your touching on this matter. But howeuer Wisedome & safety perhaps forbids the Censure of it in these, yet surely good Conscience & desire of salvation will bind vs to condemne it in ourselues as it deserues in its own Nature for a bitter fruit of infernal Malice. For so I remember I haue heard it painted out at the height of Nature & by an heathen Poet professing his hatred & detestation thereof to be like that, which he bare to the gates of Hell.

MOTHER. What Hell that Heathen man intended I know not ⟨74v⟩ but for that Hell which wee are afraid of I am perswaded a

Christian man cannot well find a readier way to leap at once into the iaws thereof then after this manner. Either [other] sins seeme to roul [roll] them, which committ them, downe the hill with more leasure. But Backbiting & this kind especially by an instant & absolute reuersing of Charitie in the Soule, Casteth a man headlong into the state of condemnation. God grant it may neuer be found amongst vs. & if it steal in at any time through frailtie or ill Example, that it may be forthwith canceld by repentance & amends made. Let vs not dare to make remonstrance of any mans Infirmities in absence, except Necessitie of preventing infection of them, which are present, enforce vs. Where we cannot speak good of them, which are away, or at least to the bettering of them, which are with vs, let vs keep silence, & by our silence, if it be not fitt to doe it by open reproof, put to silence all other erring discourses in this kind. He, that tells mee of others vertues, shall haue both eares. He, that tells me of their faults, that appertaine not to mee, shall loose me quite. My heart shall instantly depart from his societie, my body shall follow as speedily after as it may.

AFFECTIONATE. When your Resolution shall come to be known, ⟨75⟩ I doubt not but your Roome [absence] wilbe alwaies better accepted at Feasts then your Companie. It was the Patients Opinion, That Taking Wine from Feasts two thirds of the good cheare might well be saued. But debarre murmuring & backbiting, & I am perswaded, you may sett down alone, at least very simply attended, howeuer richly furnished the table bee. There is none of any spirit or fashion as the world termes it, will beare you companie, if you enioyne them this pennance. Whilest hunger is satisfying you may say & forbeare, & forbid what you please. But when wanton appetites come into the Feild & the chaps busy themselues about daintie bitts, If you allow not the tongue to walk at large & please it self in taking what it hath most mind vnto, (& to nothing at such times hath it so much mind as to slander) you cancel all former obligations & shalbe guiltie of more discurtesie, then if you went about to put muzzels on the Guests mouths.

GUARDIAN. It cannot be denied indeed, but that as generally vpon eating for pleasure their [there] springs vp in euery man an itching desire of talk, as if so be there were a necessitie of emptying the heart for the better receiuing in that, which is necessarie into the stomack. So for the most part no kind of discourse seemes ⟨75v⟩ to rellish nor suit so well with good cheare, as that, which is other mens Liues & actions, or to say more plainly, of their errors & imperfections. For that, which is good, & tends to advancement of any mans worth, & may begett loue or creditt, like honey to a full stomack breeds an instant loathing in all those, that haue not some particular interest in the person, or designe in the busines. Nay verily as the meats, which come in the reare; so must the discourse be at Feasts, tart & biting, or els the palate of the mind aswell as that of the mouth goes away cloyd & distasted. Good matter & that, which serues to others prayse, if it be sett on foot by an ignorant person, is like the sweet meats brought in at last scambled ouer [snatched] merrily by them, that make profession of wisedome, & by the rest pocketted vp to giue their Children at home, but for themselues they make no accompt at all of them.

PATIENT. It may be well counted a charitable Feast, where Taunts & Bitings of the absent serue the guests turns, that drawing of bloud & the wronging out-right of all, that come in their way is that, which most good meetings grow to before they break vp. But shall wee say that this is a natural effect of good cheare?

GUARDIAN. No verily but a necessarie consequence of the Euill disposition of mind, wherewith men ordinarily come vnto it. ⟨76⟩

PATIENT. How so I pray?

GUARDIAN. Why the contentment of sensualitie being absolutely intended by most men on such occasions, & to this end not onely by most men the yoke of Temperance quite cast of

[off], but conscience it self layd aside by them for the present, It comes to passe, that delight finding no restraint, like waters, that haue broken down the banks, spreads itself to euery pleasing obiect, when through any diversion or other impediment it cannot stay, where at first & most naturally it powres out it self, that is in the bed of wantonnes & Lust, it passeth on forwards without stop, till it settle in the filthy puddle & sink of Envie therein by sporting it self with others shame endeauouring the recompence of that satisfaction, which it is debarred of in the Exercize of its own concupiscence.

PATIENT. Your meaning, if I vnderstand it aright, is, that when through impotencie of bodie or Eminencie of Dignitie in such as are invited or any such respects (& many perhaps there be) Lasciuious discourses cannot gett open admittance at a feast, that then instead thereof murmurings & Backbitings are serued vp to giue the full complement of solace and delight to the mind aswell as to the Bodie of the Guests. But is there any such necessitie in the complement & progresse of delights, that when the corporal appetites ⟨76v⟩ haue obtained their satisfaction, Content must needs be forthwith giuen to the Affectionate part also, that it may likewise find matter to Reuell in aswell as the sensitiue doth.

MOTHER. Gluttonie is vndoubtedly one of those euill spirits, which our Sauiour tells vs, cannot dwell alone,[1] when it therefore getts possession of the heart (& alwaies it getts possession, when the soul abandons it self to the glutting of the appetites) it instantly fetcheth in more companie. This Deuill will neuer abide there, where he may not take in worse & worse wicked spirits, then himself. Hee, that may not iointly with his Gluttonie be allowed the Exercizes of some higher kind of vitiousnes, wilbe ready himself to giue it ouer. & the reason is plaine in respect of the Natural concupiscence of a man, as well as of the spiritual. The affectionate part & facultie of the soul is so linked with the

---

[1] Cannot dwell alone—This remark may be based on Luke xi, 26, or on the references to Legion in Mark v, 9 and Luke viii, 30.

sensitiue, as naturally the selfsame desires & motions, which are begun in the one, doe forthwith proportionably spring vp in the other, so that it is impossible for the soul, when it giues way to the appetites to take their free course, to restrain the will & affections from procuring their satisfactions likewise after their own way and manner to the vttermost.

AFFECTIONATE. Indeed it seemes hard to beleiue, that the soul, which ⟨77⟩ by sensual pleasure is led down to the ground, should be able to resist the Temptations of higher delights, or temper it self in the acceptation of this content, which seemes agreable to the Excellencie of its own Nature, when for the purchase of contents (for such are the best in this kind) it debaseth it self to the Nature & condition of a beast, whose proper happines lieth in the filling themselues with pleasant food.

MODERATOR. That Pleasures like the sun-beames, which though they gett entrance but at a crannie fill all the roome with lightsomenes, should spread it self through euery facultie of the soul if it getts admittance by any one, seemes very probable in regard of the diffusements of delight, & the streight coniunction, which is between the sensitiue & reasonable parts of a man. I shall easily therefore agree, that the ouerswelling of pleasures in the lower faculties must needs rise vp to the higher. & that the contentations [satisfying] of the affections must be necessarily sought, where the satisfaction of the appetites are strongly on foot. But, mee thinks, the suddaine reuolution of the soul, which you make in this case, passing without stay from one contrarie to another is not probable. If delight may not haue it [its] free swing in Lasciuiousnes, must it needs turne instantly to the Exercize of malice? Will nothing but others faults ⟨77 v⟩ rellish, when wanton discourses are put by at a Feast? That for the most part it falls out so I know: But till you raised this scruple in my mind I euer thought it to haue beene rather a voluntarie practize of the ill Natures of the guests, then any necessarie or Natural consequence of good cheare.

GUARDIAN. That Lust should be the first subiect, which delight should choose to reuell in on such occasions, if it had its own choise, you grant mee.

MODERATOR. The filling of the Belly especially with dainties setts the Body on fire. & the violence of Lust, that giues way to no other passion, challengeth the precedencie of satisfaction. In regard therefore both of mind & body this seemes the master veine of delight, which Nature would in such occasion pursue, if she might be left to her own Libertie. & in truth, if wee rightly obserue that proceeding of Nature alwaies going forward from that, which is lesse to that, which is more in euery kind, & euer carefully making provisions for the redresse of all inconveniencies, wee shall find both necessitie & reason in this progresse.

PATIENT. Wee desire to vnderstand this Reason & Necessitie, which you speak of, a little more plainly and fully.

MODERATOR. Why he, that *well marks* the faire pretence vpon which ⟨78⟩ Gluttonie getts allowance & the foul consequences, that alwaies attend it, shall plainly perceiue, that neither the good that it promiseth, can make good, nor the euill, which it apparently worketh, canne be auoided by any meanes so naturally and really, as by the bringing in of concupiscence to act her part likewise.

PATIENT. Hath Gluttonie any other pretence then the delight, which it makes tender of to the pallate?

MODERATOR. For the inveigling of the sences there needs no other bait then sensual pleasure: but the superiour Faculties of the soul look for more substantial motions, ere they will stoop so low.

PATIENT. And what more reasonable motions can be found?

MODERATOR. Why that strength receiues increase & health is conserued by meanes of good cheare?

PATIENT. You say very true. This is that painted Lure, where-with Gluttonie brings the soul from her lofty pursuits to this carrionly Game of Satietie & daintines. He, that should provoke to Gluttonie in plain termes, Now, my Masters, content the greedines and delicacies of your appetites to the vttermost, would deseruedly be interpreted to meane rather the affront, then the entertainment of guests. If they be of any Ciuil fashion, they must be touled [lured] on smoothly with arguments of Necessitie & conueniencie. That he, that pincheth ⟨78 v⟩ his Belly impaireth his strength, & he that eats not of the best as they call it, wrongs him self much. That strictnes in Diet is a perilous Errour to the Body, & a peice of superstition in Religion. These & the like are the onely inducements, which skilfull Masters of Gluttonie vse amongst Wise & sober men. As for Liquorishnes of dainties (though that be it alone, which both parties canvas for) Yet should there be any publick motion thereof, it would breed as great disorder, as the vnwary Calling for salt doth at the enchanted Banquets of Sorcerers & Witches.

AFFECTIONATE. Surely if it did not cause the good cheare to vanish, yet it would so damp the appetites, as the best dishes might be taken off from the Table, as whole as they were sett on. There is no man, that hath any witt or gouernment of himself, that will buy the satisfaction of his Gluttonie in open market. They must be brought home & that not like themselues neither but vnder the disguizes of better things & necessarie duties. There must be no notice taken of any pleasure intended in following of good cheare, but all must be interpreted as done out of care & desire to preserue the Body strong & vigorous for better imployments.

MOTHER. The matter seemes very plaine, That Gluttonie could not find admittance amongst Professours of ciuilitie, but for the faire ⟨79⟩ vizour of bettering the Natural being. But what pretence hath Lust to crowd in after, whose effects turn all to the weakning & ouerthrow of Nature.

MODERATOR. That Lust, which is so witty & skilfull to deuize Masks for all the Courts of Christendome, should want skill to help it self with a mask, were strange.

MOTHER. The fault then lies in my simplicitie, that cannot discern the business.

GUARDIAN. It's your Honour & Happines to be so little acquainted therewith, as to be ignorant of that, which is so euident.

MOTHER. If it be not vnfitt I desire to vnderstand it now.

MODERATOR. Why that, which Lust makes promise of, & by the tender whereof it gaines such readie enterance into the soul, is the propagating of the Natural being An act of highest Excellencie, if rightly ordered.

PATIENT. The Communication of good in euery kind is surely farre more noble, then the reception or conseruation of the same. Lust therefore, that vndertakes the greater & more desired service cannot but find double welcome to that, which Gluttonie hath vpon promise of that, which is farre Lesse?

MOTHER. Farre lesse indeed is the conservation or improuement ⟨79v⟩ of any particular part, which is the vttermost, which Gluttonie pretends vnto, then the Conseruation & propagation of the whole kind, which Lust vndertakes. And therefore no marvell, that it carries the inferiour appetites with such violence aboue all other passions, making shew vnto them of the Fairest obiect, that they possibly aime at. But is it probable, that the soul of man should giue way to such euident impostures, as these are. Why there is nothing that hurries men on so fast to the graue, as Gluttonie doth. Nor any thing, that so much disturbs & ruines the happy propagation of Mankind, as Lust doth. And how then can Reason giue way to their admittance knowing full well their intents and effects to be cleane contrarie to their Allegation.

MODERATOR. Reason like a false sentinel corrupted by pleasure shuts his eies, & draws back. & the inferiour faculties hearing the watchword of conservation & propagation runne out blindly to meet & entertaine this imposture instead of those holy & freindly institutions of Eating & Generation, to whose care & regiment God hath indeed intrusted & ordered the preservation of mankind both in the general & in euery particular, hauing annexed a strong & mastering sence of pleasure to the right & orderly operation of them the rather to invite ⟨80⟩ and enforce the Necessarie accomplishment of them from all sorts of creatures, that by these two meanes preserue themselues & propagate the like.

PATIENT. Were it not for this particular interest & advantage of delight, it is much to be doubted, that the Rebellious disposition of mans Nature would be as adverse from the performance of these, as it is from all other good duties. Admirable therefore is the contriuement of God both for the point of Wisedome & Goodnes in so providing & ordering, as there should be an enforcement without violence, & a compulsion without constraint to induce men gladly to performe that, which is necessarie, & freely to make choise of doing that, which the Diuine prouidence absolutely requires at their hands.

AFFECTIONATE. And surely great on the other side is the sinfulnes of sin, that in these matters takes occasion & hint to perswade worldly men to the breach & perverting of Gods institution from that selfsame pleasure & delight, which God mingled in these matters purposely to haue them the more carefully performed according to his own ordinance & institution. God hath seasonsed Food with much pleasantnes in eating the rather to draw vs on cheerfully to receiue that part, which he hath appointed for ⟨80v⟩ the Conseruation of our Liues & the better enabling vs to his seruice. & wee incited by sin with the shew of more abundance of delight goe forward powring in meats & drinks in excesse not onely beyond all the measure of Gods allowance, but to the certaine ouerthrow both of our souls & bodies.

MOTHER. How great soeuer the sinfulnes of sin appeare, yet it seemes not to ouerpasse the sencelessenes of mens hearts in this matter, that turnes ouer to the sences the cognizances of that, which is proper to the vnderstanding, & brings vp that, which ought to rule in the tribunal of Reason, immediately to attend & serue the most inferiour parts & faculties of the soul. The pleasantnes & delight in eating, that was made to hire sensitiue Nature is sett vp to controul the iudgement. The Examination of the Nature & Issue of that, which is propounded, which belongs properly to the iudgement, is referred ouer to the sences.

MODERATOR. You haue rightly obserued the progresse of this busines. The sences out of that sensible good, which they find in good cheare, conclude the larger participation in this kind to be likely to turne to more benefitt. & Reason fearing to bee challenged of Envie & ill will against the inferiour Nature, if it should call in question the issue of that, which yeelds ⟨81⟩ so much delight, giues way to the deceit, rather choosing the instant pleasure of the Body with content & satisfaction, then the real good of the whole man with offence & Contestation.

Part IX

The Patient and the Affectionate open this section by pointing out that just as the individual man will not listen to the voice of moderation within himself so the self-indulgent man will not listen to the counsel of restraint from a friend. All agree that friendship usually is not strong enough to accept interference with or criticism of self-indulgence; and the Mother, who claims to speak from her own experience, suggests that anger with a well-intentioned friend is the result rather of gluttony than of suspicion of that friend's intentions. The Guardian agrees that the glutton will not listen to reason, but confesses that the argument that lust, the natural result of gluttony, is justified as a means of propagating the race is difficult to refute. Lascivious discourse, therefore, seems natural at a feast, but the Moderator confesses that it is hard to understand why backbiting and slander should be acceptable substitutes for lustful talk. The Affectionate also demands that the relationship between such apparent opposites as hot lust and cold malice be made clear. The Guardian and Affectionate both point out that one passion often mysteriously gives way to its opposite, especially when the original is frustrated or disappointed in realization.

The practice of backbiting by the old and by others who suffer no feelings of frustrated lasciviousness merely proves that slanderous conversation is a universal pleasure. The Mother delivers a sermon on the sinfulness of those who seek to win favour by repeating slanders and gossip and finds them guilty of more heinous practices than those of the Devil himself. There follows a discussion of verses 4 and 5 from the seventh Psalm of David, in which he calls down God's wrath on himself if he has spoken evil of his friend. The Patient and the Guardian (the latter in words of great simplicity and humility) implore God's mercy in forgiveness of sins past and His strength in avoiding any future backbiting and slanderous gossip. The Guardian concludes by maintaining that he who listens to slanders and evil gossip is as guilty as he who utters them.

———————◆———————

PATIENT. That the matter should be carried in this fashion within a mans self seemes the more probable to mee because I see it euidently to passe after the same manner outwardly. & when it comes to question between different persons, he, that goes about by arguments, how well grounded soeuer they be in Diuinitie & Philosophie to restraine mens appetites at a Feast, is presently challenged of plaine Emnitie against humane Nature & Condition. He may perhaps be allowed to meane well for the spirit: But surely he is no freind to the Body, nor rightly affected to the welfare of the corporal Life, that goes about iniuriously to depriue it of those things, which sence tells to be good, & Religion teacheth to be Gods blessing. & how then can harm follow from any liberal vse of that, which is doubly warranted by its own Nature & Gods guift.

AFFECTIONATE. That euery man should eat what he likes best, & no man take vpon him to order anothers belly, nor robbe it of the delight, which God offers, as the Belly itself conceiues, seems as iust & aequall a thing to the greatest part of the world ⟨81 v⟩ as very few are, as I suppose, to be found, that suspect not their best Freinds, when they are Contrarie to them in this way, to be put forward with some spice of Malignitie against their particular satisfaction, then to be moued by sound iudgement & sincere affection of their greater & more Necessarie good.

MOTHER. There are very few, that can temper themselues from giuing euidence of manifest displeasure against whosoeuer they be, that goe about to debarre them from the vncontrouled exercize of their appetites. & howeuer they cannot answere the argument, yet will they by no meanes be brought to allow the affection of the opposers of their pleasures to be without some taint of ill will or Couetousnes. They think in their hearts & be readie to say it too, if they can gett fitten Eares to disburthen themselues vnto, That their freind, how deare so euer he hath approued his loue otherwise, yet grudgeth the meat, that he discounsells, if he haue any interest in it. & if there be no opportunitie for such calumnie, yet at least hee envies the pleasure, which himself cannot or will not take part of.

MODERATOR. That the sensual part of a man hath gott the mastery ouer the reasonable, when he thus tumults in himself or clamours to others, cannot, I think, be well denied. But shall wee say, that ⟨82⟩ Gluttonie hath gotten possession of that soul, wherein the sences beare the sway?

MOTHER. I would to God I could aswell cleare others, as I must absolutely condemne myself to be harrowed like a slaue in Chaines by Gluttonie, when I am thrust vpon the playing of [for] these goodly prizes. Is it not euident beyond all exception, that the Liquorish morsel, for the disappointment whereof I rage in heart & quarrel in words with my best freind is more deare to mee then his Loue & Freindship?

PATIENT. Els it were not possible to come to any breach of good will, & much lesse to proceed to such iniurie, as to suspect & tax him of vnkindnes & wrong for offering to take it away.

MOTHER. And shall wee not then conclude, that it must needs be Gluttonie of foure & twentie Carrats, that thus professes the satisfaction of the belly before the sacred bonds of Freindship, so as for the Loue of a good bitt it makes light to violate them in the highest degree.

AFFECTIONATE. It must needs be poore Freindship, that cannot prevail with a man cheerfully to quitt such poore delights, as a few good bitts can at best afford, though there were no other ⟨82v⟩ reason, then desire without reason alledged. I doe not see how a man with any face can deny such a request made by a freind, although he made it absolutely in his own Name, & should say for my sake forbeare this or that of meat, & for my pleasure now relinquish thine own. I know not, I say in this case, how to put of [off] any, to whom I professe freindship without plain insinuation, that I value both him & his content much lesse then that of mine own appetites, & the thing, that he discounsels, & would vndoubtedly, if so be there were no other respects then pure Loue, that Cymented vs together, rather part the Freindship, then continue & exercize it vpon these termes. But when he tells me besides, & my Conscience tells mee, hee speaks the truth, that the Leauing of what he forbids, will turn more to my good, then the eating, & yet I cannot forbeare I must needs grant, that Gluttonie hath shuffled all vnderstanding out of my head, as well as Freindship out of my affections.

GUARDIAN. It must needs be but weake Loue and Freindship & simple witt in regard of a mans own self, that is so easily ouer born by the Liquorishnes of any dainties, As to cause a man to make choise rather to disgust his faithfull friend then his false appetites, ⟨83⟩ & to hazard great preiudice afterward for the advantage of a little vile delight at the present.

MODERATOR. Whilest you goe not out of your own circuit, you may happily be allowed to proceed, as you think fitt: There lies no appeal from your iudgement touching that, which appertains to your self. If it bee want of Loue & abundance of Folly, that moues you to impatiencie, when you are crossed by your freind in the quantitie or qualitie of your diet, be it so. & if you find gluttonie to be the ground & author of disorder, lay it as home to his charge as you please, so you goe no further then the home of your own brest. but to passe the like Censure vpon others, and to condemne euery one, that cannot brook restraint in this kind without discontent, to loue his belly more then his freind, would vndoubtedly sett the whole world against you, as a false accuser, & enforce them for the maintenance of their own reputation to endeauour the ouerthrow of yours.

MOTHER. Oh by no meanes. Wee intend all this for our owne Edification & no waies to others preiudice. Think you that wee meane to tax euery one of Glutttonie, that is angry, because he is not allowed to eat freely what & as much as he list? No verily, wee loue our selues & their good will more then so. Wee know ⟨83 v⟩ its not the meat but the vnkindnes of their freind, that moues to Choler. & the maintenance of their Libertie & freedome, that they striue for, & not the contentment of their appetites. They hold as much scorn of Liquorishnes, as the best, but to be tutoured for their meat is childish basenes in their apprehension. These wee know. & Number of other invincible allegations they haue for their defence in this matter, which wee can make no vse of through a certaine scrupulousnes of conscience, that wee are of late run into, that makes vs not dare to sett a faire glosse vpon a foul matter. Wee vpon examination of the matter between God & our own Consciences find it to be the losse of the pleasant morsels & the disappointment of our Liquorish appetites, that troubles vs, otherwise wee could well enough passe ouer iniuries & allow a Freind more Mastership, then he takes in this case without taking any the least vnkindnesse or making any the lightest complaints against him for it. And therefore wee conclude resolutely, & though it be to our owne shame must confesse plainly, that it is not the misapprehension of our Freinds intents & actions, that leads vs to this distemper of affection & reason, but the distemper of Reason & affection through Gluttonie, that leads vs to the misapprehension of their intents & Actions. ⟨84⟩

MODERATOR. Well, you make Gluttonie, I perceiue, a notable iugler, that comes in boldly vnder Colour [excuse] of Loue, & thrusts out Freindship cunningly vpon pretence of ill-will. But this perhaps is the least of the two. Where Gluttonie is entertained in Triumph, as a benefactour to Life & wellbeing, Temperance & all the abettours of it must needs incurre the suspicion of Emnitie. Abstinence cannot appeare lesse or otherwise then famine & tending to wilfull murder in his conceit, whose eies Gluttonie hath so bafled, as to make her self to be taken for lawfull eating & fulnes.

PATIENT. You haue now driuen the Nail to the head. It is a certaine confused apprehension of starving, or some notable weaknes, that the heady sences run away with, when they make head against moderation & sobrietie. No marveil therefore, if they be so fierce, where they think all lies at stake.

GUARDIAN. Wee cannot leaue this matter at a fitter period then that, which you haue now brought it vnto. The maine defence, that the wisest vse, when they are crossed in their intemperance, is, You would haue vs eat nothing I think, you meane to starue folks, & other the like extravagancies, by the observation whereof a simple artist may easily calculate the predominancie, not of sence, but sencelesnes aboue reason, & all other superiour faculties ⟨84 v⟩ whereuer Gluttonie hath gott possession of the soul vnder Colour [excuse] of preseruing & bettering the particular being. To return back whence this Digression,[1] was you sayd Gluttonies pretence & offer, which being once admitted as a benefitt, I know not possibly how the much fairer allegation & promise of Lust to conserue & propagate the whole kind can by any meanes bee refused.

MODERATOR. Especially considering, that Gluttonie, whilest it seemes officious in stirring vp abundance of provision for Nature to work strength out of, doth secretly bring in the matter & Nourishment of Lust, which alwaies breaks out into very perilous inconveniencies for the body, when the proper & Naturall vent thereof is restrained & diverted.

GUARDIAN. Why then it seemes euery way for the cleansing of these superfluities, which Gluttonie cloies the Bodie with for the complement of that delight & pleasure, which the sences hunt after, & for the perfection of those designes, which Nature aimes at, there is not onely a fitting sutablenes but an absolute Necessitie of admitting Lust, as a Companion, whereuer Gluttonie getts entrance, as a Freind.

MODERATOR. That Lasciuious discourses then should haue the prerogatiue at most Feasts, if the choyse might freely bee ⟨85⟩ made by the inclination of the guests mind is no question, but how it should come to passe vpon disappointment in this kind, that they should at next Cast fall vpon that, which seemes cleare contrarie, I meane the Exercize of malice & ill-will, I doe not well vnderstand.

PATIENT. Indeed Backbiting, & Slander, & detraction are the

[1] See above, pp. 268–9.

proper fruits of hatred & Envie, howeuer there be some and too many perhaps so impudently hypocritical, as to make Pietie, & Loue, & Zeal, & other good affections the motiues & putters of them forward to the playing of [for] these kind of prizes. But No Body, I am perswaded, beleiues them one whitt, except some few of their own Corporation, who as Merchants, that pay down readie money, & receiue bills of exchange, to the intent they may gaine creditt in the like occasion, force themselues to giue creditt to that, which they know to be a manifest Ly. Sure I am when it comes to be their own case there is none so hard to beleiue, that anything, which tends to the diminution of their own creditt, is sayd or done otherwise, then out of perfect malice, as the very self same generation of men, who are most importunate to haue their own calumniating & slanderous discourses of others inter-preted pure Loue to the person, or harty ⟨85 v⟩ detestation of the vices, which they declaime against.

AFFECTIONATE. That the declaration & censure of others faults, be they true or false, where no necessitie enforceth, is plaine slander & euidently proceeds from Envy & ill-will, needs no further proof. That which I desire to be informed of, is, how it comes to passe, that the mind of a man ouermastered with gluttonie vpon the Check of its Lustfull desires, should presently abandon it self to this outragious exercize of envie, which seemes euery way a passion diametrically opposite to the other, Lust being founded in the concupiscible, & Envie in the irascible part of the soul, Lust being of an hott & fiery temper, & Envy of a cold. & manifestly aiming at the destruction & ouerthrow of mankind, the cleane contrary to that, which Lust pretends, & by the pretence whereof it so strangely captivates the soul.

GUARDIAN. Why it fares perhaps in the soul of a man, as it doth in the sea. the suddaine ebbe in any one part causeth an instant floud in that, which is ouer against it.

PATIENT. Waters & Passions haue indeed great resemblances in many things. & it may be in this they are not much vnlike. He, that marks it well shall seldome find it otherwise in these, that suffer themselues to be lead by their passions, but that this ⟨86⟩ forced stopping vp of any affection causeth a violent eruption of the clean contrarie. And so wee commonly see the interruption of excessiue mirth immediately breeds profound melancholie & oftimes (though it seemes somewhat strange to beleiue) the constrained restraint of greif, breaks forth into extreme mirth & Iollitie.

AFFECTIONATE. Wee haue euery day instance of this in little Children. They neuer are so full of game & Laughter, as immediately after they haue been ouerawed in their froward and peeuish disposition.

MODERATOR. Their example is an euident proof, it may be, that this passage from one extreme to another is Natural in the affectionate part: But I desire, if it may be, to vnderstand the reason thereof & especially in this particular that we are vpon. ·

GUARDIAN. Is there not a Necessitie of greif & iust cause of anger, when a man finds disappointment in that, which he longs after.

MODERATOR. Yes verily if the desire be of that, which is good and profitable, but Lust is euery way euill & preiudicial. & therefore the putting it aside ought as a singular benefitt to be accepted with ioy & thanks then with contrarie passion.

GUARDIAN. If men could be perswaded, as you are, these matters ⟨86v⟩ would passe, as you say. But whilest Lust appeares not onely pleasant & sutable for the fulnes of content, but almost absolutely necessarie for well-being, for most allow the soul howeuer deceiued in its apprehension of this matter to be displeased in the Losse & offended at the Authours & Occasions thereof.

PATIENT. Indeed Gluttonie is a teachy [tetchy, touchy] Beast & keeps no quarter with any thing, that in the least goes contrarie to her irregular appetites. I shall easily grant therefore, that it may egge the soul forward to wrath & choler vpon the shutting out of her deare freind & companion Lust.

GUARDIAN. Well then the storme being gathered, there's a Necessitie, that it should light some-where. The mind full of rancour & Bitternes must needs discharge it self. When therefore it discouers no ground neare at hand, it seeks further of [off] & runs out to find abroad that opportunitie, which it misseth at home, setts it self by arming complaints & picking quarrels against the absent freely to seek that teene [mischief] & splene, which it hath conceiued in it self through the disappointment of other darling contents.

AFFECTIONATE. So then the progresse of the busines, as you sett it down, should be this. Gluttonie begetts not onely a desire but a Necessitie of Lust. & Lust, when it is forcibly kept out, ⟨87⟩ lends heat & fire to Wrath. Which thus doubly enflamed by Gluttonies good cheare & supposal of iniurie will by no meanes sett down without reuenge taken some way or other. & so presently in a blind & madding rage falls a beating & wounding those, that come next to mind, if so be, it either cannot find occasion, or haue not the heart to fall out with them, that are present.

MODERATOR. That a great part of that shamefull detraction & sinfull backbiting, wherewith the great part of feasts are more stored, then with dainties, although they commonly exceed all measure & proportion, should be caused after this manner I shall easily agree vnto. Bodies prepared & minds resolued to the exercize of Lust cannot but deeply resent the constrained for-bearance of Lasciuious discourse & so perhaps in despite are harried to vent their Choler with their tongues, if they may not safely & conveniently doe it with their hands. This therefore happily may be the ground of those open & insolent raylings, which debauched minds too often run into vpon these occasions not onely going through the world with their tongues but stretching forth their mouths euen vnto heauen because they think it loures [frowns] on their desires, but surely the onely cause of all backbiting no nor [even] of the most and worst ⟨87v⟩ sort, that is now in fashion at the best Feasts & amongst the best guests. It cannot bee in regard, that wee commonly see none more forward and busie at this game of backbiting, then those, who through Age, impotencie, Conscience or for Credit sake doe not onely willingly giue out themselues, but compell others by their Authoritie to giue ouer lasciuious discourses, when they come on foot at such meetings & occasions. They can by no meanes therefore be thrust on to this open exercize of malice through any secret discontent for the losse of that, which they voluntarily depriue themselues of.

PATIENT. The frustrating of Lustfull designes cannot surely stirre vp any vnquietnes in them, that are neither fitted nor inclined to the exercize thereof. Especially where it is their own free choise besides. There being therefore no ground of wrath or greif in these mens fancies, there is no colour [excuse] of bringing slanders & backbiting in this way, besides in my apprehension this matter seemes to be purposely chosen by the greatest Number, for the pleasure that it naturally affords, rather then accidentally fallen vpon through offence taken at the diuersion of any other pleasure, that were aimed at.

GUARDIAN. Why is there any such great pleasure in backbiting and slandering? ⟨88⟩

MODERATOR. The Spaniards haue a proverb, as I haue often heard, that the Quintessence of delight lies in murmuring, so they terme Backbiting. So that let a man haue his Libertie & fill this way, & it will make amends for all other wants & sufferings whatsoeuer. A Man neither feels heat nor cold, nor hunger, nor thirst, nor pain nor wearines nor any other Necessitie of the Body & much lesse those of the mind, whilest he is either speaking or hearing Euill of others.

GUARDIAN. The strange Patience & hardines, that Pauls, Moorefeilds, the exchange & other such like places[1] infuse into the minds & bodies of those, that frequent them cheifly to this

---

[1] Disreputable places of business and amusement in seventeenth-century London.

intent shews plainly, that howeuer our English Palates agree not perhaps with the spanish in the rellish of our ordinarie diet, yet are our minds no lesse sett then theirs are on this appetite of the forbidden fruit. How many are there think you, that neither for Loue of their best freinds nor for any Necessity of their own can be won to sitt still within dores in summer, or to stay in a warme & close roome an houre or two in winter without lamenting themselues that they are sweltered with heat or frozen with cold, & yet can by no meanes be kept from running to the forenamed places, & there find, as it ⟨88 v⟩ seemes no manner of annoyance either from parching sun, or peircing wind, spinne out the whole day merrily without the help or assistance of any other advantage or satisfaction whatsoeuer then that, which they find & make to themselues in Vindicating other mens Liues & Actions.

AFFECTIONATE. The masterie, that this delight hath ouer the mind is no lesse then that, which it hath ouer the body; if it keep out the sence of all incommodities from the one it shuffles out the Care of all busines from the other. There's very few so resolute in the pursuit of any thing whatsoeuer, that a smooth-faced slander will not lure them away. The consideration of others faults instantly draws the attention from all other affaires. Euen Gamesters leaue their play, at least they mind it not to giue the better care to these bad kind of discourses.

PATIENT. But that, which shews the predominancie of it aboue all the rest in my opinion is, That it hath power to reingratiate such as know the art into the affection & esteeme of those, who are most offended with them. There is no flattering submission nor intended present, that finds so ready accesse or fauourable intertainment from the greatest Number of men & women, ⟨89⟩ when they are displeased as a cunningly deuised & neatly conveyed slander doth. He, that giues information of anothers Errours getts pardon for his own, & as the banditores in Italie vpon the bringing in of his fellow-malefactours head is instantly restored to fauour.

MOTHER. He, that thus grows into fauour, falls of [off] from grace, & brings himself into further condemnation with God by thus clearing himself with man. The vnorderly revealing of others faults corrupts innocencie it self, how much then must it adde to former guiltines. He that priuily slandereth his neighbour, him will I destroy, sayth Dauid,[1] & what then doth hee merrit, that doth it purposely adding iniustice to malice, and strengthening himself in his wickednes. A man perhaps can hardly find, if the instance be rightly taken, a larger proportion of shamelesse impudencie in any one action whatsoeuer then in this. What an impudencie of a seared Conscience[2] must it needs proceed from, for a man to offer his brothers Nakednes for the couer of his proper shame & vpon the proclamation of others errours to challenge the Cancelling of his own. He, that should make mends for himself falls vpon the punishment of his Brother & by becoming an iniust judge & cruell executioner of anothers honest Name and ⟨89v⟩ Creditt goes about to regaine the good will & Loue, which he hath deseruedly made forfeiture of in his own particular. There is a strange boldnes in the attempt & there must needs bee a strange sencelesnes in their hearts, vpon whom it takes effect. Hee, that well looks vpon the matter, shall find a double both of offence & estrangement from them, that thus endeauour to purchase reconciliation by causing more fallings out: How can he intend Loue, where he hath wronged, that offers wrong where he ows Loue? Or how can hee meane peace truely to him, that is at warre with him, that laies hands first vpon him, that is at peace with him? What greif or what shame of his own faults can such a man haue as with ioy & in triumph blazons out anothers? Or what satisfaction can he really purpose to giue them, whom hee hath offended, that so maliciously offends them, to whom he ought to afford pitty & compassion at least. The sin, which he should pray God to couer, he trumpets out to men, & when he

---

[1] Psalm ci, 5.

[2] A conscience rendered incapable of feeling. See I Timothy iv, 2.

should bow his knee to the throne of mercy in heauen, he stirrs vp
coals of wrath vpon Earth, incensing his fellow-servant, insteed of
appeasing his common Master. But let him vow what he will,
that thus demeanes himself, he getts no further credit of mee,
then that his heart is as false to the present, as his tongue is to
them, that are absent. He lies as much in the Loue he ⟨90⟩ professeth, as in the malice, that he dissembles & if occasion serued or
might be to his advantage, he would make as little scruple of
traducing them, that heare him, as he doth of them, that heare
him not. He is an hypocrite in the good will, that he pretends to
him, that giues him eare, & an hypocrite in the ill will, that he
makes shew of towards the vice, that he declaimes against. He
neither Loues nor hates either truely but for to serue his own
turne. Make him a gainer by the match, & he instantly shifts the
sides, verging about with the same breath to the flattering of
those, whom he backbites, and to the iniuring & affronts of those,
whom he seeks this way to please. Thus I condemne, myself, & lesse
I cannot suspect of others touching this matter, an ordinarie indeed
but an abominable practize, which I now as much hate, as I haue
heretofore little vnderstood, finding the venome to ly cheifly in
that, which is commonly reputed the vertue thereof. because it is
intended to the increase of Loue, & ministers much satisfaction to
distempered minds I thought it a trimme peice of Art, & pleasing
my self in the opinion of much charitie as well as policie, made
the revealing & discanting vpon others faults the ordinarie manner
of patching vp mine own reconciliation with offended freinds.
But not euery pleasing of others but that onely which is good &
in things tending to edification ⟨90v⟩ belongs to Christian
Charitie. The pleasing in euill things & tending to destruction is a
spice [sort] of hellish kindnes. The Deuill by this argument may
proue his good affection towards vs as well as wee can doe one to
another. So it be in a bad matter he is as forward as the best to
giue his furtherance. My desire of pleasing then boots mee not at
all then to hold my self any whitt better minded to my Freind

then the Deuill himself. He will not doe as much as this comes to, to second a man gladly in his sin-full content. And though hee loue not peace nor freindship, yet on these termes he will not refuse, I dare say, to become himself the brooker [broker] for it. He, that with peaching [accusing] others sues out his own pardon shall haue the Deuill not only his advocate, but Atturney & solliciter in the cause & if need bee suretie & baile too. Hee will not stick at any thing on his behalf, that will not stick to make the purchase of good-will on the one side by the exercize of malice on another. You see the reason of that speedie dispatch for pardon & reconcilement, that men gett, that goe this way to work; they haue the Deuill to second with all the might & skill, that he can afford. & how then can they misse of that, which they pretend vnto. But as they doe not commonly misse so neither can they greatly boast of what is thus gotten, if it be rightly scanned. The manner & their partner spoils the purchase cleane, & makes the re⟨91⟩conciliation & freindship thus obtained farre worse then the former Enmitie. How much lesse harm & danger were it to bee at odds through humane frailtie, then to come to agreement by the Deuils compromise & to remaine a debitour for single vnkindnes done to one, then gett free by double iniurie to another. The desire of pleasing then, that goes before, & the attainment of peace, that follows after this kind of relating & censuring others faults, mends the busines but a little since for all that it becomes no other & better, then such as likes & befitts the Deuill to be cheif agent in. And if that, which seemes good be thus amisse what shall wee say of that, which is plaine naught in this matter. The impudencie, the insolencie, the vniustice, that Men must needs yeeld themselues guilty of, when they accuse condemne & offer to punishment others Errours in stead of con-fessing sorrow & satisfaction [penance] for their own. Seemes it not to you as it doth to mee, that the busines is carried on both sides, as if there had beene a match made of emulation between vs & the Deuill, whether he should outvy vs in the promotion of that which seemes good, or wee him in the performance of that, which is euidently euill. He is for peace & pleasing on these termes as much as wee can be for our Liues & wee no whitt behind him in the very ⟨91 v⟩ worst of that, which wee can lay to his charge in this kind. Its only accusation that wee challenge him of, when we call him Deuill, & what can wee iustly obiect against him so foul, that he will not iustly retort vpon vs in this Case. Take it into the Light & see, whether to accuse lesser crimes being guilty of more heinous, to prosecute lighter Errours without repentance of greater in himself, & to offer Iniuries done to a third person in satisfaction of a mans own faults will not being put together make vp the complete body of Diabolical iniquitie for height of madnes, depth of hypocrisie & latitude of malice. But the Deuill tells faults out of ill will, & wee to gett good-will. He seeks the punishment of the accused, & wee the pleasure of the hearers, hee others harmes wee our own benefitt. Thus wee commonly deceiue others, & oftimes ourselues vpon a supposal of contrarie intentions, inferring a difference in the Nature & vpshott of this Action, & construing that to be wisedome in our selues, which wee condemne as excesse of wickednes in him. But if wee bring the matter to proof by the touchstone of veritie & not of particularitie wee shall vndoubtedly find, that the ill-will which wee shift off is not at all excluded, but onely shutt vp more priuately in our own brests, because the open shew thereof would bee to dis-advantage, ⟨92⟩ the outward fruit of this action seemes a little fairer, but the inward root is the same with that of the Deuill. There is an addition of hypocrisie more on our parts to colour [cloak] it, there is no abatement of the malice it self. Detraction & slander can haue no other foundation then hatred & Envie. What euer a man beare men in hand with, God will find him guilty of bearing ill will in his heart, that broacheth ill reports with his tongue. Out of the abundance of the heart the mouth speaketh, sayth truth it self.[1] & how then must it not needs be a

---

[1] Matthew xii, 34.

ly in graine [essence], that the bringing forth of euill and preiudicial words is without the conception of euill & preiudicial
thoughts within. There must needs be an implicit intent of malice
in this actual exercize thereof which the explicite intent of flatterie
is so farre from extenuating as it rather increaseth the deadlines
thereof. The soothing vp of ill humours casheereth a man out of
Gods household. If I please men I am not the seruant of God,
sayth St Paul.[1] How little then will it help to boulster out [sup-
port] the wronging others, that cannot beare out it self: the Malice
getts no abatement but the sin is hereby doubled. Poysons may
sometimes correct one another & a healthfull medicine be compounded of contrarie venomes: ⟨92v⟩ In regard that wee call
poisons are but accidentally euill inasmuch as they are vnpro-
portionable to the Natural Temper of man. But sin that is entirely
euill & absolutely contrarie to the spiritual welfare can by no
meanes possible be so ordered as that the addition of a second
should qualifie the first to any other benefitt then of further condemnation. He, that multiplies sin increaseth guilt, & adds to the
weight & substance by seeking to vary the shape. He, that tells
tales to gett good will becomes a plaine flatterer but leaues not at
all to be a real backbiter. The new transforming themselues is but
as laying on varnish makes the colour more firm & solid though in
it self to weak sights it oftimes makes it lesse distinguishable. This
addition then of pleasing others helps not at all the matter but to
double the crime. Nor will the substraction of malice, which they
so stand for, if it be allowed them, serue for other purpose. They
meane no harm to those, whose faults and imperfections they tell
of. Their own hearts witnesse it to themselues & reason ought to
perswade all others as much, in regard it is euident there is no
ground of offence between themselues & those, whom they speak
of & most commonly there are many great & iust causes of hearty
Loue & affection, they haue receiued kindnes, are linked in bloud,
are vnder the iurisdiction ⟨93⟩ or some way or other neerly

---

[1] Galatians i, 10.

interessed in the partie of whom they hold discourse; to suspect
them therefore of malignant intention must not only be vnkindnes, but folly too. Why what reason haue they to be spitefully
disposed against the person. & if there be no reason it must needs
be the spite, that's against reason, that challengeth them of so
foul a crime. This is the defence, which admitted for good, makes
the offence mount to such a height of wickednes on mans part,
as that worst of wickednes, which wee impute to the Deuill in
this case, falls many leagues short of it, if I mistake not the
measure. The mischeif is the same, that is done on both sides.
the Deuill accuseth, when he ought not, neither being called by
the iudge, nor interessed in the crime, & so doe wee. He provokes
wrath against those, whom he accuseth, & so doe wee. He pro-
cures infamie to those, against whom he hath provoked wrath,
& so doe wee. He puts them out of fauour, to whom he hath
procured infamie, disceasing [depriving] them of the grace &
good will aswell as the good esteeme & opinions of their freinds,
& so deceiue in the act it self & in all the circumstances of it, & in
this final issue of preiudice & wrong of the accused there's no
difference at all to be found between ours & the Deuils information,
publication & prosecution of other ⟨93 v⟩ men's Errours in this
way or manner. That, which then salues all our parts, is that wee
doe it not with malicious intent, which hee discouers & how
proue wee that? because they be our freinds, our kinsmen, our
benefactours, our Superiours in Ciuill or Ecclesiastical matters,
our Country men, our Neighbours, & if none of all these our
Christian Brethren, whose salvation & good wee know wee are
bound charily to tender vpon penaltie of making forfeiture of our
own. Wee cannot then be thought to be such monsters in Nature,
in Reason, & in Religion, as to be maliciously affected, or to doe
it with that despitefulnes of mind, which the Deuill bewraies
[betrays]. he makes proclamation of warre against whom he
proceeds in this kind, & therefore wee may be sure he meanes the
words that can bee True. & what then? Wee are sure wee meane

well & yet doe the worst that wee may, as bad as he can doe for his Life. & which shall wee say is the more Deuillish of the twain, maliciously to prosecute an enemy or mischeiuously to preiudice a freind. Hee a Deuill for accusing of men, with whom he hath nothing common in Nature or Grace. & what shall see then be in accusing one another, amongst whom there is nothing proper or seueral [distinct] either in Manhood or Christianitie, but an intire, absolute & indissoluble brotherhood in both these respects. Goe now ⟨94⟩ and aggravate the Deuills malice in his Actions, & extenuate thine own to the vttermost that witt & words can reach vnto & yet vndoubtedly, when they come into the ballance of the sanctuarie, the sin wilbe found through neernes of relation, that is between thee & the iniured much heauier then the Devuils for all the euidence of malice, wherewith he seemes fraughted [laden]. Its a Diabolical Exercize out of malice to persecute errours against thine enemy. But to persecute, whom wee pretend loue vnto for our own advantage or others pleasure is to my apprehension a degree of wickednes beyond that, which the inhabitants of Hell themselues practize. They keep better quarter one with another. I neuer yet heard any thing, that might induce the least suspicion, that one Deuill should tell tales or accuse his fellow either to God or Man. And yet it is matter of accusation & telling tales, that seemes cheifly to make them so odious, not onely on earth amongst men, but in heauen with the blessed Saints & Angels. The great iubile that is recorded by St John to be made aboue in heauen for the casting down & vtter expulsion of Satan from thence is cheifly founded vpon this ground. The accuser of our Brethren is cast down, which accuseth them before God day & night.[1] ⟨94v⟩ There's neither Falshood nor Malice layd to his charge but onely accusation, not that he is not perhaps oft guiltie of the first & alwaies of the last, but least wee should take occasion either by the truth of what wee report, or the conceit of our own freedome from malice to

---

[1] Revelation xii, 10.

iustifie our selues. The Wisedome of God hath not thought fitt, as I conceiue, to insert expressely either of these ill conditions, but simply & absolutely to brand the action it self, of accusing the Brethren, as the very quintessence & Masterpeice of Diabolical wickednes. Many differences, I know, & some maine ones may be found between that kind of accusation, which the Deuil is there so heinously taxed with & that, which wee here so commonly practize. He doth it Night and day wee but now & then. & yet that seemes rather for want of matter then good will to the busines, if wee could find what to say, wee would neuer giue ouer. It seemes to be his cheif imploiment, it is with vs but a by-work, when occasion serueth. & yet it is certain wee doe nothing more contentedly. He accuseth but before God, & wee before men that's principally intending their information yet necessarily Gods, from whose eies & ears wee know nothing can be hid, that wee doe or say. But let all those and whateuer other ⟨95⟩ differences can bee properly framed, bee allowed to the full for the increase of this Deuilish impietie & yet they will all not so alter the action, but that the very cor [core, heart] & wherein the pestilence lies in him, is that, which wee make least accompt of in ourselues, That his accusations are against the brethren, although he be a professed enemy himself is that, which fills the measure of his iniquitie. & how then will not the accusation of our Brethren to our Brethren professing Freindship on both hands make the measure of ours heaped vp, pressed down, & running ouer to the vttermost extent, that can be imagined both of guilt and Condemnation. Let who will sooth vp himself in this kind I shall neuer dare to think otherwise, then that all manner of voluntarie accusation, much more delightfull information or reuelation of others errours is a part of that office, which is proper to the Deuill. That onely in these kinds excepted, which is really & principally intended to reformation of the delinquent, iustification of the innocent, prevention of infection to them, that are whole, or to the redresse of some Notable inconveniencies. In these a good man may & oftimes is bound to make known others misdoings & though with greif, & hazard perhaps of his own safetie, hee may not refuse, when Necessitie enforceth, to become ⟨95 v⟩ informer, Wittnesse, Solliciter, & Atturney or whateuer else is needfull against those persons, that offend of malicious wickednes, & against those crimes, which by concealment endanger the Common good, or him, that committs them, more then the shame & punishment, which will follow vpon such prosecution, can doe. He that laies open his Neighbours faults with a sincere intention of remedying that, which is done amisse, or of preventing some further mischeif, deals like a good Physition, that searches wounds to cure them, & cutts of [off] rotten members to preserue the sound. But he, that for others sport & pleasure makes shew of infirmities, & tents [probes], & launceth his freinds wounds for his own advantage-sake, deserues the Name of a hangman, if he exercize his skill & doe his cures in bodily diseases: but what shall I term him when it is in spiritual affaires & those, which concern the soul, I am at a stand; to say, he plaies the Deuill in this Case will be thought too much to be born, although to say he passeth the Deuill wilbe scarce enough for what hee deserues. That I may neither offend the world therefore nor the truth Ile say nothing of others, but shut vp all in these words, which he did, from whence I learned what I haue told you in this matter: I shall esteeme in my self the malicious disclosing & ⟨96⟩ prosecution of their errours, against whom I am ill affected, a sin paralell to that of the Deuills, but the iniurious & infamous publication of their faults, to whom I owe & professe freindship, to be one, at least, if not more, degree aboue that, for which the Deuill is so odious, & for which he hath gott so ill a Name both in heauen & Earth. As for the desire of pleasing others, & the designe of recouering that fulnes of grace & fauour, which I am fallen from, with any body, I see they adde to the substance by transforming the shape of this wickednes, & I hereby proue a soothing Flatterer without ceasing at all to bee a Cursed Slanderer.

All the gain that comes by this meanes, is, that the guilt is doubled, & I run in point-blank vpon that, which Dauid so abhorres, & to which he imprecates so fearefull a reward, as vtter desolation from Gods auenging hand, Destroy thou them, o God, let them perish through their own imaginations, cast them out in the multitude of their vngodlines for they haue rebelled against thee.[1] You see the imputation of a hainous crime; you heare the thunder of a dreadfull sentence; will you know the persons to whom it belongs? Why they be the very same of whom wee speak, such as make their mouths serue scorpion-like to con⟨96v⟩-trarie effects. The scorpion embraceth with his claws & stingeth with his tail. So doe these double faced monsters in the selfsame instant bite one & lick another drawing bloud from the absent by defamation & soothing vp the present in their euill dispositions. Their throat is an open sepulcher, they flatter with their tongues.[2] The description, which gods holy spirit hath made of these enormious offendours, which euery way suiting iust to the selfsame crime, that wee are vpon. I shall alwaies condemne myself to be full & altogether guiltie of as much euill & liable to as much punishment, as the Psalmist awarded, when euer willingly I sett my self to the comitting of this detestable sin of telling tales to procure goodwill, & backbite others to gett pardon & reconciliation for my self.

PATIENT. It is a dreadfull censure, that your Master who euer he be hath passed against this cime. & howeuer according to the Anatomie [analysis], that he hath made thereof no more then it deserues, yet too dangerous for mee to bee his partner by the like application of it in mine own particular. Henceforth, God willing, I shalbe most precizely wary of keeping my self farre off from all taint of this abomination. But if I should through mine own frailtie, the Deuills driuing, or, which I most feare, the lewd enticement of perverse Example at any time vnwarily slip ⟨97⟩ into it, I should be ouermuch perhaps amated [cast down] to

---

¹ Psalm v, 10.   ¹ Ibid., 9.

haue such a heauie doome of mine own enrolment ready to be brought in against mee. He belike is very confident of neuer incurring the sin, that is so resolute & forward in aggrauating the guilt & accepting the punishment due thereunto.

MOTHER. Indeed he is very confident as he sayth not in his own strength, which is lesse then nothing, but in the mercy of God & in the power our Lord Jesus Christ, which is so much aboue all things, as assisted thereby there is nothing so hard as he dare not vndertake to keep himself vnspotted from this enormious wickednes.

GUARDIAN. But, mee thinks, that they, who are afrayd of falling into it should be rather induced to the imitation of the like, that so they might haue the greater obligation on themselues to avoid running into that, which their own tongues haue condemned to be brimme full of vnspeakable Euill & danger. I am sure, It was Dauids practize in a busines much of the same nature. If I haue rewarded euill to him, that dealt freindly with mee yea I haue deliuered him that without a cause is mine enemie, then let mine enemie persecute my soul & take it, yea let him tread my life down vpon the ground & ⟨97v⟩ lay mine honour in the dust.[1]

AFFECTIONATE. The case seemes not alike. Dauid speaks of those actions, which were past, wherein knowing his innocency he might boldly engage both soul & body to the hazard of any penaltie whatsoeuer.

GUARDIAN. True. But doth not he, that offers his head to the block in iustification of himself, if he haue done such or such a crime, bind himself to the laying of it down, & suffer it to be cutt off, if he should at any time afterwards committ the like.

PATIENT. I cannot deny verily but the consequence is so necessarie, as you may well from Dauids Example iustifie the matter. But yet mee thinks my heart serues mee not to pronounce so hard a censure against myself afore hand.

[1] Psalm vii, 4–5.

GUARDIAN. Why but afterwards belike you would make no spare nor scruple.

PATIENT. No verily. In case I had committed the sin, I should hold it the safest course to iudge my self no whitt lesse guiltie nor worthy of lighter punishment then he doth.

GUARDIAN. Why then I dare warrant, there is no difference at all between your meaning & his words. He intends not an imprecation, howeuer safe he conceiues himself from prouing liable ⟨98⟩ therevnto, but a declaration of his opinion only touching the heinousnes of the crime, & binds not himself arrogantly to the vndergoing of the punishment, which he setts vpon the faults, but binds himself humbly to that measure & manner of repentance, which is necessarie for the redeeming & clearing thereof in case it should be committed. This I conceiue to be his meaning. & sure his words if rightly scanned import no otherwise. And this I hold many waies so good & vsefull, as I desire you in the same sence to accept now likewise my protestation in this matter. Not to exclude Gods mercy if I shall vnhappily fall into this errour, but the more surely to procure it by necessitating my self to a sound & full repentance for the same according to the measure & weight of that Guilt, which I find it now clearly & iustly convicted of. It's a greiuous sin beyond that, which any words of amplification can reach vnto, for a man to speak euill & report faults, & run out into slanderous discourses for the satisfaction & pleasure of any hearers whatsoeuer, & for the advantage of obtaining of any good, though it seeme neuer so great & faire: but he, that gaines his temporal ends, looseth his soul, & incurres an absolute forfeiture [of] Gods grace by his recouery ⟨98v⟩ of mens good will after this fashion. Thus I censure my self before hand, & so I shall condemne my self afterward, and accordingly shall my sorrow, my shame, & supplications be without intermission or stint, till I haue by the infinitenes of Diuine Goodnes obtained a renewing of that holy couenant with God, which in euery branch & member I must needs yeeld to haue beene on my part vtterly defaced & cancelled, wheneuer I shall willingly & purposely committ this wretched kind of perfidiousnes against God & Man. But by the preventing & vpholding mercy of my God I shall neuer henceforth committ it againe, howeuer often heretofore I must needs confesse with blushing face & wounded heart to haue been greiuously foiled thereby. But the time past sufficeth to haue walked according to the course of the world, henceforth my conversation shalbe according to the rule of Gods word. It's much too much to haue liued so long as I haue done to the will of men, & much too little to liue that short time, that remaines, absolutely & intirely to the will of God. The darknes of the former times cannot excuse because it was in truth more effected through my wilfull shutting of mine eies, then really by the depriuation of ⟨99⟩ necessarie Light, But now the brightnes of the sun, that shines round about, would doubly condemne mee, if I should willingly stumble & fall againe into these horrible precipices. The easines of pardon for that, which was this way done amisse in time of ignorance, will increase the difficultie of obtaining it now vpon full knowledge & vnderstanding. The often escaping makes mee more timorous of adventuring vpon it any more, finding, that it was not the want of weight in the sin, but the exuberancie of Gods mercies, that hath restrained the euill influences & effects, that naturally attend it. Which I must needs expect should return double on my head if I should goe on presumptuously incensing that Diuine grace & Mercy, which hath hitherto been my safegard. No verily. Ile no more hazard my soul in this kind on any condition whatsoeuer. Ile report no bodies faults but with the intent & hope either of the delinquents amendement or of the Auditours profitt. Ile sooth vp no mans ill humours to bring him into good temper with my self, nor turn parasite to Malice for currying fauour. He shall surely be disappointed, that expects his basenes from mee. Ile report no mans errours purposely to please. & if vpon necessarie reporting I discouer pleasure ⟨99v⟩ to arise in them that heare mee, Ile purposely break of [off], if I possibly may, & to put to venture the losse of that good, that I intended rather then become guiltie of the euill, which I so much abhorre. He shall be good man in my opinion & in a good disposition for the present likely to make good vse of it, to whom I disclose errours, I meane, of any other then those, that appertaine properly to his charge & care. But if he be a good man indeed & in a good disposition hee wilbe scrupulous to heare, as I can be to make report of those Errours, that belong not to him. In regard it is vndoubtedly true what I lately read in most Diuine & Learned Sallis,[1] that the acting of slanders & the hearing of them, the playing of the Backbiter & the looking on & lending eare therevnto are so little different either in the qualitie of the sin, or the Author from whose inspiration & abetment they proceed, as it is a measuring cast[2] (as wee say) whether of the twaine is the more wicked, or shall receiue the worst punishment. Questionlesse the Deuill is alike interessed in both & both alike engaged to him. His right is as good in the one, as in the other. The one makes open Liuery & seazon[3] by his tongue, the other giues him enterance by his eares. Both invest him in full and absolute possession of his soul. I shall therefore God willing to the first ⟨100⟩ adde the second resolution, & to the protestation against telling any tales my self to pleasure others ioyne the promise of refusing to heare at all those, which shall be told by others to this intent.

[1] Sallis—St Francis of Sales. See *Introduction to the Devout Life*, Part III, Section 29, and Introduction, p. lv.

[2] A measuring cast—a competitive throw at a mark in which the results are so close as to require measurement.

[3] Liuery & seazon—livery of seisin, a legal term meaning delivery of property by use of a symbol, such as a key or piece of turf.

Part X

Encouraged by the Guardian's last statement, the Mother offers to continue despite the weariness of all. She will point out that the willingness to listen to slanders not out of malice to the accused but out of love to the complainant is a greater sin than eagerness to utter them. The Guardian speaks at length and with great eloquence on this matter and elaborates on the heinous sinfulness of giving comfort to those who complain of the backbiting by those whom they in turn malign. The Patient and the Affectionate develop the theme of false friendship and malicious good will. The Affectionate first elaborates on David's indictment of evil speakers and liars in Psalm ci and later works out a complicated simile involving the relationship between the seal and the imprinted wax to the relater and the believer of slanders and lies. The dialogue ends abruptly before the Mother has spoken again.

◆

MOTHER. Let him, that heareth, say, Come, is the Bridegromes Exhortation in the Apocalyps,[1] & well now put in execution by you, Worthy Guardian, You stay not a scholer in the lesson, which you haue beene taught; but take out a new one of your self, & become a Master to your fellows by good Counsell & example. Why this is the right course of profitting in Gods seruice, not onely to walk readily the good way that is shewed vs, but to shew it to others & to passe on as a guide to them that are behind, aswell as to follow them, that are before. You'l not onely tell no tales to please; but you'l heare none to this intent. This improuement of the first merits the declaration of the second part. Wherefore though the feare of your wearines, aswell as the feeling of mine own through this longsome digression, make it appeare lesse seasonable perhaps, yet finding it according to the zeal & good affection that I now see kindled in you likely to proue very beneficial I dare not but make offer of now acquainting you

---

[1] Revelation xxii, 17.

with the remainder ⟨100v⟩ of that, which I learned touching this point & so much the rather as mee thinks, this your continual specification of that, which is lesse in this matter of giuing eare to slanders seemes to imply, that you are not yet fully informed touching that, which is the greater: for surely else you would haue toucht vpon it. the iealousie [anxiety], that makes you keep so aloof from the shole [shoal] would vndoubtedly haue made you put off much more scrupulously from the quicksands & the Rocks, if you were aswell aware of them as of this other lighter danger.

GUARDIAN. In very truth I thought to haue stricken at the root & quite deaded the power of backbiting to be exercized by mee or towards mee, when I made my protestation of driuing away with frowns & euidencie of dislike those, that brings news & make reports of others faults to breed pleasure & giue satisfaction to their freinds & Auditours. But it seemes belike though the telling of tales & slandering in this kind be the worst of all others, yet there is some other worse & more wicked manner of hearing tales & giuing eare to slander then that, which is caused through the delight & satisfaction, that men find in hearing others euill spoken of. ⟨101⟩

MOTHER. Worse & more Wicked say you? Why to giue eare with open profession of much content & solace vpon the diuulging of others Errours, & afterwards to fall on censuring them with all manner of despight, that may be, though it swell to the full measure of the Deuils Iniquitie in this kind, yet is it in truth but like a crawling serpent to flying Dragon in comparison to another cursed practize this way, which now adaies runs currant for a singular peice not onely of good Nature, but of religious charitie. The suspition what this may be, hath filled you, I see, with wonderment. I shall double it, I am afraid, rather then allay it by the declaration of what, it is. Why it is the giuing eare to slanderous tales & backbiting not out of malice to the accused but out of Loue to the complainants, not out of ill will to the wrong-doer, but out of compassion to the iniured, not out of pleasure, that wee take in hearing any body euill spoken of, but out of pitty, that wee haue of euery bodies vnderserued sufferings.

GUARDIAN. I [Aye]. Soe men pretend indeed flattering them selues in their own sight: but not able for all these figleaues to couer or disguise the matter so but that the title of an ⟨101 v⟩ Abominable sin wilbe found grauen vpon the forhead thereof by them, that with spiritual eies & in the light of true reason look vpon it. Come hither, thou deceiued, (for so I perceiue thou art) aswell as dissembling Hypocrite, & lend mee that false eare a while to heare the truth of thy self; which thou hast so often lent to heare lies & tales of thy Neighbours. If it be Loue, that thou bearest to the partie, or pitty, that thou hast of the cause, how comes it, that thou lendest thy hand to a distempered creature to teare ope his wounds & powre [pour] in venome after? Is it not enough, that he is afflicted with humane misfortune, but that by thy vnkindnes hee must be helped forward to infernal Guiltines, & be made infinitely more miserable by his wilfull sin, then by his vniust sufferings. Were there no Receiuers there would be no Theeues. If thou offeredst not thy ready eare, like stirred & fallowed ground, hee should be forced to keep back his euill seed & all that fruitfull crop of wickednes & mischeif, that springs vp by this meanes would haue beene spared. His tumultuous thoughts would haue been strangled in his own bosome, or if they must needs break forth into Lamentations, yet finding no better then the barren Aire, they must needs haue returned like seed scattered in the wind. Its thy brooding, that giues life to those Cockatrices Eggs & armest them with poyson to the certain ouerthrow of his ⟨102⟩ soul aswell as to the further ranckling of his wounds. Thou hath helped him with a little ease at the prize [price] of his Innocencie. He hath become both to God & manward an offender, & liable by this wrong-doing to the stroakes of that selfsame Iustice, which he calls vpon for help against Wrong-sufferings. He, that prosecutes a crime before those iudges, to whom the cognizance thereof belongs not, incurres the penaltie of a Libeller, & is awarded if they doe iustice to pay Costs & dammages for his vniust vexation. howeuer true the matter bee, yet when the accusation is made to those, that cannot, or purpose not to sett in hand with the redresse, it is a meere Calumnie in the Plaintiue. For where there is no probabilitie of obtaining right, the complaint must needs bee intended onely to the working of reuenge. An end so contrarie not only to Christianitie but to Manhood, as whosoeuer setts himselfe to the practize thereof makes the vttermost of wrongs, that he can suffer, to be rightly deserued. There's no oppression so intolerable nor vnkindnes so vnnaturall, no iniury so exorbitant, that the persecution of it with a wrongfull mind will not so much advantage as to make to appeare to all indifferent eies the lesse euill of the twaine. He, that persecutes his vniust offender with despight proues himself the worst malefactour, & vndoubtedly will, if the matter come ⟨102 v⟩ before any vnpartial Tribunal, be condemned to the sorer punishment. Lo here the gaine, that thy Loue & freindship hath procured, in lending thine eare to vnprofitable murmurings, informations, & Accusations in an vndue & vneuen manner. Thou hast giuen ease as they, that help to scratch an itching soare Causing it thereby to rankle & fester afterwards with doubled torments & trebled length of time. How swoln with Rage, Confirmed in Rankour, puffed vp with self-conceit, & resolute not to beare with Patience, nor to sitt down with Humilitie, but to publish with infamie, to resist with might, & to reuenge with malice, doth this disorderly relatour of his own greifs & others iniuries goe away, when he hath done. & all this through thy cursed abettment & hatching vp of his Distempered Passions. Thy fained pitty like soft blowing to the coal hath made the sparkles of his Greif to break out in a flame. & now on thy remonstrance of a sorrowfull compassion hee faines to himself, as they, that veiw themselues in deceitfull mirrours, representing all things much larger then they bee indeed. A farre greater misery then he was before aware of. He

argues from thy fellowship the excesse of his affliction, & concludes, that it is not tolerable to be born in the full weight by
him, that proues so burthensome to thee in the bare relation.
Thus thy ⟨103⟩ false bemoanings increase his woe, & thy colloging
[sympathetic] flatteries, that alwaies come after, make it incurable.
Thou canst not giue him pitty, but thou must giue him right
likewise. Thou must iustifie his cause, whose part thou takest &
tell him, that he hath wrong, aswell as affliction. Thus soothing
him vp in the conceit of his innocency, thou bringest him into the
certainty of condemnation & into the Necessitie of further punishment. He, that grows presumptuous in the chastizement laying
the blame of what hee feels to smart on the Executioners malice
& not on his own demerrits, aggrauates the guilt & multiplies the
stripes euen whilest they are Numbered out in payment to him.
There must be an acknowledgement of Errours, a Confession of
guilt before there be a discharge of the correction, when it proceeds from the award of Gods Iustice. His own conscience directs
him this way, but thy encouragements recall him & like a deceitfull Proctour ready to retaine the cause in his own hand, thrusts
him on headlong to an impenitent iustification of himself & to an
impious prosecution of his adversarie. I know thy iudgements are
right & that thou of very faithfulnes hast caused mee to be
troubled, sayd the man after Gods own heart in the ouerswelling
of his greif:[1] & who is there amongst vs, that in euery thing walk
so ⟨103 v⟩ contrarie to Gods open iniunctions, that would in like
case dare to say otherwise, if he were left to himself, or had, as I
suppose, no worse Counsellours, then the Deuill of Hell. He puts
men often forward to plead not guiltie with their tongues, but to
make them beleiue it in their own hearts he neuer goes about,
that I haue heard. He knows, it were too palpable a ly for him,
though he be the profest Father of Lies, to suggest to this sort of
people, that their sufferings are aboue & without their deserts. But
what the Deuill hath not as it seemes either the heart or the face

[1] Psalm cxix, 75.

302

to attempt, certainly not the Libertie from God to bring to passe, a false tongue of a fellow delinquent after a fained shew of an vnfained sentence vpon the full discussion of the matter hath the power to effect. He professeth freindship to the accused, & puts on a visour of dislike against the complainant. Hee tells them they are to blame, & presseth it hard, till teares perhaps start out of the complainants eies. But all is but a cheating combination. The one weeps to sell himself for an humble Patient, the other chides to sett himself for an vnpartial iudge. Both of them haue made a match to deceiue each by an interchangeable Testimonie of false goodnes & vertue to the mutual ruine and ⟨104⟩ desolation of all true vertue & goodnes, which they driue at; & in the end this is the bargaine strock vp between them at the cost & on the head of the accused. He stands guilty of all the wrong, for as for those other matters, that were insisted vpon with such earnestnes against the plaintiue, they proue vpon examination very trifles, & that was well enough vnderstood from the very first, on both sides. & therefore the pressing of them, though it driues teares from the eies, yet it breeds no ill blood in the complainants heart, his mind bodening, that it would turn to the advantage of that, which he hunted after. & so it doth indeed. For on this ground mainly doth he build vp that glorious frame of his own innocency, which he cheifly aimed at; the integritie of the iudge, to whom he hath submitted his cause, approuing it self by such plaine reproofs, as he hath vsed, perswades him to accept the sentence giuen in his fauour, as from heauen it self. I should not haue beene spared in greater faults thinks hee, if they had beene found, that haue beene so fully prosecuted in the lighter. & found they must needs haue beene, if there had been any vpon such narrow sifting as was vsed; the iudgement is vncontroulable & therefore my innocencie infallible. I suffer wrongfully on the oppressours part; vndeseruedly on myne own, excessiuely in ⟨104v⟩ the measure & therefore intolerable in all. So Wisedome & the vprightnes of an vnpartial vmpire hath determined. Neither the presumption of others censures, nor the peeuishnes of mine own conscience shall perswade mee to the contrarie. It is but scrupulousnes, that galls mee within, it is but malice, that taxeth mee abroad. I am cleare from Errour & ought to be freed from blame, I find pitty & will pursue my right. It is necessarie to resent; it is natural to reuenge in these like cases. This is the conclusion, that this wicked plaintiue grows to. & all through thy wicked abetment of his vnruly passions. the bowing of thy compassionate eare, the complying of thy sad visage, & the soothings vp of thy mornful tongue draw him on to vnstinted Lamentations of his greif, to impudent iustification of his innocencie, to arrogant boasting of his own deserts, & to obstinate resolutions of going on in his impenitencie & Errours, to bitter exclamations against his offender, a setled purpose of Reuenge, Last of all this multiplying new sins, when he should amend the old, driuing him on to the prolonging & aggrauating of his instant affliction to the pulling down of that with more greiuous. For how iust is it the remedie should be enforced, where the euill humours gett head, Where that which is ministred to the cure of the disease is converted to the increase thereof through the malignitie of the Patient, there is a necessitie ⟨105⟩ on the Physicions behalf of proceeding to stronger & sharper Experiments, if there be a sincere intent of his recouerie. When small & gentler Simples purge not, there must be a greater quantitie & of more operatiue ingredients put in the medicine. He, that is not bettered by a lighter chastizement from the iustice of God Compells his Loue to make payment full weight. I haue brought you to the entrance & portal of that World of sin & mischeif, which is bred in the world by this Hypocriticall practize of kindnes, this Diuelish peice of Charitie. The Entrance, I say, & Beginning, the vpshot & full issue thereof no length of time would serue to recount, nor any eloquencie of Language be able to expresse, how infinite & enormious are the disastrous effects and damned consequences thereof. For Take all the murthers, violences, quarrels, Emnities, & in summe all the manner of

outrages (& innumerable they bee, which in the veiw of heauen
& with high hand here below are committed through & by the
meanes of open affronts & Calumnies, false accusations & reports)
& yet, I dare boldly say, they will not amount to the tenth part of
that mischeif either for weight of sin, or woe of misery, which is
really bred & caused in the ⟨105 v⟩ world by this priuie & secret
entertainment & hatching vp of complaints & greiuances vnder
pretence of Loue & colour of pitty. & as men perswade themselues out of singular good affection to both parties, aswell the
iniurer as the iniured, So their tongues proclaime to others &
their hearts beare wittnes to themselues. for they protest they are
as sorry for the wrong-doer as for the wrong-sufferer, both are
alike freinds to them, & they equally freinds to both. Thus
fortifying themselues in the conceit of meaning nothing but good,
& that of the best kind, no worse, then to repaire the breaches of
comfort to the distressed & to build vp themselues in charitie,
they goe stumbling on boldly to the acting of the vttermost, that
may be deuised for euill & mischeif, with vndermining & ruining
the very groundwork of all that Loue and vertue, whereon the
welfare & prosperitie of humane societie is grounded. For verily
he, that looks well vpon the busines shall perceiue, that all the
wicked Rebellions of children against Parents, the sedition of
wiues against husbands, the conspiracie of servants against
Masters, the peaching [accusing] of freinds & kinred one towards
another, the ingratitude against Benefactours, the wrong against
Neighbours, & in a word almost all these priuate iniuries, sufferings, & mutual vexations especially betweene ⟨106⟩ Superiours &
those, that are vnder subiection, which disturb & contaminate the
peace & quiet of mankind, & turn all the sweetnes of our Liues
into wormwood & gall, haue their rise, growth, & fruitfulnes in
that iniquitie & mischeife, which they produce cheifly through the
fomentation, abetment & heart, that they receiue and find from
the secret Lending eare, & compassionate soothing vp of them,
who pretend to lend their eare & to afford their pitty to com-

plaints thus brought vnto them meerly out of their Loue to the iustice of the cause, desire of releif to the oppressed, & pure good-will to all parties interessed therein.

PATIENT. Vndoubtedly the greatest part of those bitter cursed fruits, which you haue reckoned vp, would through remorse of conscience & the feare of shame, which God hath appointed alwaies to attend their springing vp, fall away like blossomes nipped by cold Winds & frosts in their very first putting forth, were it not for the shelter, warmth, & succour, which they gett vpon a fauourable audience, seconded by ruthfull Looks & solemne bemoanings of those, which carry the reputation of goodnes. There are very few brought forth so impudent by Nature, or so farre abandoned by Christian grace, as would of themselues adventure vpon the infamous publication of their errours & vnkindnes ⟨106v⟩ to whom they owe allegiance, Loue, & seruice, & in breif their own selues, as Children, wiues, & seruants doe to their parents, husbands & Masters, were they not by degrees like birds & beasts trained vp for the chase & prey, manned & fleshed[1] as it were to this inhuman kind of snarls, biting & deuouring by the perfidious encouragements & hartnings on of these kind of formal Hypocrites, that make it a work of charitie in themselues to bee the receiuers of those tales & slanders, the broaching whereof the Relatour in his own conscience knows to be the work & instigation of the Deuill. Mark well the blushing, the trembling ioynts, the faltering tongue & all other symptomes of a perplexed conscience, wherewith euery one begins at first approach & enterance into this busines of accusing & traducing superiours. & he will be forced to grant; that his own mind tells him, the profession, which he sets vp, is stark naught, & the ware, that he hath to vent altogether Contrabando so as vndoubtedly he would giue ouer the trade as wicked & vnprofitable in the first setting vp; but that from the acceptation, which he sees, they

---

[1] Manned & fleshed—accustomed, as a hawk used in falconry, to the presence of man and eager for the taste of meat.

haue with good Customers, he is perswaded to think better of his Commodities then he knows them in truth to bee. The ready vtterance, that he finds of his pestilent trash amongst those, that ⟨107⟩ make profession of dealing in nothing but sound & good wares & such as will abide the test of Gods word it self is the only warrantie, that he goes vpon for the bold putting it off; were it not for the opinion, that slanderous complaints haue their vertue & goodnes, who giue them eare & become their partners in the crime, the thing it self would appeare so monstrously deformed, as I verily beleiue the sufferings of any true iniurie would be more lighter to beare, then the weight of an undue & malicious report made against a mans freind, & there would be very few, whom the sting of conscience would not more perplex after their traducing accusations, then the sence of any wrong or vnkindnes did before. But now because these be good persons & seeme confident to haue done a good work, that haue lent willing eare to their tales, there is no cause to doubt of hauing done amisse in telling them. For were the speaking in their parts blameworthy, the hearing on the other side could not well be iustified. Thus they goe on from the supposal of vnquestionable welldoing in their partner, arguing a lawfulnes in their apparent wickednesse, hastening themselues on in murmuring & vnorderly venting their distempered passions, till at last they grow hardened to the ⟨107v⟩ presumptuous exercize of all manner of outragious calumnie, adding palpable Lies to open remonstrance of malice without any scruple of conscience or shame holding all things lawfull & good, that may tend to their advantage.

AFFECTIONATE. There's none verily at least of those, that euer I haue meet with (& too many there be, so great is the exuberancie of this sinfull crime, that I haue meet with, although my yeares be not many, nor my experience much) theres none I say of these vndue & vnorderly relatours of their greifs & iniuries, publishing where and as they ought, that euer conteine themselues in any tolerable bounds of Discretion, truth, or Charity, but after a little

whiles practize, howeuer shy & modest they begin, grow, as the
Italian proverb is, to make vp the bundle with all kind of herbs.
There's nothing, that may help their own cause or hurt their
adversaries, that they stick at. Bee their deuice neuer so vnseemely,
vnprofitable, I [aye] or euidently vntrue, yet if it may serue their
present turn, they make no bones, as wee say, of suggesting it by
way of surmize, no nor oftimes of swearing & avowing it as a
reall truth. Oh, the innumerable & monstrous fictions, that
Chimera-like raysed at first by the distempered fancies of these
irregular ⟨108⟩ Complainants, run afterwards currant for true
stories. How many Parents on this ground become branded with
vnnaturalnes? how many husbands marked out for worse then
Barbarians? how many Masters & Gouernours defamed with
oppression & Tyrannie, that in very truth haue nothing more
perhaps to answere for before God, then their too much Loue,
fondnes & Lenitie, wherewith they proceed towards their
children, wiues, & those, that are vnder their charge. but that
Enraged minds should lash out & hauing once bid adue to the
tendernes of a good Conscience, rush on impudently to the acting
of all kind of Enormities I wonder not. that, which amazed mee,
was to see the slack & cold resentment, that these compassionate
hearers of others greiuances alwaies make shew of vpon the
euident conviction of most palpable malice & vntruths in those
relations, that haue beene this way brought them. Oftimes haue
I known the disproof of all that hath beene reported by one of
these discontented persons, & the remonstrance of their euill disposition made as apparent to the light as Noone day, yet could I
neuer perceiue any one of these, who haue taken vpon them to be
private iudges & Patrons of the cause, turn against the false complainant ⟨108v⟩ with that true Indignation & Zeal, which they
ought to doe, & wherewith in very truth in all other matters they
shew to abound. They cannot endure to be guld, so they terme it,
with lies in the most trifling matters, that can be thought vpon.
they cannot away with malicious interpretations of doubtfull

actions either in themselues, or in others, whom they truely Loue. & yet notwithstanding, when they discouer themselues to haue beene abused out of all measure in this kind by a deceitfull tongue, & such as they must needs yeeld hath giuen proof of it self to loue vnrighteousnes more then goodnes, & to talk of lies more then righteousnes, They remaine notwithstanding as gentle & patient in respect of their own wrong, as if they had no gall at all, & neuer a whitt the lesse kindly affectionated to the now convicted malefactour, then they did formerly, when they conceiued him innocent & oppressed. A marveilous strong preiudice, that their compassionate patronage was not so well grounded, nor intended to that right end, with which they beare the world in hand, that is, the redresse of greif & iniuries, but rather to the multiplying of them. For were it impartial Loue to Right & truth, & not partial Loue to the complainant, or secret malice to the accused, they must needs proceed to the condemnation of that euill, that is detected with the same zeal that they ⟨109⟩ before made shew of in the consolation of the afflicted, and they would now lay on deserued shame equall to the vndeserued pitty, which they had formerly afforded. Hee shall keep the simple folk by their right, defend the children of the poore & punish the wrong-doer, sayth Dauid,[1] when he reckons vp the progresse of iustice & mercy. Whether in the prince of peace & [or] righteousnes, the sharp chastizement of wickednes is as necessarie in respect of iustice, as the stout & cheerfull defence of innocencie. & seuere correction of malicious offenders, as great a point of charitie, as the compassionate affording of help to the truly afflicted. They are combined in the son of Gods proceedings towards men, & they ought not to be seuerd in those sons of men, that call themselues by his Name, in their proceedings one towards another. What Dauid shews vs in Christ as in the supreme pattern & mould, hee setts forth for our better Imitation in his own practize as in a second draught & transcript, least wee might happily think, that

[1] Psalm lxxii, 4.

the persecution of euill deeds appertaines to Gods iustice onely &
not to mans faultines. He makes it plaine by putting himself for
an Example, that it appertaines likewise to euery man, that will
deriue his fauouring of others in their weldoing, or in their euill
⟨109v⟩ suffering from the Diuine mercy. He makes it plaine, I
say, that all such ought to be equally affected to [inclined toward]
the punishment of the guiltie, as well as to the pittying of the
afflicted, & to the protection of the innocent. My song shall be of
mercy & Iudgement, sayth hee, unto thee, oh Lord, will I sing.[1]
That is, as I haue beene taught, how they ought to be ioyntly
exercized by mee in Imitation of thee. And so as if it had beene a
president [precedent] purposely intended for the cause wee haue
in hand, he tells vs seueral degrees of correction & coertion, by
which he ment to proceed against those seueral offences, which
wee dayly find vnited in these traducing complaints & informations, that are made onely for the procuring of pitty & compassion from the Auditours. There's no deceitfull person shall
dwell in my house, sayth Dauid. He, that telleth lies shall not
tarry in my sight. a froward heart shall depart from mee. I will
not know a wicked person. Who so priuily slandereth his Neighbour him will I destroy.[2] From Expulsion of deceitfull persons
out of his Familie, he goes on to the Banishment of Notorious
Liuers out of his sight; from Estrangement towards froward
minds he proceeds to the excommunication of wicked doers &
at last comes to the capital execution of these ⟨110⟩ selfsame
Malefactours, which wee haue now at the Barre. Hee, that
vnjustly slandereth his Neighbour, him will I destroy. This was
Dauids Methode in the order of his affection & in the course of
his Actions. And if it were right as hee seemes very confident,
that it was, stiling it, that it was the way of perfection,[3] then
without doubt the common vsage of the world must needs be
very wrong. The very best of these priuie receiuers of complaints,
as farre as I could euer see, taking still the quite contrarie path to

---

[1] Psalm ci, 1.   [2] Ibid., passim.   [3] Ibid., 6.

that which he walked. How often haue wee seene the plaine remonstrance & conviction of these crimes turn to the advantage of the delinquents, & to the further charge and oppression of the accused. & as if it had beene an vnpardonable crime in the one to proue himself innocent, & nothing but misfortune in the other to haue been discouered altogether froward, false & malitious in their reports. A stronger League of freindship hath been made with the complainant, a stouter patronage of the cause hath been vndertaken, & oftimes an open persecution of the defendant hath ensued cheifly from this ground, that it was made invincibly apparent, that they were mere tales & lies & Calumnious suspitions, which had been brought against him, wherevnto they had giuen ouerforward entertainment. ⟨110v⟩

PATIENT. This last Test goes to the quick. The secret acceptation of Complaints, the serious intending them, & the solemne affording pitty to the Relatours doth so farre engage a man in the busines, as he must be a right good-man indeed (& yet how a right good-man should come within the verge of this kind of wrong I doe not well see) that had not rather haue his best freind found guiltie of what he was accused, then himself convicted for so much falshood in Freindship, so much indiscretion in respect of the world, & such a high streine of Hypocrisie in point of Religion, as are eminently conspicuous in this kind of Errour.

AFFECTIONATE. Call it, as it is, a perfidious crime against God & Man, the greatest Bane & ouerthrow of true freindship, that can be imagined. There's no man guilty of it, but hee instantly begins to hate them, whom he hath thus iniured, & pick vp matter of faultines, Errours & Imperfections against them, to the intent that he may haue ground vpon the true resolutions of his own iudgement deseruedly to continue that offence & misprizion, which he had vndeseruedly conceiued against them through others false reports & suggestions. if a scruple clearing & a single forme of restitution of credit would be desired, there's none that would more sincerely endeauour the absolute iustification of the partie accused, nor turn ⟨111⟩ more feircely for his innocence, then these priuie Receiuers of Complaints vpon the Discouery of the abuse, or if the matter might be carried altogether vpon the faultie Accusers score & his punishment make the full amends. But when they perceiue (& there is none so dull-eied, that perceiue it not in the very dawning of the Light), that their Affections, assent, beleif, & compassionate entertainment of the absurdities, wrongs, & slanderous vntruths, which they gaue vnadvised eare vnto, hath brought them in arrearages of Lenitie, vnkindnes, Hypocrisie, breach of Freindship, & Christian Charitie equall to the accuser, & that they cannot reuerse the sentence of condemnation, which they had giuen in their minds at least, howeuer reserued they were in their words against the accused without condemning themselues, nor sett him right & streight in the court of their own and others iudgements without publishing themselues to haue been in the wrong, & that in high degree. There's none of these but grow enraged in his heart at the consideration of that integritie, wherein he reads the proclamation of his own manifold errours texted out in Capital Letters. & he thinks Wisedome & Iustice & Necessitie enforce him rather to persist in the search of the accused faults, & to proceed to the casting out of [exposing] him ⟨111 v⟩ some way or other guiltie, then to yeeld himself convicted of so multiplied & notorious a huddel [mass] of iniquities as is necessarily included in the willing setling with malicious wickednes against good deserts and Innocencie. I know very well, that their confidence of better intentions & their being no waies culpable to themselues of such explicite purpose will make them think this imputation of mine too intolerable. But if they will giue leaue to scan the matter by reason & not by passion, they shall euidently perceiue the liuely resemblances of all those wicked pourtraictures, which they find engrauen vpon the tongue of the false accuser, & to be really & liuely stampt off vpon their own credulous eares. & by this eare-mark both they & wee may be so well assured, that the whole streame of wickednes, which his vnruly tongue powred out, hath sunk down setled in their harts, & there left the malice, falshood, folly & hypocrisie, & all the appurtinant euills of these heinous crimes printed of [off[as full & plaine, as in the original it self. Their consciousnes of this participated guilt is that, which makes them, as you shall euer obserue it vpon the pressing of the matter so fauourable to the delinquents, so quick in finding & so fierce in vrging arguments of excuse & extenuating on his behalf, that so by the obscuritie of his deformities they might cancell the ouglines of their own. But let them neuer so ⟨112⟩ boisterously contend in words. They can neuer calme the vproares of their own Consciences, nor silence it so much (except by long custome they haue gotten a brawn [hard skin], & become sencelesse in this kind) but it will tell them, as I now doe, that they haue their hand as deep in the paste as the principal[1] & by this reseruing [retaining of] this false coyne giuing in exchange their beleif to the thing, their pitty & compassion to the complainant & running out to the censure & condemnation of the accused made themselues liable to the vttermost of all that, which either in point of guilt or punishment is due to the minter himself. Let them well veiw & they shall see, there is no more difference in this case, then is between the seal & the printed wax. The figures are the same in both to a stroak, although perhaps to vnskilfull persons by reason of their contrarie placing they seeme in nothing agreeing: So verily, howeuer the false-reporters malice did at first blush cause the matter to be taken for a thing of a cleane other kind in him, then it is in the other, that out of tendernes of pitty gaue eare & credditt to the relation, yet in very truth, if it be rightly obserued by an vnderstanding eie, there will not be found any one stitch in this abominable work of darknes, that will not be found taken out & wrought true & as liuely on ⟨112v⟩ the soul of this vnwary receiuer of tales as on the prime sampler it self of the wicked Inventour & broacher of them. See there the knott of Lies Wherein the

---

[1] In the paste as in the principal—in the stuff by which a copy (of a coin) is made as in the original.

Deuill sports himself so merrily, & tell mee whether it shew not as plaine & fairely drawn in the beleif of the hearer, as in the invention of the Relatour. Its trodden down by malignant deuice in the mind of the one & riseth vp by malignant credulitie in the mind of the other. There's no more difference then is between engrauement & Embossement of the selfsame storie. In the one it is cutt inward, by the other it is wrought outward. Vntruth hath spred it self like a Leprosie ouer both their souls. The one hath made a ly by wicked forgerie, the other hath made it his own by willfull entertainment. He, that loues a ly, is by the last proclamation, that was made from heauen to be shutt out from thence aswell as he, that makes it.[1] how much more then must hee, for whose sake it was properly made, bee, which plaies the midwife in bringing forth a ly, & becomes a Nurse in rearing it vp, needs entangle himself in the guilt & condemnation due thereunto. Let no man that is thus ouertaken fondly sooth vp himself in the conceit of innocencie, or think, that hee is lesse free from the loathsome pollution of falsehood because it is not so layd to his charge by way of purposed invention of slander, when it lies more heinous against him in another kind. What bootes ⟨113⟩ it, that he cannot be rightly indited for false accusation, when he cannot be acquitted for false iudgement. He, that either absolues, or condemnes without full & certaine Notice of the cause, giues a false sentence howeuer true it may happen to be in regard of the crime. & he, that proceeds to the execution thereof by awarding of pittie to the one, & conceiuing of offence against the other, howeuer iust it may agree to the desert of both parties, yet makes himself altogether liable to the condemnation of an uniust iudge. But seldome in this case doth it happen but that the Issue of the busines proues altogether as wrong as the manner of proceeding was at first, & their secret vsurpation of iudgement & priuate acceptation of partial information are euer contrarie to right & equitie: so likewise is their vse & application of them most

[1] Revelation xxii, 15.

comonly to the maintenance of the worse, & to the oppression of the better part & cause. But let it proue as it will this cannot possibly bee avoyded, but that he, which makes himself a iudge by hearing complaints, censuring, & misdemeanours makes himself a false iudge by doing it vpon hearing of one partie onely, & taking half information in the Busines. Now whether a false iudge be not as bad as a false accuser, iudge you. Especially when he presumptuously arrogates the office, which he thus vnduely exerciseth. ⟨113 v⟩ But when as commonly (& scarce one time ot hundred it falls out otherwise) to vnlawfull vsurpation & vnlegal proceedings the surcharge of a false sentence giuen & put in execution comes to be added, what can you find not only worse but equivalent in the false accusers standing to the multiplicitie of Lies & mysteries of falsehood, which you see plainly wrought in the false proceedings & iudgement of this vniust hearer & Receiuer of complaints. ⟨114⟩

Bibliography

ADDINGTON, RICHARD. *The Idea of the Oratory.* London, 1966.

BASIL THE GREAT, ST. *Ascetic Writings of St Basil,* translated by W. K. L. Clarke. London, 1925.

BLACKSTONE, B. (ed.). *The Ferrar Papers.* Cambridge, 1938.

BOETHIUS. *The Consolation of Philosophy,* translated by 'I.T.' (1609), revised by H. F. Stewart. London, 1918.

BUSBEQUIUS. *The Turkish Letters of Ogier Ghuselin de Busbecq,* translated by Edward S. Forster. Oxford, 1927.

BUSH, DOUGLAS. *English Literature of the Earlier Seventeenth Century.* Oxford, 1945.

Paradise Lost in Our Time. Ithaca, 1945.

Clare College, 1326–1926. 2 vols., Cambridge, 1928–30.

CORNARO, LUIGI. *Discorsi,* translated by George Herbert. Cambridge, 1634. Herbert's translation is included in the volume called *Hygiasticon* by Lessius (see below).

DONNE, JOHN. *Letters to Severall Persons of Honour,* edited by C. E. Merrill Jr. New York, 1910.

DOWDEN, EDWARD. *Puritan and Anglican.* New York, 1910.

ELTON, G. R. *Reformation Europe 1517–1559.* Cleveland, 1964.

FRANCIS OF SALES, ST. *Introduction to the Devout Life,* translated by Fr. Michael Day. London, 1961.

GREGORY OF NYSSA, ST. *Ascetical Works,* translated by Virginia Woods Callahan. Catholic University of America Press, Washington D.C., 1967. (Vol. 58 of *Fathers of the Church.*)

HERRICK, ROBERT. *Poetical Works,* edited by L. C. Martin. Oxford, 1956.

HOOPES, RICHARD. *Right Reason in the English Renaissance.* Cambridge, 1962.

LESSIUS, LEONARD. *Hygiasticon,* translated by Nicholas Ferrar with an introduction by T. S[mith]. Cambridge, 1634.

MANUSCRIPTS

British Museum—Add. 34657, edited by Sharland (see below).
    Add. 34658, edited half by Sharland and half by Blackstone (see above).

BIBLIOGRAPHY

Add. 34659, the 'Dialogue on the Austere Life' now printed for the first time. The pages are numbered in the manuscript.

Clare College, Cambridge—Little Gidding manuscript: the 'Dialogue on the Retirement of Charles V' now printed for the first time. The pages, unnumbered in the manuscript volume, have been assigned numbers.

Little Gidding manuscript: another copy of BM Add. 34658.

Magdalene College, Cambridge—Little Gidding manuscript: another copy of the 'Dialogue on the Retirement of Charles V' with corrections and some notes by a second and later hand.

MAYCOCK, A. L. *Nicholas Ferrar of Little Gidding*. London, 1938.

MAYOR, J. E. B. (ed.). *Nicholas Ferrar: Two Lives by His Brother John and by Doctor Jebb*. Cambridge, 1855.

MOORMAN, F. W. *Robert Herrick: A Biographical and Critical Study*. London, 1910.

ROBERTSON, WILLIAM. *History of the Reign of Charles V*. 3 vols., Boston, 1857.

SHARLAND, E. CRUWYS (ed.). *The Story Books of Little Gidding*. London, 1899.

DE THOU, JACQUES AUGUSTE (THUANUS). *Histoire Universelle de Jacques de Thou*, traduite sur l'édition latine de Londres, à Londres. London, 1734.

VALDES, JUAN DE. *The Hundred and Ten Considerations of Signior John Valdesso*. Oxford, 1638. Reprinted with an introduction by Frederic Chapman, John Lane, London, n.d.

WALTON, IZAAK. *Lives*, with an introduction by George Saintsbury. Oxford, 1927.

WILLEY, BASIL. *The Seventeenth-Century Background*. London, 1946.

Index

318

INDEX

Cicero, on temperance, 185, 199

Cineas, ambition of, 7

Clare College, Cambridge, and Nicholas Ferrar, xiv

Collett, Anna (the Patient): cognomen, xxxi–xxxii; role in dialogues, xxxviii–xxxix, lxxii

Collett, Hester (the Cheerfull): cognomen, xxxii; role in dialogues, xxxix–xl, lxxiii–lxxiv

Collett, John (the Resolved): cognomen, xxx; role in dialogues, xliii–xliv, lxxi

Collett, Joyce (the Submisse): cognomen, xxxiii; role in dialogues, xl–xli, lxxi

Collett, Margaret (the Affectionate): cognomen, xxxii; role in dialogues, xl, lxxii–lxxiii

Collett, Mary (the Chief, the Mother): cognomens, xxv, xxx–xxxi; role in dialogues, xxxv–xxxviii, lxxvi–lxxviii

Collett, Susanna (the Moderator): cognomen, xxx; role in dialogues, xliv–xlv, lxxi

Conrad I, II, and III, kings of Germany, xxv

Cornaro, Luigi: *Discorsi della vita sobria*, lxxviii–lxxxi, lxxxvi; cited by Bacon, lxxix–lxxx

Crashaw, Richard, association with Ferrars, lxiv

Cyprian, St, cited by Mother, 182

David, a sober poet, 205

De Consolatione Philosophiae, Boethius, lvii

de Groote, Geert, founder of Brethren of Common Life, lii

de Thou, Jacques-Auguste, *Historia sui Temporis*, xlv–xlviii, 34 n. 2 and n. 3, 35, 44, 119 n., 120

Discorsi della vita sobria, *see* Cornaro

Donne, John: as diplomat, lxv; poetry of, lxvi, 209 n.

Eleanor of France, sister of Charles V, 30-1, 80

Eliot, Thomas Stearns, 'Little Gidding', xi, lviii n. 1

Elizabeth I, queen of England: on misery of the world, lvi–lvii; and *Richard II*, lxviii

Elizabeth, princess, daughter of James I, wedding of, lxv–lxvi, lxix–lxx

Epictetus, cited by Chief, 68

Essex, Robert Devereux, Earl of, his fall from power, lviii, lxv, lxvii–lxviii

Eve, corrupted by desire for food, 218

Ferdinand: brother of Charles V, 30-1; made Holy Roman Emperor, 78

Ferrar family: at Little Gidding, xiii–xiv; genealogical table, xiv

Ferrar, John (the Guardian): cognomen, xxx; role in dialogues, xli–xliii, lxxiv–lxxv; as educator, 114–15

Ferrar, Mary Woodnoth (the Mother, the Grandmother, the Founder), xiii: her death, xxv; cognomens, xxx; her austerity, 8

Ferrar, Nicholas (the Visitor): at Clare College, xiv; at Bourn, xv; in entourage of Princess Elizabeth, xv, 140 n. 1; and Virginia Company, xvi; becomes deacon, xvii; as organiser and editor of Charles V dialogue, xxi, xxiv, xxxiv–xxxv, 23 n. 1; cognomen, xxx; and Counter-Reformation, l–lvi; his library, l–li; as translator of Valdes, liii

Ferrar, Nicholas III, son of John Ferrar, 112

Ferrar, Susanna, *see* Collett, Susanna

Ferrar, Virginia, daughter of John Ferrar, 113

Florentius, confessor to Philip III, 18–19

Foxe, John, *Book of Martyrs*: cited by Guardian, 169; cited by Mother, 170, 182

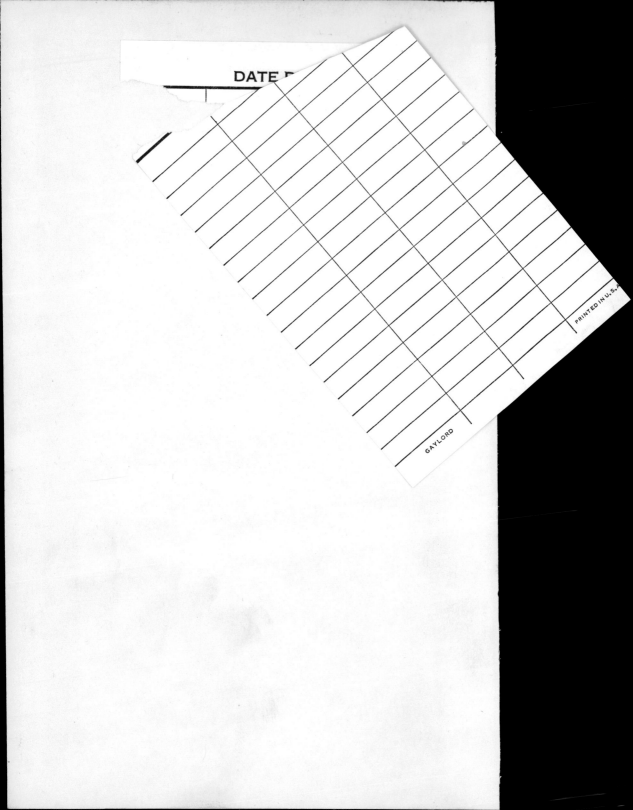

DATE

PRINTED IN U.S.A.

GAYLORD